BERIT OLAM
Studies in Hebrew Narrative & Poetry

1 Kings

Jerome T. Walsh

David W. Cotter, O.S.B.
Editor

Jerome T. Walsh
Chris Franke
Associate Editors

A Michael Glazier Book
THE LITURGICAL PRESS
Collegeville, Minnesota

A Michael Glazier Book published by The Liturgical Press

Cover design by Ann Blattner

1	2	3	4	5	6	7	8

Library of Congress Cataloging-in-Publication Data

Walsh, Jerome T., 1942–
    1 Kings / Jerome T. Walsh.
      p. cm. — (Berit olam series)
    Includes bibliographical references and index.
    ISBN 0-8146-5044-9
    1. Bible. O.T. Kings, 1st—Commentaries. I. Title.
II. Series.
BS1335.3.W35 1996
222'.5307—dc20   95-35984
                                                             CIP

for
C.A.S.G.
yāqîm 'et-ḥăbērô

CONTENTS

Principal Sites
mentioned in 1 Kings

Sidon

Damascus

Mt. Harmon   A R A M

Wilderness of Damascus

Tyre

Dan

Zarephath

LAKE
HULEH

Hazor

SEA OF
GALILEE

Aphek?

Aphek?

Mt. Carmel

KISHON R.

Megiddo   Shunem

Jezreel

Ramoth-gilead

JORDAN R.

Abel-meholah

G I L E A D

Samaria   Tirzah

Shechem

Succoth

Penuel

I S R A E L

Bethel

Gibbethon

A M M O N

Gezer   Ramah   Jericho

Gibeon

Jerusalem

J U D A H

DEAD
SEA

PHILISTIA

M O A B

Beersheba

Wilderness of Beersheba

Mi 0   10   20
Km 0   10   20

Horeb   Ezion-Geber   E D O M

Created by PC Bible Atlas 1.0

ACKNOWLEDGMENTS

It is a pleasure to confess the enormous debt I owe to the many scholars who have so richly contributed to the literature on the First Book of Kings. Those familiar with the standard commentaries and more recent studies will recognize how much they have influenced my own reading of the text. Historical critical commentaries of the past often display valuable, if not methodologically systematic, literary sensitivity, just as the more literary-oriented studies of the present never dispense entirely with reflection upon the history of composition and event behind the extant text. The suggestions for further reading at the end of this study include some, but by no means all, of the works I have found particularly stimulating.

It is equally a pleasure to thank two people whose careful reading and suggestions have made this work much better than it otherwise would have been. My editor, David W. Cotter, O.S.B., has been most helpful in raising insightful questions at the right moment and in answering my questions in timely fashion. My colleague Rev. Jean-Pierre Ruiz, S.T.D., of the diocese of Brooklyn, has generously given of his time and keen perception to help hone my analysis and polish my prose. To both, my gratitude. For the flaws, the limitations, the oversights, and the failings of what remains, I take full credit myself. My graduate assistant, Mr. Denis Sugrue, prepared the first draft of the index. I am immensely grateful for his labors.

This study was completed during a time of considerable personal turmoil, in which many have been of great support. They too, then, have indirectly contributed to whatever value lies herein and deserve thanks beyond words. Of them all, I must name Theresa, Carol, Ann, and the one to whom this book is dedicated.

INTRODUCTION

The First Book of Kings is a historical narrative. Both of those dimensions of the text deserve extended study in order to come to a full appreciation of the book. 1 Kings is historical in two ways. First, it *is* a history. However widely its canons of history writing may differ from those of modern historians, it nevertheless purports to describe real people and events from the tenth and ninth centuries B.C.E. As a work of historiography, it is subject to all the investigative techniques historians use to evaluate ancient witnesses. Second, it *has* a history. 1 Kings is the result of a long and complicated process of composition. Beginning with a wide variety of originally independent oral and written sources (each of which has its own history as well), a series of creative author-editors selected, rearranged, combined, and sometimes thoroughly reshaped the source materials to produce, eventually, a continuous text. Later editors revised this text in light of the concerns of subsequent generations; and finally centuries of scribes and copyists made further small changes, some intentional and some not. All this becomes grist for the historian's mill, for reconstructing the history *of* the text is essential to evaluating the reliability of the history described *by* the text.

The attempt to rediscover the history of the text and to use that rediscovery as evidence for retrieving underlying historical events is called "historical criticism." This approach has flourished over the last two hundred years of biblical scholarship. The work of historical appreciation and appropriation of 1 Kings has resulted in vast gains in our ability to evaluate the biblical text as a source for historical reconstruction, and the external controls furnished by archaeological excavations in western Asia have put the sometimes highly conjectural proposals of exegesis on a more solid empirical footing. Most of the standard commentaries on 1 Kings focus to a greater or lesser degree on the historical questions. (The suggestions for further reading at the end of this book list some standard historical critical commentaries.)

But 1 Kings is also a narrative, and recent attention in the field of biblical study to the nature of narrative has increased our awareness of the implications of that dimension of the text. A narrative is always in some measure the product of human literary creativity. The author wields words as a painter wields pigments, to create a world according to his or her own vision. This is no less true in historiographic writing than in fiction; for the historian has a holistic vision of the *meaning* of events, not just of their data, and must attempt to communicate that integral understanding of the events in the very process of narrating them. This is in fact the basis for the historian's inescapable task of selecting, arranging, and reshaping the source materials. The historian's hope is that the world he or she builds out of words will correspond to the "real" world in its profoundest significance and to the extent possible in its informational content as well. The *narrative* quality of a work, however, is independent of its correspondence to an external "real" world, and its appreciation requires a different avenue of approach. In the last two decades attention to the literary character of biblical texts has grown, and we are slowly coming to appreciate the depth and richness of this dimension of the Hebrew scriptures. Several recent commentaries on 1 Kings (also listed in the suggestions for further reading) combine a traditional concern for historical reconstruction with a newer sensitivity to the literary creativity in the text.

The intention of the present commentary is to focus strictly on the literary dimension of 1 Kings. Inevitably some questions of history—both the history of the text and the history recounted in the text—will arise. But my fundamental perspective is that the text of 1 Kings as we have it is a narrative and has been read as a narrative for millennia. My concern will be to explore this narrative nature.

The Text

The history of the composition of the text is not my focus. Certainly one could do a narrative study of the sources that lie behind our present text, and indeed some of the individual stories in 1 Kings that I shall analyze may in fact have been originally independent materials. But my attention is on the narrative text we call 1 Kings, that is, the final form of the text that has resulted from the long and complex process of composition.

The present commentary is based on the Hebrew text, but it does not expect that the reader knows biblical Hebrew. I have assumed that the reader will have a contemporary English version at hand. There are many reliable translations; for the sake of simplicity, I have chosen one, the New Revised Standard Version (NRSV), as my point of reference.

Wherever my commentary hinges on elements of the Hebrew text that the NRSV does not reflect clearly, I have supplied my own translation of the Hebrew and indicated the NRSV's wording in parentheses.

There are two specific differences between the Hebrew and the NRSV that ought to be mentioned. First, the NRSV follows venerable tradition in substituting LORD or GOD (note the small capitals) wherever the Hebrew text reads *yhwh* for the name of God. I have generally rendered *yhwh* as "Yahweh" to reflect the Hebrew consonantal text more closely. Second, in a few places the NRSV's numbering of chapters and verses differs from that of the Hebrew text. In those cases I have alerted the reader to the difference, and I have used the NRSV's numbering in the commentary. One other technical note: it is often necessary to refer to parts of verses rather than simply to a verse as a whole. In that case the parts of the verses are distinguished by letters. For example, verse 5a means the first part of verse 5; verse 5b means the second part; verse 5ab means the first two parts, and so on.

The Approach

What is a "narrative" commentary? In other words, what does a literary approach to 1 Kings look for? Most basically, narrative criticism approaches the text as *story*, irrespective of its referential function as historical record or interpretation. It focuses on categories drawn from the discipline of literary criticism rather than on those of historiography. In order to situate our discussion, we should consider the areas of interest that will occupy us in this commentary. Occasionally this will involve some technical vocabulary.

STRUCTURAL ISSUES

One of the discoveries literary analysts of the Hebrew Bible have made is that Hebrew has its own particular ways of signaling the organization of a narrative. Recognition of these structuring devices enables us to perceive nuances of relationship between episodes, shades of emphasis, and intimations of contrast that we would otherwise miss.

Different techniques can separate subdivisions of a narrative or conjoin them or indicate that one event is before, after, or simultaneous with another. The grammar of Hebrew prose narrative, for example, uses a specific verb form to indicate that one action follows upon another, and a different verb form to indicate a break in the narrative flow (for instance, in the case of flashbacks or simultaneous actions). Another grammatical signal, unnecessarily repeated subjects ("The king sat down . . . and the king said . . ." instead of "The king sat down . . . and he said . . ."), also indicates some sort of break in the narrative flow, rather like a paragraph indentation in English prose.

The components of a literary unit are often arranged symmetrically, according to a variety of patterns. For instance, a literary unit can begin and end with a common element, be it a word or phrase, a concept, a motif, or the like. This technique is called "inclusion," and it serves to mark the extent of a literary unit or subunit. Inclusion occurs in units from the very small (Nathan's speech in 1 Kings 1:24-27 begins and ends with the words "my lord the king") to the very large (the central section of the Solomon story is delimited by references to "building the house" of Yahweh: 5:3; 9:25). Symmetrical organization of the subdivisions of a literary unit can take various forms: they can be arranged in two or more parallel sequences (ABCA'B'C'; see, for example, the discussion of 13:11-32); or in two sequences reversed around a single center (ABCB'A', called "concentric symmetry"; see, for example, 17:17-24); or in two sequences reversed around a double center (ABCC'B'A', called "chiastic symmetry"; see, for example, 12:1-20). Creative combinations of these patterns can produce a variety of pleasing symmetrical arrangements.

Each of the three basic symmetrical patterns has its own thrust. Parallel patterns tend to invite comparison of the parallel sequences and of individual parallel elements. Comparison often reveals progression, but not necessarily opposition or contrast, between the parallel components. Concentric symmetry usually emphasizes the central element (and sometimes the first and last elements as well). The central element often contains a turning point in the narrative development. The sequences before and after the turning point or the individual corresponding elements in those sequences often contrast with one another. Chiastic symmetry also puts emphasis on the central elements, though not as strongly as concentric symmetry.[1] There is less a sense of the narrative turning on a pivot, though the sequences of elements before and after the center are frequently in contrast.

Asymmetry within a symmetrically structured literary unit calls attention to the asymmetrical element. Sometimes this is done for emphasis (for example, the prophetic condemnation episodes in chapters

---

[1]The line between chiastic and concentric structures is not always easy to determine, particularly when the central element of a concentric structure is itself complex. See, for example, 1 Kings 1:1–2:12a, where the central element comprises four scenes arranged in parallel.

20 and 22); sometimes the disruption of pattern is itself the desired effect (as, for instance, in Obadiah's frantic speech in 18:9-14). Whatever the reason, the effect of asymmetry within an otherwise symmetrical organization always warrants careful study.

Verbal Techniques

The raw materials of the literary artist are words. What words are chosen, their order, even their sounds are hues on the writer's palette. Poetry is more self-conscious about its verbal texture than prose, but literary prose is not without its aesthetic. Many of the verbal techniques of Hebrew prose are difficult, if not impossible, to preserve in translation. Yet the English reader must have some understanding of them in order to appreciate their effect on the reader of the Hebrew text. Elements that are, in English, more properly poetic can occur in Hebrew prose: rhythm, alliteration, assonance. At particularly solemn junctures, Hebrew prose may become pure poetry (for example, David's words in 1:30 and the gruesome couplet of 14:11). At other times, even when the text does not become pure poetry, an aural grace can mark the words: Elijah's "sound of sheer silence" (19:12) has a chiastic series of consonants (*qôl dĕmāmâ daqqâ;* note the sequence *q-d-m-m-d-q*).

There are several techniques in Hebrew for emphasizing a single word or phrase. One of the commonest is almost impossible to detect in translation. Hebrew verbs are highly inflected to agree in person, number, and sometimes gender with their subject. It is not necessary, therefore, to use pronouns like "I," "you," "he," "she," "they," etc., as subjects of verbs, as it is in English. When Hebrew uses such a pronoun unnecessarily, it is emphatic, contrasting *this* subject with someone else. In other words, without a pronoun, "The king said, 'You shall die'" is a simple death sentence; but with an emphatic pronoun, "The king said, '*You* shall die'" means, "*You* shall die, in contrast to somebody else, who shall not die." Since English requires the pronoun, its force is lost in translation. In the course of the commentary we shall see the effect of emphatic pronouns repeatedly.

A second very common form of emphasis is a construction that, when translated into English with any attempt to reproduce the Hebrew effect fully, sounds very odd. Hebrew has a word, *hinnēh*, that makes the following phrase vividly present to the reader. In effect, it puts us in the position of one of the characters and shows us the scene through that character's eyes. The vivid quality is strengthened because *hinnēh* is usually followed, not by a verb in the past tense, but by a present participle. The whole effect is something like: "The king looked, and here comes a prophet to speak to him!" Though a translation like this sounds contrived in English, and thereby conveys an artificiality that is not present in the Hebrew, it nevertheless manages to capture something of the immediacy of the Hebrew. In the course of the commentary I have referred to this usage as the "vivid present" construction. Finally, Hebrew can produce emphasis in ways similar to English—emphatic particles (especially *kî*, "indeed"), unusual word order, repetition, etc.

Repetition can have other effects besides emphasis. Three techniques are noteworthy in this regard. Often information given by one character or by the narrator will be repeated at a later time by a different character. Variations between the original speech and the repetitions can reveal much about the later character. A somewhat similar use of repetition occurs in cases where one character gives another a command, and the narrator recounts in similar words the second character's compliance with the command. This "command and compliance" pattern is very frequent in 1 Kings. Echoing the order in the account of compliance signals the meticulous fidelity of the obedience. Divergencies in the wording can have a variety of effects, such as alluding to other passages (17:6), creating space for narrative development (18:2), or signaling incomplete obedience (19:13). Finally, there are cases where the narrator gives us information that he later repeats in the same or similar words. This is usually a sign that one of the occurrences is actually from a character's point of view, not the narrator's (see the discussion of "point of view" below).

Another set of verbal techniques exploits double meanings. Wordplay in English is generally considered to be a form of humor (and in some circles the lowest form). That is not the case in Hebrew. Wordplay in Hebrew is not play; it is a reflection of the profound interconnectedness of all reality. As a literary technique, it can create a web of allusive echoes that tie together disparate texts. But the effect is not merely ornamental. When the narrator plays on the name Solomon (Hebrew, *šlmh*) in speaking of Ahijah of Shiloh's garment (Hebrew, *šlmh*), he is deadly serious: Ahijah tears the garment into twelve pieces both to demonstrate and to effect the tearing of Solomon's kingdom away from the house of David (11:29-32).

Double meanings function on a larger scale too. Any language is capable of ambiguous constructions, and any author can inadvertently write ambiguously. But ambiguity can be used to very pointed effect as well. Sometimes a passage is grammatically open to two (or more: see 21:25-26!) different construals, and there is no decisive reason to choose one over another. The reader makes a provisional choice but realizes that other readings are possible. In other cases a passage is apparently clear, but a later twist in the text requires that the reader go back and reconstrue differently what has already been read (for example, 22:30). Both of these situations result in double meaning. The reader does not simply forget the alternative or rejected understandings but remains as conscious of them as of the one that he or she has finally settled on. Thus even the rejected understandings contribute to the meaning effect of the passage.

NARRATIVE, NARRATOR, AND AUTHOR

What constitutes a text as a "narrative" or "story"? Fortunately the question of the nature of a narrative is much less vexed in the Hebrew Bible than in the more self-conscious products of modern literature. For our practical purposes, a narrative or story recounts a series of connected events that move from a situation of stability through a complicating process of destabilization to a situation of new (or reestablished) stability. In other words, as Aristotle said, a story has a beginning, a middle, and an end. The situations of stability are not absolute, of course. They presume antecedent and subsequent stories; in some sense, every story begins and ends *in medias res.* But the stories in 1 Kings begin and end with a relative stability that affords the reader a feeling of completeness and closure. These qualities will require us to read the stories of 1 Kings on two levels—both as self-contained narratives and as components of larger, more inclusive stories.

A concept correlative to "narrative" is "narrator." As narrative tells a story, so the narrator is the storyteller. The narrator is not the "author" (on the author, see below), but the voice within the text that we hear when all characters' voices are silent. In other words, the narrator is the voice that informs us that "King David was old" (1:1). As with narrative itself, the narrator in modern literature is a complex and problematic category. In biblical Hebrew narrative, the concept is less problematic but complex nevertheless. The narrator in our texts tells the story as an observer rather than as a participant; first-person narrators are rare though not unknown in the Bible (see, for example, Neh 1:1; Ezek 1:1, and the so-called "we" sections of Acts). And the narrator in 1 Kings is usually impersonal, that is, he[2] rarely calls attention to his own personal opinions and judgments. This does not mean that the narrator is neutral. On a few occasions the narrator will "break frame," that is, he will

---

[2]The narrator's presence in the text is not gendered, as it would be, for instance, in the case of a first-person narrator. Yet, since the narrator is the storyteller, we cannot think of the voice as inanimate. The limitations of English require a personal pronoun.

step out of the horizons of the narrated story to address the reader directly (for instance, 8:8; 10:10-12). But more often he conveys his own stance in subtler and less obtrusive ways. One of our tasks will be to discern the means the narrator uses to direct, from behind the scenes as it were, the shaping of our understanding and our judgments.

The narrator is reliable and authoritative. This means that we need not doubt either the factual information he gives us or the honesty of his judgments. (This is *within* the story world, of course. Narratorial reliability is no guarantee of historical accuracy.) The narrator's factual reliability and moral authority are based on omniscience. He has access to secret information (for example, what Nathan and Bathsheba discuss in privacy: 1:11-14); he knows the interior life of his characters (for example, Jeroboam's motivations in 12:26-28); and he has definite, if not always explicit, criteria for moral judgment (for example, 15:3, 11-14; 16:30). When the narrator withholds information from us, it is not in order to deceive us but to achieve a literary effect (see the discussion of 3:16-28). If we sometimes disagree with his judgments—and we can—we do so on the basis of different moral starting points (see, for example, the discussion of 21:25-26).

"Author," too, is a complex concept. Literary theorists speak of the "real" author and the "implied" author, both of whom are distinct from the narrator. The real author is the historical person or, in the case of biblical narratives, series of persons that produced the text. Interpretation of texts in terms of the real author requires an independent access to the historical person that is difficult, if not impossible, in the case of 1 Kings. It is, moreover, an issue of history, or history of literature, more than of narrative criticism. The implied author, on the other hand, is not a real person that exists or existed outside the text but a construct made by the *reader* from what is within the text itself. The implied author is the set of values and presuppositions that the reader must posit as responsible for the extant text in order to interpret it as a coherent unity. In a sense, the implied author is an inevitable corollary of the perceived unity of the text: if the text is coherent in organization and unified in meaning, we must assume an organizing principle. This is the implied author, to whom we conventionally ascribe the values, intentions, and dynamisms we discern in the text. When I speak in this study of the author of the stories in 1 Kings, I am referring to the implied author, not the real author.

The distinction between implied author and narrator will be clearer, perhaps, in light of an example. In 4:21-24 the narrator tells us that Solomon's daily provisions were obtained from imperial tribute. But we can discern behind the text older sources—probably lists from the royal archives—that attributed these provisions to the district officials mentioned in 4:7 and listed in 4:8-19. It is the implied author who pieces together from these conjectural sources the text we have before us.[3] The text that the implied author produces from these archival sources portrays a world in which the sources do not exist. In that world, there is a narrator who tells his audience a story about how Solomon's provisions came from imperial tribute.

PLOT AND POINT OF VIEW

Narrative recounts a series of connected events. This is a complex statement. Narrative's recital of events has a creative flexibility in at least three dimensions.

First, a narrator may recount events in the order of their occurrence or use techniques like foretelling and flashback to recount them in different order. Chronological order is the norm, and departure from it is always worthy of careful attention. Foretelling, whether everyday anticipation (for example, David's directions for Solomon's installation ceremony in 1:32-35, which are carried out in 1:38-39), or literary foreshadowing (for example, the narrator's comparison of Adonijah to Absalom in 1:6, which foreshadows Adonijah's eventual downfall and death), or prophetic prediction (for example, Yahweh's condemnation of Ahab in 21:19, which is fulfilled in 22:38), creates links that connect more or less distant passages and reveal them to be parts of a single narrative. Flashback, on the other hand, offers the narrator a means to fill in background information for the sake of characterization (for example, 18:3-4) or to create irony (see the discussion of 11:14-25).

A second dimension of flexibility is in the tempo with which a narrator recounts events. On a grammatical level, narrative with a high concentration of verbs gives the reader a feeling of rapid action. Passages with few verbs—either long sentences with complex subjects or objects, or passages with numerous verbless clauses—tend to slow the pace considerably. On a scenic level, the narrator can summarize long periods of time in a few words (for example, 19:8); or by recounting dialogue he can present a scene where reading time approximately equals the period of time described (for example, 1:15-37); or he can even stop time completely by extended descriptive passages (10:14-21) or by parenthetical asides to the reader (21:25-26). The effects of varying the

---

[3]If our reconstruction of sources and editorial processes corresponds in fact to documents and deeds of the historical past, then to that degree our implied author resembles the real author. It is certainly reasonable to draw that conclusion but difficult to see how to confirm it.

tempo of a narrative are several. The simplest are variety and maintaining the reader's interest. Slowing the pace of a scene can also add emphasis or, especially in the case of dialogue, make a scene much more vividly present to the reader. It can increase suspense by delaying resolution of a complication. Many other effects are possible, and the narrator's manipulation of tempo must be considered sensitively in each case.

A third dimension of narrative flexibility is in the point of view. This refers to the place in a scenic episode where the narrator positions the reader. An analogy from cinema can clarify the concept. Though the viewer seldom adverts to it consciously, the director chooses the angle and the distance from which the camera films a scene. So too in narrative, the narrator chooses the angle and the distance from which we view the action. The commonest point of view is that of a neutral, relatively distant observer. Certain techniques—dialogue is especially effective here—can force the reader to step onto the stage, as it were, and to draw closer to the action. When we read Jezebel's letter to the elders in 21:9-10, we feel ourselves to be looking over someone's shoulder—either Jezebel's as she writes or the elders' as they read.

Other techniques—revelation of a character's inner thoughts or feelings is an example—can associate the reader to one or another character, so that the scene is viewed from that character's point of view. The structure of Solomon's speech in 3:23, which may be spoken interiorly rather than publicly, reflects the inconclusiveness of the evidence presented and enables us to share and sympathize with him in his dilemma. A subtle signal that the narrator is showing us something from a character's point of view is when the narrator appears to repeat information he has already given us. Since we already know about David's age (1:1) and Abishag's attendance on the king (1:4), the repetition of this information in 1:15 is meant to show us David's age and Abishag's presence at his side through the eyes of Bathsheba as she enters the king's chamber. The effects of manipulating the reader's point of view include evoking (or preventing) identification with or sympathy for a character, giving (or withholding) from the reader information available only to some characters or to the narrator, and endowing (or not) particular information or judgments with the authority of the narrator.

CHARACTERIZATION

In literature as in life, characters drive events. However, unlike flesh and blood, literary characters are made, not born. Narrators construct them out of words, and the ways in which the narrator accomplishes this construction are many. Most simply, he can tell us what he wants us to know about the character: physical details (1:6); emotional or mental qualities (11:9, "Yahweh was angry"; we sometimes forget that Yahweh is as much a literary character in these narratives as any other); moral assessment (16:25-26), and so forth. More subtly, the narrator can give us a glimpse of the character's internal life (12:26-27) or show us the character in action (2:28-29) and leave us to infer characterization from what we witness. Still more complex is showing us one character through the eyes of another (1:50); in such a case we must evaluate the intermediate witness—is he or she reliable or biased, insightful or shallow?—before attempting to infer characterization indirectly. Finally, the subtlest means of all is characterization by silence: the narrator's silence, for instance, about Bathsheba's motivation in 2:13-21 intrigues us as readers to the extent that we feel compelled to conjecture character traits to explain her actions.

The Commentary

As mentioned above, the individual stories in 1 Kings are also components in larger narratives. Sometimes a linear series of individual stories makes up a single larger unit; this is the case, for instance, with the Solomon story in chapters 1–11. At other times an individual story can be embedded in a larger story that is in turn part of a still larger story. That is the case with the story of the contest on Mount Carmel (18:21-40), which is embedded in the story of the ending of the drought (ch. 18), which is part of the Elijah story.

This multiplicity of narrative levels calls for a commentating strategy adequate to its complexity. Throughout the commentary we shall follow a strategy of moving from smaller units to larger ones. We shall look first at the simplest stories in the order in which they appear. In most cases we shall work our way through the story's individual subunits; if the story is particularly complex, we shall then consider the unity of the story as a whole. When we have examined all the stories that make up a single larger narrative, we shall examine its unity and coherence. This procedure enables us to approach the text of 1 Kings as a series of four large, overarching narratives: the story of Solomon (chs. 1–11), the story of Jeroboam (chs. 11–14), the story of Elijah (chs. 17–19), and the story of Ahab (chs. 20–22).

Part One

THE STORY OF SOLOMON
1 Kings 1–11

Chapter 1

SOLOMON SUCCEEDS TO THE THRONE OF DAVID

1 Kings 1:1–2:12a

The narrative of Solomon's succession to the throne of King David, his father, is the longest single story in 1 Kings. It is an unusually complex story for the Hebrew Bible, with numerous well-drawn characters, a subtle use of timing and point of view, and a carefully constructed symmetrical organization.

The story unfolds in nine sections, which are arranged in a balanced concentric pattern:

> A. King David is dying (1:1-4)
>> B. Adonijah exalts himself (1:5-8)
>>> C. Adonijah holds a feast (1:9-10)
>>>> D. Nathan conspires to make Solomon king (1:11-14)
>>>>> E. Four scenes in David's chambers (1:15-37)
>>>> D'. Nathan and others make Solomon king (1:38-40)
>>> C'. Adonijah's feast is disrupted (1:41-50)
>> B'. Adonijah abases himself (1:51-53)
> A'. King David dies (2:1-12a)

The first two sections supply background for the narrative. (There is a grammatical technique in Hebrew for indicating where the background material ends and where the action proper begins; in this story, the action begins in verse 9.) The last section acts as a transition and link between this story and the following one about Solomon's consolidation of power. The action of the story occurs in verses 9-53, and takes place in Jerusalem and its environs during the course of one momentous day late in David's life.

Background: Sections A and B

King David had been a military and political genius. He delivered the people of Judah and Israel from Philistine oppression, welded them into a federated realm under a single king, and established them as a dominant power in the lands at the eastern end of the Mediterranean Sea. David was celebrated as Yahweh's particular favorite; and indeed God had confirmed with him, through the mouth of David's court prophet Nathan, an unconditional covenant that his dynasty would last forever (2 Sam 7).

David's personal life, however, was far less successful. The gripping and tragic story of his familial disasters is told in 2 Samuel 9–20. David had an adulterous affair with Bathsheba, the wife of Uriah the Hittite, one of David's soldiers. When the liaison resulted in pregnancy, David resorted to murder: at his order Joab, David's general in the Ammonite war, maneuvered Uriah into a dangerous mission during which several warriors, including Uriah, were killed. As if these sins had unleashed a poison in his whole house, David's sons began their own catalogue of crimes. His eldest son, Amnon, raped his own half-sister Tamar, and then spurned her. When David seemed incapable of disciplining Amnon, his third son, Absalom, who was Tamar's devoted full brother, murdered Amnon by treachery. Absalom fled David's territory, but was reconciled with David three years later through the intervention of Joab. The reconciliation was a chilly one, however; David permitted Absalom, now the heir,[1] to live in Jerusalem, but he refused to meet him face to face for another two years. Absalom's growing disaffection because of his father's treatment eventually ripened into ambition, and he mounted an armed rebellion against his father. It was now David's turn to flee Jerusalem. In the ensuing battle Joab killed Absalom, and the rebellion collapsed. This left Adonijah, David's fourth son, as heir apparent.

This, then, is the remote background: a king whose public, political shrewdness founded an empire and a dynasty but whose private, familial failures made a shambles of the succession. 1 Kings begins at the point where these two contradictory sides of David intersect. If there is to be a stable transfer of political power in the kingdom, he must act decisively on a family matter.

---

[1]David's second son, whose name was either Chileab (2 Sam 3:3) or Daniel (1 Chr 3:1), does not appear in the stories of the Davidic house. Most scholars surmise from this that he had died by the time of Absalom's attempt to usurp the throne.

KING DAVID IS DYING: 1:1-4

In the first section of our story, King David is old and his health is failing. We are told that he "could not get warm"; presumably he suffers from arteriosclerosis, but in view of the sexual innuendoes of the next verses, the phrase surely has a double meaning. The principal concern of these verses is the irreversibility of the king's feeble condition, with which the section begins and ends:

A. David's feeble condition (1:1)
    B. Plan: find a virgin to care for David (1:2a)
        C. Her specific duties (1:2b)
    B'. Abishag is found (1:3)
        C'. She carries out her duties (1:4a)
A'. David is still impotent (1:4b)

His servants, that is, courtiers who have his confidence, propose to find a young virgin to care for the king. She will be "his attendant," a role whose specific duties are spelled out in two contrasting images: she will "stand" before him (NRSV, "wait on"), and she will "lie" beside him. (Similar therapy is attested in Greek medical literature of a thousand years later, though without the sexual dimensions. The underlying theory is that the vigor and energy of the youthful person will spread to the elderly one through physical contact.) The plan is carried out with only partial success. Abishag of Shunem, a small village in the tribal territory of Issachar, becomes David's attendant and serves him, but the king's potency does not revive. The narrator's remark that "the king did not know her" (the NRSV adds "sexually" to make the meaning explicit) is a comment, not on David's restraint, but on his terminal infirmity. Since the good of the kingdom depends on the king's health and energy, David's frailty points up the pressing importance of determining the dynastic succession.

The narrator draws a poignant picture of King David. His great age is emphasized by repetition: he is not merely "old" but "advanced in years." (If we can rely on the round numbers in 2 Samuel 5:4, David was about seventy years old.) The pathetic picture of the king shivering under piles of blankets contrasts starkly with the David who was the hero of 2 Samuel. This is no longer the vigorous, decisive leader of the past but the passive object of others' actions. Grammatically, he is the subject of no active verbs; things are done *to* him, not *by* him. His awareness, however, is still sharp, whatever his physical condition. The narrator signals this obliquely by showing us Abishag from two points of view. First he tells us that David's servants sought a beautiful girl and found Abishag (v. 3a). Thus the narrator assures us of Abishag's beauty (at least in the eyes of the courtiers). Then he says that the servants "brought her to David, and she was very beautiful" (vv. 3b-4; the NRSV obscures this by translating as two separate sentences). This second allusion to her beauty is from the viewpoint of the king to whom she has just been brought, and whose eye for female pulchritude is evidently undimmed (cf. 2 Sam 11:2), even if he is no longer capable of availing himself of his opportunity.

And what of Abishag herself? At first glance she has little function in the plot beyond demonstrating David's continuing impotence. Neither her name nor her provenance is significant. She is deemed beautiful by both courtiers and king, a stereotypical prerequisite for the role she is to fulfill. Yet, to the reader aware of the story's remote background in 2 Samuel, there are indications that Abishag may be more important than she appears. Two phrases used of Abishag allude to passages about Bathsheba in 2 Samuel. First, David's perception of Abishag's beauty is described in terms similar to his reaction to Bathsheba in 2 Samuel 11:2. Second, Abishag's duty of lying in the king's bosom recalls the same uncommon image in 2 Samuel 12:3, where Nathan uses a parable about a poor man and the ewe lamb that used to "lie in his bosom," to condemn David for his adultery with Bathsheba and his murder of her husband Uriah. As the story develops, most of the principal figures in Adonijah's camp will have counterparts in Solomon's: Joab and Benaiah, Abiathar and Zadok, Jonathan and Nathan. Bathsheba's counterpart is Abishag, who has replaced her in the king's bed; Abishag's connection with Adonijah is implied also in 2:13-18, when he asks that Solomon give her to him as his wife.

ADONIJAH EXALTS HIMSELF: 1:5-8

The second section of the story introduces Adonijah, David's oldest surviving son. Since David founded a new dynasty, the principle of succession by the eldest son was not yet established by precedent in the kingdom; nevertheless, Adonijah assumed that he would succeed his father. Verses 5-6 highlight Adonijah's presumption:

> A. Adonijah's claim to be heir (1:5a)
>   B. Adonijah's actions as heir (1:5b)
>   B'. David's silence about Adonijah's actions (1:6a)
> A'. The grounds for Adonijah's claim (1:6b)

Several elements in verses 5-6 point up Adonijah's royal expectations. Throughout the Books of Kings, whenever a new king comes to the throne in Jerusalem, his mother's name is given; this reflects the importance of the queen mother (the *gĕbîrâ*, or "Great Lady") in the court of Judah. The mention of Haggith, Adonijah's mother, reminds us that the position of *gĕbîrâ* is also at stake in the struggle that is about to ensue. The narrator also draws several parallels between Adonijah and the figure of Absalom in 2 Samuel and calls attention to the parallels by naming Absalom explicitly at the end of verse 6. The retinue of chariots, horses (not "horsemen," as several English versions, including the NRSV, render the word), and runners that Adonijah assembles repeats Absalom's pretensions preceding his rebellion against David (2 Sam 15:1). David's silence in the face of Adonijah's presumption recalls his inability to call Amnon to account for the rape of Tamar and his protective indulgence of Absalom even during the latter's armed coup d'état (see 2 Sam 18–19). Adonijah is, like Absalom himself, "a very handsome man" (v. 6; cf. 2 Sam 14:25-26), and follows Absalom in the presumed line of succession. The last elements, Adonijah's good looks and his birth order, balance his boasting in verse 5a and reflect his own point of view rather than being simply objective information supplied by the narrator. Adonijah, we see, is not only presumptuous; he is also spoiled and vain, counting on his father's indulgence and his own beauty to gain him the throne.

Unlike Absalom, however, Adonijah is not actively seeking to unseat his father. His claim "I will be king" (v. 5) contains an emphatic pronoun in Hebrew. (Such emphasis is often lost in English because our language requires pronouns where Hebrew does not. Its force here is "I, and no one else, shall be king.") It is a self-satisfied comment on his status as heir, not a statement of rebellious intent, which would emphasize the verb rather than the subject. His retinue is to be seen as the honor guard of a crown prince. In view of the lack of an established policy of primogeniture, Adonijah is perhaps overconfident, but there is no indication that this small force is the beginning of an army of usurpation. David's declining health would make an attempt to take the throne by violence unnecessary and foolish. Our impressions of Adonijah to this point are hardly flattering, but the support he has from such notables as Joab and Abiathar argues that he is not a fool.

Verses 7-8 offer the first hints of conflict in the story. Adonijah's succession has the support of powerful people in David's court, but other influential figures do not back him. The two parties are presented in partially balanced fashion. There is one military leader in each party: Joab, the head of the army, who supports Adonijah, and Benaiah, the leader of David's personal guard of mercenaries, who does not. Both are identified by a parent's name. (Joab is regularly identified as the son of Zeruiah, his mother, rather than by his father's name, which would be more common Israelite practice. This may be because it was through her that Joab was related to David, who was Zeruiah's brother; see 1 Chr 2:13-16.) There is one priest in each party: Abiathar supports Adonijah, and Zadok does not. Each is identified as "the priest." In addition, those who do not support Adonijah include the prophet Nathan, Shimei and Rei,[2] and David's warriors (who were under the command of Benaiah). The narrator leaves open a tantalizing question: if they do not favor the heir apparent, whom do they support?

There is a historical and perhaps ideological division hidden behind these names. Joab and Abiathar represent the old guard; they were David's companions since his outlaw days during the reign of King Saul, before David's seven-year reign in Hebron and long before his conquest of Jerusalem. Adonijah was born during David's time in Hebron (2 Sam 3:4). By contrast, Benaiah, Zadok, and Nathan do not appear in the Hebrew Bible until after David conquered Jerusalem and established his capital there. Some scholars even suggest that Zadok and Nathan may have been functionaries of the Jebusite cult and court of Jerusalem before David took the city. Whether or not that is so, these individuals may stand for the more pluralistic and cosmopolitan viewpoint that develops in Yahwistic society after it becomes an imperial power. Solomon, born in Jerusalem, will ultimately show himself inordinately sympathetic to political and religious pluralism.

Solomon, however, has not yet been mentioned. Although as the story develops the essential conflict will be between Solomon's partisans and Adonijah's, these introductory sections do not contrast the two rivals; rather, they contrast Adonijah with David himself. David is old and infirm, confined indoors, surrounded by solicitous courtiers and a beautiful woman all concerned about his health. He is passive, acted upon but not himself acting. Our feelings toward him are sympathetic, but we recognize that he is no longer a figure to be admired and followed; his day is done. Adonijah is young and handsome, outdoors, in the midst of military might and political contention. He is active and decisive, boastful, gathering followers and marshaling political support. His personal qualities are unendearing, but his boldness elicits from us a certain grudging admiration. He has the support of shrewd and experienced people; perhaps his shallowness is only apparent and they perceive in him strengths that we have not yet dis-

---

[2]The names "Shimei and Rei," with no further descriptions, are obscure. Both are otherwise unknown, unless "Shimei" is the Shimei son of Ela of 4:18. The Hebrew text may be damaged. A small change in the Hebrew letters would yield "Shimei, the Friend," that is, "Friend [of the King]," which was an office in the royal court (see 4:5, where Zabud, son of Nathan, holds this position).

cerned. David is the past; the inevitable question is, Is Adonijah the future?

Conflict: Sections C and D

Adonijah Holds a Feast: 1:9-10

The action of the story begins in verse 9, when Adonijah holds a feast for his partisans at En-rogel, a spring a few hundred yards south of Jerusalem in the Kidron Valley. (The "stone Zoheleth" is otherwise unknown.) Since the verb "sacrificed" usually occurs in cultic contexts, the feast may have been religious in nature. Here, too, there is a parallel with Absalom, whose rebellion began with a feast (2 Sam 15:11-12); but in Adonijah's case there is no indication that the event represents anything more than a celebration of solidarity with his followers.

Verses 9b-10 list those whom Adonijah does and does not invite to his feast. His list is expansive. "All his brothers, the king's sons" suggests that his status as heir is uncontested by the younger members of the royal family. Primogeniture is the presumption, if not yet the precedent. "All the men of Judah, the king's servants" (NRSV, "all the royal officials of Judah"), however, is exclusive: Adonijah apparently does not invite royal officials from Israel, that is, the northern tribes. This may be another indication of the ideological division noted above. Adonijah's support comes from those who are more closely identified with southern concerns and interests. The phrase also recalls the "servants" who brought Abishag to care for David (v. 2). Are the courtiers who are most closely in David's confidence all from Judah? Has David, in his old age, fallen under the influence of those who would put nostalgia for old ways and old loyalties in place of the broader vision needed in the new world of empire?

The organization of verses 9b-10 is a good demonstration of how the narrator relies on our active cooperation as readers to untangle ambiguity and, literally, to *make* sense of the text. The Hebrew reads, "And he invited all his brothers, the king's sons, and all the men of Judah, the king's servants, and Nathan the prophet, and Benaiah, and the warriors, and Solomon his brother he did not invite." Clearly the list includes both the invited and the uninvited, but where are we to understand the break between the two? (The translator of the NRSV, by moving the words "did not invite" to an earlier point in the sentence, has made our decision for us.) The narrator expects us to use the information in verses 7-8 and to conclude that Adonijah's invitations are extended on a partisan basis, excluding those who do not support him as David's successor. This implies that Adonijah is aware of their opposition, and suggests too that, at least in Adonijah's mind, Solomon is their rival candidate for the throne. All these surmises will be confirmed as the story continues. Another narrative technique in verses 9-10 is also worthy of note. The narrator uses flashback to good effect. Logically, the invitations (and non-invitations) itemized in verses 9b-10 must have preceded the feast Adonijah holds in verse 9a. By recounting the feast before the invitations, the narrator builds tension and delays as long as possible introducing the name of Adonijah's rival, Solomon.

NATHAN CONSPIRES TO MAKE SOLOMON KING: 1:11-14

The scene shifts abruptly to a conversation between Nathan and Bathsheba, Solomon's mother. Nathan was David's court prophet, that is, his role was to communicate to the king God's opinion about affairs of state. It was Nathan who conveyed to David God's promise of an eternal covenant with him and his descendants (2 Sam 7), who confronted and condemned him for his crimes against Uriah (2 Sam 12:1-15), and who conferred a name of great promise on the newborn Solomon (2 Sam 12:24-25). In all those cases, where Nathan's words and activities were consonant with his holy office, the narrator is usually content simply to call him "Nathan"; he is styled "Nathan the prophet" only in 2 Samuel 7:2 and 12:25. Here, where he is embroiled in a sordid palace intrigue with no apparent divine mandate, the narrator insistently—and ironically—reminds us at almost every opportunity that this schemer is "the prophet." Bathsheba is the woman for whom David committed murder. The child of their adulterous union died, but Bathsheba soon bore David another son, Solomon (2 Sam 12:24-25). After Solomon's birth, neither he nor Bathsheba is mentioned again until this chapter.

We hear only Nathan's part of the conversation, but it is enough to reveal his political agenda and his verbal deftness. His claim that Adonijah "has become" king is a double distortion: it changes Adonijah's words in verse 5 from the future to the past tense, transforming them from an innocent assertion into an act of treason; and it implies that Adonijah intends his feast at En-rogel to be his inauguration as king. Nathan identifies Adonijah as "son of Haggith" to remind Bathsheba that the role of queen mother is also at stake, and he points out that she and Solomon are both in grave danger if her son does not succeed to the throne. He refers to David as "our" lord, thereby asserting both his solidarity with Bathsheba and his loyalty to David. Whether

Bathsheba would be motivated more by self-interest or by faithful devotion to David, Nathan offers her a reason to cooperate with his scheme.

Nathan intends to take the offensive in the struggle for succession. He proposes that Bathsheba approach David with a question about an oath the king purportedly swore to her guaranteeing her son's succession. (The very proposal contains a hidden irony, since the name "Bathsheba" may be translated "daughter of an oath"!) As Nathan phrases it to Bathsheba, her question appears to assume that David has approved Adonijah's inauguration, though Nathan is well aware that this is not the case. The approach he counsels is calculated to stir up David's anger against Adonijah without endangering Bathsheba herself. It avoids suggesting that David is no longer in control of things, but it will lead him to conclude that Adonijah thinks so and is acting as if it were the case. The question form itself implies that David must have reasons for naming Adonijah as his successor, and thus softens the tacit accusation that David has violated an oath. Nathan promises to supply "independent" confirmation for Bathsheba's claim.

Nathan's instructions to Bathsheba (vv. 13-14) center on the oath David purportedly swore:

> A. What Bathsheba should do ("go in . . . and say," 1:13a)
> B. Bathsheba's words to David (1:13b)
> C. David's alleged oath (1:13c)
> B'. Bathsheba's words to David (1:13d)
> A'. What Nathan will do ("come in . . . and confirm your words," 1:14)

Bathsheba's and Nathan's actions are complementary: she will go in to the king and speak; he will come in after her and confirm what she has said. The speech Nathan gives her to address to the king consists of two questions surrounding the oath. The first question begins with an emphatic pronoun, "you," followed by the phrase "my lord the king" (Hebrew, *'ădônî hammelek*). The second question ends with the phrase "Adonijah is king" (Hebrew, *mālak 'ădônîyāhû*). The wordplay can be appreciated only in Hebrew: Who is king *(melek/mālak)?* Is it "my lord" *('ădônî,* that is, David) or Adonijah *('ădônîyâ)?* By phrasing things this way, Nathan suggests that the fundamental struggle going on is between David and Adonijah. Since David has already suffered greatly at the hands of another son who tried to wrest the throne from him, Nathan seeks to convince David that the present contention is a rebellion like Absalom's rather than a struggle for the succession.

The oath itself contains a two-part formula. Both parts put emphasis on the subject of the sentence: *"Solomon* [no one else] shall succeed

me as king; it is *he* who will sit on my throne." The formula will
become a leitmotif echoing several times throughout the chapter,
sometimes verbatim, sometimes with modifications. It expresses succinctly the real issue of the whole story: *Who* will be David's successor?

The crucial question, of course, is whether David actually swore
such an oath or whether it is a fabrication by Nathan designed to cozen
the aged king. The conventions of biblical Hebrew narrative would
easily allow the narrator to make the situation clear. Yet there is no
information here or elsewhere in the Hebrew Bible to answer the question one way or the other. That fact is itself significant: we are *meant* to
wonder. The possibility that Nathan and Bathsheba are simply taking
advantage of David's condition to promote their own candidate raises
uncomfortable questions not only about their honesty but about the
whole process by which Solomon becomes king.

The Turning Point: Section E

The crisis is reached in the central section of the story, which consists of four scenes that take place in David's chambers. The scenes are
arranged in two parallel pairs:

> A. Bathsheba's audience with David (1:15-21)
> B. Nathan's audience with David (1:22-27)
> A'. David summons Bathsheba (1:28-31)
> B'. David summons Nathan and others (1:32-37)

BATHSHEBA'S AUDIENCE WITH DAVID: 1:15-21

In the first scene Bathsheba carries out her part in the intrigue Nathan
has devised. The narrator sets the emotional stage by repeating things we
already know, but now showing them to us from Bathsheba's point of
view. As she enters the room, she confronts two stark realities: the king is
very old, and she herself has been replaced at the king's side and in his
bed by the beautiful Abishag (v. 15). Both facts underscore how completely her future depends on her success in the next few moments.

Bathsheba makes a profound obeisance, and the king greets her with
a brief, two-syllable question; perhaps he can manage no greater effort.
Ironically, his question ("What do you want?" Hebrew, *mâ-lāk*) echoes
by coincidence the thematic term of the whole chapter, *mālak*, "to rule as
king." Bathsheba then addresses the king. Her speech is a rhetorical

masterpiece. Structurally, it begins and ends with personal references: David's supposed oath to Bathsheba, and Bathsheba's danger if Adonijah becomes king (vv. 17, 21). Inside those references are two remarks about the succession: Adonijah has become king though David doesn't know it, and all Israel looks to David to decide who shall succeed him (vv. 18, 20). Centered within the speech is a detailed description of the feast Adonijah is celebrating at that very moment (v. 19).

The changes that Bathsheba makes in Nathan's proposed script reveal much about her strong character. The essence of what Nathan told her to say is in verses 17-18a. Everything in verses 18b-21 Bathsheba says on her own initiative. Moreover, where Nathan recommended an oblique approach, Bathsheba mounts a frontal assault. Her emotional manipulation of David is quite different from what Nathan envisaged, but it is equally effective. Instead of questioning David, her words begin with an emphatic pronoun, "you," and bluntly assert that he did make the oath. Bathsheba cites the oath exactly as Nathan worded it, but she adds to the oath's weight by claiming that David swore it "in the name of Yahweh your God" (NRSV, "by the LORD your God").

Where Nathan would have Bathsheba ask why Adonijah has become king—as if David must have made the decision, but for unknown reasons—she confronts him with his ignorance of what is taking place. Unknown to David, she says, others are acting to void the oath he has made. The theme of David's "not knowing" recalls for us that he "did not know" Abishag (v. 4); his physical impotence is symptomatic of his loss of control of public affairs. The implication that David is losing his grip would wound him deeply, and the tacit accusation that he has become an oathbreaker as a result would add insult to injury. Verse 18 repeats the wordplay mentioned above: "Adonijah has become king" (*'ădônîyâ mālak*) and "my lord the king" (*'ădônî hammelek*). The latter phrase will recur three more times in Bathsheba's speech (vv. 20-21), as if to drum into David's consciousness that she is unswervingly loyal to his kingship rather than Adonijah's.

Bathsheba's description of Adonijah's feast repeats information we have already learned from the narrator in v. 9 with two variations, both of which exaggerate the solemnity of the feast. Where the narrator told us that Adonijah sacrificed "sheep, cattle, and fatlings" (the NRSV translation is not exact here), Bathsheba says he sacrificed *"oxen, fatlings, and sheep in abundance."* Moreover, since she has just said that "Adonijah has become king," David will inevitably infer that the feast is an inauguration ceremony. She also tailors Adonijah's list of invitees to suit her purposes. In verse 9b Adonijah invited "all his brothers, the king's sons," reflecting both his own point of view ("brothers") and their significance as members of the royal family ("sons"). Bathsheba, addressing David, simply calls them "the king's sons" (NRSV, "all the children of the king") in deference to David's point of view. Adonijah invited "all the men [i.e., royal officials] of Judah"; Bathsheba leaves this out, since it could suggest a wider political support for Adonijah than she wishes to acknowledge.

Bathsheba adds the names of Abiathar and Joab, whom the narrator has already identified in verse 7 as supporters of Adonijah, though they were not specifically mentioned among those invited in verse 9. The information that two of David's oldest and most faithful comrades have joined Adonijah will come as a further painful betrayal. At the same time, her description of Joab as "commander of the army" subtly introduces a threat of violence that she will invoke again at the end of her speech (v. 21). Since it turns out later that David harbors a secret, deadly grudge against Joab (2:5-6), the mention of Joab here may be a further factor influencing David to turn against Adonijah. As uninvited, she names only Solomon, though the narrator also listed Nathan (of whose exclusion she is clearly aware) and Benaiah. By naming Adonijah's supporters but not Solomon's, Bathsheba conceals the fact that the struggle is between two rivals for their father's throne and conveys the impression that it is between Adonijah and his supporters on the one side and David and those loyal to him on the other. Solomon is simply one of those loyal to David: in Bathsheba's terms, he is David's "servant," a term she does not use of Abiathar or Joab. The phrase "Solomon your servant" in verse 19 is emphasized (the inverted word order of the NRSV reproduces the emphasis well).

The phrase that begins verse 20, "You, my lord the king," is not grammatically integrated with what follows and thus has considerable emphasis. It introduces a flattering appeal to David's vanity that is particularly ironic, since it is Bathsheba who is in fact telling David who should be king after him! The flattery is well timed. After arousing mixed feelings of anger and guilt in David, Bathsheba gives him the opportunity to regain stature (at least in his own eyes) by acting decisively to name a successor. She affirms David's freedom to choose whomever he wishes. In reality, however, her earlier statements that David has sworn a sacred oath in Solomon's favor and that Adonijah has already laid claim to David's throne undercut that freedom and influence David's choice in one direction. The end of verse 20 echoes both parts of the alleged oath: "who shall sit on the throne" recalls the last words of the oath, and "after him" recalls the same word in the first half of the oath (the word is obscured in verse 17 of the NRSV behind the phrase "succeed me," which is literally "reign after me").

In verse 21 Bathsheba returns to a personal appeal. The words do not flow smoothly from verse 20 (the NRSV's "otherwise" is not in the

Hebrew), and the abruptness of the transition points up that this is the emotional bottom line for Bathsheba: she and Solomon are in danger. The phrase "lies down with his ancestors" (NRSV, "sleeps with his ancestors") is a stereotyped Hebrew euphemism for death and burial, reflecting the custom of burying several generations of a family in a common tomb, usually a cave in the ubiquitous limestone hills of Palestine. In David's case, the traditional phrase is inappropriate, since his ancestral home was in Bethlehem, where he grew up as a shepherd. As conqueror of Jerusalem, the "City of David," and as king and founder of a new dynasty, he would not be buried in the family tomb in Bethlehem but in a newly dug royal tomb in his own city. Bathsheba's use of the phrase may be nothing more than convention. On the other hand, it may recall to the king the demands of generational loyalties, and thereby underline both David's obligation to Solomon and Adonijah's alleged repudiation of those loyalties. In any case, the collocation of "sitting on the throne" and "lying down" points once more to David's feebleness: he is bedridden and moribund, no longer able to sit on the throne. The need to assure the succession is pressing.

Bathsheba does not spell out in detail the offense of which she and Solomon will be held guilty (v. 21) or the penalty which that offense will incur. Leaving things to David's imagination is an effective ploy, for, as we will see (2:5-9), David is quite capable of imagining bloody ends for those who oppose royal power. It is noteworthy, though, that Bathsheba lists her own danger ahead of Solomon's (the NRSV reverses Bathsheba's word order): "I and my son Solomon will be counted offenders." This reflects the personal quality of the appeal, but it is also a shrewd psychological move. David may or may not have a particular attachment to Solomon, but his former love for Bathsheba was the stuff of legends. If the power of that devotion can be awakened again, it will likely overwhelm less emotionally volatile issues such as primogeniture or even fitness to rule, much as it once overwhelmed moral strictures against adultery and murder.

NATHAN'S AUDIENCE WITH DAVID: 1:22-27

Nathan enters as planned. The Hebrew text is very vivid, putting us immediately into the scene: "And while she is still speaking to the king, in comes Nathan the prophet!" We must assume that Bathsheba withdraws, as would be proper when the king has speech with one of his close advisers, since later she will be summoned back to David's chambers (v. 28). The fact that the narrator does not explicitly mention her departure, however, allows the memory of her presence to hang in the air, as it were, coloring the scene for us much as Nathan's frequent repetitions of Bathsheba's very words will remind David of her. Nathan's approach to David contrasts with Bathsheba's in several ways. Unlike the wife, who can approach the king immediately, the prophet-courtier must be announced. Bathsheba "bowed," but Nathan "bowed, face to the ground" (NRSV, "did obeisance . . . with his face to the ground"). Where Bathsheba's speech was personal and emotional, Nathan's is formal and concerned about political policy. His approach befits a royal adviser: in a significant matter like the succession, he would expect to have been consulted. As in verses 8-10, the repeated mention of Nathan's position as court prophet underscores the irony of his guiding role in this palace intrigue despite the apparent absence of any divine commission to do so.

The first sentence of Nathan's speech (v. 24) is not a question in Hebrew, as the NRSV translation would have it, but a statement: "My lord the king, you have said . . . ." The pronoun "you" is emphatic and admits of no suspicion that Adonijah's succession could have occurred without David's approval. Similarly, the word order emphasizes the name Adonijah: "it is Adonijah [not someone else] who shall rule after me." Nathan's strategy thus complements Bathsheba's. Where she averred that David promised the throne to Solomon and that Adonijah's actions are done in David's ignorance, Nathan pretends to believe that David has decreed Adonijah's succession. His words, however, are carefully chosen to echo to David the oath in favor of Solomon that Bathsheba has just spoken of (cf. vv. 17 and 24).

David is caught on the horns of a dilemma. If Bathsheba is correct, he has lost control of his kingdom; if Nathan is correct, David has violated a solemn oath. We know that Nathan is not correct, of course, and David presumably realizes it as well. But if Nathan is not correct—so the conspirators hope David's thinking will run—then Bathsheba must be, and David owes Solomon the throne in fulfillment of his solemn oath. Moreover, the prophet's feigned assumption that David has acted in Adonijah's favor will only intensify the king's ire at what both Bathsheba and Nathan paint as Adonijah's presumption.

As evidence for his conclusion that David has named Adonijah to succeed him, Nathan speaks of the feast Adonijah is holding at that very moment. His description of it corresponds extensively with Bathsheba's in wording, thus further confirming to David Bathsheba's honesty and accuracy. But Nathan adds new details calculated to further the conspiracy in Solomon's favor. Lest David think that Adonijah's seizure of the throne is an accomplished fact, Nathan reveals that the feast is being held "today." It is not too late to thwart the pretender's coup! Nathan deemphasizes the list of invitees by leaving out, as Bathsheba also did, the royal officials and by substituting "the army commanders" for the more inflammatory name of Joab.[3] On the other hand, he heightens David's impression of the treasonous character of the gathering by painting the scene in vivid and explicit language as a royal coronation feast: "Here they are, eating and drinking with him, and they've said, 'Long live King Adonijah!'" To a reigning monarch, the acclamation of another as king can only be sedition; and for David in particular, who was once before driven from Jerusalem by a usurping son, the news would evoke as well all the danger, pain, and suffering of the days of Absalom's rebellion.

Unlike Bathsheba, Nathan lists several people whom Adonijah did not invite to his alleged coronation. He places himself first, in terms that strongly emphasize his precedence and loyalty: "And me, myself, your servant, . . . he did not invite." Between his own name and that of Solomon he mentions Zadok the priest to balance Abiathar's presence among Adonijah's supporters, and Benaiah to balance the military commanders. The narrator has already told us that Nathan, Benaiah, and Solomon were not invited (v. 10), and Zadok's status as a non-supporter of Adonijah (v. 8) makes it likely that he was not invited either. Nathan's interweaving of verifiable facts and unverifiable innuendoes gives his speech great manipulative power. He uses the same word as Bathsheba, "your servant," at the beginning and end of the list to mark these four as a small group still loyal to David. The implication is that loyalty to David excludes one from being numbered among those who support Adonijah. In this way Nathan achieves the same illusion as Bathsheba: he presents the conflict as being between Adonijah and David, each with his band of followers, rather than as being between Adonijah and Solomon.

Nathan's final words are a conditional statement, not a question (the NRSV translation is misleading): "If this affair has come about at my lord the king's behest, then you have not let your servants know . . . ." Nathan does not question what David has supposedly done; he simply and somewhat diffidently expresses his surprise and disappointment that David has acted without consulting his loyal retainers. The mildness of his complaint adds one more fillip of guilt to the pressure building up on David. But at the same time Nathan offers David a way out of his dilemma: the king can deny that he is behind Adonijah's actions and repudiate them.

---

[3]This is the reading of the Hebrew text and one ancient Greek translation. Another ancient Greek manuscript tradition, which the NRSV follows here, has "Joab, commander of the army."

Nathan's speech ends with the phrases that have reverberated in David's chambers since Bathsheba's opening words about David's alleged oath: "sit on the throne" and "after him." For us, the incessant repetition of these phrases (vv. 17, 20, 24, 27) unifies the speeches of Bathsheba and Nathan and reflects their character as a single, coordinated campaign. For David, it keeps forcefully in the forefront of his consciousness the decision he must make.

With this final echo of the oath, the story reaches its crisis. Bathsheba and Nathan have used an impressive array of rhetorical strategies to pit David against Adonijah and to present Solomon as the only son still loyal to David. Although they both pay lip service to David's freedom to act on the succession in any way he sees fit, their potent mixture of information and insinuation effectively narrows his options. If he favors Adonijah, he will in effect be surrendering to those who have seemingly betrayed him. If he chooses Solomon, he will both reward loyalty and thwart those who, as Bathsheba and Nathan tell it, have risen up against him.

David Summons Bathsheba: 1:28-31

The turning point occurs here, at the structural center of the story, between the two pairs of interviews in David's chambers. The narrator calls him by his full title, "King David," which also marked the beginning of the first half of the story (v. 1). The title also reflects his change from passive to active: David now becomes decisive and commanding, and will remain so until we are told of his death in 2:10. The very first word of the scene in Hebrew is an active verb, "answered." Except for the weak, two-syllable question in verse 16, it is the first thing David has said or done in the entire story.

This scene, like so many of the preceding ones, is carefully structured:

A. A statement of David about Bathsheba (1:28a)
   B. Bathsheba comes and stands before the king (1:28b)
      C. David reaffirms the oath (1:29-30)
   B'. Bathsheba bows and kneels before the king (1:31a)
A'. A statement of Bathsheba about David (1:31b)

David's statement is a summons. He calls Bathsheba into his presence to reaffirm to her the oath she claims he has sworn. Nathan has presumably left David's chambers, since he will have to be called back in verse 32, but the narrator passes over his departure in silence, just as he did with Bathsheba's in verses 22-27. The effect is similar: Nathan's influence still lingers in the room, even though the king thinks he is acting on his own initiative. The opening verb of the scene strengthens that effect: "King David *answered*." His decision to act in Solomon's favor, as original as it may seem to David himself, is in fact only a *response* to the pressures his beloved wife and trusted courtier have brought to bear upon him.

Bathsheba enters. At her first appearance before David in verses 15-16, she was a petitioner; she approached him, therefore, with a bow. Here she is a summoned subject; she therefore does not bow but "stands before the king"—the standard Hebrew phrase for being at his service. Ironically, this was the position for which Abishag was sought (v. 2: "let her stand before the king"). Bathsheba's implied victory over her beautiful rival foreshadows David's decision to support Solomon over the handsome Adonijah.

David's oath in verses 29-30 is actually an oath within an oath. He swears, in effect, to do as he has sworn, repeating at the center of his solemn speech the words that Bathsheba supplied him with as far back as verse 17. His oath begins with the standard formula, "As Yahweh lives," approximately equivalent to "so help me God" in contemporary American idiom. But he expands the standard formula with a personal reference to Yahweh's faithful care for him. We see here a glimmer of one facet of this complex king's character. Alongside his political shrewdness (which, as we shall see later, can be entirely without scruples), alongside his parental ineptitude, alongside the monumental human weakness that led him to adultery and murder, he has a deeply religious personal devotion to Yahweh.

David's oath in verse 30 contains three clauses, each one introduced by the emphatic word *kî*, "indeed." The effect is powerful and cumulative, culminating in David's present resolve: "Indeed, just as I swore . . . saying, indeed, Solomon shall sit . . . , indeed, just so will I do . . . ."

In the process of voicing his oath, David draws heavily on Bathsheba's earlier words to him, but with some significant changes. Where Bathsheba claimed that David made the oath by "Yahweh your God," David now swears by "Yahweh, the God of Israel." David's devotion to Yahweh is not only based on God's faithfulness to him personally; it also includes a recognition of Yahweh as the national God. This is a subtle repudiation of a political ideology that sees the king as principal mediator between the divine and human realms—the standard view of kingship in the Ancient Near East. For David, Yahweh is directly and immediately the God of the whole people.

A second change is found when David quotes the oath that Bathsheba "reminded" him of. David repeats her words exactly but adds the phrase "in my place" at the end of the oath. The phrase corresponds to "after me" in the preceding line and gives the whole clause better stylistic balance. In fact, it turns this formula into a poetic couplet complete with end-rhyme (which is rather uncommon in Hebrew poetry):

> Solomon your son shall reign after me (*'aḥăray*)
> And he shall sit on my throne in my place (*taḥtāy*).

The effect is twofold. First, poetry embedded in a Hebrew prose narrative often marks a particularly solemn statement. Here the words of the oath—which have been repeated often enough in the story to constitute a leitmotif—become finally effective. They become what Nathan and Bathsheba claimed they were: a royal promise determining the succession. Second, the added phrase highlights the idea contained in "after me," namely, that Solomon's accession to the throne was originally intended to take place after David died. With his next words David will change that expectation.

David's new oath is brief: "Indeed, just so will I do this day." The significant phrase is "this day," which answers to Nathan's shrewd "today" in verse 25. The phrase in David's mouth is more emphatic: not simply "today" but "*this* day." In order to circumvent what he believes is an attempt to seize the crown, David must act right away, before Adonijah's supposed coup can achieve its goal. And therefore the supposed original oath, which promised Solomon the throne upon David's death, must be revised. Solomon must become king "this day," to rule the kingdom as coregent with his father during David's last days.

Bathsheba's reaction is, first, to express her gratitude by a profound obeisance. The two terms are the same as those used for her petitionary approach in verse 16, plus the description "face to the ground" that characterized Nathan's courtly bow in verse 23. By this means the narrator reminds us of both earlier scenes where the seeds were planted that have now borne fruit. Her exclamation, too, is extravagant. She addresses David more elaborately than anywhere else in the story: "my lord the king David," and she wishes him to "live forever." The language is typical courtly exaggeration (cf. Ps 72:5), but in view of David's nearness to death it carries a certain poignant irony. After watching Bathsheba's calculated manipulation of David in verses 17-21, we are justified if her sentiments here ring a bit hollow in our ears.

David Summons Nathan (and Others): 1:32-37

David's decisive behavior continues, and the narrator continues to style him with the full title "King David." He sends for Zadok, Nathan, and Benaiah, the loyal "servants" whose names Nathan so conveniently supplied him as having "not been invited" by Adonijah. There is an irony in the Hebrew text that is lost in translation, for Adonijah's invitation and David's summons are both expressed with the same verb, *qārā'*, "to call." David's summons and the celebration to which it leads will counter and cancel Adonijah's invitation and feast. The king proceeds to give detailed instructions for a ceremony that will inaugurate and enthrone Solomon as king. We shall eventually see this ceremony from three different points of view: here from David's perspective as he plans it; in verses 38-40 from the narrator's perspective as it unfolds; and in verses 43-48 from the perspective of a supporter of Adonijah as Jonathan recounts it to the group gathered at En-rogel.

In a series of eight commands, David details who is to participate in the ceremony and how it is to proceed. First, Benaiah, Zadok, and Nathan are to assemble "the servants of your lord." The term does not mean menials but, as it did in verse 2, courtiers close to the king. Next, they are to mount Solomon on David's own mule. David calls Solomon "my son," reflecting both David's point of view and the basis for Solomon's advancement to the throne. Horses were used for pulling chariots, but they were not yet riding animals in Israel. The commoner's mount was a donkey (see, for instance, 2:40), while the mule seems to have been restricted to the elite; most references to mules in the Hebrew Bible either associate them with the royal family or list them as items of tribute brought to the king along with other exotic and valuable goods. The king's own mule was presumably a particularly notable animal, and, in fact, it is the only time a *female* mule is mentioned in the Hebrew Bible. David refers to it a bit pompously as "the mule which is mine," rather than just "my mule" (NRSV, "on my own mule"). If Solomon is seen riding David's own royal mount, it will be clear to all that his accession to the throne has David's blessing.

Third, Benaiah, Zadok, and Nathan are to "bring Solomon down" to the spring Gihon. This corresponds to Nathan's claim that Adonijah has "gone down" (v. 25) to hold his purported coronation feast. It is an ironic coincidence that David chooses the Gihon for Solomon's ceremony. That spring lies less than half a mile north of En-rogel in the Kidron Valley, where Adonijah's feast is in progress, although neither Bathsheba nor Nathan informed David of its location. Why David would choose the Gihon is unclear. It has no cultic or royal associations that we are aware of, although that may be due to our scanty information about customs in pre-Davidic Jerusalem. It was at that time the main source of water for the city, even though its principal access lay outside the city walls.

At the Gihon, David says, Zadok and Nathan are to anoint Solomon to be king over Israel. Anointing has many meanings in Israel and in other Ancient Near Eastern cultures. In this case it was a consecratory act that set the anointed person apart for unique religious functions. Priests, or according to some passages only the high priest, were anointed. But the word is most commonly applied to the king, who was sometimes called "the anointed *(māšîăḥ)* of Yahweh"; this is the origin of the term "Messiah," which originally meant simply "the anointed (king)." Solomon is to be set apart by anointing for the unique role of king over Yahweh's chosen people. Since anointing is a cultic act, Zadok, the high priest, is to perform it. As prophet, Nathan may also have actively anointed Solomon. There was precedent in the prophet Samuel's anointing of both Saul and David (1 Sam 10:1; 16:1-13), and one of Elisha's disciples will later anoint Jehu (2 Kgs 9). But he is not mentioned as having done so in verse 39, and his role may have been to pronounce a divine oracle of approbation of the new king such as the ones embedded in Psalms 2:7-9 and 110:1, 4.

Solomon will be "king over Israel." The term "Israel" here is a formal and cultic one, as befits the ceremonial language David is using. It refers to the whole people of Yahweh and comprises two originally separate political entities, Judah and Israel (in a more restricted sense). Compare, for example, verse 35, where the narrower political terms are used. The two entities had independently chosen David as their king (see 2 Sam 2:1-4; 5:1-5); his hope was to weld them into a single united kingdom. This hope expressed itself in a religious ideology: the nation was a single people, the people of Yahweh, who had chosen them for his own. Their name as his people was "Israel." The religious ideology was powerful enough to hold the kingdom together through two reigns, but the union came apart after Solomon died (see below, on 1 Kings 12).

David's next command is to sound the shofar, the ram's-horn trumpet. This was not an ordinary horn. It was used chiefly in two contexts: in times of war and in times of solemn religious observance. Its sounding here marks this occasion as singularly important. The people in the city, unexpectedly hearing the shofar in the Kidron Valley, would immediately know that it announced something portentous. After the shofar, David commands a public acclamation, "Long live King Solomon!" This answers exactly to the cry Nathan told David that Adonijah's supporters were shouting (v. 25) and marks in a vivid way the reversal of Adonijah's fortunes and the victory of Solomon's partisans.

In verse 35, David continues with two final instructions. First, the participants in the rite are to climb back up to the city (the hill up from the Gihon is quite steep), with Solomon in the lead on the royal mule. There is in this instruction another subtle allusion to Adonijah's downfall. Solomon's journey is down (v. 33), then up. By contrast, Adonijah began by rising: he "exalted himself" (v. 5; literally, "lifted himself up"); he will finish by being "brought down" from the altar and bowing low to Solomon (v. 53). Finally, David instructs that Solomon is to "enter and sit on my throne; it is he who shall reign in my place." With this decree of enthronement the thematic words originally found in verse 13 and repeated so frequently throughout the story resound again to put the seal, as it were, on Solomon's victory.

David's last words in verse 35 do not continue the series of directives about the ceremony, since the previous instruction has brought the leitmotif of the oath to fulfillment. Rather they are an explicit assertion of the king's commitment to the political decision he has just made. Several points are noteworthy. The word order strongly emphasizes Solomon: "*Him* have I appointed to be ruler . . . ." The word for "ruler," *nāgîd*, appears only here in the whole story. Everywhere else, even in David's mouth, this is a struggle for the office of king. Why the different term here? The answer lies in political history. Not only was the Davidic kingdom a federation of two entities, Judah and Israel; kingship itself was relatively new in the political life of both groups. The older term, *nāgîd*, was more deeply rooted in the traditions of the people, particularly the people of the northern area, Israel. The term "king," *melek*, still smacked a bit of Canaanite political systems. It was David's goal not only to unite the Yahwistic peoples of Judah and Israel into a single kingdom but to include the numerous non-Yahwistic elements of the population as well. He determines the same for Solomon: his son will be "king" according to the new political structures David has erected; but he will also be *nāgîd*, faithful to the older traditions of his Yahwistic subjects. Since he is thinking in terms of the political composition of his kingdom, David naturally speaks of "Israel and Judah," unlike verse 34, where the cultic context made the more comprehensive religious term "Israel" appropriate.

Benaiah responds to David's decree with great enthusiasm. Though David has not given him any explicit task to perform, his office as commander of the king's personal troop of mercenaries would be known to the ancient reader and his function as armed guard for Solomon would be evident. David's language as he describes the ceremony is formal and cultic; mention of security forces would be out of place. By allowing Benaiah to speak here, the narrator achieves two things. First, he achieves a certain balance in the scene: Zadok and

Nathan have been given tasks to perform, but Benaiah has been left out; this gives him a chance to act. Second, the narrator intimates something about Benaiah's character. He is quicker to cheer David's decision than either Zadok or Nathan. Does his alacrity reveal the kind of swift, even unquestioning obedience that is often prized in military personnel? In other words, is Benaiah a yes man? We will have more reasons in 1 Kings 2 to suspect that he is.

Benaiah's first word is a powerful one. "Amen!" is an exclamation of commitment much stronger than its use in English would suggest. Its fundamental meaning is to express the absolute reliance of the speaker on the person to whom he or she is speaking. In response to a statement, it means, "I trust your honesty and accept that what you say is true." In response to a promise, it means, "I trust your faithfulness and rely on what you promise." In response to a directive, as here, it means, "I trust your integrity and will obey what you command."

Benaiah continues with what is probably a wish: "May Yahweh ordain . . . ," though the Hebrew can be understood as a simple statement of fact expressing Benaiah's confidence in the rightness of David's decision: "Yahweh will ordain . . . ." Like Bathsheba in verse 17, he relates Yahweh directly to David ("the God of my lord the king") rather than to the whole people as David did. This may be standard court flattery, but it also reflects an aggrandizement of the intermediary role of the king that is not fully compatible with the thinking of pre-monarchic Yahwism. If his words are understood as a statement rather than as a wish, the aggrandizement is extreme: the king has said it, therefore God wills it.

In verse 37 Benaiah continues with two further wishes for the newly named king. The first desires for Solomon the same level of divine favor that David has enjoyed. The second goes beyond the first, expressing the hope that Solomon's reign will actually exceed David's. Some have read this remark as tactless, but it is not. In Israelite understanding, David's glory would live on in Solomon's. To wish that Solomon grow even greater than David is not to disparage David but to wish for him an ever increasing fame in the next generation. Benaiah ends his unrestrained outburst with the same elaborate title used by Bathsheba in verse 31, "my lord the king David."

The figure of David undergoes a startling transformation in these two scenes. In place of the feeble, passive, even unresponsive old man of the first half of the story, we witness a determined figure, able to make a firm decision and to act unhesitatingly on it. Whatever the king's physical frailties, he is clearly in complete control of his mental faculties. The narrator signals that control particularly through David's use of language. David is able to quote exactly Bathsheba's version of the oath. He recalls details of Nathan's speech (e.g., the word "today," the verb "go down," the acclamation of Adonijah) and incorporates responses to them in his speeches. Even more impressive is his rhetorical inventiveness. He elevates the oath as originally spoken by Bathsheba to solemn poetry by the addition of a single word, and he structures his own oath around three repetitions of "indeed" that bring it gradually to a powerful climax. His directives for Solomon's inauguration ceremony are organized symmetrically:

> A. Solomon is to be seated on the king's mule;
> B. He is to be led down to the Gihon;
> C. He is to be anointed king;
> D. The shofar is to be sounded;
> C'. Solomon is to be acclaimed king;
> B'. He is to go up, leading the people;
> A'. He is to sit on the king's throne.

Furthermore, David distinguishes clearly and appropriately between cultic and political language. When he orders the ceremony, his sentences use parallel syntax and cultic vocabulary (for example, "Israel" as the whole people of Yahweh). Each sentence begins with an imperative verb or its equivalent; the whole series of commands has a regularity and cadence that befit the rubrics of a cultic celebration. On the other hand, when he speaks in political terms at the end of verse 35, he breaks the pattern of the series of commands to emphasize Solomon's primacy and uses politically sensitive terms like *nāgîd* and "Israel and Judah." Perhaps most striking of all is David's unprecedented decision to establish a coregency immediately. This reveals both a sharp insight into the demands of the current moment and an ability to formulate creative solutions to those demands.

These evidences of David's mental alertness further complicate the unresolved issue of the genuineness of the oath. There are reasons to consider it a fabrication intended to dupe a dotard king; for example, if it was genuine, Bathsheba, to whom the oath was allegedly made, should have raised the issue, not Nathan. Yet, if it was a fabrication, it is unlikely that it would have succeeded, for a dotard this David plainly is not. The ambiguity is never resolved and in fact forms part of a covert pattern of ambivalence that runs through 1 Kings 1–11 (see the discussion of the characterization of Solomon, p. 33).

Resolution: Sections D', C', and B'

The next three sections of the story unravel the twisted strands of conflict. The first describes Solomon's inauguration ceremony as it unfolds at the Gihon spring. The second shows Adonijah's faction as it receives the news about Solomon's victory. The third brings the two rivals face to face to determine Adonijah's fate.

Nathan and Others Make Solomon King: 1:38-40

The scene of Solomon's anointing is succinct but conforms closely to David's instructions. However, instead of repeating David's formal, step-by-step directives, the narrator reorganizes the elements for greater narrative interest. He situates our vantage point, as it were, at the Gihon. From there we watch the procession come down the slope of the Kidron Valley from the city: the first word of verse 38 is the verb "went down." This necessitates recounting the events out of chronological order, since several of the details mentioned later (for instance, mounting Solomon on the king's mule and taking the horn of oil from the tent) must have preceded the descent to the Gihon. It is a mark of the narrator's deft artistry that we do not sense the temporal dislocation as disrupting the flow of the story.

Verse 38 identifies the principal members of Solomon's entourage, whom David commissioned to perform the ceremony. For David's "the servants of your lord" the narrator substitutes the "Cherethites and the Pelethites," mercenary soldiers who made up David's personal bodyguard. The terms are of uncertain meaning; most scholars think that they are etymologically related to "Cretans" and "Philistines," that is, to various seafaring groups that came out of the west and settled on the Mediterranean shore of Palestine in the century or so before David's rise to power. David chose them for his closest guard precisely because they were drawn from neither Israel nor Judah; they owed allegiance to neither of the political components of the kingdom but to David alone. At this time they were under Benaiah's command.

Before Zadok anoints Solomon, the narrator inserts a note that Zadok had taken the oil from "the tent," that is, the tent that David constructed in Jerusalem to house the ark of Yahweh (see 2 Sam 6:17). This holy oil, itself consecrated by being in the presence of Yahweh, will in turn consecrate Solomon king. The shofar is blown and Solomon's kingship is acclaimed, as David ordered. Of note here is that "all the people" voice the acclamation. Since the entire ceremony is done hurriedly in order to forestall Adonijah's supposed coup, it is improbable that any effort is made to gather the populace. It is more likely that the fateful sound of the shofar draws a curious throng to the Gihon, who then join spontaneously in the ceremony.

At this point the narrator adds a graphic description of the crowd's joyous celebration, "piping" and "rejoicing" as they follow Solomon back up to Jerusalem. He ends with a startling image: their tumult is so great that it splits the earth! The claim is certainly an exaggeration, but it serves an important narrative purpose: it assures that the noise is loud enough to be heard a half-mile away, where Adonijah and his supporters are feasting unawares. Since the narrator has situated us at the Gihon, we watch the procession return to the city, but we do not join it. The last of David's directives, therefore, namely the enthronement of Solomon, is not yet mentioned, since it takes place out of our sight. Instead of climbing to Jerusalem with the procession, we turn south a few hundred yards down the Kidron Valley to En-rogel to watch as Adonijah's partisans learn of what has transpired.

Adonijah's Feast Is Disrupted: 1:41-50

The loud noise of the crowd at the Gihon serves as the bridge to carry us to En-rogel, enabling us as readers to keep our temporal bearings despite the shift in our vantage point. In fact, the transition is instantaneous, for the noise we heard at the Gihon in verse 40 is just being heard by Adonijah and his guests in verse 41. The assembled guests hear the general uproar; the battle-trained ears of Joab pick out of the din the ominous sound of the shofar, though he does not mention it to the others. His question is oddly phrased in Hebrew and may be a colloquialism something like "Why this noise of the city a-roaring?" The parenthetical remark that the guests have just finished eating when they hear the noise is prophetic: the noise means, in fact, that Adonijah and his partisans no longer have any reason to celebrate. The party is over in every sense!

The next verse begins vividly. "While he [Joab] is still speaking, here comes Jonathan!" The expression is identical with that used in verse 22 and points up a comparison of Jonathan and Nathan that we shall examine in a moment. Adonijah welcomes Jonathan warmly as an *'îš ḥayil*, a barely translatable phrase that means something like "a worthy fellow," "a solid character," "a man of substance." In this context it implies Jonathan's loyalty to Adonijah and the latter's awareness and appreciation of his support. Adonijah blithely assumes that because Jonathan is a friend, his news must be good. Adonijah's complacency and vanity have not changed from our first introduction to him in 1:5-8. Unknown to him, however, his star has fallen. The narrator has brought us to En-rogel just in time to savor the irony of his impending disillusionment.

Jonathan's first word intensifies the irony. The NRSV translates it "No," as if Jonathan is aware that his news will spell disaster to Adonijah. But the Hebrew word carries this meaning only in texts composed much later than this passage. At the time that this scene was probably written, the word conveys strong agreement: "Yes, indeed!" Either Jonathan is using the word sarcastically ("Ha! *Sure* I bring good news!"), or he naively presumes that Adonijah and his guests will be overjoyed that David has finally acted and named a successor, even if that successor is Solomon. In the latter case, we have to visualize Jonathan giving an eager and excited account of Solomon's consecration and enthronement, oblivious to the horror dawning on the faces of his audience. The narrator offers us no sure way to resolve this ambiguity. On the contrary, he piles irony upon irony. The word Jonathan uses, *'ăbāl*, sounds almost exactly like an entirely separate Hebrew word, *'ābal*, meaning "to mourn." Whether he realizes it or not, Jonathan's news sounds in Adonijah's ears as a reason to mourn.

Jonathan recounts the events that have taken place. First, the pith of the message: "Our lord the king David" (note the elaborate formula already used by Bathsheba and Benaiah; like them, Jonathan seems truly devoted to David) "has made Solomon king." He goes on to describe the details of the inauguration ceremony from the perspective of an observer. We have already seen those details from David's viewpoint and from the vantage afforded us by the narrator. How does Jonathan's view differ? Unlike the narrator in verses 38-40, he tells the story in the order in which the events occurred. But he abbreviates or even leaves out some events that he probably considers of secondary importance. For example, he mentions all the participants, including the mercenary guards under Benaiah's command, but he telescopes the procession to the Gihon into one clause. He recounts the anointing but does not speak of the shofar, the presence of "all the people" (vv. 39-40), or their acclamation of Solomon's kingship. He mentions the procession back up the hill and the rejoicing but not the pipes. He answers the question Joab was asking when he arrived, but not in quite the way we expect. He does not identify the noise Adonijah and his companions heard as the crowd's joyful tumult on the way back up to the city. He says rather that it was an uproar in the city itself, one that presumably broke out as the news spread through the streets.

With those words Jonathan's description turns to things we did not see from our position at the Gihon. The rest of his speech is punctuated by three repetitions of *wĕgam*, "and what's more" (the NRSV obscures the repetition; *wĕgam* is the first word of verses 46, 47, and 48); each occurrence introduces a separate bit of news. The first item is something we can anticipate, since it was part of David's original directives: Solomon has taken his seat upon the throne.

The second and third items are as much news to us as they are to Adonijah. The second item recounts a scene in David's chambers. David's "servants" (the courtiers of verse 2? the Cherethites and Pelethites?) come to David to congratulate him and offer blessings on the reign of his son. Their wishes are very similar in spirit to those voiced by Benaiah in verses 36-37, including the use of a title that links God personally to David (the Hebrew of verse 47 has "your God" where the NRSV has simply "God"). David acknowledges their words by "bowing upon the bed." The odd image seems to confirm that David was bedridden (cf. Gen 47:31).

The third item is David's prayer in response to his servants' good wishes. Several of his words recall earlier elements of the story. He uses the national term "God of Israel," as he had done also in response to Bathsheba. His "today" recalls Nathan's words in verse 25 and David's repetition of the term in verse 30. The phrase he uses for Solomon's kingship, "sit on my throne," echoes the familiar thematic words of the oath. The narrator, too, slips an ironic echo into David's speech: the verb the NRSV translates as "granted" is *nātan*, which is also Nathan's name! Nathan may appear to us to be the moving force behind Solomon's victory, but David assures us that it is really Yahweh who is responsible. The whole prayer reminds us of the devout side of David's character, about which we have already had occasion to comment.

This is not the only play the narrator makes on Nathan's name. The figure of Jonathan is introduced here not as a highly developed character—he appears nowhere else in 1 Kings—but to add depths of allusion and irony to the tale. One aspect of this is the way in which the narrative function of Jonathan (= "Yo-Nathan") contrasts with that of Nathan. Nathan began the conflict with his announcement to Bathsheba that "Adonijah has become king and our lord David does not know it"; "Yo-Nathan" ends it with his announcement to Adonijah that "our lord the king David has made Solomon king."

A second aspect of Jonathan's presence in the story is that he is a further thread in the narrator's tapestry of allusions to the earlier struggle for the throne between David and Absalom. The story is recounted in 2 Samuel 15–17. When Absalom's forces temporarily drove David from Jerusalem, several of David's loyalists remained in the city. Ostensibly they transferred their allegiance to Absalom, but in reality they acted as spies, sending information to David in the wilderness. These included Hushai, an adviser of David, and the priests

Zadok and Abiathar; the priests' sons, Ahimaaz, son of Zadok, and Jonathan, son of Abiathar, acted as messengers. They did not enter the city but stayed at En-rogel to receive their intelligence from their fathers. From there they brought it to David. The contrast of the two stories is strong. In both, Jonathan is a messenger. But in 2 Samuel he comes *from* En-rogel, bringing word to David (who will ultimately be victorious) about his eldest son's seizure of the throne. In 1 Kings he comes *to* En-rogel, bringing word to the eldest son (who has been defeated without knowing it) about David's awarding the throne to another.

Jonathan's speech provides another example of the narrator's ability to manipulate narrative time. Realistically, Jonathan could not have seen what he claims to have knowledge of: he arrived at En-rogel just as Joab was reacting to the sound of the shofar; Solomon's enthronement, the wishes of the servants, and David's prayer had not yet occurred. Yet the distortion of time is so deftly done that we scarcely notice it. If we did, we would have to suspect some strange campaign of deception on Jonathan's part; but we do not. We accept his recital at face value, since the events of which it informs us accord entirely with our expectations. The temporal telescoping simply adds to the speed with which the events seem to unfold. We sense a sort of breathless rush—Jonathan must have run all the way to En-rogel—that his repeated "and what's more" only intensifies.

Jonathan's news quells any spirit of celebration at En-rogel. The reactions of Adonijah's guests in verse 49 are compared and contrasted with Adonijah's own in verse 50. (Adonijah's name is emphasized at the beginning of verse 50, which could be translated: "But as for Adonijah, he feared . . . .") The guests "tremble"; Adonijah's fear is more specific: he "fears Solomon." The guests "get up and go, each his own way"; Adonijah also "gets up and goes," but his way, too, is more specific: he goes to the altar, where he claims sanctuary by grasping the "horns of the altar." The altar in question is not further identified, though it is probably the altar at the tent housing the ark of Yahweh. Later Joab will seek refuge there as well (2:28). The "horns of the altar" are projections on the four corners of the altar's flat top; several examples of such altars have been found in archaeological excavations in Palestine. These projections were smeared with the blood of sacrificial animals and were considered the holiest part of the altar. To grasp them was to put oneself under the protection of the deity, a protection that could be annulled only for very grave cause.

In terms of unraveling the narrative conflict, Adonijah's refuge at the altar temporarily checks the resolution of the story. Two elaborate, contrasting movements here reach a momentary stalemate:

Adonijah's movement	Solomon's movement
large entourage gathered	small entourage gathered
descent to spring En-rogel	descent to spring Gihon
feasting	anointing
the shofar heard	the shofar blown
news of Solomon's kingship	acclamation of Solomon's kingship
entourage scattered	entourage increased ("all the people")
refuge at the altar	sits on the throne

Solomon sits on the throne, with royal and military power to back him; he has won. But Adonijah clings to the altar, with divine sanctuary to protect him; he has not admitted defeat. One more step is necessary to resolve the issue: the rivals must meet.

ADONIJAH ABASES HIMSELF: 1:51-53

The third section of the resolution finally brings the two rivals together, although even here their meeting is delayed until the very last words of the scene. Since Adonijah cannot leave the altar without relinquishing his asylum, negotiations between him and Solomon take place through intermediaries. Thus the narrator can put their encounter off until the last possible moment.

This scene is linked to the preceding one by the repetition of the mention of Adonijah's fear followed by his taking sanctuary at the horns of the altar. Adonijah's reaction to Solomon's victory is ambiguous. We have not yet seen Solomon in action and know very little about his character; Adonijah presumably knows him better than we do. Is Adonijah's fear of bloody reprisals from Solomon an accurate reading of Solomon's character? Or is it perhaps a projection of how Adonijah himself would have acted had he been victorious (compare Nathan's warning in verse 12 and Bathsheba's plea in verse 21)? Below we will examine the narrator's use of suspense and ambiguity in revealing Solomon's character to us.

Adonijah's actions show that he knows Solomon has won. His words, however, attempt to salvage at least a degree of personal safety from the wreckage of his ambitions. Through the anonymous messengers he asks of Solomon an oath of amnesty before he will agree to leave his place of refuge. The fact that Adonijah thinks he still holds any cards to bargain with is consistent with the naive complacency that has characterized him throughout the chapter (for example, in verses 5 and 42). It is not the last time that Adonijah will reveal this trait; eventually it will prove his undoing (see 2:13-25).

What Adonijah says is a curious mixture of the tactless and the tact-
ful. He phrases his request baldly and does not use the small forms of
social politeness that are available in Hebrew. For example, he says,
"Let Solomon swear to me . . ." instead of "Let Solomon swear to me,
if he will . . . ," and "that he will not kill me" instead of "that I shall
not die." Yet he calls himself Solomon's "servant," implying that he
acquiesces to Solomon's lordship.

Solomon's response is shrewd. He apparently accedes to Adonijah's
request, but in fact he holds back on two important counts: he does not
swear an oath, and the amnesty he grants is conditional rather than
absolute. Moreover, the conditions are couched in vague generalities
that offer Adonijah nothing in the way of real security. The first condition is that Adonijah must prove to be a *ben ḥayil*, virtually the same
phrase Adonijah himself had used of Jonathan in verse 42. It might be
translated here "worthy" or "noble"—but who is to say what specific
behavior will satisfy such a condition? The second condition is even
vaguer: "wickedness" must not "be found" in him. Again, who defines
"wickedness," and who will do the finding? The answer is clear:
Solomon will decide, as and when he wishes, whether the conditions
have been fulfilled.

The negotiations completed, the narrator quickly brings the scene
to an end: verse 53 speeds through these final actions with five verbs
in fifteen words. Adonijah does not "come down" from the altar;
rather, Solomon has him "brought down." Does Adonijah realize that
Solomon's mercy is only superficial and refuse to leave the altar voluntarily? In contrast to their subtle and wordy negotiations through
intermediaries, their encounter is brief and terse. Adonijah acknowledges Solomon with a silent obeisance, and Solomon dismisses him
with two words: "Go home!"

Solomon's final command is one more allusion to the Absalom
story. Before Absalom's rebellion he had been in self-imposed exile
because he feared David's reprisals for having murdered Amnon (see
above, p. 4). The reconciliation that Joab engineered brought Absalom
back into the country but not into David's good graces. David would
not see him face to face but sent him "to his home" (2 Sam 14:24). The
command does not impose a form of house arrest—at least not in
Adonijah's case—since it is clear from the next chapter that he still had
access to the palace. But it can hardly be called a cordial reunion. In
Absalom's case, his dismissal by David was only a partial and temporary resolution of the conflict. His attempt to seize the throne materi-
alized afterward. Will a similar pattern occur with Adonijah? We sense
that it might and, in view of the vagueness of the conditions Solomon
imposes in verse 52, it seems that he thinks so too.

The narrator's language reflects Solomon's ascendancy and Adonijah's defeat. Adonijah is named in verse 51, and never again in the scene. It is as if his significance as an individual evaporates with his hopes for the throne. On the other hand, the narrator names Solomon seven times in the three verses, four of those times by the full title "King Solomon." The title is used first by the messengers, then by Adonijah as reported by the messengers (both in verse 51). In verse 53 the narrator uses the title twice, the second time reflecting Adonijah's viewpoint as he abases himself before the monarch.

The Characterization of Solomon

The lack of characterization of Solomon throughout the whole story to this point is striking—until this scene he is almost entirely absent! Despite his centrality in the plot, the narrator keeps him at a distance from us. For example, in verses 5-7 we meet Adonijah, we learn his mother's name, his birth order, his handsomeness, his actions as heir apparent, and the names of his supporters. By contrast, we are never told explicitly that Solomon is Adonijah's rival, nor do we learn much personal about him. We know only how other characters perceive him: Adonijah seems to consider him a competitor for the throne; Nathan, Benaiah, and others apparently favor him. But we do not know whether he shares their hopes or is even aware of them, or whether the narrator favors Solomon or Adonijah.

Solomon himself does not appear on the scene until verse 38. Even when David summons the participants in Solomon's ceremony of anointing and enthronement (v. 32), he does not summon Solomon himself! When we finally see Solomon in verses 38-40, it is as if from a distance, and he is completely passive. He is seated on the mule, he is led to Gihon, he is anointed by Zadok, the people go up after him. He is the subject of no verbs, he speaks no words, he performs no actions. The only active thing he does is "sit on the throne" (v. 46), and this we hear of only through the words of another character, Jonathan. Solomon has become king, and we have learned virtually nothing about him!

When we arrive at the scene where Adonijah and Solomon will meet face to face, we are justifiably curious. The narrator's strategy has built up considerable suspense about this unknown who has unexpectedly emerged as David's successor. How he treats his erstwhile rival will give us our first insight into his character. Adonijah expects the worst; Solomon's judgment, however, turns out to be merciful, even if it is framed in politically cautious language.

Our first impression of the new king is accordingly positive. We
sense, however, beneath the vague conditions with which he hedged
Adonijah's amnesty, that Solomon is not a simple and straightforward
character. In addition, the unresolved question of David's alleged oath,
even though it reflects on the integrity of Nathan and Bathsheba more
than on Solomon's, nevertheless casts a shadow of doubt over the
entire series of events that won him the throne. This narrative strategy
will mark the next several chapters of the Solomon story: on the surface he will be presented generally in a positive light; beneath the surface the narrator will strew gaps and ambiguities that invite a much
more critical appraisal of Solomon.

Transition: Section A'

The first scene of chapter 2 serves as a transition between the stories in 1:1-53 and in 2:12b-46. The scene comprises a narrative frame,
2:1 + 2:10-12a, and a lengthy speech by David, 2:2-9. The frame, which
recounts David's death, completes the concentric pattern described
above (see p. 3) and brings the story of chapter 1 to a close. The speech
looks forward to the events that follow in chapter 2, where Solomon
acts to eliminate those he considers threats to his security. By interweaving the two elements in this way, the narrator is able to give us
simultaneously a sense of closure and a sense of smooth continuance.

NARRATIVE FRAME: 2:1, 10-12a

Most of the action of chapter 1 happened in a single day, as the frequently repeated "today" made clear (vv. 25, 30, 48, 51; in verse 51 the
NRSV translates it "first"). This scene appears to take place some time
later. It is not clear how much time has passed, but we do not get the
impression that it has been very long. The opening words, "David's
time to die," remind us that the decisive David of 1:28-35 is still the old
man of 1:1. His energetic words do not change the fact that he remains
bedridden (1:47). His death cannot be far off. Now that time has come.
The words thus establish a connection with chapter 1, particularly
with 1:1-4, despite the apparent lapse of time since those events. They
also point forward to 2:10-12a, the end of the present scene, which
recount David's death, burial, and succession by Solomon.

Biblical heroes often deliver themselves of long speeches when
they are at the point of death (see, for instance, Jacob in Genesis 49,

Moses in Deuteronomy 31–33, Joshua in Joshua 23–24, and Samuel in 1 Samuel 12). And the verb "to charge, to command" is sometimes used to describe a deathbed speech that expresses the dying person's last wishes (for example, Gen 49:29; see also 2 Sam 17:23 and 2 Kgs 20:1, where the NRSV translates the verb "set [your house] in order"). David's words in verses 2-9, therefore, are presented as a sort of last will and testament, conveying the final thoughts and desires of Israel's greatest king. (See below, p. 37, for a discussion of the speech itself.)

The account of David's death and burial and the succession of Solomon follows a common pattern for marking the transition from one king's reign to another's (see below, p. 206). David is said to "sleep with his ancestors," a stereotyped reference for dying in peace, as opposed to dying violently by assassination or in battle, and being buried in one's family tomb. (Bathsheba used the same formula in 1:21.) In David's case the conventional phrase is only half appropriate: he dies peacefully but he is buried, not in his ancestral tomb at Bethlehem, but, as the next words state, in the "City of David." This term for Jerusalem reflects that David's conquest of the city (recounted in 2 Samuel 5:6-10) was accomplished using his own private troops, not forces from the tribes of Judah or Israel. Jerusalem thus became David's private holding, crown property rather than part of either of the larger political entities that made up David's kingdom. As founder of a new royal dynasty, David would be buried inside his own capital; subsequent royal tombs would be located in the same area. (Several very large tombs have been unearthed in Jerusalem on the southern end of the Ophel hill, where David's city was situated. Many archaeologists suspect that they were the royal tombs of the kings of Judah, though they were used as quarries in Roman times and no identifying marks have survived. The present tourist site in Jerusalem known as "King David's Tomb" is almost certainly based on later, inauthentic traditions.)

David's reign is computed at forty years. The number may be conventional for "a full generation," since "forty" is a traditional length for periods of time and particularly for reigns.[4] On the other hand, the specification that the forty years included seven at Hebron and thirty-three at Jerusalem, and the similarity of this information to that in 2 Samuel 5:4-5, may indicate that, in David's case, forty years is approximately accurate. The narrator neatly balances religious and political

---

[4]See, for example, the phrases "forty days" in Genesis 7:4, 12; 8:6; Exodus 24:18; 34:28; Numbers 13:25; and "forty years" in Genesis 25:20; 26:34; Exodus 16:35; Numbers 14:33. Rules of "forty years" are mentioned in Judges 3:11; 5:31; 8:28; 1 Samuel 4:18; 1 Kings 11:42; 2 Kings 12:1.

perspectives. He uses "Israel" in the religious sense of the whole people. But by recalling that David's reign had two phases, Hebron (where David ruled only over Judah) and Jerusalem (where he ruled over both Israel and Judah), the narrator gives due weight to the fact that David's kingdom never entirely lost its character as a federation to become a truly unified nation.

The standard notices, or "regnal formulas," that mark the end of a king's reign usually conclude with the statement that "so-and-so succeeded him" (literally, "reigned in his place"). The regnal formulas are so conventional and stereotyped that the use of a different phrase here for Solomon is noteworthy. The words "sat on the throne of David his father" are still another echo of the leitmotif of David's oath from chapter 1. They answer, finally, the question Bathsheba voiced in 1:20 and bring the whole drama of chapter 1 to an appropriate conclusion.

Before we go on to look at David's speech, which will orient us forward toward the events of 2:12b-46, we should pause to appreciate the overall narrative artistry of the story we have just examined in detail. The narrator has in fact created two different stories and told them side by side. The first is a story that contrasts Adonijah and Solomon as two rivals for David's throne. This contrast is established narratively by equipping each rival with a similar band of supporters: a mother, a priest, a military commander, and miscellaneous others (Adonijah invites "all the king's sons, and all the men of Judah"; Solomon is accompanied by "the Cherethites and Pelethites, and all the people"). The contrast is furthered by the way in which each principal is characterized: Adonijah is depicted directly, and we see him as vain, naive, presumptuous, and complacent in his future as heir. For the most part, Solomon is depicted indirectly, as others see him or act upon him. We learn virtually nothing directly about him until near the end of the story, and what we learn then is compromised by its ambiguity. The story is a form of "victorious underdog" tale so typical of the Hebrew Bible, where younger sons supplant older ones with such regularity that the pattern becomes almost predictable (for example, Ishmael and Isaac; Esau and Jacob; Perez and Zerah in Genesis 38:27-30; Manasseh and Ephraim in Genesis 48:8-20). Adonijah, the heir apparent, is handsome, well-known, and has influential support for his claim on the throne. Nevertheless, he loses out to a shadowy figure of whom we know little at the start of the story and little more at the end.

The second story is the one crafted by Nathan and Bathsheba to tell David. It presents the struggle for the throne as a conflict between Adonijah and David himself. As Bathsheba and Nathan portray them, Adonijah's actions are an overt attempt to seize the throne. This naturally influences David to decide against him. But the two conspirators carefully avoid presenting Solomon as an alternative candidate for succession. They do not compare him with Adonijah, nor do they give any indication that the two sons have similar groups of supporters. Yet Bathsheba and Nathan manage to inform David of all the necessary names, with their respective allegiances; and their repeated protestations about the loyalty to David of those who are in fact Solomon's partisans direct his attention where they want it to go.

The theme of Absalom serves to unite the two stories. For David, Adonijah's alleged grab for the kingship cannot avoid raising the specter of Absalom's earlier rebellion, with all its attendant social and political upheaval as well as the personal suffering and grief it entailed for David himself. This supplies motivation for David's decision to act definitively by naming Solomon as coregent immediately, lest another civil war break out. Yet, surprisingly, none of the textual allusions to the Absalom stories occur in conversation directed to David, where they would strengthen his perception of Adonijah as a usurper. Rather, most of them are found in the narrator's own words; they are all for the reader's benefit. Since the narrator never gives us any reason to believe that Adonijah's actions are an attempt on the throne, we know that that is not the link between him and Absalom. The link is that both were heirs apparent, and neither obtained the throne. Thus the narrator foreshadows failure right from his first mention of Adonijah, where the allusions to Absalom begin (1:5). The foreshadowing extends to chapter 2 as well, where Adonijah, like Absalom, will lose his life.

DAVID'S SPEECH: 2:2-9

David's speech has long troubled commentators. It is an uneasy combination of religious platitudes and unscrupulous violence. The juxtaposition of verses 2-4 and 5-9 is jarring, and many scholars have suggested that verses 2-4 are an insertion by a later deuteronomistic editor.[5] The reason for such an editorial insertion would be to put in

---

[5] "Deuteronomistic" is the term scholars use to refer to the theological school of thought in the eighth to sixth centuries B.C.E. that produced the final forms of the books of Joshua, Judges, 1–2 Samuel, and 1–2 Kings. These works are collectively called the "Deuteronomistic History," since they take their theological inspiration from the Book of Deuteronomy. The theological passages composed by members of this school can be identified by characteristic vocabulary and style (for example, "statutes, commandments, ordinances and testimonies") and by characteristic theological preoccupations such as the importance of the Temple in Jerusalem, "the place that Yahweh your God has chosen for his name to dwell" (see, for example, 1 Kgs 8:29).

David's mouth—and thus endow with Davidic prestige—unalloyed deuteronomistic theology. Similar deuteronomistic ideas are found in the farewell speeches of Joshua (Josh 23) and Samuel (1 Sam 12). Many passages of the Hebrew Bible underwent such editorial modification in the course of the centuries before they became recognized as sacred texts, and it is indeed possible that something similar has happened here. That should not prevent us, however, from attempting to understand the text as a coherent product in the shape that its final editor gave it. In this instance there are three observations that can enable us to make sense of the undeniable disparity between the two parts of David's speech.

First, there is the character of David himself as we find it particularly in 2 Samuel. He is surely the most richly drawn, complex, and multifaceted human figure in the Hebrew Bible (only the character of Yahweh is more complex). We have already had occasion to refer to David's deep and sincere religious devotion to God, which nevertheless did not prevent him from committing adultery and murder or protect him from failing completely as a parent. David also showed himself capable of bloody vendetta (2 Sam 21:1-9), as well as of profiting from political murder while his own hands remained clean (e.g., 2 Sam 4). It is certainly not inappropriate that his final speech, meant to "set his house in order," reflects these same extremes of character.

Second, there is the character of Solomon as we will see it revealed in 2:12b-46. He is always attentive to the niceties of legal observance, yet he is not above twisting evidence and, if need be, falsifying it in order to gain what he wants. The ambivalence in David's speech between pious obedience to the law and ruthless expediency aptly foreshadows the ambiguity we will find in the narrator's characterization of Solomon.

Third, there is the possibility of reading the speech as having a consistent tone throughout. To do so, we must remember that when a narrator puts pious deuteronomistic language in a character's mouth, it is no longer a narrator talking, much less a deuteronomist. The language must now be read in the context of the character and the entire situation. David may use deuteronomistic language for purposes quite different from a deuteronomistic theologian. Here, for example, David is in the process of giving Solomon his final advice, one king to another, on how to assure his success. But David's suggestions are made by innuendo, indicated by oblique references like "act according to your wisdom" (v. 6) and "you are a wise man; you will know what to do" (v. 9). David expects Solomon to be shrewd enough to read between the lines of his advice. The deuteronomistic platitudes in verses 2-4 function much like the references to wisdom. Solomon is to hear both platitudes and pragmatism and to read between the lines: "Obey the law (you know what I mean) and make sure you protect yourself from your enemies."

David's opening sentence shows that he is aware he is about to die and that these will be his last words. We anticipate, therefore, that what he tells Solomon will be weighted with the solemnity of the moment. His first command to his son is "Be strong! Be a man!" In terms of the whole speech, the command points forward both to the discipline necessary to be faithful to Yahweh's law and to the brutality of the advice David will impart in verses 5-9. "Being strong," for David, means religious obedience; it also means ruthlessness.

The exhortation to obedience is couched in generalities. The "law of Moses," from a deuteronomistic point of view, would mean the Book of Deuteronomy (cf. Deut 17:17-20, which may have been written with the disastrous example of Solomon's reign expressly in mind). From a reader's point of view, however, the phrase would refer to whatever was currently thought to be the "torah" in David's time. After the first five books of the Hebrew Bible became "*the* Torah" in the last centuries B.C.E., a reader would have understood "the law of Moses" as meaning the Pentateuch. Since David is not specific about what this law entails, the issue does not become significant for the narrative's development. The reason for obedience is eminently practical: success. This too is standard deuteronomistic thought, but in the context of David's subsequent advice, it smacks of an opportunism far from deuteronomistic morality.

There is a second reason for obedience; verse 4 is grammatically parallel to the end of verse 3 (read "so that the LORD may . . ." for the NRSV's "Then the LORD will . . ."). Obedience will assure the fulfillment of a promise Yahweh made to David. The divine "word" of which David speaks is not found elsewhere in these exact terms, but the reference is almost certainly to Yahweh's promise to David in 2 Samuel 7:12-16. That oracle, delivered to the king by the prophet Nathan, assured David that Yahweh would never abandon his successor, and that David's dynasty, kingdom, and throne would endure forever. The most significant difference between the oracle in 2 Samuel 7 and David's recollection of it here is the addition of a condition. David's descendants are assured the throne *on condition that* they are ardently faithful to Yahweh. Nathan's oracle included no such qualification; in fact, 2 Samuel 7:14-15 is explicitly unconditional. This is the first appearance of a motif that will grow in importance through the entire story of Solomon. Indeed, it is one theological key to the whole drama of Israel in the Books of Kings: the promise to David of an eternal kingdom depends upon the kings' fidelity to Yahweh's ways. There is as yet no mention of what will happen if they are unfaithful; that will become clearer as the motif develops through the book.

David's last words in verse 4 pick up the term "throne" from the earlier oracle (2 Sam 7:13, 16) but use it in a way that recalls yet again the oath formula from chapter 1. There is one other modification. Neither in chapter 1 nor in the original oracle was the throne called "the throne of Israel." Given the two meanings of "Israel"—the religious meaning referring to the whole kingdom and the political meaning referring to the northern group of tribes in the federation—what is at stake? Will infidelity threaten the unity of the federation—in other words, the throne of Israel (that is, the northern tribes) will be lost to the Davidic king? Or will it threaten the dynasty itself—the throne of Israel (that is, the whole kingdom) will fall into other hands? As the long, tragic story of 1–2 Kings will show, both are at stake. The breakup of the federation will occur first, and quickly: at Solomon's death the northern tribes will reject his son and choose a non-Davidid to rule them. And eventually Jerusalem, the kingdom of Judah, and the Davidic throne itself will fall to the armies of Babylon.

The second part of David's speech is of very different character. David instructs Solomon on how he should treat three individuals whose actions have had an impact on David's career. Two are to be destroyed, one is to be rewarded. The commands for destruction surround the one for reward and are much longer and more detailed. This gives these verses a predominantly violent, negative tone. The structure of the speech is balanced, with an internal variation in the reward section:

> A. Joab's punishment (2:5-6)
>   a. reason for punishment
>   b. order to punish
> B. Barzillai's reward (2:7)
>   b'. order to reward
>   a'. reason for reward
> A'. Shimei's punishment (2:8-9)
>   a". reason for punishment
>   b". order to punish

Verse 5 begins with a linking word and an emphatic pronoun ("and besides, *you* know").[6] The effect is to draw Solomon's attention to an

---

[6] There is much disagreement between the standard Hebrew text and the ancient translations on the exact wording of verse 5. The NRSV follows the Hebrew, as we shall.

unspoken connection between David's preceding remarks about the law and past events of which Solomon is already aware. The connection, we surmise, is that Solomon must never lose sight of obedience to the law of Moses as a condition for the dynasty's continuance; therefore, when he carries out David's subsequent instructions, he must do so with caution and cleverness. The events of which David will remind him will supply him with grounds for action that will not jeopardize the divine promise.

David's next words, "what Joab . . . did *to me*," reveal that David is acting out of a personal sense of injury. He perceives the murders of Abner and Amasa with which he charges Joab as personal affronts, affronts which, despite the passage of many years, David has neither forgotten nor forgiven. The story of Joab's killing of Abner is told in 2 Samuel 3, and his murder of Amasa is recounted in 2 Samuel 20. In both cases Joab may have had a legitimate political mistrust of his victim. But he also had strong personal reasons for doing away with them: Abner had killed Joab's brother (though it was in self-defense; see 2 Sam 2:18-23), and Amasa had been appointed by David to take Joab's job (2 Sam 19:11-15). David claims that Joab's deeds were acts of war done in time of peace and so deserve punishment. David may also want to suggest that Joab's guilt implicated David as well, since he was Joab's superior and therefore responsible for his actions.[7] In that case, only Joab's death will expiate his crimes and remove the onus of bloodguilt from the house of David.

David's directive is not direct. Instead of telling Solomon what to do, he fixes Solomon's attention on himself. "Your wisdom" (v. 6) is a way of signaling to Solomon that it will be up to him to figure out how best to deal with the situation David is leaving him. All that David is concerned about is the bottom line, and even this he couches in euphemisms like "gray head" for "old age," "go down to Sheol" for "die," and "in peace" for "of natural causes" (v. 6). The images are all lovely, but the message is brutal: old, faithful Joab is to be killed.

The second instruction is to reward the sons of Barzillai the Gileadite by giving them a royal pension (that is the meaning of "eat at your table"—v. 7). This repays loyalty with loyalty, since Barzillai supplied David with food when the king was fugitive from Absalom's seizure of the throne (the story is in 2 Samuel 19:31-40).

The third instruction concerns one Shimei, son of Gera. David says that Shimei is "with Solomon." This could mean no more than that Shimei is living in Jerusalem, but it reminds us that among those who

---

[7]One ancient Greek translation strengthens this suggestion by reading "*my*" belt, waist, sandals, and feet instead of "his."

"were not with Adonijah" is a Shimei (1:8). We do not know whether this is the same Shimei, since in 1:8 the narrator does not tell us his father's name. Nor do we know if the Shimei of 1:8 is one of Solomon's partisans, though most of whose who "were not with Adonijah" turned out to be on Solomon's side. The possibility that they are the same person is disturbing. If they are, then David is about to tell Solomon to turn on one of his own allies because of an ancient offense that ally committed against David. The contrast with Barzillai, where David told Solomon to reward loyalty with loyalty, is stark.[8]

The story of David's dealings with Shimei is told in 2 Samuel 16:5-14 and 19:16-23. In the first passage David is fleeing from Absalom, who has captured Jerusalem. On his way he is accosted by Shimei, a relative of King Saul, whose family David disenthroned. Shimei curses David for his violence against the Saulids. When one of David's military retainers threatens to kill Shimei, David orders him spared: "Let him alone, and let him curse, for Yahweh has bidden him." The second passage takes place after Absalom has been defeated; David is making his victorious way back to Jerusalem. Shimei comes to meet him again, this time with an obsequious apology for his earlier behavior. The same retainer again wants to execute him, but David grants him pardon and swears an oath that he will not be killed. David justifies his leniency as an amnesty to celebrate his restoration to the throne; but the careful reader may suspect that the presence of a thousand Benjaminites backing Shimei had some influence on the king's decision (2 Sam 19:17)!

David's account of his dealings with Shimei is selective. He leaves out his earlier assertion that Shimei cursed him at Yahweh's bidding; he leaves out Shimei's apology; and he leaves out the thousand Benjaminites whose presence compromised the freedom and sincerity of the royal pardon. In this way he portrays Shimei's crime of *lèse majesté* in the worst possible light, and his own leniency in the best. Even more deceptive is the way David rewords his oath. His promise to Shimei in 2 Samuel 19:23 was without loopholes: "You shall not die." When he recounts this to Solomon, he rephrases it to "I shall not put you to death by the sword," leaving open the possibility that someone else, such as Solomon, could do so, or even that David himself could do so by some other means. David's instruction for dealing with Shimei is as round-

---

[8]This uncertainty is never completely resolved. Much later in the Solomon story the reader will learn that there is another Shimei, son of Ela, whom Solomon made one of his high officials (1 Kgs 4:18). At that point it will become reasonable to assume that this is the Shimei of 1:8, but until the reader reaches that point, the discomfort is unrelieved.

about as his directive about Joab and uses very similar language. Solomon is to use his wisdom again, and Shimei is to die a bloody death.

What motives lie behind David's bloodthirsty advice to Solomon? What moves the dying king to leave as his last words to posterity such violence? There are three possibilities, and all of them have some support in the text.

First, there is the most straightforward reading of the text. David may be concerned that the past actions of Joab and Shimei pose a continuing threat to Solomon. The bloodguilt Joab incurred by the murders of Abner and Amasa could bring divine displeasure upon Solomon if it were not expiated by Joab's death. In Shimei's case, the danger is his curse. The ancient concept held that a curse was an effective force which, once uttered, continued to work its ruin unless God intervened or the one who uttered the curse died. Shimei, therefore, has to be killed in order to protect Solomon from its inevitable effects.

Second, David may be genuinely concerned for Solomon's future security. David knows that Joab supported Adonijah; if the canny general is not disposed of, Solomon's cause will always be in jeopardy. And Shimei is a Saulid; his connections to the former king Saul and his history of hatred for the Davidic house make him a continuing threat to Solomon's welfare. David is aware, however, that Solomon cannot act despotically without violating the condition David mentioned in verse 4. He therefore supplies Solomon with legal pretexts for removing both of these dangerous men. David's words support this view by emphasizing the connection between the demands of the law of Moses and the instructions of verses 5-9 and by counseling shrewdness and subtlety with his repeated references to Solomon's wisdom.

Third, David's words may reveal the vengeful hatred of a vindictive old man. David had more reasons than the murders of Abner and Amasa to wish Joab ill. Joab was also responsible for the death of Absalom, which David took particularly hard. Furthermore, when David's grief over Absalom became excessive, Joab rebuked him severely (2 Sam 18-19). David's words in verse 5, "what Joab . . . did to me," suggest that David may have had these more personal affronts in mind. In Shimei's case, David's skewed account of the events indicates that he still harbors resentment for Shimei's bitter words.

With this enigmatic and ambiguous speech, David's career comes to a close. Few characters in ancient literature are more complex than this king, sinful saint, man of blood, and obedient servant of Yahweh. What strikes us, as we reflect on his final words, is David's assumption that Solomon will be like him, able to combine in a single life faithful obedience to God and ruthless, bloody, political expediency. David's references to Solomon's "wisdom" are the first appearance of the theme that will characterize this king for the ages. As the term recurs over and over again in the remaining chapters of the Solomon story, Solomon's wisdom is a divine gift, admirable in its exercise and positive in its results. But here, at its origin, the theme is shadowed by the violence of the advice to which David attaches it.

Chapter 2
SOLOMON'S THRONE IS SECURE
1 Kings 2:12b-46

The second story in the account of Solomon's reign is very different from the first. Instead of a relatively long, complex narrative, we find a series of four shorter, more or less independent dramatic episodes. Several factors unify the series, however, and show that the narrator intends us to read the episodes as a single literary unit. There is, first of all, their common content: each describes how Solomon eliminates, either by execution or by exile, someone he perceives as a danger to his throne. Second, there is a similarity of structure in three of the four episodes. The stories of Adonijah, Joab, and Shimei are much longer than the episode about Abiathar. Each of them has a basically bipartite structure and ends with a line about the execution of the victim by Benaiah, son of Jehoiada. Third, the narrator uses a very noticeable inclusion in verses 12b and 46b to mark the beginning and end of the literary unit. Finally, as we will see below, the subtle strategy for characterizing Solomon is the same in all four units.

The overall structure of the story is easily discerned. The inclusion forms a frame around the whole. Within that frame are the stories of Adonijah, Abiathar, Joab, and Shimei, and an administrative note about the replacement of Abiathar and Joab. The result is an alternating pattern of short and long elements that affords a certain regular rhythm to the whole unit:

A. Narrative frame (2:12b)
    B. THE EXECUTION OF ADONIJAH (2:13-25)
C. The exile of Abiathar (2:26-27)
    B'. THE EXECUTION OF JOAB (2:28-34)
C'. Replacement of Joab and Abiathar (2:35)
    B". THE EXECUTION OF SHIMEI (2:36-46a)
A'. Narrative frame (2:46b)

Frame: 2:12b, 46b

The technique called "inclusion" is used frequently in Hebrew, both in prose and in poetry, to delimit literary units. It consists of repeating a word, phrase, or concept at or near the beginning and end of the unit. We have already encountered an example of inclusion in 2:1-12a, the transitional section that links the story of Solomon's succession in chapter 1 to the present unit. In 2:1 the narrator mentions "David's time to die," and in 2:10 he mentions David's death. In that case the inclusion is conceptual, not verbal, since the narrator avoids the word "die" or "death" in 2:10 and uses the euphemism "sleep with his ancestors." An example of verbal inclusion is Nathan's use of the phrase "my lord the king" at the beginning and end of his speech in 1:24-27. The inclusion in the present passage is verbal ("kingdom" and "established"), although there are minor variations in the Hebrew words used. It should also be noted that 2:12a has verbal links both forward and backward. The thematic phrase "sit on the throne" connects it closely with chapter 1. The name "Solomon" points ahead to what follows: it is the first word in v. 12a and the last word in v. 46b. Verse 12a, then, acts as a kind of hinge holding the two stories together.

Both parts of the frame announce that Solomon's kingship is established. The words used for kingship in the two places are related though not the same. The NRSV translates them both "kingdom," but they carry the meaning of "royal power," not just that of "realm" (the nuance of power is stronger in the word used in v. 12b). Solomon's actions in this chapter aim not at assuring the security of his territory but at consolidating his own sovereignty.

The two statements do more, however, than simply frame the literary unit. They set a context within which we must evaluate the intervening actions. If Solomon's sovereignty is already "firmly established" *before* he purges those he considers enemies, then the ensuing executions are not necessary to consolidate his power. To what purpose, then, is the bloodbath? The narrator gives us a small hint by deleting "firmly" in v. 46b and adding "in the hand of Solomon." These changes suggest that v. 12b represents the narrator's view of Solomon's power, while v. 46b gives us Solomon's own perception of it. In other words, though the narrator informs us that Solomon's sovereignty is "firm" as soon as he succeeds to sole possession of the throne of David, Solomon himself does not feel that he has things under control ("in hand") until he has disposed of those he thinks of as dangers to him. This reading is supported, as we shall see, by several indications throughout vv. 13-45 that Solomon is preoccupied with his own security and with his own "establishment" on the throne.

Already in the frame surrounding these episodes the narrator signals the strategy he will use throughout the chapter to characterize Solomon. On the surface he will say positive things, but between the lines he will undermine the positive picture with a series of gaps, innuendoes, and ambiguities that invite a much more critical evaluation of the king. We shall discuss the characterization of Solomon after we examine the four episodes.

The Execution of Adonijah: 2:13-25

The story of Solomon's elimination of Adonijah is told in two scenes: Adonijah's audience with Bathsheba (vv. 13-18) and Bathsheba's audience with Solomon (vv. 19-24), followed by a brief narrative note about Adonijah's execution by Benaiah (v. 25). As is common in Hebrew narrative, the narrator tells us nothing directly about the thoughts and motivations of his characters; we are obliged to infer their inner life from their words and actions. In this story Adonijah and Bathsheba act in ways that allow divergent readings; the narrator leaves us free to choose among the different possibilities.

ADONIJAH'S AUDIENCE WITH BATHSHEBA: 2:13-18

The first scene begins with Adonijah's appearance before Bathsheba. The narrator identifies both characters by an additional name, Adonijah by his mother's and Bathsheba by her son's. This fuller introduction of the characters is appropriate at the beginning of a new narrative unit, but it also sets up complex resonances between the two. First, the names reflect the *characters'* viewpoints. Adonijah approaches Bathsheba precisely because she is the king's mother; he hopes that she will have decisive influence over him. Furthermore, as "Great Lady" (*gĕbîrâ*), a role held by the queen mother, Bathsheba is in charge of the women who belong to the king's harem. For her part, Bathsheba sees in Adonijah, not her son's brother nor even David's son (and therefore Solomon's rival for the throne), but the son of Haggith, Bathsheba's own rival for the position of queen mother.

A second dimension of these resonances is on a psychological level: Adonijah is the son of a mother; Bathsheba is the mother of a son. Perhaps this complementarity will allow a mutual understanding and engender in Bathsheba a sympathy for Adonijah's cause. Thus from the first words the narrator opens two possible paths of development:

Bathsheba will react negatively to the son of her rival, or she will react positively out of her own maternal compassion.

The remainder of the scene is a concentrically structured dialogue:

A. Bathsheba's question (2:13b)
  B. Adonijah's answer and request (2:13c-14a)
    C. Bathsheba's one-word answer, "Go on" (2:14b)
      D. Adonijah's lengthy speech (2:15-16a)
    C'. Bathsheba's one-word answer, "Go on" (2:16b)
  B'. Adonijah's request (2:17)
A'. Bathsheba's response (2:18)

Concentric structures like this generally highlight the central element, in this case, Adonijah's longest speech. This is where we would normally expect to find the main point of the scene expressed. Yet the narrator puts off until the last words of verse 17 Adonijah's explicit request to have Abishag as his wife. The effect is twofold. First, we pay special attention to what Adonijah has to say in the central speech. Then, since that speech still leaves us wondering what Adonijah wants, the narrative tension increases even more in the second half of the dialogue.

Bathsheba's question uses the word *šālôm*, which can mean much more than simply "peace." Depending on the context, it can be translated "health, welfare, well-being, wholeness," etc. Here it means, approximately, "Do you come in good faith and not to make trouble?" Adonijah answers, *šālôm*. Repeating the key word of the question is a common way of saying yes in Hebrew. The emphasis on this word is another example of the narrator's play on names, much like the play on *'ădônî hammelek* and *mālak 'ădônîyāhû* in chapter 1 (see pp. 11 and 13). Here the play is on *šālôm* and the name *šělōmōh*, "Solomon," which is from the same root. The *šālôm* at issue in this episode is reconciliation between brothers. It remains to be seen whether the wordplay signals harmony between the two terms or opposition, as it did in the first chapter. In other words, will Solomon's actions promote or hinder *šālôm* between himself and Adonijah?

Adonijah continues with one of those obvious, meaningless phrases people use to fill the silence when they're struggling to say something else: "I have something to talk over with you." We recognize that Adonijah is nervous. Bathsheba's first words have put him on the defensive, and he does not know whether she believes his answer. He is not quite ready to plunge to the heart of the matter, so he temporizes. Bathsheba's reply is laconic (one word in Hebrew) but not impolite. The NRSV's "Go on" captures it very well.

Adonijah's central speech consists of a lengthy exposition of the grounds upon which he will base his request (v. 15), and a further evasion of his real point (v. 16a). He begins with an emphatic pronoun, *"You* know that . . . ." In this way he tries to focus attention on Bathsheba, since she is the one he is dependent on for help. Unfortunately it becomes clear as he continues that he is still full of himself and the wreckage of his dreams. The word order of the next two phrases emphasizes Adonijah: "that to me the kingdom belonged and toward me all Israel looked . . . ." His word for kingdom is different from those used in vv. 12b and 46b; it emphasizes the office of king, with all its trappings, more than power. This is consistent with what we saw of Adonijah in chapter 1, where he was concerned about display—his retinue, his handsomeness.

The second phrase claims that "all Israel" expected him to succeed. There are two reasons to read this as a bit of self-delusion. First, the phrase "all Israel" is usually used in 1 Kings to refer to the population of the northern kingdom (Israel in the political sense), whereas Adonijah's influential supporters in chapter 1 seemed to reflect greater allegiance to Judah. Second, the only expression of popular support in chapter 1 was directed not at Adonijah but at Solomon, whose accession was celebrated by "all the people." Here too we see traits consistent with what we already know of Adonijah: his complacency, his self-satisfaction, and his naiveté about political realities.

When Adonijah acknowledges his defeat, he personifies the kingship as itself turning aside from him and becoming Solomon's. The personification underscores the connection between this and the request Adonijah will voice in a few lines: he has been abandoned by the kingship (which is a feminine noun in Hebrew); he will ask for the woman Abishag as a sort of substitute. Phrasing his defeat this way also enables him to put off as long as possible the bitter admission he will make at the end of verse 15, namely, that his defeat eventuated "from Yahweh." Adonijah refers to Solomon here neither by name nor as "your (Bathsheba's) son" but as "my brother." Since he is trying to impress on Bathsheba his sincere loyalty to the king and the *šālôm* he is committed to, he emphasizes the family relationship between himself and Solomon rather than the rivalry. Finally, he acknowledges that Yahweh was responsible for his loss of the kingdom.

After setting out the basis for his request, Adonijah would, we expect, say what he wanted. But he is still not ready. He temporizes again with "Now I have one request to request of you." The "something" Adonijah wished to talk over in verse 14 has become "one request"; other than that small change, these words do not advance the conversation at all. Their virtual emptiness, their verbosity ("one request to request"), and the unnecessary word "one," by which Adonijah attempts to minimize the significance of what he is about to say—all work together to give us a sense of his growing nervousness as he nears the heart of the matter. This in turn suggests that Adonijah realizes that his "one request" is anything but trivial and that he runs a risk in putting it forward. Bathsheba's response is identical to that in verse 14b, a single word, "Go on." In view of Adonijah's obvious unease, it is an encouragement to continue, but it neither affirms nor denies sympathy for Adonijah's cause.

Adonijah's nervousness reaches the point where he becomes almost incoherent. "Please ask King Solomon"—he uses the formal title here because he puts himself into the role of ordinary petitioner before his monarch, requesting a royal favor. Then he interrupts himself once again to flatter Bathsheba by calling her attention to her influence over Solomon. The idiom he uses, literally, he will not "turn your face back" (NRSV, "refuse"), will become a refrain over the course of the next few verses. Finally he can delay no longer and blurts out what he wants: "Let him give me Abishag the Shunammite as wife."

The significance of this request can only be seen in its political context. One of the privileges of a monarch was to inherit his predecessor's harem. Any claim on the wife or concubine of a living monarch was tantamount to a claim on the throne. Examples of this custom in the Bible include 2 Samuel 3:6-8, where Saul's son and successor, Ishbaal (sometimes called Ishbosheth), accuses his ambitious general Abner of having intercourse with one of Saul's concubines. Abner's defense shows that the charge impugns his loyalty to the house of Saul. Another example is in 2 Samuel 12:8, where Yahweh's word to David through the prophet Nathan reminds David that Yahweh made him Saul's successor; the phrase Yahweh uses is "I gave you your master's house and your master's wives into your bosom." A third example occurs during Absalom's rebellion against David. Once David has fled from Jerusalem and his son's forces occupy the royal palace, Absalom's counselor Ahitophel advises him to make a public show of his seizure of the throne. By making the breach between himself and his father irreparable, he will strengthen his own supporters' resolve. The way to do this, says Ahitophel, is to have intercourse with the concubines David left behind to care for the palace; that way "all Israel will hear that you have made yourself odious to your father" (2 Sam 16:20-22).

In the present case, it is difficult to determine whether this custom is pertinent. One of Abishag's duties was to sleep with David, but the narrator carefully assured us that David did not have intercourse with her (1:4). Is she then a concubine or not? If she technically is not, then Adonijah can request her for himself without necessarily implying a claim on David's throne. On the other hand, as David's bed-partner she was certainly part of the royal harem, and therefore now belongs to Solomon. Given Abishag's beauty and Solomon's youth and virility (he has already fathered at least one son), her status as royal concubine is unlikely to remain uncertain for very long, if indeed it has not been resolved already. Even if Adonijah's request does not imply a claim on David's throne, it could imply one on Solomon's.

Why would Adonijah risk giving Solomon such an opportunity to take offense? One explanation might be that Adonijah has indeed not given up his hopes for the throne, and that his request for Abishag is in fact the covert claim that Solomon will make it out to be. The structure of the dialogue supports this reading by centering our attention on Adonijah's nostalgic yearning for the kingship he nearly obtained. His obsession with it raises the suspicion that he may not be as resigned to his loss as he would like Bathsheba to believe. Against that are Adonijah's avowals that he comes in *šālôm* (2:13) and that the kingdom belongs to Solomon "from Yahweh" (2:15). But these statements, spoken to Bathsheba as part of Adonijah's attempt to gain her support, may well be more politic than sincere. An alternative reading is that Adonijah is simply so self-centered and spoiled (1:6), and so unrealistic about his status, that he thinks he still has some leverage in the situation and cannot imagine Solomon refusing him. That would be consistent with the complacency and self-absorption he showed in chapter 1. His roundabout approach to Bathsheba and his dithering diffidence in voicing his request suggest that he is aware of some danger in his course of action, but he may not realize its full extent.

The narrator does not give us enough information to choose between these two characterizations of Adonijah. In a work of historiography, the openness of the story to such different interpretations could be a serious flaw; but from a literary perspective it can be appreciated as a narrative strategy of great richness, allowing a variety of satisfying readings. We will see in a moment that the characterization of Bathsheba involves the same ambiguity of motivation and openness to divergent understandings.

Bathsheba's reply to Adonijah (v. 18) is badly served by the NRSV. "On your behalf" suggests that Bathsheba is willing to support Adonijah's request. The Hebrew contains no such implication. What Bathsheba says is, "Very well. *I* [emphatic pronoun] will speak to the king about you." The force of the emphatic pronoun is to remind Adonijah pointedly of his situation: he is the petitioner who requires someone to intercede for him with the king; *she* has the influence. The rest of the sentence is noncommittal. She does not comment on his request or even say that she will speak to Solomon about it. She will speak about *him*.

Bathsheba's Audience with Solomon: 2:19-25

The second scene begins as the first one did, with a narrative line. Bathsheba comes to Solomon "to speak with him about Adonijah" —exactly as she said she would. The narrator uses the full title "King Solomon," both because it is his first appearance in this literary unit and to underscore that Solomon will be acting in his royal capacity in this scene. Bathsheba is approaching him to ask for a royal judgment, not for a favor from her son. By contrast, "Adonijah" is not further identified; the narrator is not ready to let us know whether Bathsheba still thinks of Adonijah as a rival ("son of Haggith") or has come to view him more sympathetically ("brother of Solomon").

Solomon greets his mother with a display of courtesy that is as warm as it is courtly. He rises to meet her and does obeisance to her. In chapter 1, when Bathsheba approached David she bowed to him (1:16); now, however, she holds the office of *gĕbîrâ*, and the king treats her as almost an equal. He takes his seat on the throne and places a throne for "the mother of the king" at his right hand. The unexpected appearance of this phrase, "the mother of the king," which sounds like a title, reinforces the formality of the scene and probably expresses the viewpoint of others who are present: courtiers, advisers, servants, etc. Behind the narrator's voice one can almost hear Solomon's command to a handy servant: "Set up a throne for the mother of the king!" This audience, then, is not a private meeting but a public occasion that we witness from a vantage point among the bystanders.

The dialogue begins in a way very reminiscent of Bathsheba's conversation with Adonijah. Compare verses 16-17 with verses 20-21:

2:16-17	*2:20-21*
one request to make of you	one small request to make of you
do not refuse me	do not refuse me
go on	make your request, my mother
please ask King Solomon	
for he will not refuse you	I will not refuse you
let him give me	let Abishag be given
Abishag as wife	to your brother Adonijah as wife

In the midst of these strong parallels, the few differences are worth noting. First, Adonijah already tried to minimize the significance of his request by calling it *"one* request." Bathsheba goes even further and calls it "one *small* request." Second, where Bathsheba's response to Adonijah was laconic in the extreme—a single word, polite and encouraging but noncommittal—Solomon's reply to Bathsheba is warm and personal (he calls her "my mother"), and promises to give her whatever she wants.

Third, Adonijah's use of the active voice ("let him give me") could be construed as an indirect way of ordering Solomon's actions; Bathsheba's use of the passive avoids any hint of that. Finally, Bathsheba characterizes Adonijah as "your brother," emphasizing the familial ties between him and Solomon rather than the rivalry that has divided them.

To this point the scene has several parallels to the preceding one. They have identically constructed opening narrative lines (obscured a bit in the NRSV translation), very similar dialogue, and comparable moods: Bathsheba is civil to Adonijah, even if she is not as cordial as Solomon is to her. Since the first scene remained polite to the end, we anticipate that this one will too. Solomon promises to grant whatever Bathsheba asks; and Bathsheba, at least on the surface, supports Adonijah's request. Everything leads us to expect an amicable resolution to the situation.

Solomon's response, however, brutally disrupts both the mood and our expectations. The narrator reflects the sudden change of mood from warmth and courtesy to anger and autocracy by using the full title, King Solomon, from here to the end of the scene. The king begins by lashing out at his mother as if the request were her own idea (and in fact Bathsheba has not told him that it originated with Adonijah). He claims that asking for Abishag is practically the same as asking for the kingship (using the same word for it that Adonijah used). He takes Bathsheba's reminder that Adonijah is his brother and turns it against Adonijah: "He is my *older* brother"—which was the basis for Adonijah's claim to the throne in the first place. The last words of verse 22 are grammatically awkward, as if Solomon's emotions are so strong as to render him a bit incoherent. If the Hebrew text is correct, it can only be translated as the NRSV renders it: Solomon thinks of his rivals, Adonijah, Abiathar, and Joab, as a single group who are maneuvering to rule the kingdom.[1]

In the next two verses King Solomon swears a double oath. The first oath, verse 23, begins with a stereotyped oath formula and pledges that the request will cost Adonijah his life. Solomon has either figured out that Adonijah himself is behind the request, or he has decided to assume it. The second oath begins with a different but equally common oath formula, "as Yahweh lives." Solomon embellishes the formula by recalling Yahweh's deeds in his favor: God "established me" (the same verb as in verses 12b and 46b, where it is the "kingdom" that is established) and "seated me on the throne" (the thematic phrase

---

[1]A slight emendation of the Hebrew text produces a smoother reading of the verse: "Ask for him the kingdom as well! For he is my elder brother, and the priest Abiathar and Joab son of Zeruiah are on his side!"

from chapter 1). The next phrase, "made me a house as he said," refers to the dynastic promise Yahweh made to David in 2 Samuel 7:11, which Solomon here appropriates to himself. These phrases, with their repetition of the pronoun "me," reveal to us what is uppermost in Solomon's concern: the security of his own position. The last words of the second oath confirm Adonijah's death sentence and add the word "today." Since, in Solomon's judgment, Adonijah has forfeited his amnesty, there is no need for further confrontation or discussion. The execution is to be carried out immediately. The "today" also echoes the motif word of chapter 1 (1:25, 30, 48, 51): Adonijah's todays have run out.

How shall we read Bathsheba's behavior in this scene? Her faithful delivery of Adonijah's message seems to indicate support for his request, and the slight changes she makes in the wording all contribute to polishing the original message and making it even more presentable to Solomon. Yet the political implications of the request are so evident, and Solomon is so quick to seize on them, that we must wonder whether Bathsheba does not anticipate just such a reaction. In her speech to David in chapter 1, she showed herself quite shrewd in palace intrigue and skilled in manipulative rhetoric. Can her speech here be understood as similarly manipulative? As *gĕbîrâ* she certainly is aware of the reigning king's rights over the harem. Adonijah's request is potentially explosive and hardly merits the term "small," unless Bathsheba is speaking ironically. The passive construction ("let Abishag be given") changes the word order of the original request, building narrative tension slightly by putting the name of Solomon's rival a bit later in the sentence. Reminding Solomon that Adonijah is "your brother" recalls not only familial ties but also the basis of Adonijah's strong claim on the throne, as Solomon is quick to point out.

The character of Bathsheba in the episode, then, like that of Adonijah, is open to very divergent readings. She may be exactly what she appears to be: a woman trying to reconcile estranged brothers by arranging a marriage. Against this reading is the difficulty of harmonizing such a Bathsheba with the shrewd conniver of chapter 1. Or she may be knowingly and gleefully bringing her son what he wants most: an excuse for disposing of a dangerous rival. The narrator leaves us free to choose.

The episode ends with a narrative verse recounting the execution of Adonijah. Solomon sends Benaiah to do the deed. The Hebrew says, literally, "King Solomon sent by the hand of Benaiah," which is the standard phrase for sending a messenger. In this case Benaiah's message is, in fact, his "hand" and the sword it wields. Benaiah obeys immediately and without comment (we have already noted his readiness to respond to whatever the king says—1:36-37). What Benaiah does is "come upon" Adonijah; the verb used, *pāga'*, does not usually connote the idea of violent attack as it does here. It is a relatively uncommon word; in 1 Kings it occurs only in this chapter. But here it becomes a motif word, since it occurs several times, always in the sense of violent killing.

The Exile of Abiathar: 2:26-27

The brief episode that recounts Solomon's exile of Abiathar is different from the three stories of Adonijah, Joab, and Shimei. It consists of a single scene depicting Solomon's command banishing Abiathar and a comment by the narrator on the event. There is no narrative tension or plot development within the episode itself. In the larger context, however, this episode contributes to the narrative unity of the whole section. In verse 22 Solomon named three enemies—Adonijah, Abiathar, and Joab. He disposes of each of them in turn and appoints replacements for Abiathar and Joab in verse 35.

Solomon's speech to Abiathar begins with the command to go to his holdings in Anathoth, a small village about three miles northeast of Jerusalem. He is, presumably, to remain on his estate there and live from its income. The implication is that Abiathar is forbidden to return to Jerusalem and, therefore, to continue in the role of high priest, which he shared with Zadok. The command is followed by a series of explanations. First, Solomon says that Abiathar is, literally, a "man of death" (NRSV, "you deserve death"). Coming from the king, this is not merely a comment on Abiathar's guilt but a formal death sentence. The very next words, however, suspend the sentence, though only for the time being, and give the grounds for Solomon's leniency: Abiathar's longstanding and faithful service to David. Solomon cites two specifics: Abiathar carried the ark of Yahweh before David and shared David's hardships. The first does not appear anywhere in the scriptures. It may refer to the occasion when David brought the ark of the covenant into Jerusalem (2 Sam 6), although the account does not mention Abiathar's role in the ceremony. The second reference is both to David's days of outlawry when Saul was persecuting him and to David's flight from Jerusalem during Absalom's rebellion. (For Abiathar's role in these events, see 1 Samuel 22–23 and 30 and 2 Samuel 15.)

In verse 27 the narrator makes explicit what is only implicit in Solomon's decree of banishment, namely, that Abiathar is to be excluded from the priesthood of Jerusalem. This, the narrator informs us, is part of a much larger divine intention. Several generations earlier Yahweh spoke a word of condemnation against the priesthood of the sanctuary at Shiloh, in the person of Eli and his sons (1 Sam 2–3). Abiathar, according to notes scattered through 1 Samuel (14:3; 22:9; 30:7), can trace his lineage back to Eli. The narrator sees Abiathar's exile as the inexorable working out of the divine punishment.

The narrator's purpose in informing us of this is not simply to supply us with an erudite bit of trivia. He wishes to remind us of three important dynamics in Israelite history as he presents it. First, the story of Israel is a seamless whole. Individual chapters, such as the story of Solomon, can be isolated for narrative purposes, but we must not lose sight of the fact that those chapters gain even richer meaning in a larger context. Second, that history can never be seen apart from the working of God's hand. No matter how far removed an event seems to be from divine influence, it can contribute to God's larger purposes. Finally, individuals can, as Solomon does here, fulfill the divine plan and yet be completely unaware of what they do. This is no guarantee of the moral rightness of the individual's motives; it merely demonstrates the inevitability of God's designs.

The exile of Abiathar points forward to a significant moment in the later history of Israel as well. The royal ukase is not the last word. Centuries later a priestly prophet will return to Jerusalem from Anathoth, bringing Yahweh's decree condemning the throne of David and the Temple that Solomon himself built and announcing the coming exile of God's unfaithful people (Jer 1:1-3).

The Execution of Joab: 2:28-34

The episode of Joab's execution, like that of Adonijah's, has two main scenes. The scenes have basically parallel structures, but each scene contains one element not paralleled in the other.

> A. NARRATIVE LINE ABOUT JOAB (2:28)
>   B. FIRST SCENE (2:29-30b)
>   a) report to Solomon about Joab (2:29a)
>   b) Solomon's command to Benaiah (2:29b)
>   c) Benaiah attempts to carry out the command (2:30a)
>   +) Joab's response to Benaiah (2:30b)
>   B'. SECOND SCENE (2:30c-34a)
>   a') report to Solomon about Joab (2:30c)
>   b') Solomon's command to Benaiah (2:31a)
>   +) justification of the command (2:31b-33)
>   c') Benaiah carries out the command (2:34a)
> A'. NARRATIVE LINE ABOUT JOAB (2:34b)

FIRST SCENE: 2:28-30b

Joab hears "the news"—presumably the news both of Adonijah's execution and of Abiathar's exile. Believing that this signals a purge of Adonijah's partisans, Joab "flees"—a humiliating action for the brave old general—and takes refuge, as Adonijah did, at the altar of Yahweh. (See the comments on 1:50, p. 30; here the altar is specifically identified as associated with the tent that David built to house the ark of the covenant.) He hopes, perhaps, to negotiate the same sort of conditional amnesty that Adonijah obtained. The remark that Joab supported Adonijah but not Absalom reminds us that Joab's loyalty to David was unbroken, even during Absalom's rebellion (in stark contrast to David's disloyalty to Joab in advising Solomon to kill him; see 2:5-6), and Joab's support of the heir apparent simply continued his loyalty to the dynasty. Any animosity Solomon bears him is based on personal affront, not on true treason.

The narrator arranges verse 28 oddly. In Hebrew the motive clause ("for Joab had supported Adonijah") would normally follow the action it motivates. In this case we would expect to find the clause at the end of the verse: "Joab fled to the altar because he had supported Adonijah." In its present position, however, the clause is ambivalent: it can also be read as explaining why Joab is informed of Solomon's purge: "Joab heard the news, for Joab had supported Adonijah . . . ." The implication of this reading would be that Adonijah's partisans still have an effective communications network, and that Joab's impression of a purge against Adonijah's party is shared by others as well.

When Solomon is informed of Joab's flight to seek asylum at the altar, he sends Benaiah to strike him down, in apparent violation of the right of sanctuary. The motif verb *pāgaʿ* appears for the second time in Solomon's command. Benaiah begins to obey immediately, as usual, but even with a royal mandate he hesitates to violate the holy ground. He dissembles, saying that Solomon's command ordered Joab out of the sanctuary but not admitting that Solomon has decreed his death. If Benaiah can get Joab to abandon his refuge, he can kill him without qualms. Joab, however, is too suspicious to fall for such a ploy, and he retorts, with emphatic word order, "No! It is *here* I shall die!" Joab's gamble, presumably, is to force Solomon to choose between public violation of the hallowed right of sanctuary and negotiation of some sort of amnesty.

SECOND SCENE: 2:30c-34

Benaiah reports back to Solomon the standoff he reached with Joab. Benaiah's words reflect a device sometimes used in Hebrew narrative. Rather than repeat Joab's words, the narrator simply replaces them in Benaiah's speech with the word "thus." The meaning here is that Benaiah reported what Joab said exactly. Solomon's response is to repeat his original command, then to explain in a lengthy speech the reasons for Joab's execution and the legal basis for annulling his right to sanctuary. To the original command Solomon adds two elements. First, the king's opening words in verse 31 are a brutal response to Joab's dare: the gamble loses. Solomon has a way out of the dilemma Joab is trying to force on him. Second, Solomon makes one concession by adding a further command to Benaiah's original orders: he is to strike Joab down (the motif verb *pāgaʿ* again) and also to bury him. Since in Hebrew thought lack of burial often meant that the unburied person was under a divine curse, Solomon's concession is an act of magnanimity designed to protect Joab from a disgraceful fate.

Solomon's lengthy justification of Joab's execution has a concentric structure. The NRSV changes the order of the clauses slightly; what follows reflects the order in the Hebrew text.

    A. David's house will be freed of bloodguilt (2:31b)
      B. Punishment will fall on Joab's head (2:32a)
        C. He killed two men better than himself (2:32b)
          D. My father David did not know it (2:32c)
        C'. Abner and Amasa (2:32d)
      B'. Their blood will be on Joab's head (2:33a)
    A'. David's house will have peace (2:33b).

This structure focuses attention on the innocence of the house of David, past and future, by placing that idea at the beginning, middle, and end of the pattern. In contrast, Solomon calls bloodguilt down upon Joab's head in elements B and B'. Joab's specific crime is spelled out in elements C and C'.

Solomon's emphasis on the need to remove bloodguilt from the house of David will appeal to Benaiah's proven loyalty both to David and to Solomon. His claim that that bloodguilt belongs properly on Joab, and that David was not a party to the murders Joab committed, will demonstrate to Benaiah that killing Joab is sufficient to restore justice. And his description of the murders as "without cause" and as "attacks" (the thematic verb *pāgaʿ* again) will convince Benaiah that Joab has no right to sanctuary, since this was provided only for involuntary manslaughter, and murderers could be forcibly removed from the altar and put to death (Exod 21:12-14).

Several details of Solomon's speech are worth noting. First, in verse 31 he claims that Joab's death will remove bloodguilt from *him* and from his father's house. Solomon's first concern is his own escape from the effects of Joab's deeds, and only secondarily the dynasty's. Second, Solomon describes Joab's murders in terms very similar to those David used in 2:5-6; one difference is that where David spoke of the "two commanders of the armies of Israel," Solomon calls Amasa a "commander of the army of Judah." Solomon is more accurate, politically speaking. But the shift could also reflect a different set of priorities: for David, the religious unity of the whole kingdom as "Israel" is paramount; for Solomon the political distinction between "Israel" and "Judah" is uppermost. Finally, the play on Solomon's name appears once more: Solomon (*šĕlōmōh*) claims that his ultimate purpose in executing Joab is to guarantee the *šālôm* of the Davidic throne.

Solomon's arguments satisfy Benaiah's scruples, and he returns to the tent, where he strikes Joab down (*pāgaʿ* again), apparently ignoring the legal stipulation that the victim be removed from the altar lest the sanctuary be defiled by the execution. A final narrative line informs us that Joab was buried (though it does not say that Benaiah himself did so). The burial was on Joab's own property in Bethlehem (see 2 Sam 2:32: Asahel was Joab's brother). The terrain there, described as "wilderness" (Hebrew, *midbār*), is not true desert but rather land too arid to farm but sufficient to supply grazing for sheep and goats.

The Replacement of Joab and Abiathar: 2:35

To the victor belong the spoils. Having removed two influential figures who supported his rival, Solomon replaces them with his own creatures. Benaiah, Solomon's ready hatchet man, replaces Joab. There is a bitter irony in this appointment. One of the murders of which Joab was guilty was that of Amasa, "commander of the army of Judah." Amasa held that post, however, only because David appointed him to it as a replacement for Joab; by killing him, Joab regained his old position. Now Benaiah, in his turn, gets the job by killing his predecessor Joab. Zadok replaces Abiathar as high priest.

The order of verse 35, mentioning Joab's replacement and then Abiathar's, reverses the order in which their removals were recounted. The reversal enables the narrator to wrap these two episodes together with a precise inclusion: in the Hebrew text, "Abiathar" is the first word in verse 26 and the last word in verse 35. This marks the tale of

the elimination of Adonijah's supporters as a kind of subplot within
the whole literary unit of 2:12b-46.

The Execution of Shimei: 2:36-46a

The episode that recounts Shimei's downfall comprises two scenes
of confrontation between Solomon and Shimei separated by a narrative section. Structural parallels between the two outer scenes give the
whole episode a concentric pattern:

> A. Shimei before Solomon (2:36-38a)
>   B. Narrative (2:38b-41)
> A'. Shimei before Solomon (2:42-45)

This pattern is extended and strengthened by the generally concentric
structure of the narrative section (see below). The episode ends just
like the episodes about the executions of Adonijah and Joab, with a
narrative line about Benaiah carrying out the death sentence.

SHIMEI BEFORE SOLOMON: 2:36-38a

The first scene contains a lengthy speech of Solomon to Shimei and
Shimei's response. Shimei is not identified as "Shimei, son of Gera,"
against whom David advised Solomon to act in 2:8-9, but Solomon's
words later on (2:44-45) will make it clear that this is the same person.
Whether he is also the Shimei mentioned in 1:8 as not supporting
Adonijah is unclear (see pp. 41–42).

The king's command to Shimei restricts his movements to the city
of Jerusalem. He is to take up permanent residence there and not to
leave the city for any reason. From a political point of view, this action
is reasonable. Shimei is a member of the house of Saul, from which
David wrested control of the throne of Israel. Saulid opposition to the
house of David is by no means ended, and Shimei's vilification of
David (2 Sam 16) marks him as a prominent dissident. It is understandable that Solomon wants to keep Shimei under observation and
his movements under control.

Solomon puts two prohibitions on Shimei. He is not to leave
Jerusalem to go anywhere at all, and specifically he is not to cross the
Kidron Valley. The first prohibition would chafe as time went by, since
Jerusalem was a rather small area; scholars estimate the size of the city
in those days at around eleven acres. The second prohibition restricts

Shimei's contact with his hometown of Bahurim, where his Saulid support systems would be strongest. Bahurim was just east of Jerusalem, separated from the city only by the Kidron and the long ridge known as the Mount of Olives. Solomon underscores the second prohibition in several ways. He attaches a death threat to crossing the Kidron, using emphatic language: "Know for certain that you shall certainly die." Having spelled out clearly the consequences of disobedience, Solomon disavows personal responsibility. Should Shimei incur those consequences, he alone will bear the responsibility. (Note how Solomon's words "your blood will be upon your own head" echo David's instructions in 2:9.)

Shimei's response accepts the king's commands without demur. Of course, Shimei has little choice in the matter, and we may question the sincerity of his words, "The sentence is fair" (literally, "The word is good"). But he goes on to call the king "my lord" and to speak of himself as "your servant"—indicating at least a recognition of where the power lies and an intention to comply with Solomon's orders.

NARRATIVE: 2:38b-41

The narrative section recounts how Shimei comes to violate the restrictions Solomon imposed on him. The section is organized concentrically by a lengthy series of words, phrases, and grammatical constructions. Not all the parallel elements can be preserved in translation, but enough survive to demonstrate the pattern. The following very literal rendering shows most of the parallels in capital letters:

A. AND DWELT (Hebrew, *wayyēšeb*)
  B. SHIMEI IN JERUSALEM for many days.
    And at the end of three years, two servants that were Shimei's fled to Achish, son of Maacah, king of Gath.
    C. AND THEY TOLD TO Shimei,
      D. YOUR SERVANTS are IN GATH.
        E. AND SHIMEI arose,
          F. and saddled his donkey
            G. and he went to Gath to Achish
          F'. to seek his servants.
        E'. AND SHIMEI went
      D'. and brought HIS SERVANTS FROM GATH.
    C'. AND IT WAS TOLD TO Solomon
  B'. that SHIMEI had gone FROM JERUSALEM to Gath
A'. AND RETURNED (Hebrew, *wayyāšob*).

There is one asymmetrical element, the lengthy sentence between B and C. It is wordy, and, with only one active verb in the whole sentence, slows the narrative pace considerably by comparison with the rest of the section. The effect is to signal the passage of the time indicated by the preceding phrase "for many days" before returning to the regular narrative flow.

The asymmetry of this element within the larger concentric pattern calls attention to it and to its informational content. It establishes important circumstances surrounding Shimei's disobedience. First, he has complied with Solomon's strictures for three years. Second, his reason for violating Solomon's command is to retrieve two runaway servants; such a loss would be a serious economic blow to a household of that day. The third detail in the asymmetrical element is an ironic allusion to the time when David himself fled from his master, Saul, when Saul wanted to kill him. David too sought refuge with Achish, king of Gath (1 Sam 21:10), and later became his vassal (1 Sam 27:1-6). Now once again servants are fleeing from a member of Saul's family to Achish of Gath, but this time the result will be the death of the Saulid at the hand of David's son.

The narrative passage begins and ends with words which, though pronounced differently, are written with identical consonants (ancient Hebrew did not write vowels): *wyšb*. This clear example of inclusion calls attention to the fact that Shimei's actions do not change his situation: he dwells in Jerusalem, and he returns to Jerusalem. His departure has no political agenda, nor is it an attempt to escape Solomon's control. It violates the letter of Solomon's prohibitions but not their spirit.

The central element in the section, and therefore the most prominent, is the line "and he went to Gath to Achish." The narrator focuses our attention on Shimei's destination. (Note, too, the insistent repetition of the word "Gath" throughout the narrative section; it occurs five times in less than three verses.) This emphasis on Gath is, as we shall see, the key to recognizing that Solomon executes Shimei on false charges.

SHIMEI BEFORE SOLOMON: 2:42-46a

The final scene begins with Solomon confronting Shimei about his disobedience. He accuses Shimei with questions intended to demonstrate Shimei's guilt. Yet Solomon's questions and the accusations implicit in them falsify the matter on two counts. First, Solomon claims that he made Shimei swear by Yahweh. If this were true, Shimei would be guilty not only of disobeying Solomon's order but of violating a sacred oath as well—a serious crime in itself. But there is no evidence in the earlier dialogue that Shimei bound himself by oath to obey the king. He agreed to do the king's bidding, but without any oath formula or invocation of the divine name. Secondly, Solomon claims that he said, "on the day you go out and go to any place whatever, know for certain that you shall die" (v. 42). But this, too, is untrue. Solomon forbade Shimei to leave Jerusalem and to "go out from there to any place whatever" (v. 36), but he did not attach the death penalty to this prohibition. That was linked to a much more specific offense: "on the day you go out and *cross the Wadi Kidron,* know for certain that you shall die" (v. 37). (Note how the verbatim repetition of verse 37 in verse 42 spotlights the way in which Solomon misquotes his own earlier words.) In fact, Shimei's journey was to Gath, as the narrative section insisted. But Gath lies southwest of Jerusalem; such a journey would not have taken him across the Kidron, which is to the east. Shimei therefore has violated the king's first order but not the command to which Solomon attached the death penalty.

Since Solomon's claims are false, we expect Shimei to defend himself. This expectation is strengthened by the close structural parallels between the two scenes of confrontation. Each scene comprises two speeches; each speech is introduced by a narrative line. The similarities of the narrative lines establish the parallel (those similarities are slightly obscured in the NRSV):

> A. "The king sent and called Shimei, and said to him" (2:36)
> B. "And Shimei said to the king" (2:38)
> A'. "The king sent and called Shimei, and said unto him" (2:42)
> B'. "And the king said to Shimei" (2:44)

The variation in verse 44 is significant. Since the king is already speaking in verse 43, the words "and the king said to Shimei" are redundant. (The NRSV smooths over the awkwardness by adding the word "also.") The only effect this narrative line has is to establish the structural parallel with the first scene, and thereby to point up the fact that Shimei does *not* speak where we expect him to. Where Shimei should have his chance to answer the king's questions and their implied accusations, the king goes right on talking. Given the falsity of Solomon's claims, it is not surprising that he does not allow his victim a chance to respond.

The continuation of Solomon's speech in verses 44-45 suggests a great deal about his hidden agenda. His first word is an emphatic pronoun: "*You* know . . . ." The emphasis has a double thrust. First, it suggests that Shimei knows something that others do not. Solomon goes on to say that Shimei committed evil against David, but this is certainly public knowledge. What only Shimei knows is that there is a connection between that evil and the sentence Solomon has just passed. Publicly, Shimei is to be executed for disobedience to a royal command. Privately, Solomon informs him that he is really being punished for his offense against David many years before. The second effect of the emphatic pronoun is to draw a contrast between "you" (that is, Shimei) in verse 44 and "King Solomon," who is named, also in emphatic position, at the beginning of verse 45. The sentence Solomon has just passed on Shimei will result in evil for Shimei but in blessing for Solomon.

The wording of verse 44 is quite awkward in Hebrew, and may have been corrupted in transmission. The NRSV rearranges the text to produce a smooth reading, but the Hebrew runs:

> *You* know all the evil
> which your heart knew
> which you did to David my father
> And Yahweh will bring your evil back on your head.

If we accept the Hebrew text of verse 44 as it stands, the second line emphasizes that Shimei committed his crime against David with full knowledge. (The word "heart" in Hebrew refers to the center of understanding and will, not to the center of emotion as in English. The word "mind" is actually closer to what the Hebrew means.) According to Solomon, Shimei was guilty of premeditated *lèse majesté* and therefore fully deserves whatever punishment he gets. The first and last lines use the word "evil" to turn the situation into an example of talion law: Shimei committed "evil" against David and will suffer "evil" in return.[2] (Shimei's "evil," of course, was the curse against David that David reminded Solomon about in 2:8-9.) In the last line Solomon makes Yahweh responsible for Shimei's punishment. The king's pious invocation of the divine will would be more credible if he had not already decided the issue by royal decree. As it stands, it is another instance of a pattern by which Solomon consistently places responsibility for his victims' death either on the victim himself (2:23, 26, 31) or on God (2:32, 44).

In verse 45 Solomon contrasts his own blessed destiny to what has just been said of Shimei. The parallel construction of the first two clauses of the verse suggests that the last words of the verse apply to both clauses:

[2]The "law of talion" refers to the biblical principle of "an eye for an eye and a tooth for a tooth." Originally this was intended to lessen violence, since it *limited* the amount of vengeance a person could take: one could not claim, for instance, a life for an eye. The Hebrew Bible frequently uses similar or identical vocabulary in describing a crime and its punishment to imply that the situation satisfies talion law. In modern terms we might say, "The punishment fits the crime."

But King Solomon will be blessed [before Yahweh forever]
and David's throne will be established before Yahweh forever.

There are three points of note in these words. First, here as in verse 31
Solomon names himself before the symbol of the royal dynasty: in his
view, his own future takes precedence over the future of the house and
family of David. Second, he refers to himself in emphatic position and
in overly formal language as "King Solomon." His title and the power
and position it implies have become central to his self-image. Third,
the motif word "establish" recurs here as in verses 12b, 24, and 46b, recalling once more the thematic issue of the whole chapter: Solomon's
concern for the consolidation of his own power.

The concluding narrative line of the Shimei episode (v. 46a) depicts
Solomon's ever-ready executioner Benaiah at work once more. The remark takes on almost the character of a refrain, since it appears at the
end of the three major episodes of this literary unit. The motif verb
pāgaʿ occurs again. It is found only in this chapter in 1 Kings, but, as we
have seen, it appears often. (The NRSV renders it by "strike down" in
verses 25, 29, 31, 34, 46 and by "attack" in verse 32.) Its frequency here
and its absence elsewhere in the book single it out for notice, though
at this point it is not clear why the narrator wishes to call our attention
to it. It is part of an overarching narrative strategy that we will discuss
below (see the remarks on 5:4).

The Characterization of Solomon

The narrator's strategy for characterizing Solomon is consistent
through the four episodes of this section. On the surface he depicts
Solomon positively: his decisions are always justified, and sometimes
they are even merciful. But beneath the surface the narrator uses a variety of subtle narrative devices to suggest a different, much more negative picture. We have already discussed this strategy in connection
with the narrative frame (vv. 12b, 46b); we will now examine how it is
used in the four episodes.

POSITIVE CHARACTERIZATION

The execution of Adonijah must be seen in the context of 1:51-53,
where Solomon granted him amnesty on condition that he remain loyal
to Solomon. Since Adonijah's request for Abishag can be construed as

a covert claim on the throne, he has violated the condition of loyalty. Solomon offered his brother a chance to escape punishment, but Adonijah throws away the opportunity. Adonijah himself is to blame for his own destruction, as Solomon says explicitly in 2:23.

Abiathar's exile is an act of mercy. He is deserving of death, but Solomon commutes that sentence to exile in view of Abiathar's faithful service to David. Since Abiathar has estates at Anathoth, the exile, while depriving him of his exercise of the high priesthood, will presumably permit him to live comfortably from the proceeds of his holdings. The narrator reminds us that Solomon's actions are also in harmony with the divine plan as articulated by an ancient prophet.

Joab is executed for the premeditated murders of Abner and Amasa. Since David charged Solomon to this duty, Solomon has two justifications for his decision: long-delayed justice to a murderer and filial obedience to David's last wishes. Solomon's mercy is evident, however, in his insistence that Joab be buried on his ancestral land. In this way Solomon recognizes and rewards Joab's years of loyalty to David.

David's instructions to Solomon also called for the elimination of Shimei, but Solomon was content to confine Shimei's movements to Jerusalem. Only when, after several years, Shimei violates the royal command does Solomon decree his death. Thus Shimei's fate is his own doing, and Solomon again has a double justification for executing him: Shimei's disobedience and David's dying request.

Negative Characterization

Alongside these positive elements, each episode contains covert indications that point to a negative characterization of Solomon as well. Some of them were mentioned in our discussion of the individual episodes; others were not.

In the case of Adonijah, the intensity of Solomon's reaction to Adonijah's request is striking. His instantaneous rage at Bathsheba, the incoherence of the last words of verse 22, and the unprecedented double oath in verses 23-24 (no comparable example of a double oath occurs elsewhere in the Hebrew Bible)—all combine to point up how strongly Solomon feels threatened by the request. The depth of his emotions suggests that a great part of his response is fear for his own security. His mention of Adonijah's precedence in age and of his influential supporters shows that, whatever Adonijah's motivations for his request, Solomon has never stopped thinking of him as a rival. Solomon's repeated use of "me" and the appearance of the motif word "establish" in verse 24 reveal his preoccupation with himself and his concern to eliminate all threats to his position. The inference is that Solomon does not have Adonijah executed simply because of the request for Abishag; rather the request supplies Solomon with a convenient excuse to eliminate a rival he still perceives as a danger.

The commutation of Abiathar's sentence of death to mere exile seems merciful, until we ask one question: On what basis does Solomon impose the death sentence in the first place? Certainly Abiathar committed no crime by supporting the heir apparent. The only possible reading is that anyone Solomon perceives as opposed to him deserves death. But if Solomon has no legal basis for executing Abiathar, then the death sentence is unjust, and commuting the death sentence to exile is merely a smokescreen to conceal Solomon's vindictiveness toward Abiathar for supporting Adonijah. And even the commutation of the unjust death sentence is qualified: Solomon says he will not put Abiathar to death "at this time," which leaves open the possibility of doing so in the future for unspecified reasons. This is essentially the same ploy that Solomon used with Adonijah in 1:52.

The narrator gives another pointer to a negative evaluation of Solomon by a wordplay placed, ironically, in Solomon's own speech. The first word in Solomon's speech to Abiathar is "Anathoth" (*'ănātōt*), the name of the village of Abiathar's exile. The end of the speech makes reference to Abiathar's having "shared hardships" (*hit'annîtā*) with David. The implication of the wordplay is that exile to "Anathoth" is one more in the series of "hardships" that Abiathar has suffered because of his loyalty to David.

Joab takes refuge at the altar when he hears "the news"—that is, the news about the execution of Adonijah and the exile of Abiathar. Joab's flight means that he believes Solomon is eliminating anyone identified with Adonijah's claim on the throne. When Solomon first commands Benaiah to execute Joab, he does so without expressing any reason for the command. This invites the reader to conclude that Joab's suspicion is correct. It is only when Benaiah's scruples prevent him from violating Joab's sanctuary that Solomon persuades him with arguments borrowed from David's instructions in 2:5 that negate Joab's right of asylum. The inference is that these arguments are only intended to salve Benaiah's conscience and that they do not express Solomon's real reasons.

Is there any indication that Solomon's real motive in condemning Joab is to eliminate another of Adonijah's supporters? Yes. In verse 22 Solomon shows that he continues to think of Adonijah, Abiathar, and Joab together as threats. The narrator has arranged the episodes in the same sequence—Adonijah, Abiathar, Joab—and has closed the sequence with verse 35 to mark the end of the subunit. The episode about Joab is thus more closely linked to the one about Abiathar than it is to the one about Shimei. This is what we would expect if Solomon's principal reason for disposing of Joab is the same as it was for Abiathar (they both supported Adonijah). If his principal reason were to fulfill David's instructions, we would expect the narrative structure to link Joab more closely with the other object of David's hatred, Shimei, than with Abiathar.

Finally, Solomon's untruths in the matter of Shimei clearly portray the king in a negative light. But the narrator does not make them obtrusive or comment on them. They are evident only when one compares the speeches of the king before and after the narrative of Shimei's journey. Similarly, only a careful comparison of the structures of the two scenes reveals that Solomon prevents Shimei from defending himself against the false charges.

A further negative element in the characterization of Solomon consists in something the narrator passes over in silence. Solomon carries out without qualms the two executions David urged on him in 2:5-9; but nothing is said about the generosity David recommended toward the sons of Barzillai (2:7).

Chapter 3
THE EARLY PROMISE OF SOLOMON'S REIGN
1 Kings 3:1-15

In 1 Kings 1–2 the narrator described how Solomon came to succeed David on the throne of Israel and how he rid himself of persons whom David and he considered threats to his security. Now the narrator turns to his account of Solomon's reign. He begins with two passages that sound a keynote, as it were, for the remainder of the narrative. The first passage is a brief summary statement by the narrator himself (vv. 1-3). It introduces three themes that will thread their way through the Solomon account, marking both the high points and low points of Solomon's career. The same three themes will recur in another summary statement near the end of the whole story (11:1-8), but the bright optimism of the early days will have darkened into tragic failure. The second passage is a single narrative scene that describes a dialogue between God and Solomon during a divine appearance to the king (vv. 4-15). It introduces other themes that supply the organizational principles for much of the following material. It is also the first of a series of divine encounters that punctuate the Solomon account and trace the gradual fading of the early promise of Solomon's reign.

The two passages do not form a self-contained story; there is little narrative tension or plot development in them. In examining them we shall concentrate on three issues: the internal structure and logic of each passage; the elements in each that contribute to the narrative unity of the whole Solomon account (discussed further on p. 150); and the contribution these passages make to the continuing characterization of Solomon.

Narrator's Summary Statement: 3:1-3

The narrator's remarks focus on three themes: Solomon's marriage to Pharaoh's daughter, his building projects, and the use of the high places for sacrifice. These themes interconnect the three verses, which are otherwise only very loosely linked with one another. The mention of Solomon's marriage to Pharaoh's daughter leads naturally to the remark about her temporary residence in the City of David until after Solomon built the palace and Temple. This prepares the way for the notice that, in the absence of a Temple, the people continued to worship on the high places. This in turn connects to the statement that Solomon, too, offered sacrifice on the high places. Each theme also continues the narrator's strategy of characterizing Solomon in positive terms on the surface but suggesting a more negative view in subtler ways. In the following discussion we shall show how each theme conveys these positive and negative views.

Solomon's Marriage to Pharaoh's Daughter

The narrator speaks of Solomon's marriage first in roundabout terms: the Hebrew reads, literally, "Solomon became Pharaoh's son-in-law" (NRSV, "made a marriage alliance with Pharaoh"). Even the next phrase, which uses the standard Hebrew idiom for marriage ("he took Pharaoh's daughter," that is, to himself as wife), de-emphasizes the marital relationship by omitting the usual elements "to himself" and "as wife." The wording is significant, because it points up clearly that in reality the union is a political alliance between Solomon and the king of Egypt; it is not primarily a relationship between Solomon and a foreign woman. In fact, as the narrator points out in verse 3, Solomon's love is directed wholeheartedly at Yahweh.

Yet the same Hebrew verb, "to become [someone's] son-in-law," also carries negative connotations in all its other occurrences in the Hebrew Bible. In every case the man who "becomes son-in-law" to another man makes himself subservient to his father-in-law or vulnerable to the harmful influence of his wife. In particular, the word appears in warnings against marriage between Israelite men and non-Israelite women (for example, Deut 7:3; Josh 23:12). To use the term here of Solomon's alliance with Pharaoh can imply that Solomon is in some measure subordinate to Pharaoh; it can also suggest that Pharaoh's daughter will adversely affect Solomon's behavior. Both possibilities will be borne out in later passages. In 9:16, Pharaoh captures Gezer from the Canaanites and gives it to his daughter; yet this city lies only twenty miles from Jerusalem, deep within Solomon's own territory. Apparently Pharaoh's might is greater than Solomon's and can achieve decisively even inside Solomon's own kingdom what Solomon himself cannot. In 11:1-8 we will see that Solomon's foreign wives, of whom Pharaoh's daughter is certainly the most prominent, lead him into idolatry.

It is noteworthy that the narrator puts the foreign marriage alliance first in his account of Solomon's reign, since other issues, particularly Solomon's building projects, will dominate the subsequent chapters. The emphasis accorded to the foreign marriage by its primary position in this passage alerts us that it will play an important role as the tale of Solomon's reign unfolds (see p. 134).

Solomon's Building Projects

The narrator lists Solomon's building projects between two place names: the "City of David" (where Solomon houses Pharaoh's daughter until his building projects are completed) and "Jerusalem." The difference is due to the building projects themselves. When David conquered the city, he used his own personal military forces rather than troops from either Israel or Judah; the city thus became his own crown property, therefore, the "City of David." It was located on a spur of rock between two steep valleys: the Kidron to the east and the Tyropoean to the west. North of the city rose a prominent height on which Solomon was to construct the Temple and the royal palace, but this hill lay outside the defensive walls of the City of David. Consequently Solomon had to build a new wall incorporating this site, thereby increasing the city's area considerably. This new, larger city is "Jerusalem," and it contains the "City of David" as its older section.

Solomon's constructions include his palace complex (Solomon's "house"), the Temple (Yahweh's "house"), and the defensive wall around the expanded city of Jerusalem. Each of these is important, and each benefits the whole people: the palace complex houses the public administrative buildings of Solomon's kingdom; the Temple offers a central shrine for worship of the God of Israel; and the wall strengthens the city's defenses, particularly on its vulnerable northern flank. We shall learn later that Solomon's works are vastly more ambitious than this, but the narrator chooses from their great number these three particularly praiseworthy endeavors to highlight how Solomon's reign contributes to the national good.

At the same time, the narrator lists the projects in a telling sequence. Later chapters will recount that Solomon built the Temple first, and only then turned to the construction of his palace; yet here the narrator places the palace before the Temple, as if to suggest that Solomon's house precedes Yahweh's on the king's list of priorities. And, in fact, later remarks by the narrator will support this inference: as we shall see, Solomon will spend nearly twice as long building his palace as he will building the Temple.

The third theme is worship on the high places. These were open-air sites, usually located on natural or artificial elevations (hence the name), where sanctuaries to various deities were situated and sacrifice was offered. Later on (in other words, in the days of the author and original readers of our text), worship on the high places was synonymous with idolatry, since approved sacrificial worship of Yahweh could be carried on only at the Temple. In fact, in the rest of the Books of Kings, a king's attitude toward the high places will be one of the criteria on which the narrator judges him: if he attempts to destroy them, he is good; if he leaves them alone, he is mediocre; if he worships there, he is evil to the core. The narrator must explain to his audience that in the early years of Solomon's reign the situation is different: the people offer sacrifice to *Yahweh* on the high places, and this worship is acceptable, since Solomon has not yet built the Temple. Even Solomon himself offers such sacrifice to Yahweh, whom he loved.

Yet here too the narrator inserts an implied criticism of Solomon. In the Hebrew text the lines about the people's worship (v. 2a) and about Solomon's (v. 3b) both begin with the word *raq,* which is used to introduce some idea that contrasts with what precedes it. (In verse 2a the NRSV moves the word to the end of the clause and translates it "however"; in verse 3b the NRSV renders it by "only.") In both cases the word reflects badly on Solomon. In verse 2a the contrast with verse 1 is difficult to see. (That is probably why the NRSV moved the word to the end of the clause: it smooths the awkwardness somewhat.) What is common to the two verses is the mention of Solomon's building of the Temple. For the narrator, worship on the high places was undesirable, though the people had an excuse for it before Solomon built the Temple. But it was incumbent upon Solomon to complete the Temple as quickly as possible so that the practice might end. In effect, the narrator says, "Solomon was going to build the Temple; however, the people were sacrificing on the high places because he had not yet built it."

In verse 3 the situation is different. The second clause begins with *raq;* it thus qualifies the first clause by suggesting that Solomon's worship on the high places, legitimate as it was, tarnished his love for Yahweh. In other words, "Solomon loved Yahweh; however, he still sacrificed on the high places." The inference is that Solomon should not have offered sacrifice there but somewhere else. There was a more acceptable alternative: the altar in front of the tent holding the ark of the covenant, where both Adonijah and Joab had sought asylum. And in fact, Solomon himself will offer sacrifice there in 3:15.

There is a second implied criticism as well. The narrator says that Solomon "walked in the statutes of his father David." Elsewhere in the Hebrew Bible the phrase "walk in the statutes of (someone)," meaning "behave righteously," always refers to Yahweh's statutes, not to those of a human being. It might be argued that "David's statutes" could also mean righteousness, since he is elsewhere held up as the model king. But the usage is without parallel anywhere in the Hebrew Bible.[1] Moreover, in the present context, the most recent activity we have seen on David's part is his giving of vindictive, bloodthirsty directives to Solomon for the liquidation of Joab and Shimei—"statutes" that Solomon has indeed obeyed to the letter.

Solomon's First Encounter with Yahweh: 3:4-15

Two speeches dominate the scene of Yahweh's appearance to Solomon at Gibeon: Solomon's prayer and the Lord's response. A double inclusion frames the dialogue:

A. Solomon offers sacrifice at Gibeon (3:4)
  B. "And Yahweh appeared to Solomon in a dream" (3:5a)
    C. SOLOMON'S PRAYER (3:5b-9)
    C'. THE LORD'S RESPONSE (3:10-14)
  B'. "And Solomon awoke; it had been a dream" (3:15a)
A'. Solomon offers sacrifice at Jerusalem (3:15b)

The two speeches of the dialogue have similar introductions (vv. 5b-6a and 10-11a) and are further unified by the theme of the "heart," which runs through both speeches (vv. 6, 9, 12), and by another inclusion: the righteous ways in which "David my/your father walked" are mentioned at the beginning of Solomon's prayer (v. 6) and at the end of the Lord's response (v. 14). Both motifs, the "heart" and the example of David, are of special import in what follows.

Narrative Frame: 3:4-5a, 15

The outermost frame recounts a sacrifice that Solomon offers at Gibeon before his encounter with Yahweh and another that he offers at

---

[1] There are several other occasions where someone is said to "walk in the statutes of" a human being. But without exception these uses refer to *unrighteous* behavior.

Jerusalem after it. The change of place is significant. The narrator makes clear that Gibeon was originally the preferred location: it was the most important high place, and it was Solomon's custom to offer extravagant sacrifices there. (Gibeon is about seven miles northwest of Jerusalem; the impressive nearby prominence known today as Nebi Samwil— "mountain of the prophet Samuel"—was probably the location of its high place. Nebi Samwil is the highest point on the northern horizon of Jerusalem.) But after his encounter with Yahweh, Solomon returns to Jerusalem to offer sacrifice at the altar of the ark of the covenant. This move foreshadows the effect Solomon's building of the Temple is to have on the cultic life of the people: they, too, are to abandon the high places and center their worship in Jerusalem.

The inner frame identifies Solomon's encounter as an appearance of Yahweh in a dream at night. (Solomon apparently spends the night at the sanctuary, perhaps in the hope of receiving just such a revelation.) This is not intended in any way to cast doubt upon the experience. It was common belief in the Ancient Near East, including Israel, that deities used dreams and visions to communicate with human beings. Since the narrator has already told us in verse 5 that Solomon's experience occurs in a dream, the repetition in verse 15a that "it had been a dream" is intended to reflect Solomon's point of view and to assure us that Solomon realizes that he has experienced a divine visitation.

SOLOMON'S PRAYER: 3:5b-9

Solomon's prayer has two parts with parallel structures:

A. *"You* showed great loyalty to your servant my father David" (3:6a)
    B. A description of David's obedience (3:6b)
        C. "And you gave to him . . . ." (3:6c)
A'. *"You* made your servant king in place of my father David" (3:7a)
    B'. A description of Solomon's inadequacy (3:7b-8)
        C'. "Give to your servant . . . ." (3:9)

The emphatic pronouns that begin each part highlight Solomon's belief that both David's kingship and his own are the results of Yahweh's initiative. Solomon's request will be for the gifts necessary to respond to that initiative as Yahweh wills.

In the first part Solomon attributes David's obedience to, among other things, his "uprightness of heart" (or "mind"; "heart" in Hebrew refers to thinking and willing, not to emotion). Solomon identifies his own succession to the throne as Yahweh's reward to David for his obedience. This leads smoothly to the second part, where Solomon speaks of himself and his duties as king. Solomon describes his own inadequacy in picturesque language. He is "a little child"—something of an exaggeration, since his son Rehoboam was born before Solomon came to the throne (cf. 11:42 and 14:21). He does not know how to "go out or come in"—an idiom for the military leadership expected of an Ancient Near Eastern king (see 1 Sam 18:12-16). The people over whom Yahweh has placed him cannot be numbered or counted—also an exaggeration, since David took up a census of the whole country less than a generation before (2 Sam 24). Unlike David, he does not have the qualities of "heart" necessary to carry out what Yahweh expects of him; he asks, therefore, for such a heart. His request is, literally, "Give your servant a listening heart to judge your people, to discern between good and evil" (the NRSV correctly renders this with "an understanding mind to govern"). The task of "judging" *(šāpaṭ)* and its corresponding noun "judgment" or "justice" *(mišpāṭ)* is broader in Hebrew than in English. These terms include both aspects of the ancient ruler's duties: the making of just decrees (Hebrew, *mišpāṭîm*) and the making of judicial decisions (also *mišpāṭîm*) that enforce those decrees. We can see an example of this usage in the term "Judges," which refers to the charismatically chosen rulers of Israel before the rise of the monarchy, whose stories make up the Book of Judges. Solomon's request, therefore, is for the ability to carry out the entire range of royal responsibilities entailed in government.

THE LORD'S RESPONSE: 3:10-14

God's answer to Solomon's prayer is also in two parts, but they are unequal in length and are arranged chiastically:

A. Three things Solomon did not ask for (3:11a)
B. One thing Solomon did ask for (3:11b)
B'. God grants what Solomon did ask for (3:12)
A'. God grants what Solomon did not ask for (3:13-14)

The three things Solomon did not ask for were not unworthy; they were expected divine blessings upon a favored king. God's praise of Solomon, therefore, is not because he chose something good over something bad; it is because he chose something better over other goods. What he requested would benefit the whole of God's people, not just Solomon himself. In Hebrew, verse 11 has the flavor of an enumeration, but this is somewhat lost in the NRSV:

"Because you asked for this request,
   and you did not ask for length of days for yourself,
   and you did not ask for riches for yourself,
   and you did not ask for the life of your foes,
   but you did ask to discern to listen to justice for yourself,
behold, I have acted according to your request."

This list, almost exactly in reverse order, is what God grants Solomon: first, "a wise and discriminating heart"; next, "riches"; then, in place of the destruction of his enemies, "honor"; and finally "length of days."

Several comments are in order. Twice God refers to the one gift Solomon asked for, but in slightly different terms (vv. 11b and 12a). Together the two paraphrases use all four key words of Solomon's request—"heart," "listen," "discern," and "judge" (in the corresponding noun form, "justice")—and add two new qualities, "wise" and "discriminating" (a variant form of the word "discerning" in Hebrew). The implication is that God grants even the gift Solomon asked for in greater depth and breadth than he requested. Verse 12b emphatically underscores the unique character of the gift: Solomon will exceed all others in this respect.

Solomon's honor, too, will surpass that of all other kings (v. 13b). In this way God transforms the supremacy of violence that Solomon did not seek ("the life of your foes") into a supremacy of prestige above rulers of other nations. This supremacy will last "all your days" (the NRSV has erroneously attached the phrase "all your life" to "riches and honor"; it belongs at the very end of verse 14).

But it is precisely those days that are shadowed. Unlike the other gifts God grants Solomon, "length of days" is conditional. "If you walk in my ways," says the Lord, "then I will lengthen your days." This "if" sounds a cautionary note in an otherwise unrestrained celebration of divine bounty.

The Characterization of Solomon

We have already seen how the narrator continues his strategy for characterizing Solomon in verses 1-3: positive impressions on the surface, negative impressions conveyed by subtler means. He continues the same strategy in verses 4-15. The dominant picture of Solomon in the scene at Gibeon is very positive: his sacrifices portend the future building of the Temple and the transfer of Yahweh worship there; his prayer is humble and his request is unselfish; most significantly, the narrator himself tells us that the Lord was pleased with Solomon (v. 10a). Yet even in this scene there are a few negative notes.

Solomon sees in his own accession to the throne Yahweh's hand at work (v. 7). It is noteworthy that this claim is made several times in these chapters (see also 1:37, 48; 2:15, 24), but it is always made by Solomon himself or by some other character. Neither Yahweh nor the narrator ever confirms the claim. That is, Yahweh never tells Solomon anything like "I have given you the throne of David your father" (contrast Yahweh's words to David in 2 Samuel 7:8; 12:7). Certainly the claim is never expressly denied, but the narrator's silence leaves open the possibility that God approved Solomon's kingship only *post factum*, after Nathan and Bathsheba succeeded in gaining him the throne (for a similar situation, see Yahweh's words to Samuel about Saul in 1 Samuel 8:7-9). One can also ask if Solomon's humility is not a bit overdone. In view of his Machiavellian methods of ridding himself of Adonijah, Joab, and Shimei, his protests that he is only "a little child" and that he doesn't understand the "ins and outs" of leadership are disingenuous, to say the least.

Finally, the condition that Yahweh attaches to the gift of long life adds a new and ominous twist to the tradition of the dynastic promise. The original promise Yahweh made to David was unconditional (2 Sam 7). David's advice to Solomon in 2:2-4 already introduced a condition into the promise: long-term continuation of the dynasty was contingent upon the continuing obedience of David's heirs. Here Yahweh makes the issue much more immediate: Solomon's personal longevity is at stake, and there is no mention of a dynastic future.

Chapter 4
SOLOMON USES HIS GIFTS
1 Kings 3:16–4:34

The three gifts that God grants Solomon unconditionally—a listening and discerning mind, riches, and honor—are the organizing concepts for the next major section of the story of Solomon. To illustrate Solomon's use of these gifts, the author draws on a wide variety of sources, including folktales and royal archives. Only the first section is a true story, complete with dramatic tension. The sections corresponding to the second and third gifts contain primarily descriptive data, although here too the author arranges and sometimes changes his source materials to convey particular viewpoints, including the continuing strategy of ambivalent characterization of Solomon.

The Gift of "a Listening Mind"—Solomon's Judgment: 3:16-28

The tale of Solomon's judgment in the case of the two prostitutes is surely the best-known story from the entire Solomon account, and with good reason. It combines vivid character contrasts and poignant human interest with the intellectual challenge of a mystery story. It is small wonder that similar tales are found in a wide range of cultures. (An early twentieth-century scholar found twenty-two versions of the story in literatures from India to East Asia.)

The narrator focuses our attention on the inner life of the characters—the intellectual dilemma and the psychological maneuverings—rather than on external actions. He accomplishes this in two ways. First, he names none of the characters: we are to concentrate on them as types, "king" and "prostitutes," not as individuals. How does a "king," the ultimate arbiter of justice in the realm, respond to a perplexing case brought by representative members of society's quintessentially lowest classes? Second, dialogue dominates the story. While this is not uncommon in biblical Hebrew narrative, the extent of the dominance is striking in this case. Aside from narrative lines like "he/she said," "they spoke," and "he answered," the only narrated action in the course of the story is "they brought a sword before the king" (v. 24b). Everything else is reflected through the characters' speeches.

The effect of this preponderance of dialogue is different in the two parts of the story. In the first half, where the speeches of the women dominate, we listen along with the king and conclude along with him that the case is insoluble from the evidence presented. In the second half, the king's shocking command drives the action of the story. We hear it along with the women, and our instinctive horror is the basis from which we judge their different reactions. Finally, the king's resolution of the dilemma confirms the correctness of our instinct but points out concrete evidence that our rush to judgment overlooked and that the king's wisdom perceived.

THE DISPUTE: 3:16-23

The story opens with a connective word (NRSV, "later") that links it to the scene at Gibeon. This points up the narrator's intention to use this story as well as the information in chapter 4 to expand upon the Gibeon narrative. As we shall see, this story illustrates Solomon's "mind that listens to discern between good and evil."

A modern reader of the story is likely to mistake the narrator's purpose in identifying the contending women as prostitutes. There are two assumptions we need to understand: the role of prostitution and prostitutes in ancient Israelite society and the role of the king in juridical disputes.

First, there are two very different sorts of activity that go by the name of prostitution in the Hebrew Bible. One is often called "cultic prostitution," referring to a presumed practice of sexual activity in the worship of such deities as Baal, whose cult continued for centuries in Israel alongside that of Yahweh. Such activity (if it actually occurred, which some scholars doubt) is consistently condemned not because it was sexual but because it was idolatry. The vocabulary for cultic prostitution is quite specific and does not occur in this story. The other type of prostitution involved congress between a man and an unmarried woman for recompense, but with no cultic dimension to the activity. This sort of prostitution was not considered morally wrong, though it certainly was not a very respectable profession. It was often the only resort for a woman who had no man to support her, such as a widow with no living father, brother, brother-in-law, or adult son. The identification of the women as prostitutes, then, is not intended to cast them as sinful and to depict the king's dilemma as how to do justice in a fundamentally immoral situation. It is intended rather to cast them as among the lowest and most disadvantaged members of society, and to depict the king as attending to justice even in a case involving the least important of his people.

This observation leads to the second assumption that we could easily overlook. In ancient Israel, as in the Ancient Near East generally, any citizen had access to the king. Naturally most juridical cases were handled on a lower level, but in theory every person had a right to a royal hearing. Other examples of the same phenomenon in the Hebrew Bible are seen in 2 Samuel 14:4-7, where, even though her case is a pretext, the woman of Tekoa can present her petition directly to David, and 2 Kings 8:3-6, where a Shunammite woman comes before the king of Israel. The story is not intended to show Solomon doing something extraordinary in hearing the prostitutes' case, but to show him carrying out fully the duties of his office.

The narrator simply introduces the speaker as "one woman." He does not tell us whether she is the mother of the living child or not, as he will in the second round of speeches (v. 26). This puts us in the same position as the king. We hear what he hears, we know what he knows, we have exactly the same basis for judgment as he. Will our insight match his?

"One woman" presents her case. Her speech is a model of clarity and rhetorical effectiveness. She lays out the facts that both parties agree on: two women were living in the same house, each with a newborn; no one else was present when the events took place. She emphasizes the last point by unnecessary repetition, to rule out the presence of a third party either as potential killer of the child or as witness to what really happened.[1] She describes her version of the events poignantly: the tragic way the child died, the tenderness of waking to nurse him, the anguish of finding him dead, the mistaken identity in the early morning darkness, the unexpected discovery that he was not dead but stolen by a presumed friend. Her account is coherent and plausible.

Several elements in her speech converge to sway our responses as readers. First, she is polite and formal, as befits someone addressing the king. Second, she is clearly the woman who no longer possesses her son. Whether through death or through seizure, she is bereft and her rival

---

[1]The statement that "there was no one else with us" (literally, "there was no outsider with us") refers to the women's clients. But it may suggest that the women offered their home as an inn for travelers as well. There is evidence that some prostitutes did so (see, for instance, Josh 2:1), and one of the ancient translations of the present passage calls the two women "innkeepers" instead of prostitutes in verse 1.

holds the living child. This predisposes us to sympathy for her. Third, the pathos of her recital of events intensifies our emotional response to the situation. Fourth, she consistently refers to her rival as "this woman." The phrase conveys her disdain for the other woman (and also furthers the narrator's emphasis on anonymous types rather than individuals).

Most readers find themselves sympathetic to the speaker and moved, if not to some degree persuaded, by her speech. Yet this is a good example of the saying from the Book of Proverbs, "The one who first states a case seems right, until the other comes and cross-examines" (Prov 18:17). We tend to overlook a serious inconsistency in her argument. How could she know how the child died and what her rival did about it if she was asleep at the time? Plausible as her case seems at first, it is in the last analysis one woman's word against the other's. This is the point of the precisely balanced chiasm in the women's words as they turn to address each other in verse 22ab:

> A. "The other woman said,
> 　B. 'No! Rather my son is the living one,
> 　　C. and your son is the dead one.'
> A'. But this one was saying,
> 　　C'. 'Rather your son is the dead one,
> 　B'. and my son is the living one.' "

The verb form in the second half of the verse ("this one was saying") conveys that these two statements are not made consecutively, as accusation and response, but simultaneously, as in a quarrel. The women stop speaking *to* the king and turn on one another *before* the king (v. 22c).

The rhetorical polish and emotional power of the first woman's speech do not mislead the king. He realizes that there is no reliable evidence on either side, and that the equal weight of the women's claims is perfectly symbolized by the balance of their words in verse 22. He shows this by repeating those words almost exactly:

> A. "This one is saying,
> 　B. 'This, my son is the living one,
> 　　C. and your son is the dead one.'
> A'. But this one is saying,
> 　　C'. 'No! Rather your son is the dead one,
> 　B'. and my son is the living one.' "[2]

---

[2]The NRSV renders verse 23 differently from verse 22ab, presumably for variety. The Hebrew of the two verses is virtually identical.

The king does not address the women; his words express rather his pondering the case before him. In fact, the verb in the introductory phrase "the king said" sometimes refers to inner speech ("the king thought" or, in our idiom, "the king said to himself"). We have here an example of something relatively unusual in biblical Hebrew narrative: the narrator gives us direct access to the internal life of one of the characters.

The wordiness and extensive repetition in verses 22-23 bring the pace of the narrative to a temporary halt. The evidence is inconclusive, and the dilemma seems impossible of resolution. For the reader, the feeling is one of stalemate. Unless something unforeseen occurs, the plot has miscarried and the story is over.

THE RESOLUTION: 3:24-28

The king's next words are certainly unforeseen: "Bring me a sword"! Throughout the first part of the story we could identify with the king as he listened to the words of the women. Even at the end, when his insight into the insolubility of the case proved deeper than our own, we could appreciate his reasoning. This, however, goes beyond us. We have no idea what the king is about, and we stand with the women, apprehensive of the violence implied in the command. The only narrated action in the whole story is verse 24b: "and they brought a sword before the king." The effect is chilling. In the first half of the story, the central role was the women's; they began by standing "before the king," and they ended by arguing "before the king." Now their place "before the king" is taken by a sword.

If the cold brutality of the king's order is shocking to us, we can only imagine how it must have stunned the women. His callous condemnation of the child is not the only affront; by it the king also mocks the bereaved mother's sorrow. It is as if he says, "You want justice? I'll give you justice—both of you shall grieve equally!" The unnecessary phrase "in two" ("Divide the living child in two") recalls the first woman's redundant "only the two of us were in the house" (v. 18). And the king's repetitive words, "give half to the one and half to the one" (NRSV, "to the other") parody the repetitiveness of the women's arguing in verse 22.

In the face of such a threat, the two women react very differently. One of them speaks first. The narrator interrupts to assure us that she is the true mother of the living child and to give us a glimpse into her inner life: her "motherly love" is stirred up. (The Hebrew term, *raḥămîm*, is derived from *reḥem*, "womb." It can be used broadly of "tender compassion," but in this case the etymological connotation surely comes to the fore.) The interruption confirms that we no longer share the king's point of view—we now know who the true mother is, but he does not—and strengthens our identification with the true mother, desperate to save her son's life. The true mother is willing to give up her child rather than see it killed. One word in her speech is particularly noteworthy. To this point in the story, the women have consistently called the child *ben*, "son." The king once used the ordinary word for "child," *yeled* (v. 25). Here the true mother calls him a *yālûd*, a much less common term whose connotations recall the moment of birth (literally, "the born"; compare the dialectal English term "bairn"). The term is presumably more poignant and intimate than *yeled*, and is perhaps captured well in English by "baby." The true mother's compassionate anxiety for her infant shows through in her language.

The other woman speaks at the same time: the verb is the same as in verse 22b and connotes simultaneity here as it does there. She insists that the king's dreadful order be carried out. We do not know whether she does this because her grief has curdled to vindictive envy of the true mother or because she hopes that by agreeing with the king she will sway him to award her the child. The narrator gives us no insight into her inner life. (There is reason for the narrator's restraint: to do so would enable us to understand her better and perhaps to identify more sympathetically with her pain. This in turn would draw our attention more to the psychological drama of the two women and away from the intellectual theme of the king's gift of discerning judgment.)

Since the narrator has already told us which woman is the true mother, we are content to let the contrast between the one's self-sacrifice and the other's harshness confirm what we already know. We forget that the king does *not* know and must determine his course of action on the basis of what the women reveal about themselves by their words. When he speaks, he demonstrates that, indeed, he has the gift of "a mind that listens to discern between good and evil." Despite the wording in the NRSV, the king's words are virtually identical to those of the true mother, including the telling emotional word *yālûd*. "Give her the living *yālûd*, do not kill him!" It is clear that the king is quoting what he has just heard her say. He makes only one small change: he uses a different word for "not," thereby strengthening the woman's expression ("do not kill him") and giving it the force of a royal command. His last words show that he has, by listening, been able to resolve the mystery: "She is his mother."

The final verse is the narrator's summary of the long-term results of the event on the king's reputation. All Israel comes to know of his decision *(mišpāṭ)* and to realize that he possesses a gift of divine wisdom for achieving justice *(mišpāṭ)*. The key words in the summary verse, "wisdom" and "justice," point back to the terms Yahweh used in conferring the gift of "a wise and discerning mind" on Solomon (3:11-12).

THE CHARACTERIZATION OF SOLOMON

The narrator continues his strategy of characterizing Solomon positively on the surface and more negatively in subtler, covert ways in this passage. The positive picture is quite clear: confronted with an insoluble case, Solomon devises an effective ploy to induce the women themselves to reveal the truth. The ploy succeeds, and the king uses his God-given ability to hear the nuances of their words and to discern the truth they reveal.

There are, however, three elements in the text that can support less complimentary readings. First, the king's words in verse 27 use pronouns: "Give *her* the living baby . . . . *She* is its mother." We naturally tend to read these pronouns as referring to the true mother, who spoke in verse 26. But after she spoke, the other woman also spoke. Grammatically, the other woman is the antecedent of these pronouns. (Most translations, including the NRSV, recognize the difficulty; that is why they substitute something like "the first woman" for the pronoun "her" in the king's words.) This allows us a very uncomfortable reading as an alternative to the one given above. The king correctly discerns the identity of the true mother, as he demonstrates by quoting her words exactly, especially the term *yālûd*. But he accepts at face value her desperate offer to yield her son to her rival and declares that this makes the other woman the child's mother. The narrator gives us no indication which of these opposite readings we should choose.

A second troubling element is in the popular reaction to Solomon's judgment. The verb used is *yārē'*, whose basic meaning is "to be afraid." In Hebrew the verb often refers to the awed reverence one has before God, but even here the root sense of fear underlies the reverence: the distance between what is awesome and what is fearsome is not great. When they heard of Solomon's judgment, all Israel "feared" (NRSV, "stood in awe of") the king. The reaction is understandable, given the divine quality the people perceive in Solomon's wisdom, but it does not disguise the fact that the first result of the exercise of Solomon's gifts is fear.

Finally, in verse 28 the narrator attributes to the populace the opinion that the king possesses and exercises divine wisdom. He does not indicate whether he shares their view. This is similar to his strategy of allowing various characters to acclaim Solomon's accession to the throne as due to Yahweh's initiative but never confirming the opinion with his authority as narrator. The long-range effect of this reticence on the narrator's part is to raise an unspoken question about his own view of Solomon and to invite us to suspect that the covert indicators of a negative evaluation of the king may be closer to the narrator's opinion than the more apparent positive portrayal.

The Gift of "Riches"—Solomon's Administration: 4:1-28

The author has taken the material in 1 Kings 4 from different sources. Some of the information almost surely goes back, by a complicated process of transmission, to official archives of Solomon's reign. This diverse and complex genesis has produced a chapter full of textual and historical problems. For example: in the list of Solomon's twelve officers (vv. 8-19), the names of several of them are missing and only their fathers' names are given. (The NRSV obscures this a bit by retaining the Hebrew *ben*, "son of," as if it were the whole of the individual's name. "Ben-hur," for instance, simply means "son of Hur.") Could it be that the author's copy of this evidently official list was damaged along one edge? Historians and archaeologists wrestle with those questions. Here, however, our questions are different. How has the author used these materials to further the recounting of Solomon's reign? What is their narrative effect? Our first observation is that the chapter contains no stories at all. There is nothing like the dramatic tales we saw in chapters 1–3. Our focus in discussing this passage, therefore, will have to be on two issues: the literary qualities that the author has given to the material, notably its organization, and the way the passage contributes to the larger narrative effect of the whole Solomon account.

There are two technical details that must be mentioned before we begin. The traditional chapter-and-verse numbering in English translations differs from that in the Hebrew text. The translation we have been referring to, the NRSV, follows English tradition in this regard, as do most modern English versions. A few others follow the Hebrew numbering, which starts chapter 5 earlier than the English system:

English		*Hebrew*
4:1-20	corresponds to	4:1-20
4:21-34	corresponds to	5:1-14
5:1-18	corresponds to	5:15-32

We will follow the NRSV's chapter and verse numbers in our discussion. More confusing for our purposes is the practice of those translators who are convinced that the text is out of order. In their translations they rearrange the text according to their reconstruction of its "original" state. This is the case with the New American Bible and the New Jerusalem Bible. In both cases the English translation does not follow the order of the material in the Hebrew text, as a look at the chapter and verse numbers will show. In our discussion we will follow the order of the text in the NRSV, which is the same as that of the Hebrew Bible.

The narrator organizes the text in two main blocks dealing with domestic affairs and international affairs respectively. Each block begins with a statement about Solomon's rule and ends with a statement about how that rule affected Judah and Israel. The narrator follows the two blocks with a brief passage about Solomon's chariots and horses. The entire passage thus runs:

> A. "Solomon was king over all Israel" (4:1)
> B. Discussion of domestic affairs (4:2-19)
> C. "Judah and Israel were numerous . . . ." (4:20)
> A'. "Solomon was sovereign over all the kingdoms" (4:21a)
> B'. Discussion of international affairs (4:21b-24)
> C'. "Judah and Israel lived in safety . . . ." (4:25)
> Addendum: Solomon's chariots and horses (4:26-28)

The three sections are unified by the motif of food and drink mentioned repeatedly throughout the passage (vv. 7, 20, 22-23, 25, 27, 28).

DOMESTIC AFFAIRS: 4:1-20

The first block begins with the statement that Solomon was king over "all Israel." The phrase has a certain ambivalence here. "All Israel" can sometimes refer to the entire realm, including both the northern territory (Israel) and the southern (Judah). An example of this usage occurs in an exactly parallel passage introducing the list of David's high officials (2 Sam 8:15-17). The narrator of 1 Kings, however, often uses the phrase to distinguish the northern territory from the southern. Which is the narrator speaking of here? The ambivalence raises a question: Will Solomon's governance be different over "all Israel" and over "Israel"? Will his policies and practices be equitable for the two parts of the realm?

The description of Solomon's administration of internal affairs comprises two separate lists. The first enumerates high officials of Solomon's central government—what we might call his cabinet. It is fairly clear that the author's source has already had a complicated history: verse 2, for example, where Zadok's son is "the" priest (presumably the high priest), must reflect a later time than verse 4, where Zadok himself (and Abiathar!) are (high) priests. The system of "forced labor" (v. 6) of which Adoniram was in charge entailed temporary conscription to carry out public works projects. The system is not new; David already employed it (2 Sam 20:24). But it will become a significant factor in the achievements of Solomon's reign and in its ultimate failure.

The second list describes the administrative districts into which Solomon divides the kingdom and names the officers he appoints to gather taxes (in the form of provisions) from each district. (The NRSV calls them "officials," but this is misleading, since the word is entirely different from the "high officials" of 4:2.) Since many of the place names are unknown to us, it is impossible to reconstruct these districts on a map. Indeed, the information does not seem to be a description of borders so much as an enumeration of regions and settlements answerable to each officer. To the extent that we can compare this with other Israelite traditions, the districts are neither entirely congruent with the traditional tribal boundaries nor entirely in conflict with them. The striking thing about the list, however, is that the twelve districts are all in the northern territory: here the phrase "all Israel" (v. 7) clearly refers only to the north. Since each district is to supply the royal household with provisions for one month of the year, the list implies that Judah is not subject to this form of taxation. The last words of verse 19 strengthen this suspicion: "And there was one officer who was in the land [of Judah]." The officer is not named, his duties are not spelled out, and his territory is described only in general terms.[3] The statement sounds like a parenthetical afterthought, attached to the preceding list to assure the reader that Solomon's administrative structures do not neglect Judah. The clear implication is, however, that Judah is not divided into districts as Israel is. The possibility that Judah may not have to supply Solomon's provisions as the northern districts do reminds us of the ambiguous "all Israel" in verse 1, with its suggestion that Solomon's policies may treat the two parts of the realm differently.

The last line of the block on domestic affairs declares that Solomon's policies bring prosperity and happiness to Judah and Israel. Even if

[3]The Hebrew text is problematic here. The last words of verse 19 in the Hebrew text read, "And there was one official who was in the land." The word "Judah" does not appear. Since verse 20 begins with the word "Judah," some scholars suspect that the text originally had the word twice in a row, once to end verse 19 and once to begin verse 20, and that an early copyist accidentally left one of the words out. That is why the NRSV translator put the word "Judah" into verse 19. Even if that speculation is incorrect, however, there is little doubt about the meaning of the verse, since the term "the land" often refers to Judah.

Solomon's policies toward the north and the south are different, their results are positive.

International Affairs: 4:21-25

The second block begins with the statement that Solomon's authority extends from the Euphrates River to the "border of Egypt" (this phrase generally refers to the Wadi el-Arish in the Sinai desert). Historians doubt that Solomon actually held sway over such a vast territory, but clearly the narrator wishes to give that impression. His Solomon is sovereign over a far-flung empire. Narratively this raises the stakes, so to speak. We are not simply following the inconsequential tale of some local chieftain; the story of Solomon is played out on an epic scale and a world stage. Yahweh promised Solomon riches and honor surpassing that of all other kings (3:13); this promise, the narrator assures us, is fulfilled completely.

The list of Solomon's provisions for one day is astounding. We are to surmise that Solomon supplies thousands upon thousands of people with their livelihood. This suggests the magnitude of the state apparatus: central administration, military forces, and conscripted labor would all draw their sustenance from the king's supplies. We should note, however, that this list of provisions undoubtedly belonged originally with the list of officers who supplied the provisions (vv. 7-19). The author has transferred it here to give us the impression that Solomon obtains this vast quantity of food, not by taxing his own people, but as tribute from his international vassals (v. 21b).

The block ends with the remark that Solomon's international hegemony results in peace and security for Judah and Israel.

Chariots and Horses: 4:26-28

The brief addendum about chariots and horses contains two small textual difficulties. First, the NRSV mistranslates one word: Solomon has twelve thousand "horses," not "horsemen." Second, his "forty thousand stalls" may be a copyist's error for "four thousand" (in 2 Chr 9:25 the figure is given as "four thousand"). The lower figure makes sense. In Solomon's day, horses were not yet ridden; their military function was as chariot horses, not as cavalry. Chariot horses worked in teams of three. If each team were kept in a single large stall, the number of stalls and the number of horses would correspond. The addendum as a whole focuses on the provisioning of the horses. Like verses 22-23, verse 27 surely belonged originally with the list of district officers in verses 7-19 (in fact, it refers explicitly to "those officers"). By placing the verse here, the author includes the provisioning of the horses (v. 28) among the officers' duties, thus assuring us that the bounty of Solomon's kingdom extends even to the animals.

THE CHARACTERIZATION OF SOLOMON

The characterization of Solomon is less direct in this passage than it has been, since we do not have stories that depict him acting in particular situations. Nevertheless, we do get some impression of Solomon from the way he controls and disposes of the material wealth he enjoys. The dominant picture is positive, but here too the narrator continues his strategy of inserting subtler signals of more negative aspects.

Solomon's organization of his own realm is innovative, efficient, and productive. His imperial sovereignty is unchallenged and brings great wealth into the kingdom. On both levels, Solomon's success is beneficial to all his people. They are prosperous, happy, and secure. Even his animals share the benefits of his enlightened administration. The overall impression is that Solomon uses the riches Yahweh promised him wisely and well.

On the negative side, the suggestion that Solomon's administrative policies were different for Judah and for Israel, particularly in regard to taxation, would sound a sour note for the Israelite reader of the text. Even though Israel and Judah were both prosperous and happy at this point, the Israelite reader would surely be aware that Solomon's kingdom fell apart immediately after his death and largely on account of his discriminatory policies. Similarly, the phrase "during Solomon's lifetime" in verses 21 and 25 would remind the Israelite reader that the peace and security enjoyed by Israel and Judah were only temporary. From Solomon's death on, the history of Israel and Judah was a history of warfare and strife, with times of peace and security rare indeed. The phrase (literally, "all the days of Solomon") also recalls the fact that Yahweh promised Solomon "length of days" only conditionally (3:14), and therefore the peace and security of Solomon's kingdom are likewise contingent upon his obedience to Yahweh's will.

Finally, the juxtaposition of the statement that Judah and Israel lived in safety (v. 25) with the statistics about Solomon's military forces (v. 26) is jarring. It suggests the exorbitant costs of the kingdom's security: the creation of a vast chariot corps, with all the attendant expenses in vehicles, animals, materiel, housing, provisions, and personnel. The necessity of such an armed force suggests that the people's security was less the result of Solomon's glorious administration of the empire than of brute strength, and that the tribute Solomon exacted from his vassals was wrested from them only at swordpoint.

NARRATIVE EFFECT

What is the narrative effect of inserting such material into the account of Solomon's reign? Primarily, it is one of plausibility or, in technical terms, verisimilitude. By including official-sounding lists of names, titles, and territorial descriptions, and by enumerating in detail the types and quantities of food consumed by the royal household in one day, the narrator gives his account the feel of a factually grounded, well-researched document. This is not to suggest that it is not! Quite probably the author *has* used facts and figures that derive from official sources. But it is also clear that he has rearranged those facts and figures for his own purposes; for example, he has separated verses 22-23 from verses 7-19 in order to suggest that Solomon's vast provisions were supplied by vassals rather than by his own citizens.

The feeling of verisimilitude is particularly important at this point in the text because it is precisely here that the narrator exaggerates other issues. We have already mentioned that some historians doubt whether Solomon's hegemony extended "from the Euphrates to the border of Egypt." It is also possible that the quantity of Solomon's daily provisions is exaggerated; estimates of the number of people they would support range from four thousand to thirty-two thousand. The size of his chariot forces, too, is suspicious. His twelve thousand horses could equip four thousand chariots, yet according to 10:26 he has only fourteen hundred chariots. By comparison, a century later King Ahab of Israel could field only two thousand chariots at the battle of Qarqar—and this was by far the largest chariot corps in that huge and bloody conflict. The impression of verisimilitude conveyed by the administrative lists affords the entire passage credibility. As readers, we tend to accept the less plausible data because of the apparent reliability of the lists.

The Gift of "Honor"—Solomon's Renown: 4:29-34

The third of Solomon's unconditional gifts is "honor" or "glory" such that "no other king shall compare with you" (3:13). This is the theme of these verses. Here too there are no stories; the narrator simply describes Solomon's wisdom and its results. Although the opening line celebrates Solomon's "wisdom, discernment, breadth of understanding," the focus of the passage is the repeated claim that Solomon's reputation spreads far and wide throughout the world, bringing people and kings from other lands to learn from him.

The passage is structured in two parallel parts, much like 4:1-25. After the introductory line, each part contains three statements: a general statement, particular examples, and a statement of Solomon's international renown:

> Introductory line (v. 29)
> A. General statement: Solomon's wisdom (v. 30)
>   B. Particular examples (v. 31a)
>   C. International fame (v. 31b)
> A'. General statement: Solomon's utterances (v. 32)
>   B'. Particular examples (v. 33)
>   C'. International fame (v. 34)

The opening line uses language very close to Yahweh's terms for Solomon's first gift, "a wise and discerning mind" (compare 4:29 with 3:11-12). Yet the central issue in the passage is Solomon's international fame, which corresponds to the third gift, "honor above other kings." By bringing these two motifs together, the narrator makes Solomon's justice-producing wisdom, rather than his riches or some other quality, the basis for his glory.

The first part of the passage compares Solomon with "people of the east," whose wisdom was legendary in the ancient world. He is wiser than all of them. (Unfortunately, we have lost any ancient traditions about the exemplary sages Solomon is compared with.) As a result, he gains an international reputation for wisdom. The second part goes beyond the first by offering evidence of Solomon's wisdom. He produces a copious outpouring of wise sayings and songs (the numbers are probably conventional, meaning "several thousand" and "a thousand and more"). His scientific and classificatory knowledge covers plants from the largest to the smallest and animals of every kind; similar scientific compendia are known from surrounding Ancient Near Eastern cultures as well. As a result, his reputation not only flourishes internationally but draws people from all nations to come to him and learn from him. Among these people are official representatives of their kings as well: this is the meaning of the last phrase of verse 34 (NRSV, "from all the kings of the earth").

The characterization of Solomon is entirely positive in this passage. His divinely given wisdom benefits not only Israel and Judah but the whole world. It also redounds to his glory, thus fulfilling the third of Yahweh's promises. The final note, that representatives come to Solomon from other kings, points forward to the next verses, the story of Solomon's negotiations with the representatives of King Hiram of Tyre.

Chapter 5
BEFORE BUILDING THE TEMPLE
1 Kings 5:1-18

The last words of chapter 4 tell of kings hearing of Solomon's wisdom and sending representatives to him. This leads smoothly into chapter 5, which begins with King Hiram of Tyre hearing of Solomon's accession to the throne and sending "servants"—probably ambassadors—to his court. The focus of the narrator's attention shifts from Solomon's wisdom, however. The central concern of the entire Solomon story is the building and dedication of the Temple, which occupies the middle third of the whole narrative (chs. 6–8). This chapter looks forward to the building of the Temple by recounting Solomon's preparations for the project, specifically his arrangements for materials and labor.

The chapter is in two parts. The first narrates the negotiations between Solomon and Hiram for choice woods that have to be imported from Lebanon because they do not grow in Israel. The second part tells of the system of conscription Solomon uses to get the indigenous labor and materials needed to carry out the construction. Only the first part qualifies as a real story, for the negotiations between the two kings contain a degree of narrative tension and resolution.

Negotiations with Hiram for Materials: 5:1-12

The story revolves around the exchange of diplomatic messages between Hiram and Solomon. Structurally, two messages are the focus of attention: Solomon's proposal to Hiram to arrange the importing of timber from Lebanon and Hiram's response. Each message is followed by a brief narrative passage, and narrative remarks frame the whole exchange.

A. Narrative frame (5:1)
   B. Solomon's proposal
      1. Solomon's message (5:2-6)
      2. Narrative passage (5:7)
   B'. Hiram's response
      1. Hiram's message (5:8-9)
      2. Narrative passage (5:10-12a)
A'. Narrative frame (5:12b)

The differences between the terms Solomon offers and those Hiram counters with produce the narrative tension of the story.

NARRATIVE FRAME: 5:1, 12b

The narrative line that opens the story links it to the end of chapter 4 by casting Hiram as one of the kings who sends an embassy to Solomon because of what they hear of him. In this case, however, there is a precise issue at stake: "Hiram had always been a friend to David" (so the NRSV; the Hebrew is literally, "Hiram had been loving David"). The language is a standard political euphemism and means that Hiram and David were political allies. The "servants" Hiram sends to Solomon are no doubt diplomats charged to discover whether Solomon is inclined to continue the alliance and, if so, to renew it. Similar political language occurs at the end of the passage, thus forming an inclusion around the whole story: "There was peace (*šālôm*) between Hiram and Solomon; and the two of them made a treaty" (v. 12b). By enclosing the story of the negotiations in this frame, the narrator suggests that the relationship reflected in the agreement Solomon and Hiram reach in regard to timber is representative of the general terms of the treaty they make. That connection is reinforced by an idiomatic expression in Hebrew: the usual Hebrew phrase for making a treaty is "cutting a treaty"; the negotiations for "cutting" trees (v. 6) result in "cutting" a treaty (v. 12b; NRSV, "made a treaty") as well.

SOLOMON'S PROPOSAL TO HIRAM: 5:2-7

Hiram sends his servants to Solomon; Solomon responds by sending his proposal to Hiram. The message is a marvelous example of diplomatic discourse, with several messages being communicated at once. Solomon begins by explaining the background of the request he is making of Hiram. The first part of his message (vv. 3-5a) is wrapped around a balanced series of phrases:

A. "my father David"
  B. "to build a house for the name of Yahweh his God"
    C. "surrounded him"
      D. "Yahweh put them"
      D'. "Yahweh gave me"
    C'. "all around" (NRSV, "on every side")
  B'. "to build a house for the name of Yahweh my God"
A'. "my father David"

The chiastic structure conveys a double message to Hiram. First, the two halves contrast David and Solomon, explaining both why David did not undertake to build the Temple and why Solomon will do so. But the identity of vocabulary in the two parts underscores the continuity between David and Solomon as well. The contrast is due to circumstances, not to ideological differences. Solomon portrays his intention to build the Temple as a natural development from David's own unfulfilled designs. In this way he suggests that his policies will be similar to his father's, thus tacitly answering Hiram's larger question and assuring him that he is willing to renew the political alliance between their nations.

Centered between this structure and the following one is a single line in which Solomon quotes Yahweh's own words to David (from 2 Sam 7:12-13) to the effect that David's successor will be chosen by Yahweh and will build the Temple (v. 5b). Solomon is implying, of course, that he himself is the promised successor and that his project has divine approval. The rest of Solomon's message (v. 6) expresses his request to Hiram. Between two references to cutting trees, which is the actual request, Solomon offers his terms: his workers will assist Hiram's in the project, and Solomon will pay the wages of Hiram's workers. The second reference to cutting trees ends Solomon's business proposal with a note of flattery.

There is another set of terms in Solomon's message that also conveys a significant diplomatic signal. The initial words in each major part of the proposal form their own pattern. (Note that in Hebrew the word for "you" [*'attâ*] and the word for "now" [*'attâ*] sound almost identical.)

A. "*You* [emphatic pronoun] know . . ." (5:3)
  B. "And now . . ." (5:4)
    C. "And indeed *I* [emphatic pronoun] . . ." (5:5)
  B'. "And now . . ." (5:6a; NRSV, "Therefore")
A'. "*You* [emphatic pronoun] know . . ." (5:6b)

This structure conveys a sense of the delicate political shadings in the negotiations. With diplomatic politeness, Solomon begins and ends by emphasizing Hiram's position. (The wordplay with "you" and "now" adds even more force to the emphasis on Hiram.) Yet the even stronger grammatical form and the centered position of the pronoun "I" offset the emphasis on Hiram with a similar emphasis on Solomon himself. While such nuances cannot be measured exactly, the two techniques seem to balance each other and to suggest a relationship of equals, with neither claiming preeminence over the other.

The first half of the story ends with a brief account of Hiram's reaction to Solomon's proposal. Hiram rejoices, praises Yahweh, and comments favorably on Solomon's wisdom (for which Solomon already had a wide reputation: 4:34). Though it may surprise us to see the king of Tyre praising the God of Israel, it is not really so extraordinary. In the polytheistic belief systems of the ancient world, each nation had its own deity, and responsibility for that nation's affairs was imputed to that deity by all peoples.

HIRAM'S RESPONSE TO SOLOMON: 5:8-12a

Hiram's response is no less a diplomatic tour de force than Solomon's original proposal. It is framed by an inclusion and filled with emphatic pronouns:

A. "*I* will fulfill all your needs . . ."
  B. (Logs:) "My servants shall bring [them] down . . ."
    C. (Rafts:) "And *I* shall make them into rafts . . ."
      D. "to the place which you indicate to me"
    C'. (Rafts:) "And I shall break them up . . ."
  B'. (Logs:) "And *you* shall take them away,"
A'. "And *you* shall fulfill my needs . . ."

Our first impression is of a balance between Hiram and Solomon comparable to that found in Solomon's original proposal. The first and last lines balance the emphatic pronouns "I" and "you," and each pronoun occurs once more in the speech; the central line mentions both Solomon and Hiram (the NRSV leaves out the phrase "to me," which is in the Hebrew).

A closer look, however, revises this impression. Under the guise of agreement ("I will fulfill all your needs"; literally, "I shall do whatever you want"), Hiram in fact rejects Solomon's terms completely and renegotiates them in his own favor. The first of Solomon's terms proposed that his own laborers work alongside Hiram's. This may have been to cut down on expenses, or it may have been an attempt on Solomon's part to learn some of Hiram's logging techniques (see v. 6b). The narrator does not bother to tell us. Whatever Solomon's motives, Hiram is having none of it. *His* workers will do all the logging and deliver the timber by sea to wherever (presumably in Israel) Solomon specifies. That way, Tyrian income is maximized, there is no infiltration of Hiram's territory by foreigners, and no industrial secrets are lost. The structure of Hiram's response subtly reflects this arrangement. The first half of the response, like Lebanon, is Hiram's territory: Solomon is not mentioned. The second half is Solomon's territory, but, like the servants who will deliver the rafts to Solomon's coast, Hiram enters Solomon's verbal territory as well ("I shall break them up").

The second of Solomon's terms had to do with payment. Solomon proposed to pay "the wages you set for your servants." This would be an understandable and equitable business arrangement, but it would also mean that Hiram's workers become employees of Solomon—at best an encroachment on Hiram's sovereignty and potentially a source of divided loyalties among the Tyrian laborers. In place of Solomon's proposal, Hiram defines payment as "providing food for my household" (v. 9b). This separates the issue of payment from questions of materials and labor and makes it a direct arrangement between kings—more a matter of international treaty (which is the context of the whole story: vv. 1, 12b) than a simple business deal. The wording of Hiram's response reflects this too. The parallel statements at the beginning and end, "I shall fulfill . . ." and "you shall fulfill . . . ," make it clear that the arrangement is quid pro quo: Hiram will do what Solomon wants about the timber, and Solomon will do what Hiram wants about the food. But the key phrase itself (literally, "do whatever [the other] wants") puts the arrangement officially into the category of a courteous exchange of gifts between friendly kings.

After Hiram's response comes a series of four remarks by the narrator all linked by the main verb "gave" (vv. 10-12a; in verse 10 the NRSV translates the verb "supplied"). The first three remarks spell out the terms Hiram and Solomon finally agree on. Hiram gives Solomon two kinds of wood (note that Solomon only asked for one in verse 6; Hiram offered both in his response). The first wood is the famous "cedar of Lebanon"; the second (NRSV, "cypress") is less certain. In this passage it probably refers to a species of tall, straight-growing fir indigenous to the Lebanese highlands. In return, Solomon gives Hiram agricultural products not widely produced in Tyrian territory: wheat and first-quality olive oil (hand pressed rather than crushed between stones, to avoid including crushed olive pits and debris from the millstones).

How much of each commodity Solomon pays is uncertain. Estimates of the Hebrew "cor" range from five to twelve bushels for dry measure and from forty to one hundred gallons for liquid measure; these figures mean that Solomon sends Hiram between 100,000 and 240,000 bushels of wheat and between 800 and 2,000 gallons of the finest olive oil. The narrator's third remark reveals that this extravagant expenditure is not a one-time cost but an annual outlay! The narrator's fourth remark about "giving" recalls that Yahweh too "gave" Solomon something: wisdom. This echoes Hiram's reaction to Solomon's original proposal, where he praised Yahweh for Solomon's wisdom (v. 7).

THE CHARACTERIZATION OF SOLOMON

The narrator continues his established strategy of presenting an apparently positive picture of Solomon but including in the text subtler pointers to a more negative evaluation. On the surface the story depicts a successful diplomatic exchange that results in the reconfirmation of an existing alliance and in a business arrangement that permits Solomon to begin the most important work of his reign, the building of Yahweh's Temple. Hiram sees in the agreement a sign of Solomon's divine endowment of wisdom, and the narrator confirms that judgment with his own authority (v. 12).

There are, however, several elements that complicate this positive picture. The most obvious is the fact that Hiram rejects Solomon's original proposal and renegotiates its terms in his own favor. That in turn raises questions about the meaning of Hiram's remark in verse 7. If Hiram's reaction to Solomon's words is joy and acknowledgment of Solomon's wisdom, why does he insist on terms that are completely different from Solomon's? And if Solomon is so wise, why does he agree to terms that so favor Hiram's interests and include such exorbitant annual costs? It is plausible to read Hiram's remark in verse 7 as an ironic comment on the reports he has heard about Solomon's wisdom (4:34): he rejoices not only that relations between their kingdoms will remain peaceful but also that this reputedly "wise" son of David is offering him such an opportunity to profit from the prosperity of "this great people" (literally, "this numerous people"; compare 5:7b with 4:20).

In this case the narrator's reference to Yahweh's gift of wisdom may also be ironic. The sequence of sentences in verses 10-12a is suggestive. In Hebrew the first two sentences are linked by "and" and should be read as a pair. They appear to detail the terms of the business deal: what Hiram gives and what Solomon gives. Not until the third sentence do we learn that what Solomon gives is a recurrent annual payment. The third and fourth sentences are also linked by "and," which suggests that they, too, should be read together. The Hebrew verb of the fourth sentence is to be read as a past perfect: "And Yahweh *had given* wisdom to Solomon, as he promised." If this is a comment on the quality of Solomon's business acumen as reflected in the terms he has just agreed to, it is more likely to be sarcastic than complimentary: "And Yahweh had given Solomon wisdom [but he certainly didn't use it]!"

A further negative element concerns the payment itself, both in its description and in its amount. Hiram rejects Solomon's proposal to pay wages and requires instead that he supply "food for my household." In the last chapter we learned that the "food for Solomon's household" came from taxes imposed on his own people (4:7) and from tribute from foreign kings over whom Solomon ruled (4:21-22). Far from being an arrangement of equality and balance, the agreement Solomon makes with Hiram puts him into the same position vis-à-vis Hiram that Solomon's own vassals have toward him. The quantities Solomon sends are also extreme. His annual income from the whole empire is approximately 33,000 cors of choice flour and meal (4:22); his annual outlay to Hiram is 20,000 cors of wheat,[1] not to mention the vast amount of hand-pressed olive oil. The "wise" Solomon has not gotten a bargain.

A final negative element involves two echoes in Solomon's vocabulary. He tells Hiram that he is now free to build the Temple because "there is neither adversary nor misfortune" to distract him (v. 4). The word "misfortune" (*pega'*; literally, "stroke") is a very rare word in Hebrew and occurs only one other time in the Hebrew Bible. But it echoes strongly with the related verb *pāga'* that was such a motif word in 2:12b-46, where it was used several times to mean "violent killing." Solomon may placidly describe his reign as lacking in (literally) "evil strokes," but the victims of the ready strokes of Benaiah's sword, Adonijah, Joab, and Shimei, would be unlikely to agree. The word "adversary," too, will echo ominously later in the Solomon story. Despite Solomon's blithe denial here, dangerous "adversaries" dogged Solomon's entire reign, as we shall see in discussing chapter 11.

---

[1]Experts estimate ancient milling as producing three measures of flour and meal for every four measures of wheat. Solomon's outlay of wheat would produce approximately fifteen thousand cors of flour and meal, or just under half of his annual income. See John Storck and Walter Dorwin Teague, *Flour for Man's Bread: A History of Milling* (Minneapolis: University of Minnesota Press, 1952), p. 88.

Conscripted Labor: 5:13-18

The account of the labor force Solomon assembles in preparation for building the Temple is an administrative note rather than a story, since it has no plot development and no narrative tension. The narrator gives us statistics about two different groups of workers: a conscripted force (Hebrew, *mas*) of 30,000 (vv. 13-14) and another group of 150,000 carriers and quarriers, together with their overseers (vv. 15-17). The last verse summarizes the whole chapter.

The conscripted labor force serves for three months in rotating shifts. One month is spent in Lebanon. The narrator makes no attempt to resolve the apparent contradiction between this claim and Hiram's insistence that all work in Lebanon be done by his own workers (v. 9). Perhaps we are to surmise that Hiram compromised with Solomon on this point. If so, Solomon's bargain is even worse than it seemed: he not only pays an exorbitant annual sum to Hiram but he also supplies (and supports) a vast amount of the labor Hiram should furnish. The other two months are spent in Israel, working on the Temple. (The NRSV's "at home" is misleading; the Hebrew is "in his house," meaning the "house" Solomon is building for Yahweh.) We are probably to assume that the work continues year round, with four different groups being conscripted over the twelve-month period. The discordant note in these verses is that the laborers are taken from "all Israel" (v. 13), a term that, as 4:7 made clear, refers to the northern tribes. Judah, the homeland of the Davidic family, is exempt from forced labor, just as it is from the system of taxation described in 4:7-20. The brief note that "Adoniram was in charge of the *mas*" repeats information from 4:6 and singles out Adoniram as a person of particular note. Nothing more is made of him here, but he will reappear tragically in the story of the breakup of the kingdom after Solomon's death (12:18).

The second labor force works within Israel to obtain the indigenous limestone needed for the Temple. Its "supervisors" (literally, "officials of the officers") answer to the twelve officers Solomon appointed as tax collectors over the northern tribes (4:7). This labor force, too, like the conscripted *mas*, is an extension of Solomon's taxation system of "all Israel." Their task is to quarry, transport, and dress the large ashlars that will be the foundation stones for the Temple. The triple phrase in verse 17, "great stones, costly stones, dressed stones," emphasizes strongly both the size of the stones and the skill required to prepare them. The last verse reveals that Solomon's laborers are complemented by foreign workers, not only from Hiram of Tyre but also from farther away: the "Giblites" are from Byblos, farther north along the Mediterranean coast beyond Hiram's territory. The position of this information following verse 17 suggests that the foreigners are not involved in the early work of quarrying and transporting, but in the later work of dressing the ashlars and laying the Temple foundations. They are, then, highly skilled artisans—a further drain on Solomon's treasury. The last words of verse 18 are a concluding summary of the two sections of the chapter, mentioning both the timber of verses 1-12 and the stone of verses 13-17.

Chapter 6

THE CONSTRUCTION AND DEDICATION
OF THE TEMPLE

1 Kings 6:1–9:10

The heart of the whole story of Solomon is the account of the construction of the Temple and its dedication ceremony. The passage takes up over one-third of the Solomon narrative, from the announcement of the beginning of the project in 6:1 to the announcement of its completion in 9:10. It falls into two roughly equal parts, the construction proper (6:1–7:51) and the dedication (8:1–9:10); the two parts are like the two panels of a diptych at the center of the Solomon story. The first panel consists principally of descriptions of the building and its appointments; the second contains some narrative material about the ceremonies of dedication but mainly comprises Solomon's speeches and prayer on that occasion. There are no real stories in the section, and, for the most part, no narrative tension. Our focus will be the way in which the narrator orders the material, including interruptions in the logical organization, and the narrative effect the material is intended to have on the reader.

The Construction of the Temple: 6:1–7:51

The account of the construction of the Temple is obscure in its organization and daunting in its detail. Numerous attempts have been made to extract from the data sufficient information to create a model of Solomon's Temple. Unfortunately, several factors foil the project, not all of which are to be laid to the narrator's account. First, the text contains numerous technical terms for architectural and design elements whose precise meanings are lost to us. Second, while it is quite possible that the author had access to archival data about Solomon's Temple, he or she was writing at some remove from Solomon's day (see, for example, 8:8). It is therefore likely that the description includes elements that had changed in the Temple in the meantime. Third, despite the detail, the information is incomplete. As we shall see, the narrator is not interested in an engineer's or architect's view, but in what we might call a tour guide's view of the building.

ORGANIZATION OF THE PASSAGE

The organization of the material is difficult to discern because of two passages that disrupt an otherwise logical progression. The two passages are a divine word to Solomon (6:11-14) and the account of the building of the royal palace complex (7:1-12). When these two passages are recognized as interruptions, the remainder is quite orderly:

> A. Frame verse (6:1)
> B. Work in stone (6:2-8)
> A. Frame verse (6:9a)
> B. Work in wood (6:9b-10, 15-36)
> A. Frame verse (6:37-38)
> B. Work in bronze by Hiram of Tyre[1] (7:13-40a)
> A. Frame passage (7:40b-45)
> B. Work in gold by Solomon (7:46-50)
> A. Frame verse (7:51a)

There are some minor irregularities in this pattern (for instance, 7:46-50 includes information about Solomon's work in bronze as well as gold), but the main lines are clear enough.

The frame verses are all general references to "building" or "finishing" the "house of Yahweh." The longer frame passage in 7:40b-45 is a bit more complicated. It contains a more or less standard frame verse, "So Hiram *finished* all the work that he did for King Solomon on the *house of Yahweh*" (v. 40b), together with a list of what Hiram's work included (vv. 41-45). Since that work was already described at length in 7:13-40a, the list serves to summarize the whole preceding passage as well as to set it off from what follows. The final verse, 7:51, also does double duty. The first half is a standard frame line, "Thus all the work

---

[1]This is not the king of Tyre whom we met in 5:1-12 but a master craftsman in bronze (see 7:13-14).

that King Solomon did on the *house of Yahweh* was *finished.*"[2] The second half is a sort of literary hinge connecting the two parts of this diptych. The mention of "the silver, the gold, and the vessels" that David dedicated points back to 7:48-50, where Solomon also makes vessels of gold for the Temple. But "bringing in" the vessels also points forward to "bringing up" the ark and holy vessels that were in the tent, which begins the account of the dedication ceremony (8:4).

The four passages about work in stone, wood,[3] bronze, and gold proceed logically from structural work to decoration and furnishings. We begin with the ground plans (6:2-3), we watch the building grow to three stories (6:6), we see the wooden structural elements of stairways and roofing put in place (6:8-10). This is followed by wooden interior construction in cypress and paneling in cedar (6:15-17), ornamented and gilded interior woodwork (6:18-22), and furnishings of olivewood (6:23-33). After the interruption about the building of the palace complex, the narrator describes the metalwork: Hiram's works in bronze from largest to smallest (7:13-40a), and Solomon's works in gold, likewise from largest to smallest (7:48-50).

The Interruptions: 6:11-14; 7:1-12

The first interruption is the passage about the word of Yahweh in 6:11-13; 6:14 returns to the description of the construction of the Temple by repeating verbatim the frame verse that preceded the interruption (v. 9a). This passage is the second in a series of four encounters between Solomon and Yahweh. We have already seen the first encounter, Solomon's dream at Gibeon (3:4-15), and we will later examine all four encounters as a coherent set (see p. 154). In all four cases Yahweh reacts to something Solomon does. Here the divine word is placed after the basic structure of the Temple is completed and before interior and dec-

---

[2]The verb used in 7:51a for finishing the house (*šlm*) is different from the one usually used in the frame verses (*klh*). The verb *šlm* occurs at two points in the narrative where "finishing" is particularly noteworthy: the completion of all the Temple construction (7:51a) and the completion of the entire section of the Solomon story that is concerned with the construction of the Temple (9:25b). It is also a wordplay on the name Solomon (*šlmh*).

[3]Some of the identifications of wood are unsure. "Cedar" is the well-known "cedar of Lebanon," but "cypress" translates a Hebrew term of uncertain meaning (see above, on 5:10, p. 97). The NRSV's term "olivewood" in 6:23-33 for the Hebrew *ʿēṣ šemen* (literally, "oil wood") is most likely wrong, since the olive tree is generally called *zayit* in Hebrew. The tree in question may be a species of pine, though other scholars suggest a type of oleander.

orative work begins, and it comments on the project Solomon has undertaken. Unexpectedly, however, Yahweh is cautionary rather than congratulatory. God's first words are, "This house that you are building," a phrase that stands out starkly because it does not fit grammatically into what follows. (The NRSV's word "concerning," which smooths the syntax somewhat, is not in the Hebrew.) There is an abrupt shift of subject to "If you will walk in my statutes . . . ," as if to jar Solomon to the realization that what is at the top of his priorities, the building of the Temple, is not of first importance to Yahweh. Yahweh's desire is obedience.

As with so much of the Solomon story, we can read these words on two levels. At first Yahweh seems to say that the ultimate success of Solomon's undertaking—that is, whether or not Yahweh will choose to dwell in the house Solomon is building—is contingent upon Solomon's obedience. But in fact Yahweh says nothing at all about the Temple. He speaks of dwelling "among the children of Israel," not "in the Temple." This raises the stakes considerably. Solomon's obedience does not simply affect divine acceptance of the Temple as a house; it is necessary even for God's continued abiding with the people. Disobedience carries the threat that God will "forsake my people Israel" (v. 13b).

The second interruption is quite different. In 7:1 the account turns from the construction of the Temple (Yahweh's "house") to the construction of the palace complex (Solomon's "house"). This includes not only the royal residence but important administrative buildings as well. The transition is smooth, since both passages concentrate on architectural details. Yet when the text returns to discussing the Temple in 7:12b, it becomes clear that the intervening verses form an interruption in the larger account.

The passage about the palace complex has its own unified structure:

A. Transition from Temple to palace complex (7:1)
  B. The House of the Forest of Lebanon (7:2-5)
    C. The Hall of Pillars (7:6)
      D. The Hall of Judgment (7:7)
    C'. Two private residences (7:8)
  B'. Construction materials (7:9-12a).
A'. Transition from palace complex to Temple (7:12b)

(Notice how the "four rows of cedar pillars with cedar beams," with "three rows" of rafters between, in verses 2-5 are echoed by the "three rows of dressed stones" and "one row of cedar beams" in verse 12a, where the NRSV translates the Hebrew word "row" as "course" and "layer.") The whole section centers on the "Hall of the Throne, where he was to pronounce judgment, the Hall of Justice (*mišpāṭ*)," recalling the key word from Solomon's request of Yahweh in 3:9.

Besides reminding us of Solomon's duty to administer justice, the interruption raises two other issues more subtly and without comment. The first is the length of time Solomon spends on the palace complex. The immediately preceding frame verses (6:37-38) calculate that Solomon spends seven years building the Temple (from his fourth year, 6:1, to his eleventh year, 6:38). The transition to the account of the building of the palace complex reveals that he spends thirteen years on that project. Since the palace complex houses the central administration of the whole empire, the issue is not a simple contrast between Yahweh's Temple and Solomon's private residence, as if Solomon were being accused of spending all that time on his own luxury and glory. Nonetheless, the juxtaposition of 6:38 and 7:1 invites us to infer that the governmental buildings are far more important to Solomon than the religious one. In view of the ruinous annual tariff Solomon is paying Hiram, it is quite clear which project brings Solomon to the brink of bankruptcy.

The second issue is still more subtly evoked. The entire passage is not only a logical interruption in the flow of the account of building the Temple; it is also chronologically out of place. The narrative's view of Solomon's works—no matter how unrealistic this might be in terms of the actual construction process—is that he spends seven years building the Temple (6:1, 38); then, when he finishes it, he spends the next thirteen years building the palace complex (7:1). Together the two projects take twenty years (9:10). To describe the construction of the palace complex in the middle of the account of building the Temple is, therefore, an anachronism. This reinforces the interruptive character of the passage and focuses our attention on it even more.

But within the passage itself there is a further anachronism. In verse 8b the narrator mentions the construction of the house for Pharaoh's daughter, which is not to take place until after both the Temple and the palace complex have been completed (3:1; 9:24). (The NRSV translation is incorrect; the Hebrew is "Solomon *was* also *to make* a house like this hall for Pharaoh's daughter . . . .") This interruption within an interruption points to a motif that runs through the entire Solomon story: his entanglements with foreign women and the disaster they eventually bring upon him. We will look more closely at this motif later (see p. 134).

NARRATIVE EFFECT

What is the narrative strategy that motivates these chapters? In other words, to what purpose does the narrator spend such an inordinate amount of time on details of construction and decoration? The main effects are three. First, the detailed description of the construction places the Temple itself squarely in the center of our attention, much as it places it in the center of the whole Solomon story. For the ancient Israelite reader, the Temple would be of intense and immediate importance; it may have been still standing (see 8:8[4]), and it was the focal point for Israelite worship. For a modern reader, the text's appeal is less to immediacy than to imagination. We are invited to rebuild in the mind's eye what once stood in glory in Jerusalem.

Even the ancient Israelite reader, however, would have to use imagination. For the narrator, acting almost as a tour guide, intends to show his readers the entire Temple, including those inner sanctums inaccessible to the ordinary Israelite. We have already seen how the narrator organizes his description in terms of material (stone, wood, bronze, gold) and in terms of construction (foundations, superstructure, finishing and decoration, furnishings and appurtenances). This method also allows the narrator to usher his readers through the Temple, pointing out noteworthy sights along the way.

We approach the building from a distance, where we can clearly see its foundations and dimensions, its stories and stairways, and its roof and outbuildings (6:2-10). We enter the building and admire the interior woodwork: flooring and paneling, interior walls that separate the inner sanctuary from the nave, and the ornamentation in the nave (6:15-18). We stand "in front of" the inner sanctuary (not in the "interior," as the NRSV would have it in verse 20) and marvel at its gilded cedar walls and altar and the solid gold chains that bar access to the interior (6:19-22). But our guide even leads us inside the inner sanctuary itself to see the monumental statues that will overshadow the ark of the covenant, once it is installed in its place (6:23-28). This is the turning point of the tour, and so we take a last look at the interior carvings and gilded floor (6:29-30), go through the doorway back into the nave (6:31), admire the carving and gilding on the outside of the doors (6:32), go through another doorway back into the courtyard (6:33-34), admire the carving and gilding on those doors (6:35), and find ourselves in the courtyard (6:36). After the guide points out to us the nearby palace complex (7:1-12), we can wander around the courtyard and gaze in wonder at Hiram's heroic bronze pillars (7:15-22), his gigantic

---

[4]Though the narrator's words imply the continued existence of the Temple, this may be artistic license. It does not necessarily date the account to a time before the Temple's destruction in 587 B.C.E. The remark invites the reader, ancient or modern, to enter a narrative world where the Temple still stands, whether or not it does so historically.

bronze "sea" (7:23-26), and the ten huge bronze stands and basins against either side of the Temple building (7:27-39).

The second effect of this passage is to convey a sense of verisimilitude. The extravagance of the description is balanced by the precision of the particulars to counter any impression of exaggeration. The meticulous detail—of sizes, of quantities, of ornamental embellishments, of remote locations (e.g., 7:46)—gives the entire account the ring of factual accuracy. (In chapter 4 the narrator used a similar combination of lavish description and detailed administrative data to the same purpose; see p. 90.)

The third effect of the passage is to bring the pace of the narrative, which has been slowing gradually, to a complete halt. The Solomon account began in chapter 1 with a complex, suspense-filled story. This was followed by the episodic narratives of chapter 2. Though chapters 3–5 contained some stories, they were dominated by non-narrative materials on a number of topics. This slowing culminates in chapters 6–7, where narrative development comes to a standstill. Like extended descriptive passages in modern literature, these chapters are used to establish an atmosphere. The description of the Temple is exuberant: unusual care (6:7), costly imported materials (6:15), exquisite decorations (6:18, 29, 32, 35), extravagant gilding (6:20-22, 28, 30, 32, 35), monumental sculpture (6:23-26; 7:15-16), sumptuous appointments (7:23-26), bronze implements beyond counting (7:47), and numerous items in solid gold (7:48-50; the word "gold" is used six times in these three verses). The narrator's enthusiasm is unmistakable, and the cumulative impression is one of breathtaking glory. Whatever happens in the rest of the story, however the destinies of Solomon and of Israel turn out, this remains: the magnificence of the house of Yahweh. For that alone Solomon shall be remembered with praise.

The Dedication of the Temple: 8:1–9:10

The account of the dedication ceremony of the Temple comprises three lengthy speeches given by Solomon and surrounded by narrative passages. The narratives and speeches are arranged concentrically:

A. narrative: gathering of the assembly (8:1-13)
  B. speech: Solomon "blessed all the assembly" (8:14-21)
    C. speech: Solomon's prayer (8:22-53)
  B'. speech: Solomon "blessed all the assembly" (8:54-61)
A'. narrative: dismissal of the assembly (8:62-66)

Only in verses 1-13 is there any dramatic tension; narratively, the rest of the account serves mainly to fill out the developing picture of King Solomon's character.

The report of the Temple dedication is followed by a third encounter between Solomon and Yahweh marked by the same sort of frame verses seen in chapters 6–7:

> D. frame verse (9:1)
> E. Solomon encounters Yahweh in a vision (9:2-9)
> D'. frame verse (9:10)

NARRATIVE FRAME: 8:1-13, 62-66

Together the two passages frame the intervening speeches with several strong inclusions. They describe how Solomon convoked (v. 1) and dismissed (v. 66) the assembly gathered to celebrate the dedication of the Temple. Each passage also describes the gathering as a "festival" (vv. 2, 65) and recounts the prodigal sacrifices offered on the occasion (vv. 5, 63).

The first passage situates the dedication ceremony "at the festival in the month Ethanim, which is the seventh month." As a month name, "Ethanim" was probably as strange to the ancient Israelite reader as it is to us, since the narrator has to explain it. It derived from a Canaanite calendar that was archaic even in the author's time and corresponded to late September and early October. The great festival during that period was the seven-day Feast of Booths, which was in origin a celebration of the harvest. A ceremony of dedication in the seventh month, however, accords poorly with the earlier notice that Solomon finishes the Temple in the eighth month of his eleventh year (6:38). It is unclear whether the dedication ceremony is rushed ahead, even though the last of the construction is not yet complete, or whether the Temple sits ready (but unused?) for eleven months between its completion and its dedication. What is clear is that the festival of the seventh month is an important enough occasion in and of itself to warrant some adjustments to the timetable.[5]

---

[5]If, as some scholars believe, the Solomonic period celebrated the New Year in the autumn, the dedication of the Temple may have coincided with such a festival. But since the narrator (and presumably his readers) counts late September as "the seventh month," he must be assuming the spring New Year that was later Israelite practice. The only festival he could have in mind, then, would be the autumnal Feast of Booths. One possible indicator of this is the word used in 8:7 for the cherubim's wings "covering" *(skk)* the ark. This is the same root used for the "booths" or huts *(sukkôt)* lived in during the feast.

The reader who is aware of two factors will detect a strong element of suspense in the passage. First, to transfer the ark from one sanctuary to another is a dangerous and unpredictable business. The story of David's two attempts to bring the ark into Jerusalem shows clearly the risks involved and the advisability of frequent sacrifice along the way to placate the discommoded deity (2 Sam 6:1-15). Second, the ark of Yahweh was never before housed in a permanent structure, nor did Yahweh ever express such a desire; see, for example, 2 Samuel 7:6-7. (The idea was in fact an innovation from Canaanite paganism.) God promised David that he would permit David's "son" (2 Sam 7:13; the word can also be used of more remote male descendants) to build him a temple, but he has not confirmed that Solomon is the "son" he had in mind or that this particular Temple pleases him. Even his word to Solomon when Solomon undertook the building spoke only of dwelling "among the children of Israel" and did not comment on the building itself (6:11-13). The suspense, then, is twofold: Will the transfer of the ark proceed without tragedy? And will Yahweh be pleased with his new "house"?

Suspense is heightened by several elements that retard the narrative flow and defer the resolution. Generally speaking, the whole passage is much wordier than Hebrew narrative commonly is.[6] It takes, for instance, three verses to identify all the groups present at the start of the procession (8:1-3). The piling up of different terms builds a sense of solemnity and inclusiveness, but it also delays considerably the start of the action. The procession is described in verses 4-6 with much verbiage and little action: there are only three main verbs in the three verses, and two of them are the same. The installation of the ark in its place stops the action dead with four separate phrases to describe the location: literally, "unto its place, unto the inner sanctum of the house, unto the holy of holies, unto beneath the wings of the cherubim" (v. 6). This finally resolves the first issue: the ark has been transferred successfully and without incident. But will Yahweh approve his new house? The question remains suspended while the narrator expatiates on the cherubim's wings (v. 7) and on the visibility of the ark's handles (v. 8a). He then steps entirely outside the narrative to address the reader directly and at length (vv. 8b-9).[7] Only in verses 10-11 do we return to the story and

---

[6]Scholars commonly attribute the wordiness of the passage to a series of editors, each of whom inserted vocabulary, motifs, and theological concerns characteristic of his or her particular viewpoint. While this may be true, the result of such an editorial history is a text with a coherent narrative effect on a sensitive reader.

[7]The NRSV, along with most translations, treats verse 9 as part of the narrative: "There was nothing in the ark . . . . " The Hebrew, however, is more correctly rendered in the present tense as part of the narrator's aside to his contemporary reader: "There *is* nothing in the ark . . . ."

learn that Yahweh accepts the Temple and consents to fill it with the cloud that embodies his glory.

Solomon utters a brief (and probably ancient) poetic catch to confirm the divine presence. (Hebrew narrative prose sometimes breaks into poetry at especially climactic moments.) The first line[8] recognizes Yahweh's ultimate freedom: the "thick darkness" in which he chooses to dwell is not only the windowless holy of holies deep within the Temple; it is also the obscurity of the cloud of glory in which Yahweh moves as he will, and it is, most of all, the hiddenness of his mystery. The next lines are Solomon's formal gift of the Temple as a royal palace for Yahweh and his throne. The NRSV's translation is possible, but a better rendering would be:

> "I have built you indeed a princely house,
> a firm base for your Seat for the ages."

Throughout this whole chapter it is important to be aware that the Hebrew verb *yšb*, which the NRSV regularly renders by "dwell," can also mean "sit." In other words, the frequent references to Yahweh's "dwelling" somewhere may in fact be references to his having a throne there rather than to his being in residence.

The closing narrative passage (8:62-66) has no narrative development comparable to that in verses 1-13. It culminates the dedication ceremony in a scene of grand sacrifice and celebration (similar to the celebration that climaxed David's transfer of the ark in 2 Samuel 6:17-19). The participants are described as "all Israel," which in 1 Kings usually refers only to the northern territory; but in this instance the term explicitly includes the whole people (v. 65). According to the Hebrew text, the celebration lasted twice as long as the usual Feast of Booths (v. 65 reads "seven days and seven days, fourteen days"; the NRSV follows the ancient Greek translation here and reads simply "seven days"). In this passage, too, the narrator breaks out of the frame of the story to address the reader directly ("Yahweh *our* God," v. 65); the effect is to intensify our identification with the scene by reminding us of our continuity with the people whose worship we witness.

---

[8]Some ancient Greek versions preserve what may be a more original form of the beginning of the poem:

> "Yahweh (who) made known the sun in the skies
> has said he would dwell in thick darkness."

In this reading the contrast is between Yahweh's power to create the sun and his choice to conceal himself in impenetrable mystery.

In the course of these two passages the narrator has been at pains to weave together a number of theological traditions. These include traditions associated with the Exodus from Egypt and traditions connected with David. Among the former are the "tent of meeting" (Exod 27:21; 40:1; etc.), the tablets in the ark (Deut 10:1-5), and the cloud that signals Yahweh's presence (see, for example, Exod 13:21; 14:19; 40:34; Num 10:11-12); the narrator had already used the Exodus as an important reference point for the building of the Temple in 6:1. The Davidic traditions include the procession with the ark (2 Sam 6:1-15), the holy vessels (v. 4; cf. 7:51b), and the unique relationship between Yahweh and David (v. 66). The point we as readers are to take from this is that, for the narrator, the Temple is the culmination and synthesis of all that has gone before in Israel's history.

Solomon's Speeches: 8:14-21, 22-53, 54-61

Narrative lines that describe Solomon's actions separate his three speeches from one another and from Solomon's preceding poetic lines in verses 12-13. We are to imagine him speaking verses 12-13 facing the sanctuary, for in verse 14 he turns to address the assembly. In verse 22 he turns back to face the altar and stands with his arms raised. In verse 54 he rises from a kneeling position and once more faces the people. (The disagreement between standing in verse 22 and kneeling in verse 54 is trivial. It may be no more than the sort of slip of the pen that even the most careful authors and editors, ancient and modern, occasionally commit.) The first and third speeches form a pair. The narrator emphasizes their correspondence by calling both blessings of the assembly (vv. 14, 55), even though the first speech does not fit that description at all. Both begin with the words "Blessed be Yahweh," followed by a praise of God for faithfully fulfilling his promises to David and Moses respectively. The second speech is a lengthy prayer of petition that Solomon offers to Yahweh. Repeated phrases link it to the "blessings" that surround it: "with his hand he has fulfilled what he promised with his mouth" (vv. 15, 24) and "the plea/cause of his servant and the plea/cause of his people Israel" (vv. 52, 59).[9]

[9]Most scholars see in the wording and theology of all three speeches the work of several generations of deuteronomistic theologians before, during, and after the Babylonian Exile. In this view, the deuteronomists have used Solomon as spokesman for their own later theological views. That may be an accurate assessment of the editorial history of the text, but it leaves unanswered the narrative question of how these speeches shape our understanding of the king who makes them. In other words, what does it reveal about the character of Solomon that he gives these speeches on this occasion?

A major theme of the first speech is Yahweh's promise to David in 2 Samuel 7. It is recalled in the opening praise Solomon offers Yahweh (v. 15) and by paraphrased quotations from 2 Samuel 7 that alternate with commentary by Solomon himself. After the initial praise, two references to the Exodus from Egypt bracket the rest of the speech (vv. 16, 21). In this way Solomon makes the same link of Davidic and Mosaic traditions that the narrator makes in the narrative frame. But where the narrator uses the Davidic traditions to enrich the theology of the Temple, Solomon puts them at the service of his own importance. His first quotation of Yahweh's words, based on 2 Samuel 7:6-8, makes the personal election of David the culmination of Israel's history to that moment. (Note the implied contrast in verse 16: "I have not chosen *a city* . . . , I chose *David*.") The second quotation, based on 2 Samuel 7:12-13, goes on to make David's son the ultimate heir of that election. (In verse 19 the Hebrew uses emphatic pronouns for contrast: "*you* shall not build the house, but your son . . . , *he* shall build the house.") Solomon then claims that heritage for himself and reinforces it with a wordplay: "Yahweh *raised up* his word [NRSV: "upheld his promise"] . . . , and I *rose up* in the place of my father David" (v. 20). The series of first-person verbs that end the speech reflects Solomon's self-absorption: "I have risen up, I have sat, I have built, I have provided" (vv. 20-21).

A second theme that pervades the whole speech is that the Temple is "a house for the name" of Yahweh (vv. 16, 17, 18, 20). This odd-sounding phrase can be understood by analogy with the term "the City of David." Jerusalem was called "City of David" not simply because David lived there but because his conquest of the city with his own private army made it his personal possession. Likewise, the Temple is known by Yahweh's name, it is "the Temple of Yahweh," not because it contains him but because it is his possession. In this way Solomon acknowledges that Yahweh remains free and sovereign, notwithstanding his willingness to exchange his mobile sanctuary, the tent of meeting, for a permanent structure.

Solomon's second speech is a long prayer of petition to Yahweh, with whose name the speech begins and ends (8:23-53). Its organization is quite intricate and difficult to reproduce in translation. The main sections of the speech are a series of three addresses to Yahweh about "that which you spoke to your servant David, my father" (vv. 23-24, 25, and 26-30a) and a series of seven specific cases to which Solomon asks Yahweh to be attentive (vv. 31-51, with v. 30b as an introductory refrain to the series). The last two verses summarize the whole prayer by picking up the last words of each part (compare vv. 28-30a with v. 52 and v. 51 with v. 53). As in the first speech, Solomon links traditions about Moses and the Exodus (vv. 51, 53) to those about David.

The first three addresses celebrate Yahweh's faithfulness to David in the past (v. 24: "you have kept"), present (v. 25: "keep"), and future (v. 26: "let your word be confirmed"). Two shifts in vocabulary are noteworthy. First, the term that characterizes David's relationship to Yahweh is "servant" (vv. 24, 25, 26). As his prayer progresses, Solomon claims that term for himself as well (vv. 28, 29, 52). The term can reflect both sides of the relationship: David's loyal obedience and Yahweh's fidelity to his promises. The emphasis throughout the passage, however, is almost entirely on Yahweh's fidelity. (There is only a brief reference to the necessity of obedience by David's descendants in verse 25.) Second, Solomon begins by addressing Yahweh as the Deity of the whole people: "God of Israel" (vv. 23, 25, 26). But this too gives way to a focus on Solomon's personal relationship to God: "Yahweh, my God" (v. 28), "my lord Yahweh" (v. 53). In both cases the turning point is Solomon's exclamation in verse 27 about "this house that I have built." After that Solomon's vocabulary shifts to emphasize himself as fulfillment of the promises made to David and as heir of a unique closeness to God. In Solomon's mouth, "I have built" is at least as important as "this house."

The seven specific examples of prayer that Solomon enumerates envision an individual Israelite (vv. 31-32), a foreigner visiting the Temple (vv. 41-43), and the whole people in various straits (military defeat: vv. 33-34; drought: vv. 35-36; disasters of various sorts: vv. 37-40; war: vv. 44-45; exile: vv. 46-51). Several of the examples allude to traditional punishments that Yahweh will inflict on the people if they are not faithful to the covenant (compare the curses in Deuteronomy 28). The seventh example is particularly noteworthy because of its exceptional length and because of a complex series of wordplays on the roots "take captive" *(šbh)*; "return, repent" *(šwb)*; and "dwell" *(yšb)*. Each example follows the same general pattern: the petitioner is in a situation of need, the petitioner prays in or even toward the Temple, Yahweh hears from his heavenly Seat. The common thread that runs through all seven cases is that the petitioner's prayer is directed toward Yahweh *in the Temple* ("this house" or "this place" occurs in each example); such emphasis is to be expected in the context of the dedication ceremony. In the last three examples, however, Solomon again points up his own role by expanding the phrase to "this house that I have built."

The narrator calls Solomon's third speech a "blessing of the assembly," a description that fits the third speech better than it did the first. Like the first speech, this one begins with a praise of Yahweh for fulfilling his promise; here the promise in view is the one made to Moses rather than to David. Specifically, it is the promise to "give rest" to Israel, a term used elsewhere of Israel's entry into the Promised Land (v. 56; see Deut 12:10). This is followed by two invocations of Yahweh's favor, one over the nation, that Yahweh be with them and strengthen their obedience to his commands (vv. 57-58), and one that Solomon's own preceding prayer to God will win a favorable hearing (vv. 59-60). The speech ends with a brief exhortation to the people to obey the commandments (v. 61).

NARRATIVE EFFECT OF SOLOMON'S SPEECHES

The narrative strategy that we have seen consistently in earlier chapters continues here as well. The overt characterization of Solomon is positive; the negative elements are more subtle. Solomon's speeches contain a rich and sophisticated theology. He is aware of the breadth and complexity of Israel's religious traditions—the Exodus, the desert wanderings, the covenant and commandments of Sinai, the punishments for covenant disobedience, the entry into the Promised Land, the religious symbolism of the ark, the promises to David, and so forth—and he integrates them all into a single theological synthesis centered on the Temple. He recognizes that a fixed sanctuary is a radical innovation in Israel's tradition but manages to include this innovation in his synthesis without compromising Yahweh's sovereign freedom and mystery. He protects that freedom with a profound theological concept, the divine "name." Not only does that idea explain how the Temple can be Yahweh's "house" without limiting his freedom, but it also explains how the Temple can function as the place where communication with the transcendent One takes place: when one invokes Yahweh's name in prayer at or toward the Temple, Yahweh, in his heavenly abode, will hear and heed. Solomon's attitude toward Yahweh manifests grateful praise, reverence, and trust, as well as a realistic understanding of the role of obedience and repentance for sin in the life of the people. In short, we see here a dimension of Solomon's character we have not had occasion to witness before. Like his father David, he is sincere in his devotion to Yahweh and the religious traditions of Israel even if, also like his father, he does not always prove to be a paragon of sanctity in his private life.

On the other hand, the words the narrator puts in Solomon's mouth suggest two less attractive characteristics. The first is his self-absorption, a trait we have seen already in earlier chapters. This shows, for example, in his emphasis on himself as the fulfillment of Yahweh's promise to David, in his frequent reference to the Temple as "the house that I have built," and in the order in which he mentions himself ahead of the people in verses 52 and 59. The second characteristic is Solomon's apparent obliviousness to his own responsibility for obedience. On two occasions Yahweh has reminded Solomon that he must be obedient, lest dire consequences overtake him and all the people (3:14 and 6:12-13). He heard similar advice from David (2:4), and indeed he himself can quote Yahweh to the same effect (8:25). Yet on his own he never speaks of obedience as a personal obligation. It is something for the whole people that only Yahweh himself can make happen (8:58); it is something to which Solomon can exhort his hearers (8:61). More ominously, it is something that he believes no one can achieve perfectly ("for there is no one who does not sin," 8:46). But he always describes his personal relationship to Yahweh in terms of Yahweh's promises and gifts, never in terms of his own faithful obedience.

Solomon's Encounter with Yahweh: 9:1-10

Frame verses that mention "building" or "finishing" the "house of Yahweh" surround the account of Solomon's third encounter with Yahweh; these frame verses continue the series that punctuated chapters 6–7. The first one (9:1) expands the list of finished projects to include "the king's house and all that Solomon desired to make," as if the subsequent vision were Yahweh's response to all of Solomon's constructions, not just to the dedication of the Temple, although in fact the vision will mention only the Temple. The effect is to cast the scene as a conclusion to the whole story of Solomon's building projects. But that aura of finality comes at the cost of a clumsy chronology, and it is a tribute to the narrator's finesse that we hardly notice the awkwardness: placing Yahweh's appearance to Solomon after he finished "the king's house and all that Solomon desired to make" means that at least thirteen years (see 7:1) would have passed between Solomon's dedicatory prayer and Yahweh's response to it!

The second frame verse (9:10), coming after the account of the king's vision, can be more explicit. It mentions the twenty years Solomon spent on the Temple and palace complex (6:38b–7:1). On the other hand, it omits mention of Solomon's subsequent constructions, since they will be detailed shortly (9:15-19). With the mention of twenty years, the central diptych that began in 6:1 ends. In 6:1 the narrator dated the beginning of the Temple construction to the 480th year after the Exodus. According to 9:10, therefore, exactly five hundred years have elapsed since Yahweh and his people left Egypt, and only now has the promise of "rest" been fully realized (8:56).[10] (On the grammar of 9:10 and its connection with the verses that follow it, see the next section.)

---

[10]Although the narrator makes no direct allusion to it, the tradition of celebrating the fiftieth year as a jubilee may have added to the ancient Israelite reader's

Solomon's vision of Yahweh begins with a narrative line (v. 2). Then comes Yahweh's speech, which has three parts: a direct response to Solomon's prayer (v. 3), an address to Solomon (vv. 4-5), and an address to the whole people (vv. 6-9). The last two parts are more clearly distinguishable in Hebrew than in English, since Hebrew has distinct words for "you" singular and "you" plural. In verses 6-9 all the second-person forms are plural.

Structurally, this encounter with Yahweh at the end of the dedication of the Temple balances the word of Yahweh that Solomon received near the beginning of its construction (6:11-13; on the whole series of encounters, see p. 154). The narrative line, however, identifies this encounter as a "second vision" and invites us to compare it to Solomon's first vision of Yahweh at Gibeon in 3:4-15. The comparison reveals both similarities and differences.

In both visions Yahweh's speech begins by answering favorably a preceding request by Solomon; in both cases God's words echo the king's. In 3:9 Solomon asks for "a listening mind to judge your people, to discern between good and evil"; Yahweh promises him "discernment to listen to justice" and "a wise and discerning mind." In 9:3 Yahweh uses phrases from Solomon's speeches in chapter 8: "prayer and plea" (8:28); "this house that I have built" (8:13, 27, 43, 44, 48). Yahweh's statement that his "eyes" and "mind" (NRSV, "heart") will be on the Temple corresponds to Solomon's prayer for Yahweh's eyes to be open and for him to listen to Israel's petitions (8:29-30, 52).

In both visions Yahweh's favorable response goes beyond what Solomon has requested. In 3:13 he adds two unconditional gifts, riches and honor, that Solomon has not sought. In 9:3 he "consecrates" the Temple—Solomon's prayer did not ask for this—and, to Solomon's frequently expressed desire that the Temple be marked by the presence of Yahweh's name, God responds that he is placing his name there *forever* and that his eyes and his mind will be on the Temple *for all time*.

In both visions Yahweh continues with a conditional gift. In 3:14 he promises Solomon long life on condition that Solomon obey him as had David his father. In 9:4-5 Yahweh imposes the same condition in almost identical terms but enhances the rewards enormously. Solomon's obedience will no longer win just his own long life; it will also assure him an unending line of royal descendants. The promise of an eternal dynasty that Yahweh once made to David will now be Solomon's.

---

appreciation of this text (see Lev 25:8-12). In the jubilee year, debts were to be remitted, patrimonial land was to return to its original family, and the soil was to lie fallow. The five hundredth year could be understood as a sort of superjubilee.

The vision of chapter 3 ends at that point. In 9:6-9, however, Yahweh's speech continues, and its tone changes abruptly. It shifts from singular to plural, and from conditional promise to conditional threat. Emphatic pronouns in verse 4 ("As for *you* [singular]") and verse 6 ("*you* [plural] or your children") underscore the shift to the plural. The change is unexpected and ambiguous. Yahweh is still addressing Solomon, but he is now apparently speaking through him to a larger group. Who is this larger group? It may be the whole line of Solomon's successors, which Yahweh has just promised would be eternal; or it may be the whole people of Israel, whom Solomon, as their king, represents. But third-person forms would express either of these meanings more clearly and more smoothly: "If your sons turn aside from following me," or "If the Israelites turn aside from following me . . . ." The second-person plural forms are obtrusive and force themselves on the reader's attention almost as a direct address. It is as if the voice of Yahweh breaks out of the confines of the narrative to warn the hearers themselves, "If you people turn aside from following me . . . ."

The demand is for an obedience identical to that required of Solomon (though without the evocation of the example of "David your father," of course, since that would be appropriate only for Solomon himself and his descendants), and the threat is ominous. Disobedience will result in exile of the people and destruction of the Temple itself. The house that Yahweh promised to keep before his eyes he will cast out of his sight. Where Yahweh's name was once enshrined in glory, Israel's name will become a byword of mockery. The end of Yahweh's speech is bleak. In verses 8-9 the Temple is gone and the people are unmentioned. All that remains is a heap of ruins[11] and a nameless "they," spoken of in horrified whispers by strangers.

The last three chapters have centered the reader's attention on Solomon and the Temple. This passage widens the reader's purview. Over against the importance of sacrifice and prayer it recalls the primacy of obedience to commandments. Over against Solomon's focus on himself it envisages the line of his successors and indeed the whole people. Over against glory it sets responsibility and the threat of disaster. Most importantly, over against concentration on the past it engages

[11]This reading is based on a correction of the Hebrew text of verse 8, which does not make sense in the context: "This house will become exalted [*ʿlywn*]." The NRSV and most commentators follow some of the ancient translations in reading "a heap of ruins" (*ʿyym* or *ʿyyn*), on the suspicion that an ancient scribe intentionally or unintentionally misread the original word when copying the Hebrew manuscript. The term *ʿyym* is used elsewhere in reference to the destruction of Jerusalem and the Temple (Jer 26:18; Mic 3:12; Ps 79:1).

the reader in the present and future. Here the seeds planted by the narrator in 8:8-9 and 8:65 bear potent fruit. There he broke out of the narrative frame to address his readers and draw a connection directly between them and the glories of the Temple; here Yahweh himself reminds the readers that the present and future destiny of Temple and people depends on their obedience.

Chapter 7
SOLOMONIC SPLENDOR
1 Kings 9:10–10:29

For the narrator, the building and dedication of the Temple is clearly the climax of Solomon's reign, but it is by no means the end of the story. It ushers in an era of widespread construction projects, of far-flung international contacts, and of unparalleled economic gain. Though the next two sections do not contain much in the way of complex narratives, they describe this period in glowing terms. Nevertheless, beneath the omnipresent glitter of gold, there are signs that all is not well in the Solomonic empire.

After Building the Temple: 9:10-25

The narrator described Solomon's preparations for building the Temple in 5:1-18. They involved obtaining materials, particularly timber imported from Lebanon by arrangement with Hiram, king of Tyre, and the assembling of an indigenous labor force to carry out the construction. The present passage recounts developments in both of these areas after the construction of the Temple was completed. The first part tells briefly of the negotiations between Hiram and Solomon about payment for what Hiram supplied. The second part relates how the labor force is put to further service in additional construction projects. The last words bring to a close the entire section of the Solomon story that is concerned with the Temple. Although the first part clearly assumes some conflict between Hiram and Solomon, nothing in the passage has the kind of narrative tension, development, and resolution that would qualify it as a "story." Our interest will be in the contribution the passage makes to the continuing narrative progress of the larger Solomon story.

NEGOTIATIONS WITH HIRAM FOR PAYMENT: 9:10-14

Unlike the frame verses in chapters 6–7, 9:10 is a subordinate clause, grammatically dependent upon what follows it. In this way it acts as a hinge to connect the account of the building of the "two houses" in chapters 6–7 with the material in 9:11-25. The grammar of verses 10-12 is awkward in Hebrew. The problem is to determine which is the main clause and, therefore, which of the statements in these verses is to be understood as the main point of the account. The NRSV reads verse 11b as the main clause. In this reading, the emphasis falls on the fact that Solomon gives Hiram twenty cities; the inference is that Solomon is no longer able to meet Hiram's fees of wheat and olive oil (5:11) and has to make up the difference by ceding territory. However, that is not the only, or even the most probable, understanding of the present Hebrew text. Awkward as it is, the following modification of the NRSV's translation of 9:10-14 is more likely:

> At the end of twenty years, in which Solomon had built the two houses, the house of Yahweh and the king's house (King Hiram of Tyre had supplied Solomon with cedar and cypress timber and gold, as much as he desired, while King Solomon gave to Hiram twenty cities in the land of Galilee), then Hiram came from Tyre to see the cities that Solomon had given him. But they did not please him, and he said, "What kind of cities are these that you have given me, my brother?" So they are called "the land of Kabul" to this day. (Now, Hiram had sent to the king 120 talents of gold!)

In this reading, the main point is Hiram's dissatisfaction with the cities Solomon cedes him and the sharp contrast between the apparently poor quality of the territory and the enormous amount of gold Solomon gets in exchange.[1] The overt effect of the passage, then, is to depict Solomon as a shrewd and successful bargainer. He is able to turn a huge profit

---

[1]Two details require explanation: the "land of Kabul" and the amount of gold. The meaning of "land of Kabul" (Hebrew, *kābûl*) is obscure. Traditionally it has been explained as a wordplay meaning "like nothing" (Hebrew, *kĕ* + *bul*, except that *bul* is not attested elsewhere in Hebrew). The ancient Greek translation read the Hebrew *kbwl* as *gbwl*, "boundary" or, here, "Borderland." The exact location of this territory is unknown, but there is today a village called Kabul about eight miles southeast of Acco. Since place names sometimes survive for millennia in the Ancient Near East, this may point to the original location of the "land of Kabul." As to the gold, the "talent" was a measure of weight. Unfortunately for our understanding, the weight of the talent varied between 45 and 130 pounds during the centuries of Israel's history. At the very least, this means that Hiram sends 5000 pounds of gold to Solomon, and the figure may be up to three times as much.

on relatively worthless land, and since Hiram continues to use treaty language ("my brother"), Solomon does it without nullifying the treaty between Tyre and Israel.

By now, however, we have learned to look for two layers of meaning in the narrator's depictions of Solomon. Solomon may get an excellent price for the territory, but the bottom line is that Solomon gives up land. In the immediately preceding passage, Yahweh spoke of "the land that I have given" to Israel and specified separation of Israel from the land as the ultimate punishment for covenant infidelity (9:7). Solomon's readiness to sell off what Yahweh himself bestowed on the people foreshadows a disastrous destiny for the nation: after Solomon's death, the whole northern half of his territory will secede from the control of the Davidic throne; in the eighth century, the now separate northern kingdom will be obliterated by the Assyrians; and in the sixth century, the southern kingdom will fall to the Babylonians.

The mention of gold is new in the negotiations between Hiram and Solomon. We know that Hiram sent Solomon timber that was unavailable in Israel (5:8), but why does Solomon need so much gold that he surrenders land for it? The narrator gives us no indication. Even in the next section, where he lists Solomon's vast and grandiose series of additional construction projects, the narrator does not suggest that Solomon finances them with the gold he got from Hiram. At this point the remark about gold only introduces the theme. The narrator will elaborate on it in chapter 10.

CONSCRIPTED LABOR: 9:15-25

Grammatically, the focus of this passage is the contrasting clauses in verses 21b-22a. Everything that precedes those clauses is subordinate to them, and everything that follows them is elaboration. The central statements make two claims: Solomon conscripts forced labor from resident non-Israelites; he does not conscript Israelites.

The opening verse gives a title for the section: "This is the account of the forced labor that King Solomon conscripted." The title is extended by a purpose clause with an unusually long series of direct objects listing Solomon's building projects. These include four projects in Jerusalem: the Temple, the palace complex, the Millo, and the city's fortification wall. The ancient reader probably knew what the "Millo" was, but today we no longer do. The Hebrew word means something like "filling." The most common conjecture in recent years is that it may have been terracing on the steep slopes of the hill upon which Jerusalem was built; such terraces, surrounded by retaining walls, were necessary to create solid, level foundations for the weighty buildings that rested on them. The list continues with six cities, named from north (Hazor) to south (Tamar, in the arid region south of the Dead Sea), all of which guarded strategically important approaches to Jerusalem. A parenthesis interrupts the list of cities: Pharaoh captured and reduced Gezer, and then presented it to his daughter on the occasion of her marriage to Solomon. (The NRSV calls it a "dowry," but this translation is inaccurate and implies more than the Hebrew does. The Hebrew word means literally a "going-away gift.")

Next are cities where Solomon stores provisions and quarters his chariotry and his horses (not "cavalry," as the NRSV translates). The list ends with a general remark about "all that Solomon desired to build in Jerusalem, in Lebanon, and in all the land of his dominion." The reference to building in Lebanon is surprising, since we know of no such projects; but in the context of verses 10-14 it confirms our impression that the discord between Hiram and Solomon is not allowed to abrogate the treaty they signed. (As we shall see in the next section, cooperation between Solomon and Hiram is too lucrative to let a petty dispute disrupt it.) "All the land of his dominion" (Hebrew, *mmšlt*) is a reference to 4:21: "Solomon had dominion (Hebrew, *mwšl*; NRSV, "was sovereign") over all the kingdoms . . .'"; but here too we are told nothing of any specific projects beyond the borders of Israel.

The central claim is twofold: Solomon enslaves non-Israelites; he does not enslave Israelites. Those enslaved are the descendants of indigenous peoples whom the Israelites were not able to exterminate according to the directives of Yahweh in Deuteronomy 7:1-5; 20:16-18. Israelites, by contrast, are put into responsible military and administrative positions. At first these statements seem at odds with that in 5:13 that Solomon "conscripted forced labor out of all Israel," that is, out of the Israelites of the northern tribes; but they can be reconciled. There is apparently a difference between the labor force of 5:13 *(mas)* and that of 9:21 *(mas 'ōbēd,* "slave labor"). The former involves a three-month term of service (5:14), and the narrative implies that its purpose is to construct the Temple. (In this way the narrator assures us that non-Israelites are not directly involved in building the Temple. In 7:14 he carefully explains that even the master artisan Hiram of Tyre has an Israelite mother!) The *mas 'ōbēd,* however, is probably to be understood as permanent state slavery ("to this day," v. 21) assigned to the rest of Solomon's projects under Israelite overseers. These are the "chief officers" who are over the work (v. 23); the same term occurs in 5:16, where the NRSV translates it "supervisors." Literally, they are "officials of the officers"—in other words, subordinates to the administrative officers listed in 4:7-19. Their lesser number (550 here; six times that in 5:16) implies that the *mas ʿōbēd* was much smaller than the original *mas*.

Verse 24 picks up on the mention of Pharaoh's daughter in verse 16 and the mention of the Millo in verse 15. Unlike the anachronistic 7:8b, this verse is in its proper place: according to 3:1, Solomon builds a house for Pharaoh's daughter only after he has finished his other projects in Jerusalem.

Verse 25 is textually difficult and has almost certainly been miscopied somewhere along the line of manuscript transmission. The basic meaning of the verse is clear, however; the NRSV captures it accurately. The verse does not refer to a single event but to Solomon's customary practice, once he completes the Temple, of celebrating the three principal Israelite feasts there with various sacrifices. This reference to future cultic ceremonies is an appropriate way to wrap up the long account of the building and dedication of the Temple. The last, brief statement concludes the whole account: "So he completed the house" (see the comment on 7:51a). The whole verse includes an elaborate wordplay on the name Solomon *(šlmh)*: three *(šlš)* times each year, the king offers "sacrifices of well-being" *(šlmym)*; and so he "completed" *(šlm)* the house.

The characterization of Solomon continues to be double-edged. The passage is almost overwhelming in its enumeration of Solomon's building projects in Jerusalem and Israel, and in its claim that his projects extend to other lands as well. It credits him with establishing a successful system to supply an adequate labor force for all those projects without undue imposition on the Israelite citizenry. (Our modern horror at the institution of slavery should not blind us to the fact that in the ancient world it was an unquestioned part of society. The ancient Israelite reader would not have considered the *mas ʿōbēd* a bad thing, as long as it did not include Israelites.) And the narrator depicts Solomon as regularly participating in the worship of Yahweh.

There are shadows, however. It is startling to learn that Pharaoh's army is in Israel (Gezer is just twenty miles from Jerusalem!), and that he is able to capture a city that apparently neither David nor Solomon has yet taken. It is also discomfiting that Pharaoh gives this city not to Solomon but to his own daughter as a "going-away present." A strategically significant site remains, symbolically at least, in non-Israelite hands. In the context of 9:7 and 9:10-14, the case of Gezer is yet another presage that Israel will someday be cut off from the land. The *mas ʿōbēd* implies an even more serious problem. The issue is not slavery but extermination. Yahweh's directives to the Israelites in Deuteronomy 7:1-5 and 20:16-18 were clear: under no circumstances was Israel to come to an accommodation with "the Hittites, the Girgashites, the Amorites, the Canaanites, the Perizzites, the Hivites, and the Jebusites" living in the land. Yahweh's command to destroy them was unqualified, lest they lead Israel to the worship of other gods. To enslave these peoples rather than eliminate them is to disobey Yahweh and run the risk of being led into idolatry, the very sin against which Yahweh has just warned Solomon in 9:6-9.

With these ominous threats alloying the otherwise glorious gold of Solomon's accomplishments, the account of the Temple comes to a close.

Solomon Uses His Gifts: 9:26–10:29

This section of the Solomon story, like that in 3:16–4:34, contains material of very disparate origins. The story of Solomon and the queen of Sheba is the only passage with narrative character. Our principal concern outside of that story will be the organization the narrator has imposed on his materials and the way in which this passage furthers the developing characterization of Solomon.

SOLOMON'S MERCANTILE FLEET: 9:26-28

This is the first of three mentions of oceangoing trading fleets that ply the waters of the Red Sea and Indian Ocean for Solomon and Hiram of Tyre (see also 10:11-12 and 10:22). The continued cooperation between Solomon and Hiram confirms our impression that their disagreement over the quality of the twenty cities (9:11-14) did not annul the treaty between them. Indeed, Hiram's collaboration would be essential in this venture, since Israel had no earlier tradition of shipbuilding or of maritime activities.

Ezion-geber was situated on the north coast of the Gulf of Aqaba, the eastern finger of the Red Sea lying along the east coast of the Sinai Peninsula. With Hiram in control of the major Phoenician ports and Solomon in control of Ezion-geber, their cooperation gave them an overland connection between the Mediterranean Sea and the Indian Ocean, and thus a stranglehold on trade between the Mediterranean basin and East Africa and India. Ophir's gold was of legendary quality. The figure of 420 talents is extravagant (somewhere between five and fifteen tons; see the note on 9:14), but it sets the tone for what follows: the motif word "gold" occurs fifteen times in these thirty-two verses. The mention of Ophir also prepares the way for the story of the queen of Sheba. Ophir and Sheba, as far as we can determine, were both located near the south end of the Red Sea, either eastward in South

Arabia or westward in Africa. The journeys of Solomon's fleet to Ophir explain how the queen of Sheba "heard of the fame of Solomon" (10:1).

THE QUEEN OF SHEBA: 10:1-13

The story of Solomon and the queen of Sheba shows many signs of careful artistry. Unfortunately most of those signs are difficult to reproduce in English, for example alliteration, unusual word order, and the like. Grammatical indicators divide the story into four "paragraphs":

    A. Narrative introduction (10:1-3)
      B. The queen observes Solomon's glory (10:4-5)
      B'. The queen speaks about Solomon's glory (10:6-9)
    A'. Narrative conclusion (10:10-13)

The first and last paragraphs are linked by theme (the queen arrives, the queen departs) and by vocabulary (spices, gold, and precious stones). They thus form a narrative frame around the central elements.

Like other rulers (see 4:34), the queen of Sheba—a ruling monarch in her own right, not merely the wife of a king—hears of Solomon's reputation and comes to Jerusalem to see if what she heard is true. She decides "to test him with hard questions" (literally, "with riddles"; royal riddle contests are attested elsewhere in antiquity as well). Though this plot line could afford the narrator a rich opportunity for suspense, he eschews all narrative tension and tells us immediately that "Solomon answered all her questions." The center of the narrator's interest lies elsewhere, namely, in the queen's reaction to the splendor of the Solomonic court. The narrator describes the queen's appraisal of Solomon's court with a lengthy list of what she sees. The long series of direct objects stops the action completely and thereby conveys to the reader not only the thoroughness of her observations but also the reflective deliberation with which she evaluates what she sees. Pride of place goes to Solomon's "wisdom," that is, the ease with which he deals with her riddles. Then his palace, his hospitality, his household, even his cultic offerings pass in review. The whole experience "takes her breath away" (a better rendering than the NRSV's overly literal "there was no more spirit in her").

The queen's response to all this magnificence is a speech of two parts. References at the beginning, middle, and end to "hearing" about Solomon's "wisdom" unify the first part (vv. 6-8); the second part is a praise of Yahweh (v. 9). Her speech begins emphatically: "Truth it was, the report I heard . . . ." She admits her earlier doubt about

Solomon's reputation but confesses her error with even stronger emphasis; the Hebrew might be paraphrased, "But what a sight! They didn't tell me the half of it!" In verse 8 she exclaims on the fortunate circumstances of those privileged to live amid Solomon's glory on a daily basis, his courtiers and servants.[2] The second part of her speech has careful rhythmic and grammatical balance:

A. "Blessed be *Yahweh* your God,
  B. who *has delighted* in *you*
    C. *so as to* put you on Israel's throne,
A'. because of *Yahweh's* eternal love for Israel,
  B'. and *has made you* king
    C'. *so as to* execute justice and righteousness."

The fourth line, which slightly disrupts the grammar of the sentence in English, expresses Yahweh's motivation for both the preceding (BC) and following (B'C') actions.

It is not surprising that a foreign monarch would praise the God of Israel (see the remarks above on 5:7). It is, however, striking to hear such characteristically Israelite theology as "Yahweh's eternal love for Israel" and the duties of the king "to execute justice and righteousness" on the lips of the foreigner. As impressed as the queen is by the majesty of Solomon's court, she does not lose sight of the fundamental purpose of his, or any, rule: to assure justice and righteousness for the people.

The conclusion describes the exchange of gifts between the queen and Solomon. The description is interrupted by the second reference in the section to ocean trade. The queen's gifts are lavish: she gives Solomon as much gold as Hiram did for twenty cities (9:11-14), as well as gems and an unprecedented quantity of the spices for which Sheba was famous. The interruption closely parallels the queen's gifts to Solomon:

A. The queen gave gold, quantities of spices, and precious stones (10:10a).
B. Never again did such spices come (10:10b).

[2]The ancient Greek translation (followed by the NRSV) reads "wives" here (literally, "women"). The Hebrew text reads literally "men" (that is, court personnel). The textual difference between the readings is very slight in Hebrew ("men" is *'ănāšîm;* "women" is *nāšîm*), and it is difficult to determine which was the original reading. The narrative difference, however, is considerable. The Greek text depicts the queen in a stereotypically "womanly" way, interested primarily in domestic matters. The Hebrew text portrays her much more strongly, interested, as any ruling monarch would be, in the administrative personnel and procedures of such a successful international power.

A'. The fleet brought gold, quantities of almug wood,[3] and precious stones (10:11).

B'. Never again did such almug wood come (10:12b).

The effect of the interruption is to remind us that the queen's gifts, no matter how rich, are modest compared with the income Solomon obtains from the Red Sea trade (9:28). As befits the wealthier monarch, Solomon outdoes the queen in extravagance: like the breadth of his wisdom ("Solomon answered all her questions," v. 3) is the depth of his generosity ("Solomon gave her every desire that she expressed," v. 13). The last sentence describes how the queen "returned to her own land with her servants"; this forms an inclusion with the words "she came to Jerusalem with a very great retinue" at the beginning of the story (v. 2).

CHARACTERIZATION

The queen of Sheba holds center stage in this story. In order to investigate rumors about a new maritime power in her sphere of influence, she is willing to undertake an arduous journey (Sheba was over twelve hundred miles from Jerusalem). She is skeptical about what she has heard, and she subjects not only Solomon himself but his entire court and administration to careful scrutiny. When he proves even greater than rumor made him, she is also forthright enough to admit her error. Her acclaim of Solomon's glory is unstinting, with no hint of jealousy or envy, and it issues in a remarkable and profound praise of Yahweh as ultimate source of the king's blessings as well as of his responsibilities. Her gifts to Solomon are lavish. In short, the narrator portrays her as a determined, honest, generous, and thoroughly admirable monarch.

By contrast, the picture we get of Solomon in this story is very sketchy; the queen is much more vibrantly drawn. The narrator tells us that Solomon was able to answer all the queen's "hard questions." Indirectly, through the queen's eyes, we see the splendor of his royal court. Finally, the narrator mentions Solomon's generosity to the queen in general terms, but not in the detail with which he described the queen's gifts to Solomon. The deeper contribution this story makes to the ongoing characterization of Solomon will appear only when we view it in a larger context (see below).

---

[3]This is called "algum wood" in 2 Chronicles 9:11, but other ancient sources clearly indicate that "almug" is the correct spelling. Unfortunately, none of the ancient sources enables us to determine exactly what kind of wood it was.

Solomon's Glory: 10:14-29

The remainder of the chapter comprises four paragraphs that describe Solomon's wealth and fame from several angles. The motifs of "gold" and "silver" unify the various materials, although the underlying organization is not obvious. There are numerous textual problems throughout these verses, including a high concentration of rare words of uncertain meaning. For example, three different adjectives are used to describe Solomon's gold; the NRSV translates them "beaten gold" (vv. 16-17), "finest gold" (v. 18), and "pure gold" (v. 21), but in fact the meaning is unclear in all three cases. Similarly, the identification of some of the foreign imports (NRSV, "ivory, apes, and peacocks," v. 22) is very unsure. The effect of the unusual vocabulary is to give the whole passage an air of exotic luxury far removed from everyday life.

According to verse 14, Solomon receives 666 talents of gold "in one year." This does not mean "in every year," as if the sum represents Solomon's annual income. Rather it indicates a single particularly profitable year, perhaps the one during which Hiram gives him 120 talents (9:14), the fleet returns from Ophir with 420 talents (9:28), and the queen of Sheba gives another 120 talents (10:10). This is corroborated by the remark in verse 15 that this gold is over and above the normal sources of revenue: tariffs on traders and merchants and taxes and tribute from subject territories. The sum of 666 talents is vast: somewhere between thirty and eighty-five tons of gold (see the note on 9:14).

The remainder of the first paragraph (vv. 16-21) recounts in detail what is done with that wealth. Solomon has decorative gold shields made for display in the House of the Forest of Lebanon (one of the public administrative buildings: see 7:2-5). An honor guard would carry them in solemn royal processions as well. He also has crafted a magnificent gilt and ivory-inlaid throne, which the narrator describes in minute detail. It is a fitting embodiment of the literary theme that dominated the first part of the story: "Who shall sit upon the throne of David?" An interesting detail that does not survive in translation is that the lions standing beside the armrests of the throne are female, while those standing on the steps leading up to the dais are male. Sets of gold vessels are created both for the king's table and for use at state functions. The latter are fashioned from a type of gold that is presumably especially fine, since it was also used in the most sacred part of the Temple (6:20-21; NRSV, "pure gold").

The second paragraph contains the final reference to Solomon's and Hiram's maritime trade (v. 22). Here we learn that there are at least two fleets cooperating in the venture: Solomon's fleet of "ships of Tarshish" (the Hebrew idiom for large, oceangoing vessels) and Hiram's fleet.

Moreover, Solomon's "ships of Tarshish" may not be the same fleet spoken of in 9:26-28, since there the fleet is only said to travel to Ophir, whereas the regular three-year circuits and exotic cargo mentioned in 10:22 suggest longer voyages, perhaps as far as India.

The third paragraph (vv. 23-25) describes how Solomon's fame also benefits his burgeoning treasury. The focus of the narrator's arrangement of materials is the king's wealth: notice how he puts Solomon's riches before his wisdom in verse 23. Like the queen of Sheba, people from every country hear of Solomon's reputation, come to listen to his wisdom, and leave valuable gifts behind. The last words (NRSV, "so much year by year") are awkward but may mean something like: "This was an annual occurrence." In this way the narrator assures us that Solomon's income was not limited to the triennial profits brought by his ships.

The last paragraph (vv. 26-29) tells of Solomon's chariot forces and his international trade in chariots and horses; it includes a general remark about the prosperity of Jerusalem (v. 27). The figures in verse 26 reveal that Solomon's chariot corps is smaller than 4:26 implied. He may have the stables and the horses, but he does not have enough chariots to make use of them. Verse 27 recalls the remark in verse 21 about silver, but it follows verse 26 because verses 26-27 share the horizon of Jerusalem, whereas the description of Solomon's wealth in verses 14-21 concentrates exclusively on the royal palace buildings. The last two verses describe the international trade through which Solomon acquires his horses and chariots. One source is Kue (to the north of Israel, in modern coastal Turkey just north of Cyprus); a second source is Egypt.[4] Solomon's agents also act as middlemen exporting chariots and horses to other nations, presumably swelling Solomon's coffers still more with duties and other profits.

THE CHARACTERIZATION OF SOLOMON

The narrator continues to offer a double portrayal of Solomon. On the surface the portrait is positive; beneath that surface are subtler indications of a negative evaluation. To see these less obvious traits, we must recognize how the narrator organizes this section to invite a comparison with 3:16–4:34. The three gifts Yahweh gave Solomon in 3:10-13 supply the fundamental organizing principles for the section, as they did for 3:16–4:34. The following table illustrates the parallels:

[4]This is according to the current Hebrew text. Many scholars suspect a confusion here between Egypt (Hebrew, *mṣrym*) and Musri (Hebrew, *mṣry*), a region just north of Kue.

GIFT	3:16–4:34	9:26–10:29
1) A LISTENING MIND	3:16-28	10:1-10, 13
2) RICHES		
domestic affairs	4:1-20	10:14-21
international affairs	4:21-25	9:26-28; 10:11-12, 22
chariots and horses	4:26-28	10:26-29
3) HONOR	4:29-34	10:23-25

Here the story of the queen of Sheba illustrates Solomon's gift of "a listening mind." When the queen tests him with her riddles, he is able to answer all her questions (10:2-3). Solomon's gift of "riches" is the dominant theme of the whole section, but it is particularly the topic of 10:14-21, which describe the abundant gold of Solomon's palace, of the three passages that describe Solomon's international maritime trade, and of 10:26-29, which describe Solomon's trade in chariots and horses. Solomon's gift of "honor," or international renown, is the motivating force of 10:23-25.

The positive characterization of Solomon is measured by magnificence. All of Solomon's gifts are fully and brilliantly manifest. His wisdom shines not only in his ability to explain everything to the queen but also in his radically innovative ventures into international commerce. His international renown, already attested in 4:29-34, is a beacon that draws people from "the whole earth" (10:24) and even attracts a foreign monarch herself to make the trip to Jerusalem to see the truth of Solomon's reputation. But most of all, it is Solomon's wealth that dominates the section. "Gold" glitters everywhere—in the holds of ships, on the royal throne, on wall decorations and even table utensils. Exotic wood and spices and rare animals with strange-sounding names give the whole passage an aura of mysterious luxury. Like the queen of Sheba, we find that Solomon's glory takes our breath away.

Solomon's omnipresent gold, however, also reveals the negative side of the king's use of his gifts. In 3:16–4:34, Solomon's gifts benefited others. They resolved the difficult case of the two harlots, provided prosperity and security for Judah and Israel alike, and produced works of erudition for the whole world. But now, like the tragic King Midas, everything Solomon touches turns to gold. Where his listening mind once resulted in justice for the lowliest of Israelites, it now brings Solomon gold. The only mention of "justice" is on the lips of a foreigner, and there it sounds more like a reminder to Solomon of his duty than a praise of his deeds. Where Solomon's efficient administrative system once assured prosperity and security for Judah and Israel, it now assures nothing but gold and more gold for the royal coffers. There is no mention of the people's benefit, nor indeed of "Judah" and "Israel" at all; all the wealth Solomon amasses goes to decorate the palace complex. The meticulously detailed descriptions of the numbers of shields, the weight of gold in each, and the decorations of the throne and its dais give an impression of ostentatious display that is strengthened by the hyperbolic claim that "nothing like it was ever made in any kingdom" (v. 20). Where Solomon's chariots and horses were once evidence that his providence extended even to his animals, they are now an additional source of revenue. Where Solomon's international fame was once based on his prodigious learning, it is now nothing more than a source of more gold. The narrator reminds us that God, not Solomon, is the source of the king's wisdom (v. 24). But that gift no longer flows through him to others. Solomon produces no proverbs, no songs, no erudite works of natural history; he simply acquires more gold.

The contrast is pointed. Yahweh remains faithful to the promises given at Gibeon, but the king has changed: his own glory and wealth have become more important than the good of Yahweh's people.

Chapter 8
THE END OF THE STORY
1 Kings 11:1-43

The tone changes abruptly in chapter 11. Although we have pointed out throughout the preceding material the undercurrent of negative characterization of Solomon, the dominant note was always positive toward him. This chapter contrasts sharply. In three sections the narrator shows us Solomon's infidelity and his condemnation, the external threats that are part of his punishment, and finally the internal rival God chooses to wrest Israel from the Solomonic line.

The Tragic Failure of Solomon's Reign: 11:1-13

The first part of chapter 11 is not, strictly speaking, a narrative, though it is full of dramatic movement. It tells in general terms, rather than through scenic depiction, of Solomon's infidelity to Yahweh and the consequent punishment Yahweh decrees. Most of the material is in the form of a narrator's summary (vv. 1-8); this is followed by a report of the fourth and last encounter Solomon has with Yahweh (vv. 9-13).

NARRATOR'S SUMMARY: 11:1-8

The narrator's summary describes the circumstances that lead to Solomon's apostasy (vv. 1-3), then the specific deeds of which Solomon is guilty (vv. 4-8). The narrator organizes each subsection carefully, although the pattern does not show clearly in the NRSV.

A. "King Solomon loved many foreign women" (11:1a)
B. description of the women (11:1b)

> C. "they will turn away your mind" (11:2a)[1]
> A'. "Solomon clung to these in love" (11:2b)
> B'. description of the women (11:3a)
> C'. "and his women[2] turned away his mind" (11:3b)

The second subsection has a similar structure:

> A. Solomon's women turned away his mind (11:4a)
> B. not like his father David (11:4b)
> C. "Astarte of Sidon and Milcom of Ammon" (11:5)
> A'. Solomon did evil in Yahweh's sight (11:6a)
> B'. not like his father David (11:6b)
> C'. "Chemosh of Moab and Molech of Ammon" (11:7)
> A''. He did the same for all his foreign women (11:8)

Recognizing this structure enables us to follow more easily the narrator's flow of ideas.

Verses 1-3 highlight the nature of Solomon's "love" and its consequences. It focuses on foreigners: the daughter of Pharaoh is only the first of a vast harem of foreign women. It is inordinate: the series of plurals in v. 1b (Moabites, Ammonites, etc.; the NRSV obscures this) already prepares us for the extravagant numbers of verse 3a.[3] It is dangerous: Yahweh gave dire warning against such entanglements, but Solomon ignores the warning and falls prey to the blandishments of his foreign women anyway. Verses 4-8 describe Solomon's indulgence of his foreign women (elements A and A'') and categorize it bluntly as "evil" (element A'). Specifically, this evil involved furthering the cult of

---

[1]The NRSV translates "they will surely incline your heart" here, but the verb is the same as in verses 3, 4, and 9, where the NRSV regularly uses "turn away." Moreover, "mind" is a better rendering of *lēb* than "heart" in all these verses, since the Hebrew refers to a commitment and adherence of the will, not to an emotional attachment.

[2]Hebrew uses the same word *(nāšîm)* where English has two different ones, "women" and "wives." The NRSV tries to capture the proper nuance to translate each case. My discussion tries to reflect the way *nāšîm* becomes a motif word in the Hebrew text.

[3]The NRSV translation of verse 3a is misleading. Read: "He had seven hundred princess-wives and three hundred concubines." The statement that his seven hundred wives are "princesses" does not imply that they are royalty by birth, taken into Solomon's harem in a series of diplomatic marriages like his marriage to Pharaoh's daughter. It means that they are recognized as legitimate wives, gaining royal status by their marriage, in contrast to the three hundred concubines who have no such status.

several foreign deities (C and C') by building sanctuaries or "high places" for them. In this way Solomon departed from the model of faithfulness to Yahweh set by his father David (B and B').

Several details in the wording of the passage deserve mention. Most of them are difficult to preserve in translation, and the NRSV does not attempt to do so; but they are indicators of a high verbal artistry in the passage. The inclusion of the daughter of Pharaoh at the head of the list in verse 1a is done with a strained syntax that the NRSV smooths out considerably. A closer rendering of the Hebrew would run: "King Solomon loved many foreign women—and the daughter of Pharaoh—Moabites, Ammonites . . . ." The intrusive feel of the phrase has a double effect: it emphasizes this individual, thus linking the earlier mentions of Pharaoh's daughter (3:1; 7:8b; 9:16; 9:24) with the "foreign women" motif that dominates this passage; secondly, it makes Pharaoh's daughter the principal object of Solomon's "love" —a situation that was implicitly denied in 3:1-3 (see the remarks on that passage). It is clear from the context that "Solomon clung to these in love" (v. 2b) refers to his wives. Nevertheless, there is an ambiguity. The narrator could have used a feminine pronoun for "these" that would point unambiguously back to the "foreign women" of verse 1. Instead, he uses a pronoun that can refer equally well to the "gods" of whom Yahweh's warning speaks. In this way he foreshadows that Solomon's "clinging in love" to his foreign women contains within it the seeds of his later idolatry.

In verse 4 Solomon's heart "was not true" to Yahweh. The Hebrew word for "true" here is *šālēm*, a pun on Solomon's name *(šĕlōmōh)*. In turning away after other gods, Solomon leaves behind not only the example of David but his own deepest identity as well. The names and descriptions of the foreign gods are distorted in order to insult them. "Astarte" was the name of a popular Ancient Near Eastern goddess; the Hebrew here reads *ʿaštōret*, combining the consonants of the goddess's name with the vowels of the word *bōšet*, or "shame." The name for the Ammonite god Milcom *(milkōm*, v. 5) is deformed into Molech *(mōlek*, v. 7) in the same way. Finally, the term "abomination" replaces the term "god" in three of the four descriptions of foreign deities. In this way the narrator contrasts his own orthodox contempt for other gods with Solomon's faithless involvement with them.

Yahweh's Final Word to Solomon: 11:9-13

A lengthy narrative sentence (vv. 9-10) introduces Yahweh's word of condemnation (vv. 11-13). The introduction refers explicitly to

Solomon's apostasy by repeating the motif phrase "his mind had turned away." Yahweh is described as "the God of Israel" to contrast with the other national deities named in verses 5 and 7. The concept here is very different from our own. The narrator presumes a polytheistic world view: other gods besides Yahweh existed, and each deity had its own national sphere. The text does not understand Solomon's apostasy as turning away from the only true God to worship false gods. Solomon's evil is that he supported in Israel, Yahweh's own nation, the worship of Yahweh's rivals.

The narrator reminds us that Yahweh appeared to Solomon twice before. This alerts us to read this passage in comparison with those earlier appearances (3:4-15 and 9:2-9). The contrast with the first is striking. In 3:10 we learn that "the matter was good in the sight of the Lord" (NRSV paraphrases, "It pleased the Lord"); here, "Solomon did what was evil in the sight of Yahweh" (11:6). There, Yahweh promises Solomon long life on condition that he "keep my statutes and my commandments" (3:14); here, he condemns Solomon because he does not "keep my covenant and my statutes which I have commanded" (11:11). The second appearance, too, links directly to this phrase. There, Yahweh promises Solomon that if "you do according to all that I have commanded you, and keep my statutes," then his dynasty will never fail (9:4-5). Later, in the plural section of that speech, Yahweh defines disobedience to his commandments and statutes as "turning aside from following me" and "going after and serving other gods" (9:6). Here, the narrator recalls this definition explicitly and employs the same terms to describe Solomon's sin (11:9-10).

The punishment Yahweh decrees corresponds to the threat implied in 9:5: Solomon's kingdom shall not pass to his successor. The decree has two parts: the fundamental punishment, followed by two mitigations. Since Solomon's sin is personal, the punishment is by rights imposed on him: Yahweh will deprive him of the kingdom and give it to one of Solomon's servants. This points forward to the narrative in 11:26-40, where a prophet symbolically "tears" the kingdom and gives it to Jeroboam, one of Solomon's officers. However, Yahweh softens the decree in two ways, neither of which compromises its integrity as a fulfillment of 9:5. First, he delays the punishment so that it will fall after Solomon's death. Second, Solomon's successor will not lose the entire kingdom; he will retain a single tribe. As we shall see, the entire northern part of Solomon's territory, the kingdom of "Israel" in the narrower sense of the term, will follow Jeroboam. (Yahweh's use of the "tribe" as the fundamental unit of the kingdom also implies a rejection of Solomon's restructuring of Israel into administrative districts that do not follow traditional tribal boundaries; see the remarks on 4:1-20.)

Both moderations of the punishment are "for the sake of David." Yahweh's two mentions of David correspond to the narrator's two remarks that Solomon's behavior is not like that of "his father David" (11:4, 6). Yahweh, however, calls David Solomon's "father" only once, and "my servant" the second time. In this way Yahweh reminds Solomon that descent from David is not the only thing that matters; faithful service of Yahweh according to the example of David is the criterion of reward. There is also an ironic echo with the phrase "your servant," to whom Yahweh intends to give Solomon's kingdom. Solomon's son will not succeed to the throne of Solomon's father; but Solomon's servant will succeed to the throne of Yahweh's servant. The second moderation is also "for the sake of Jerusalem, which I have chosen" (11:13). This too corresponds to something in the narrator's remarks. Solomon builds high places for foreign deities "on the mountain east of Jerusalem" (literally, "on the mountain facing Jerusalem," that is, the Mount of Olives). Yahweh's Temple faces his rivals' sanctuaries across the Kidron Valley. But Yahweh "has chosen" Jerusalem, and for its sake—and the sake of the Temple Solomon built there—he will neither abandon the city nor strip Solomon's son of it. The two mitigations of the fundamental punishment point forward to the narrative of 12:1-19, where Solomon's son and successor, Rehoboam, fails to win acceptance as king from the people of the northern tribes but does retain control of the tribe of Judah and the city of Jerusalem.

THE CHARACTERIZATION OF SOLOMON

The narrator's presentation of Solomon's character plainly undergoes an essential change here. Instead of an overtly positive characterization with covert negative elements, we have an unambiguously negative report. Both the narrator and Yahweh categorize Solomon as disobedient to the divine commands, and the narrator describes in detail the apostasy that constituted that disobedience.

The picture grows still darker when we expand our view to broader contexts. Any Israelite reader familiar with the Book of Deuteronomy would have recognized how Deuteronomy 17:16-17 is a systematic disapproval of the Solomon portrayed in this and the preceding section:

> [When you set a king over you,] he must not acquire many horses for himself, or return the people to Egypt in order to acquire more horses, since Yahweh has said to you, "You must never return that way again." And he must not acquire many wives for himself, or else his mind will turn away; also silver and gold he must not acquire in great quantity for himself (Deut 17:16-17, NRSV, modified).

Each phrase has its counterpart in 1 Kings 10–11. Solomon has assembled a large stable, including horses imported from Egypt (10:26, 28). He has gathered a considerable harem, and they have turned his mind away from Yahweh (11:3). He has amassed vast quantities of gold and silver (10:14, 21, 27).

Moreover, comparison with the narrator's remarks in 3:1-3 is even more damning. Two factors invite such a comparison: parallels in structure and the recurrence of the same themes in both passages. Structurally, both 3:1-3 and 11:1-8 are evaluative remarks of the narrator preceding an encounter between Solomon and Yahweh; thematically, both passages focus on Solomon's marriages to foreign women, his building projects, and the high places. In 3:1-3 Solomon's marriage to Pharaoh's daughter was nothing but a political alliance ("he became Pharaoh's son-in-law," 3:1); his love was reserved for Yahweh (3:3). In 11:1-8 Solomon "loves many foreign women," he "clings to them in love," and they turn him away from Yahweh. In 3:1-3 three building projects were mentioned: the royal palace, the Temple, and the city wall. All three projects were praiseworthy and beneficial to the populace. In 11:1-8 the only thing Solomon builds are idolatrous shrines to foreign deities. In 3:1-3 the high places were sanctuaries of Yahweh; though not ideal, the situation was tolerable, since the Temple had not yet been built. In 11:1-8, instead of the high places being supplanted by the Temple, Solomon builds new ones as sanctuaries for Yahweh's rivals, Astarte and Milcom and Chemosh.

Solomon's Throne Is Not Secure: 11:14-25

Chapter 11 continues with three stories of men whose careers pose serious threats to Solomon's political power. The first two adversaries are active outside Israel, one to the southeast in Edom, the other to the northeast in Aram. Their stories are meant to be read together, as is clear from the very similar introductions (11:14 and 23) and from the way verse 25 compares the two. The third story, that of Jeroboam of Israel (11:26-40), forms a separate section.

The first two stories are riddled with textual difficulties. Several sentences are extraordinarily awkward in Hebrew, and at one point it is clear some words have dropped out of the text. (In verse 25, where the NRSV has "making trouble as Hadad did," the Hebrew has only "and the evil which Hadad.") The NRSV's rendering of the passage is as faithful to the Hebrew as possible, and where the Hebrew is impossible, the NRSV's reconstructions are restrained and reasonable.

HADAD OF EDOM: 11:14-22

Grammatical indicators divide the story of Hadad into four paragraphs: introduction (vv. 14-17), Hadad's flight (v. 18), Hadad in Egypt (vv. 19-20), and Hadad's return (vv. 21-22).

The introduction begins with the narrator's assertion that Yahweh is responsible for Hadad's appearance on the scene as a foe of Solomon. The grammatical form makes this statement the consequence of what precedes it, thus implying that this story begins the punishment God decreed in 11:9-13, even though nothing was said there about external enemies. The introduction supplies us with background information from the previous generation. When David and his general Joab were ruthlessly slaughtering Edomites, Hadad, a young member of the royal family, fled to Egypt with some family retainers. (David's campaign against Edom is mentioned only in a brief remark in 2 Samuel 8:13-14.) The account of Hadad's flight, though only one verse long, contains seven very short coordinate clauses: they set out, they came, they took, they came, he gave, he assigned, he gave. (The NRSV combines clauses and uses subordination to produce more acceptable English style.) The impression the Hebrew wording conveys is almost of a forced march, moving relentlessly from one point to the next. Note too that Hadad himself is the subject of no verbs; the young refugee does not act on his own yet.

Once Hadad has become settled in Egypt, the clauses grow longer and more complex, though Hadad takes scarcely any initiative here either. Except for the basically passive idea that he "found favor" with Pharaoh, Hadad is still not the subject of any verbs. Pharaoh gives him a wife, his wife gives him a son, his sister-in-law adopts his son into Pharaoh's own family, his son lives in Pharaoh's house.

Finally, after learning that both of his nemeses are dead, Hadad acts—or at least he speaks of acting. The dialogue between Hadad and Pharaoh reveals something about both of them. Hadad's first words request permission to leave Egypt. Pharaoh sounds offended, but the basis for his hurt feelings is lost in translation. Pharaoh has given Hadad "land" (Hebrew *'ereṣ*, v. 18); now Hadad wants to abandon Pharaoh's gift to return to his own "land" (*'ereṣ*, vv. 21, 22; the NRSV obscures the connection by translating the word "country" here). Hadad's reply ignores Pharaoh's question and simply reiterates his original request, now in much more emphatic fashion. His words are at best abrupt, and perhaps even rude.

Strangely, the story ends there. We are not told that Hadad returns to Edom, nor what he does once there. Even the fragmentary sentence in verse 25 ("and the evil which Hadad") lacks any verbs to flesh out

Hadad's career or to explain in what way he acts against Solomon. Furthermore, there are numerous unresolved loose ends and other narrative weaknesses: What about the people Hadad's party brought to Egypt from Paran? Whatever happened to his son Genubat? Did his wife and son return to Edom with him? The narrator's purpose is clearly not primarily to spin a well-told tale about Hadad. What that purpose is we shall examine after a brief look at the story of Rezon of Damascus.

Rezon of Damascus: 11:23-25

The "story" of Rezon is little more than a short notice, but in its brief compass there are parallels to the story of Hadad. Like Hadad, Rezon is raised up by God to trouble Solomon. Like Hadad, Rezon was a refugee from David's depredations. (David's campaign against Zobah is recounted in 2 Samuel 3–8.) Like Hadad, Rezon will eventually come to reign over a country bordering Israel.

Narrative Effect and Characterization

The narrative contribution these two stories make to the account of Solomon's reign is hidden in some of the details that would have spoken more forcefully to the ancient Israelite reader than they do to us. Hadad of Edom's career has several parallels with that of Moses: Midian was where Moses fled from a murderous king (Exod 2:11–4:20), and Paran was one of the places Israel camped when Moses led them out of Egypt (Num 12:16–13:26). Like Moses, Hadad's son is adopted into Pharaoh's family and raised in his household. Like Moses, Hadad goes to Pharaoh to ask him to let him go out of Egypt to his own land. Rezon's career, on the other hand, has parallels to that of David. Like David, Rezon is originally the servant of a king and not of royal blood himself (David was Saul's armor-bearer). Like David, Rezon becomes the leader of a band of outlaws, and with them eventually captures the city that is to become his capital. Like David, Rezon becomes a king.

The effect of this heaping up of parallels is to recall that both Moses' and David's careers were divinely directed, and thereby to intensify considerably the impact of the claim that "God raised up" Hadad and Rezon. The same Yahweh who raised up Moses as Israel's savior, the same God who raised up David to be Israel's ideal king, now raises up adversaries to oppose Solomon. The punishment of Solomon and the impending disintegration of his empire become part of the sacred history of Yahweh's dealings with Israel, on a par in importance with the Exodus and the covenant with David.

Since Solomon does not appear in these stories, there is nothing that directly furthers his developing characterization. There is, however, one indirect element. The narrator describes both Hadad and Rezon as Solomon's "adversaries" (vv. 14, 23, 25). The Hebrew word is *śāṭān*, from which, after much later theological elaboration, comes our English word "Satan." In classical Hebrew, however, the fundamental meaning of the word is simply "adversary" or "opponent," with no moral or diabolical implications. The word is relatively uncommon and occurs only one other time in 1 Kings. Its repeated appearance here evokes an echo with that other, earlier passage. In 5:4 Solomon alleges to Hiram that "Yahweh my God has given me rest on every side; there is neither adversary *(śāṭān)* nor misfortune."[4] Yet here in 11:14-25 we learn not only that Solomon has two such adversaries but that at least one of them was an adversary "all the days of Solomon." We realize only here at the end of the story of Solomon that early in his reign the king was either ignorant of or cavalier toward serious external danger.

There is another character in this passage whom we have not considered before but whose actions will become increasingly important throughout 1 Kings: Yahweh. While it may seem odd to treat God as a literary character, we must never lose sight of the fact that we know Yahweh in these texts in precisely the same way as we know any other character: through his own words and deeds, through others' words and deeds in response to him, and through information the narrator shares with us. In other words, the "Yahweh" we encounter in 1 Kings is just as much a literary creation of the author—a figure "built out of words"—as the "Solomon" we encounter.

One of the striking things about the Solomon story is how rarely Yahweh appears. There are few narratives in the Hebrew Bible where Yahweh stays more in the background than in these chapters (two examples are 2 Samuel 9–20 and the shorter, Hebrew version of the Book of Esther). To this point in 1 Kings we have seen Yahweh doing relatively unsurprising things: appearing to the king, addressing him with words of reward or warning, hallowing his Temple, and the like. Here, for the first time in the Solomon story, Yahweh directly furthers the development of the action: he raises up the adversaries. And what an unexpected form his intervention takes! The use of Moses and David parallels in the stories of Hadad and Rezon implies that Yahweh's action encompasses their whole careers, not just their eventual appearance as enemies of Israel. Hadad's flight to Egypt, his relations with Pharaoh's family, Rezon's flight from Zobah, his conquest of Damascus—all are part of

---

[4]On the implications of the word "misfortune" for a negative characterization of Solomon, see the remarks on 5:4.

Yahweh's enterprise. The God of Israel is able and willing to manipulate events in far-flung countries in order to achieve his purposes in Israel. (And this is the God, we remember sadly, from whom Solomon "turned away his mind" to build sanctuaries to other, inevitably lesser deities!)

Jeroboam of Israel: 11:26-43

The third section of chapter 11 tells of Jeroboam, son of Nebat (vv. 26-40). While the passage does have a narrative flavor, as a story it is rather oddly shaped. Over half of the story is a single speech; and what we expect to be the central action, Jeroboam's "rebelling against the king," is never described at all. The overall impression a reader gets is that the focus of the passage is the speech, and the narrative setting is supplied to highlight it. The passage has four parts: background information (vv. 26-28), narrative introduction (vv. 29-30), Ahijah's speech (vv. 31-39), and narrative conclusion (v. 40). After the story there is a brief notice about the death and burial of Solomon and the succession of his son Rehoboam (vv. 41-43).

BACKGROUND AND NARRATIVE INTRODUCTION: 11:26-30

The NRSV's rendering of verse 26 rearranges the sentence somewhat. The Hebrew reads: "Now Jeroboam, son of Nebat, an Ephratite[5] from Zeredah—his mother's name was Zeruah, a widow—was a servant of Solomon; and he raised his hand [NRSV, "rebelled"] against the king." It is unusual to mention the name of both parents of a biblical character. One reason, perhaps, for mentioning Jeroboam's mother is that his father is dead. But there is another undertone as well. So far two royal mothers have been named in 1 Kings, Solomon's and Adonijah's, both in the context of their sons' potential for becoming king.[6] Later, as we shall see, whenever a king succeeds to the throne of David, his mother's name will be given. Naming Jeroboam's mother

---

[5]There were apparently at least two places in Israel called Ephrat or Ephratah, one to the north in Ephraim, the other to the south near Bethlehem in Judah. A person from either place is called an "Ephratite" (*'eprātî*) in the Hebrew text. To avoid confusion, whenever someone from the northern Ephrat is spoken of in the Hebrew Bible, the NRSV translates the term *'eprātî*, "Ephraimite," as it does here.

[6]The only mother named in 1 Kings whose son is not royal is Joab's mother, Zeruiah. According to one Israelite tradition, however, Zeruiah was King David's sister (1 Chr 2:13-16), which would relate Joab closely to the royal family.

here is a subtle prefiguring of his royal destiny. The Hebrew text of verse 26 also puts more emphasis than the NRSV on the words "a servant of Solomon." This is an explosive phrase. In 11:11 we learned of Yahweh's intention to give Solomon's kingdom to one of his servants. But that threat was left hanging through the stories of two foreigners, Hadad and Rezon, who, enemies though they were, did not fit the description of Solomon's servant. Now that expectation is finally met: the fulfillment of Yahweh's threat is at hand.

Verse 27a contains an important wordplay that escapes translation. Literally, the Hebrew reads, "This is the word *(dābār)* that raised a hand against the king." As well as "word" or "speech," the Hebrew *dābār* can mean a story or an affair. This is the sense in which the NRSV takes it: "The following was the reason he rebelled," in other words, "This is the affair that caused him to rebel." But the Hebrew can be understood equally well in another way. The *dābār* in question is, literally, a divine "word," the prophetic oracle Ahijah delivers in verses 31-39; and it is this word itself that causes rebellion ("raises a hand") against the king.

The last background verse tells us of Solomon's favorable impressions of the young Jeroboam and of the advancement he enjoys because of it. He is promoted to oversee one contingent of Solomon's work force in the tribal areas of Ephraim and Manasseh, in other words, in Jeroboam's own home territory. Ephraim and Manasseh (these two tribes make up the "house of Joseph"; see Gen 46:20) constitute the major portion of the northern kingdom, that is, "Israel" as distinct from "Judah." (The NRSV is not correct in saying that Jeroboam is placed in charge of the "all the forced labor." The group of workers Jeroboam oversees is numbered separately in 5:13-15 from the conscripted labor. Jeroboam is in charge of "haulers," or, in the term the NRSV uses in 5:15, "laborers," in the territories of the two tribes.)

The action of the story begins with the introduction of a prophet, Ahijah, from Shiloh, a town in the tribe of Ephraim. A few generations previously, Shiloh was the religious center of Israel. The ark of the covenant rested in the sanctuary there until it was lost to the Philistines during the time of Saul. Ahijah, therefore, has roots in the venerable religious traditions of the northern tribes. He comes to meet Jeroboam "when Jeroboam was leaving Jerusalem"—an apt emblem for what Ahijah is about to announce: that Jeroboam is to lead the northern tribes as they depart from the control of the Davidic king in Jerusalem.

Ahijah wears a "new garment." The narrator emphasizes its newness (vv. 29, 30) because Ahijah will employ it in a sacred, prophetic act. And he uses a particular term for garment that allows him a powerful wordplay: *śalmāh*. Since ancient Hebrew was written without vowels, this word is indistinguishable from the name "Solomon" (*šĕlōmōh;*

the letters *ś* and *š* are identical in consonantal writing). When Ahijah tears the *šlmh* into twelve pieces, it is symbolically the destruction of *šlmh* himself. In Israelite understanding, when a prophet performs a symbolic action like this, it is not simply a demonstration to illustrate his words. Together the prophet's oracle and the symbolic action have power: they unleash what they announce. When Ahijah tears his garment and gives most of it to Jeroboam, the disintegration of the kingdom begins. God has spoken, and God's word is his deed.

AHIJAH'S SPEECH: 11:31-39

Ahijah's lengthy speech makes up the bulk of the passage, but most of it is not Ahijah's own words. Except for the first few phrases, the entire speech comprises an oracle that Ahijah speaks in Yahweh's name. The oracle is organized in two parallel series:

A. I am tearing the kingdom from Solomon's hand (11:31a)
  B. and I will give you ten tribes (11:31b).
    C. One tribe will be his (11:32a)
      D. for the sake of David my servant (11:32b)
        E. and for the sake of Jerusalem, my chosen city (11:32c).
          . . . (11:33a)
        F. Because they[7] did not walk in my ways (11:33b)
          G. and do what is right in my sight (11:33c)
            H. my statutes and my ordinances (11:33d)
              I. as David his father did (11:33e).
                J. I will not take the whole kingdom from him (11:34a).
                  . . . (11:34b)
A'. I will take the kingship from his son's hand[8] (11:35a)
  B'. and I will give you ten tribes (11:35b).
    C'. One tribe will be his son's (11:36a)
      D'. for the sake of David my servant (11:36b)
        E'. before me in Jerusalem, my chosen city (11:36c)

---

[7]The NRSV follows the ancient translations in verse 33 and puts the verbs "has forsaken, worshiped, and has not walked" in the singular. In the Hebrew text all are plural, implying that the people have followed Solomon's lead into idolatry.

[8]The NRSV leaves out the word "hand" here for stylistic reasons. It is in the Hebrew text.

> . . . (11:37)
> F'. If you walk in my ways (11:38a)
>> G'. and do what is right in my sight (11:38b)
>>> H'. my statutes and my commandments (11:38c)
>>>> I'. as David my servant did (11:38d)
>>>> . . . (11:38e).
>>>>> J'. I will not punish David's seed forever (11:39)

The extensive parallelism invites us to compare the two halves of the oracle and take note of their differences. These include the basic difference—the first half speaks of Solomon, the second half of his son—and the elements in each half that do not correspond to elements in the other half.

By focusing on Solomon, the first half directs our attention to the present and the past. Yahweh's words begin with an emphatic present construction: "Look! I am tearing the kingdom out of Solomon's hand!"[9] They continue by recalling the sins of idolatry and disobedience that warrant this punishment (v. 33), and conclude with Yahweh's plans for the rest of Solomon's life. The second half concentrates on the future: Yahweh's plans for Solomon's son and the ultimate destiny of the Davidic house (v. 39), and his plans for Jeroboam himself (vv. 37-38).

Aside from those differences, there are only two points of divergence in elements A/A' through E/E'. In both halves Yahweh reserves one tribe for the Davidic house "for the sake of David and Jerusalem," but the specific wording is different in each case. In verse 36 Yahweh wants to assure for David a "lamp" (Hebrew, *nîr*) in Jerusalem. The Hebrew word is obscure, and the metaphorical usage here is even more uncertain. Perhaps the "lamp" refers to a "glimmer of hope" for the future of the dynasty, still burning in the midst of the dark doom Yahweh is bringing upon Solomon. We shall see below that God unexpectedly leaves room for hope that the Davidic dynasty's punishment will one day end (v. 39). A second difference is the way Jerusalem is described in the two halves of the oracle. The descriptions are complementary rather than contradictory and express why Yahweh's plans do not affect Jerusalem: it is his own city, chosen from all the tribes and marked with his own name. Its true king is neither Solomon nor Jeroboam but Yahweh himself.

There is an apparent mathematical problem in both halves of the oracle. Ahijah tears his garment into twelve pieces, gives ten to

---

[9]The NRSV translates this as a future: "I am about to tear." But the grammatical forms in Hebrew and the fact that the words accompany a power-laden symbolic gesture argue for a present tense in English.

Jeroboam and reserves one for the Davidic house. What happens to the twelfth piece? The ancient Greek translation avoided the issue by simply reading "two" where the Hebrew text has "one" in verses 32 and 36. Modern scholars have offered several different answers, all based on tribal affiliations in the divided kingdoms of the next generation. From a narrative point of view, however, the story does not seem to make an issue of the detail at this point. It is a minor loose end that we could easily overlook; in fact, however, even this loose end will be tied up in chapter 12 (see the remarks on 12:20-21).

The next part of the oracle contains more striking contrasts. In the first half it begins (v. 33a) with an explicit reference backward to 11:5-7, the list of foreign deities for whom Solomon built sanctuaries; and it continues by identifying this idolatry as disobedience. In the second half it begins (v. 37) with an explicit reference forward to 12:20, where Jeroboam becomes "king over all Israel"; and it continues, in words very similar to the first half, by urging him to obedience. It ends, in words that have no parallel in the first part of the oracle, by promising Jeroboam the same sort of blessings David enjoyed if his obedience is modeled on David's. In this context such a promise is problematic. What can it mean to promise "to build for you an enduring house, as I built for David" in the middle of an oracle announcing Yahweh's devastating punishment on that very house of David? David's kingdom is about to disintegrate because of Solomon's disobedience and will endure only in severely reduced circumstances. Is this a presage of a tragic destiny for Jeroboam as well?

In the last part of the oracle there is little vocabulary common to the two halves. The similarity is that both halves declare a mitigation of the announced punishment (element J/J'). In the first half the beginning of the punishment is in view. Solomon will not himself lose the kingdom; rather, God will make him ruler (a somewhat reduced title from "king") "all his days." The punishment, therefore, will be deferred until after his death (this echoes 11:12). In the second half the end of the punishment is in view. God will not afflict the house of David "for all days." This sounds a new note, one of hope that the punishment will not be permanent.

NARRATIVE CONCLUSION: 11:40

After such an oracle we expect to hear how Jeroboam, acting at Ahijah's behest, rebels against Solomon. Instead, the narrator tells us of Solomon's unexpected attempt on Jeroboam's life, without revealing why Solomon so abruptly reverses his earlier favor toward his servant. Is it because Solomon got wind of Ahijah's oracle? Probably not. The narrator has taken pains to assure us that Ahijah and Jeroboam "were alone in the open country" (11:29). Perhaps Jeroboam acted on Ahijah's incentive, but the narrator gives us no indication that this is the case. If anything, this reminds us of the insecure Solomon of 2:22-24, ready to lash out at anyone he considers a potential threat to his throne. We shall see below that Solomon's behavior here is part of a texture of allusions to the stories of Samuel and Saul.

Jeroboam's flight to Egypt reminds us of the refuge Hadad of Edom had found there a generation earlier (11:18-20). The irony is strong. Early in the Solomon story we learned of a great political coup: Solomon became Pharaoh's son-in-law (3:1). Frequent mentions of his marriage to Pharaoh's daughter (7:8; 9:16; 9:24; 11:1) kept before our eyes the presumably harmonious relations that continued between Egypt and Israel. Only here in chapter 11 do we learn that both before and after Solomon's marriage, Pharaoh's court was home to two of the greatest enemies Solomon would ever have to face.

Solomon's Death Notice: 11:41-43

The last words of verse 40 tell us that Jeroboam "remained in Egypt until the death of Solomon." The very next verses recount Solomon's death. This suggests that even though the story of Solomon is over, the story of Jeroboam will continue. And indeed there are major subplots that remain unresolved. Yahweh has decreed the dismemberment of the Davidic kingdom, and Jeroboam has been identified as one who "rebelled against King Solomon." Both of these important potentials in the plot are yet to be realized.

Throughout 1–2 Kings the narrator uses a more or less set formula to describe the transition from one reign to the next. The information in verses 41-43 is one example of this formula. (We saw something similar at David's death in 2:10-12.) We will discuss the technique and its narrative effect below (see p. 206).

Narrative Effect and Characterization

The first noteworthy narrative effect of the Jeroboam passage is to unify the separate parts of chapter 11. It picks up two narrative threads from the first part of the chapter: the nature of Solomon's sin (compare 11:33 with 11:5-7) and the "servant" who will be Yahweh's instrument of punishment (compare 11:26 with 11:11). Both of these threads were held in abeyance through the stories of Hadad and Rezon. But the Jeroboam account connects smoothly with 11:14-25 as well in being the third in a series of stories of individuals who, having once fled from the hostility of Israel's king, now pose threats to Solomon's security. Beyond this, the passage furthers but still leaves open important plot lines: the rebellion, and the fulfillment of Yahweh's decree of punishment. It thus also offers a link to subsequent material. It serves, then, as a sort of hinge connecting the story of Solomon in chapters 1–11 to that of Jeroboam in chapters 11–14. We shall see later that this linking function is reflected in the overall structures of both stories as well.

A second important literary effect in the passage is to establish a series of correlations between the story of Jeroboam, Solomon, and Ahijah and the story of David, Saul, and Samuel. That latter story is told in 1 Samuel. In brief, Samuel became a prophet of Yahweh at the sanctuary in Shiloh. He anointed Saul to be the first king of Israel. After Saul committed an act of disobedience, Yahweh rejected him as king. Samuel then anointed David, son of a man from Bethlehem named Jesse. David entered Saul's service and rose high in his court. Saul suddenly became jealous of David and attempted to kill him. David fled from Saul, took service with a foreign king, and eventually replaced Saul on the throne of Israel. The general similarities between this story and that of Jeroboam are clear, but there is detailed evidence that the narrator is evoking the parallels deliberately. Ahijah, like Samuel, is a prophet from Shiloh. Solomon, like Saul, comes to the throne through anointing by a prophet (compare 1 Sam 10:1 with 1 Kgs 1:34). Solomon, like Saul, is rejected for disobedience (compare 1 Sam 13:13-14 with 1 Kgs 11:11). Ahijah's symbolic gesture (1 Kgs 11:30-31) recalls an accidental but equally symbolic gesture of Samuel (1 Sam 15:27-28). Solomon's replacement, like Saul's, is introduced as "the son of an Ephratite," whose name and place of origin are then given (compare 1 Sam 17:12 with 1 Kgs 11:26; see note 5 on p. 142). Solomon seeks to kill Jeroboam, just as Saul sought David's life (compare Jonathan's words in 1 Sam 19:2 with 1 Kgs 11:40; the sentences are much more alike in Hebrew than in the NRSV). Finally, 1 Kings 11:38 makes explicit the parallel between Jeroboam and David.

The effect of this series of parallels is a kind of *déjà vu*. The narrator invites us to interpret the present situation in terms of the past. Jeroboam's career marks a new beginning, as David's did. Jeroboam has the potential to become a new David if he continues to model himself on David's fidelity to Yahweh. The parallels, however, are double-edged. David's fidelity was not enough: his son's disobedience results in disaster. Even if Jeroboam follows David's example, will his successors?

The passage adds little to the characterization of Solomon except to parallel him to Saul in their respective attempts to kill their servants. Saul's hostility toward David in 1 Samuel is based on jealousy and resembles a classic case of paranoia. This strengthens the impression we get from 1 Kings 11:40 that Solomon's hatred of Jeroboam is equally baseless.

Surprisingly, the characterization of Jeroboam is very slight. We learn a few general things from the narrator: that Jeroboam "rebelled against the king," that he was "very able," that he fled to Egypt. We learn of Solomon's favorable impressions of him, then of his enmity. And we learn of Yahweh's plans for him. But Jeroboam himself says nothing in the passage, and the only action he performs is to flee. Rather like Solomon in 1 Kings 1 (see p. 33), Jeroboam remains something of an enigma. What is he really like, and how well will he live up to the destiny to which Yahweh calls him?

Of Yahweh we learn something subtle but important. Two things show that he does not give up. First, the parallels to the Samuel-Saul-David story demonstrate that Yahweh is ready, over and over again, to effect a new beginning. When Saul forsook him, Yahweh raised up David. Now that David's son has forsaken him, Yahweh raises up Jeroboam. There is no assurance that God will *always* allow a new beginning, but the precedent is strengthened each time it happens. Second, the last words of Ahijah's oracle demonstrate that Yahweh's faithfulness to the Davidic dynasty transcends even Solomon's sin. The story of Solomon may end in tragedy, but the story of David goes on in hope.

Chapter 9

THE WHOLE SOLOMON STORY

1 Kings 1–11

The whole can sometimes be greater than the sum of its parts. Now that we have examined in detail the individual passages that make up 1 Kings 1–11, we look to the broader sweep of the Solomon story as a whole. These chapters are not a mere loose collection of episodes; they form an organized and coherent literary unity. Two factors manifest the unity of 1 Kings 1-11: structure and motifs.

The Structure of 1 Kings 1–11

Like many of the shorter passages we have examined, the entire story of Solomon has a symmetrical structure. It comprises twelve major units, chiastically arranged. Corresponding elements of the chiasm match even in details of their internal composition. This sort of structure has a double effect. It emphasizes the central elements, and it invites a comparison of the corresponding elements preceding and following the center.

THE CENTRALITY OF THE TEMPLE

For the narrator, the Temple occupied the center of ancient Israelite life, just as it occupies the center of the story. Its position in chapters 1–11 and the disproportionate amount of the text the narrator devotes to the account of its construction and dedication reveal the importance the Temple has for him. And the enthusiasm with which he guides us through the building, even into its most restricted precincts, shows that he assumes it will have an equal fascination for his reader. The

Figure 1
THE STRUCTURE OF 1 KINGS 1–11

A. A PROPHET INTERVENES IN THE ROYAL SUCCESSION: 1:1–2:12a
  1. Nathan gains the throne for Solomon: 1:1–2:9
  2. Formulaic notice of David's death: 2:10-12a
  B. SOLOMON ELIMINATES THREATS TO HIS SECURITY: 2:12b-46
  1. Adonijah: 2:12b-25
  2. (Abiathar and) Joab: 2:26-35
  3. Shimei: 2:36-46
    C. THE EARLY PROMISE OF SOLOMON'S REIGN: 3:1-15
    1. Narrator's evaluative summary: 3:1-3
      (foreign marriage; building projects; high places)
    2. Solomon's first encounter with God: 3:4-15
      D. SOLOMON USES HIS GIFTS FOR THE PEOPLE: 3:16–4:34
      1. "a discerning mind": 3:16-28
      2. "riches": 4:1-28
        (internal affairs; external affairs; chariots and horses)
      3. "honor above kings": 4:29-34
        E. PREPARATIONS FOR BUILDING THE TEMPLE: 5:1-18
        1. Negotiations with Hiram: 5:1-12
        2. Conscripted labor: 5:13-18
          F. SOLOMON BUILDS THE TEMPLE: 6:1–7:51
            (including Solomon's second encounter with Yahweh)
          F'. SOLOMON DEDICATES THE TEMPLE: 8:1–9:10
            (including Solomon's third encounter with Yahweh)
        E'. AFTER BUILDING THE TEMPLE: 9:11-25
        1. Negotiations with Hiram: 9:11-14
        2. Conscripted labor: 9:15-25
      D'. SOLOMON USES HIS GIFTS FOR HIMSELF: 9:26–10:29
      1. "a discerning mind": 10:1-13
      2. "riches": 9:26-28; 10:14-22, 26-29
        (internal affairs; maritime affairs; chariots and horses)
      3. "honor above kings": 10:23-25
    C'. THE TRAGIC FAILURE OF SOLOMON'S REIGN: 11:1-13
    1. Narrator's evaluative summary: 11:1-8
      (foreign marriages; building idolatrous high places)
    2. Solomon's fourth encounter with Yahweh: 11:9-13
  B'. YAHWEH RAISES UP THREATS TO SOLOMON'S SECURITY:
  11:14-25
  1. Hadad of Edom: 11:14-22
  2. Rezon of Damascus: 11:23-25
  (3. Jeroboam of Israel: see next section)
A'. A PROPHET DETERMINES THE ROYAL SUCCESSION: 11:26-43
  1. Ahijah prophesies the throne for Jeroboam: 11:26-40
  2. Formulaic notice of Solomon's death: 11:41-43

heart of the Temple is the "innermost sanctuary," or holy of holies. That is the high point of the narrator's tour of the building (6:23-30), and it is the scene of Yahweh's mysterious manifestation at the dedication ceremony (8:6-11). Solomon's poetic greeting to the Lord at that moment epitomizes the essential significance of the Temple: it is an exalted house where Yahweh will be enthroned (NRSV, "dwell") forever (8:12-13). Nevertheless, the narrator's joy over the Temple is not unalloyed. He interjects into the story of the building of the "house of Yahweh" an account of two other "houses," the "house of the king" (that is, the royal palace, including the governmental administration buildings) and the "house for Pharaoh's daughter" (7:1-12). By interrupting the Temple account with information about much later projects, and by using the term "house" for all three, the narrator intimates a certain rivalry between the projects.

The implication of competition between Yahweh's house and the king's is strengthened by the assertion in 6:38–7:1 that Solomon spent twice as long on his palace as on the Temple; and it foreshadows chapter 10, where Solomon's plentiful gold goes to beautify his own palace buildings, while Yahweh's Temple gets only a bit of almug wood (10:12). Competition between the Temple and the house of Pharaoh's daughter is more symbolic. Solomon's readiness to build this house for Pharaoh's daughter is not in itself blameworthy. But it is a harbinger of his later willingness to indulge his multitude of foreign wives by building sanctuaries for their gods across the Kidron Valley from Yahweh's own Temple. Thus even at the joyous heart of the story, the narrator has given us forebodings of its tragic outcome.

COMPARISON OF ELEMENTS: THE CHARACTERIZATION OF SOLOMON

The most apparent organizational principle of the Solomon story is chronology. The story begins with Solomon's accession to the throne, then describes his consolidation of power, the administrative apparatus he sets up, his major building projects, the glory of his completed court, and his infidelity in his old age. It ends with his death. Yet there are surprisingly few precise temporal indicators, and much of the material could be set at any time during his reign. In a few places, moreover, the account is clearly not in chronological order. Solomon exiles Abiathar in 2:26-27, but he is still listed as high priest in 4:4. The construction of the royal palace and of the house for Pharaoh's daughter interrupts the account of the construction of the Temple, even though the Temple is supposedly completed before the other projects are begun. The narrator does not reveal the existence of adversaries from before Solomon's reign until the very end of the story. Given the careful symmetric organization of the whole story, these irregularities indicate that some factor other than chronology is also at work.

That factor is the developing characterization of Solomon. We have seen that, prior to the condemnation of Solomon in chapter 11, the narrator uses a strategy of ambivalence. The overt characterization of Solomon is positive, but it conceals more negative elements. Comparison of the corresponding elements before and after the material on the Temple reveals a similar ambivalence. Sections before the Temple are positive; sections after the Temple are negative. In A, Solomon becomes king; in A', Yahweh announces the loss of much of his kingdom. In B, Solomon eliminates rivals; in B', Yahweh raises up new adversaries that Solomon fails to eliminate. In C, the narrator's evaluation is positive, and Yahweh expresses his pleasure with Solomon; in C', the narrator's evaluation is negative, and Yahweh expresses his anger. In D, Solomon uses his God-given gifts in ways that benefit both Israelites and non-Israelites; in D', he uses his gifts in ways that do nothing but enrich his treasuries. In E, he establishes friendly relations with Hiram of Tyre and organizes an apparently temporary labor force to build the Temple; in E', he jeopardizes the treaty with Hiram and transforms conscripted labor into a permanent institution.

The narrator does not entirely abandon his strategy of ambivalence even in chapter 11. Hidden in the unrelieved condemnations of Solomon is one grace note of sympathetic irony. In 3:14, after unconditionally granting Solomon gifts of a discerning mind, riches, and honor, Yahweh makes a fourth, conditional promise: If Solomon obeys Yahweh's commandments according to the model of David, Yahweh will grant him long life. In the very nature of things, the fulfillment of such a promise can only be determined at the end of Solomon's life. We learn in 11:4 that Solomon turned away from Yahweh "when he was old." The promise, therefore, was fulfilled, and Solomon must have lived his life, almost to the very end, satisfactorily obedient to the commands of Yahweh. We see in his aged apostasy, not the culminating crime of an evil life, but the tragic stumble of a runner just short of the finish line.

Unifying Motifs

Other signs of unity include several motifs that run through the story like continuous threads. We have already examined the motif of "marriage to Pharaoh's daughter" (3:1; 7:8; 9:16; 9:24; 11:1) and the way it expands in 11:1-8 into a condemnation of Solomon for following the idolatrous ways of his many foreign wives. Three other pervasive motifs are Solomon's encounters with Yahweh, Solomon's wisdom, and the figure of David.

Solomon's Encounters with Yahweh

At four places in the Solomon story, the king receives either a vision or a word from God. Two of those encounters explicitly refer back to earlier ones; see the discussions on 9:1-10 and on 11:9-13. But the four encounters together also form a single series, unified by several links. In each case Yahweh reacts to something Solomon says or does. In the first and third encounters, Yahweh responds to Solomon's preceding prayer. In the second and fourth encounters, he responds to Solomon's building of sanctuaries, either to Yahweh himself or to rival deities.

All four encounters also contain conditional language, references to "David your father," and steadily increasing negativity in their attitude toward Solomon. In the first encounter, Yahweh approves Solomon and makes him a conditional promise: "If you obey, I will give you long life." In the second, there is neither approval nor disapproval; there is simply the conditional promise. In the third encounter, the conditional element of the promise expands considerably and is balanced by a threat. In the fourth encounter, Yahweh is angry and condemns Solomon for his failure to fulfill the conditions imposed on him.

The effect of this series of encounters is to inject into the entire Solomon story a reverberant cautionary note. This is particularly striking in the two encounters that occur during the construction and dedication of the Temple, where the splendor of the building and the rites could blind Solomon—or us—to what is really important. The Temple is magnificent: all hewn stone and cedar and bronze and gold; and the dedication ceremony is lavish: hundreds of thousands of animals, vastly more than the altar could accommodate (8:5; 8:63-64). But what Yahweh wants above all remains unchanged: obedience.

Solomon's Wisdom

Solomon's wisdom is the emblem for which he has become legendary. The tradition begins in these chapters: the words "wise" or "wisdom" are used of Solomon over twenty times, and synonyms like "understanding" and "discernment" occur several times as well. The term "wisdom" is broader in Hebrew than in English and can include such morally neutral ideas as shrewdness, cleverness, and even skill at handicrafts. (See, for example, the description of the bronzemaker Hiram of Tyre in 7:14. The NRSV's "skill and intelligence" translates the Hebrew words "wisdom and understanding.") The development of the motif as it applies to Solomon is essentially harmonious, but it is not without a few notes of discord.

The first voice to call Solomon wise is David's (2:6; 2:9). At this initial appearance, however, the word is at its least savory. David counts on Solomon's wisdom to enable him to devise successful plots against Joab and Shimei. "Wisdom" here is the ability to steer a shrewd course between the demands of the commandments of God and the political expediency of eliminating potential enemies. At its next appearances the term is both precise and morally admirable (3:9-12; 3:28). It is the quality that Solomon prays for and receives to give him a "listening mind" and enable him to "discern what is right"; it is, therefore, the foundation of justice in his kingdom. From this point on, the term occurs either in the sense of intellectual erudition or in a vague, unspecified sense. After 3:28 there are no more examples of Solomon exercising his wisdom to "discern between good and evil." Moreover, the wisdom for which he becomes world famous is not an ability to listen but an ability to speak. People come from other nations to listen to his wisdom (4:34; 10:8; 10:24).

Except for David's usage, the motif does not contribute directly to the negative characterization of Solomon in the story. Yet indirectly it reflects the progressive darkening of the portrayal of Solomon by moving away from the moral high-water mark of wisdom for the sake of justice to wisdom for the sake of display and gain.

David

The last motif is the frequent reference to David. Even after David's death and burial in 2:10-12, he is named forty-six times, most of them in speech either by Solomon or by Yahweh (including Yahweh's words as delivered by Ahijah in 11:31-39). The differences between Solomon's and Yahweh's invocations of David's name are revealing. In speaking of his father, Solomon regularly recalls the promises Yahweh made to David in the past or the future blessings Yahweh will impart to the Davidic dynasty. On only one occasion does Solomon recall David's faithful obedience to Yahweh (3:6), and then he recalls it as the reason for Yahweh's blessings in the past. He never speaks of David or his obedience as a model for his own behavior. In contrast, Yahweh regularly speaks of David in two contexts. First, David's obedience is held up as the example Solomon and eventually Jeroboam (11:38) must follow if they are to obtain the conditional promises Yahweh makes to them. Second, Yahweh cites David as his reason for mitigating Solomon's punishment; on one occasion that reason is specifically David's obedience (11:34). For Yahweh, "David" stands for law and obedience. For Solomon, "David" stands for promise and blessings. The fundamental and ultimately fatal flaw in Solomon's character could scarcely be summed up more succinctly.

A second effect of the motif of David is to expand the horizons of the Solomon story in both directions. The David we know within this story is an enfeebled old man, whose only decisive actions are to choreograph the installation ceremony of his successor and then to deliver himself of morally ambiguous dying advice. This can hardly be the model of obedient service Yahweh has in mind. The motif of David, then, points to a preceding story of David, outside the bounds of the Solomon story, that tells of David's paradigmatic fidelity to Yahweh. Similarly, the fact that Yahweh continues to insist on David as the operative model for Jeroboam (11:38) points forward to a further story, that of Jeroboam, to answer the implied question of whether Jeroboam will succeed where Solomon failed. In this way the story of Solomon is caught up into something even larger than itself: the story of Yahweh's search for a faithful king of Israel according to the model of David.

Part Two

THE STORY OF JEROBOAM
1 Kings 11:26–14:20

Chapter 10

THE SEPARATION OF THE KINGDOMS

1 Kings 11:26–12:25

The story of Jeroboam recounts how the prophesied disintegration of Solomon's kingdom comes to pass, and how Jeroboam, Solomon's erstwhile servant and now the first king of the independent northern kingdom, fails in his turn to satisfy Yahweh's demands for faithful obedience. Jeroboam's sins result in a further deterioration of the religious unity of the people of Yahweh and, ultimately, in God's repudiation of Jeroboam's royal house.

Ahijah's Oracle to Jeroboam: 11:26-43

The account of Ahijah's oracle to Jeroboam does double duty in 1 Kings. It brings the Solomon story to a close, and it opens the story of Jeroboam. In this way it is a kind of hinge, a unifying force binding together two large blocks of material in 1 Kings. We have already examined the details of the passage in our study of Solomon. We will discuss its linking function more fully when we look at the structure of the whole Jeroboam story.

The Schism at Shechem: 12:1-20

The account of the northern tribes' secession from the federated kingdom forged by David describes how Rehoboam, Solomon's son and successor, alienated the representatives of the northern tribes and thereby precipitated their withdrawal from the united kingdom. An ironic inclusion marks the beginning and the end of the account: the Israelites come to Shechem to make Rehoboam king (v. 1), but they eventually make Jeroboam king (v. 20). The narrative has six chiastically arranged parts:

> A. Narrative introduction (12:1-3a)
> > B. The first interview with Rehoboam (12:3b-5)
> > > C. Rehoboam consults with the elders (12:6-7)
> > > C'. Rehoboam consults with the youngsters (12:8-11)
> > B'. The second interview with Rehoboam (12:12-17)
> A'. Narrative conclusion (12:18-20)

NARRATIVE INTRODUCTION: 12:1-3a

Rehoboam's journey to Shechem reminds us of the dual nature of the Davidic kingdom. It is not really a single political entity but a union of two originally distinct territories, "Judah" and "Israel" (the latter is often called "all Israel" in 1 Kings). David himself acquired the crowns of the two territories on different occasions. He became king of Judah while in Hebron (2 Sam 2:1-4). Seven years later the elders of Israel came to him at Hebron and asked him to be king over Israel as well (2 Sam 5:1-5).

There is no evidence in our texts that the northern tribes had any say in Solomon's accession, but there were two unusual factors at work in that instance. First, Solomon did not become king after David's death but while he was still alive. Perhaps as coregent he could presume to share the mantle of acceptance that still cloaked the living David. Second, Solomon's installation was done quickly (recall the frequent motif word "today" in 1 Kings 1) to forestall Adonijah's alleged seizure of power. There was no time to seek the approval of the northern tribes. Nevertheless, this lack of explicit ratification of Solomon's kingship by the tribes of "all Israel" points to a deeper problem of which we had hints in the Solomon story: What was Solomon's relationship with the northern tribes? Was his treatment of Israel equitable, or did he favor his own ancestral tribe of Judah? (See the comments on 4:1-20 and 5:13-18.)

In Rehoboam's case, there are no extenuating circumstances, and he is obliged to travel north to Shechem to obtain the allegiance of "all Israel." Shechem was an important city and figured in sacred Israelite traditions dating from long before David's day. The setting itself, therefore, bespeaks the relative autonomy of "all Israel" vis-à-vis the Davidic throne and hints that Rehoboam's confirmation is not a mere formality.

Yet the presumption is in his favor, since the representatives of the northern tribes have come to Shechem "to make him king."

The remainder of the introduction describes how the leaders of Israel recalled Jeroboam from Egypt after the death of Solomon. The Hebrew text is awkward, though not impossibly so. The NRSV smooths over some of the difficulties. The following incomplete sentence is a literal rendering of the Hebrew: "When Jeroboam son of Nebat heard (he was still in Egypt where he had fled from King Solomon, and Jeroboam had lived in Egypt, and they had sent and called him) . . . ." The NRSV, following the ancient Greek, has Jeroboam "return" (Hebrew, *wayyāšob*) from Egypt upon hearing "of it" (the words are not in the Hebrew); then, having returned, he receives the summons of the Israelites to come to the assembly at Shechem. In the Hebrew, the Israelites summon him from Egypt, where he has "lived" (Hebrew, *wayyēšeb*) since his flight from Solomon; and it is by means of this summons that he hears of the events that have transpired in Israel. In the Hebrew text, then, the Israelites have kept contact with Jeroboam even in his distant exile, and they alert him as soon as it is safe for him to return. This implies a much higher respect (and destiny?) for Jeroboam than we infer from the NRSV, where his convenient return simply makes him available to serve as head of the team negotiating with Rehoboam.

The First Interview with Rehoboam: 12:3b-5

The representatives of the northern tribes, presumably led by Jeroboam, present their agenda to Rehoboam. They are willing to accept him as king if he will redress the grievances they have against the crushing burdens his father imposed on them. Though their complaint is not specific, we saw in the Solomon story how both taxation and conscripted labor were demanded of the northern tribes but apparently not of Judah. The speech is respectful but firm and straightforward: it contrasts the past deeds of Solomon ("your father") with the future policies the Israelites hope for from Rehoboam ("*you*— emphatic pronoun);[1] and in return for a lessening of the service (*'bdh*) expected of them, the Israelites pledge to serve (*'bd*) the new king. Rehoboam asks for and is given time to consider his answer.

[1]The NRSV ignores the emphatic pronoun, which is even more strongly emphasized in the Hebrew by similar-sounding "now" following it. "You [*'attâ*], now [*'attâ*], lighten the hard service . . . ."

Rehoboam Takes Counsel: 12:6-11

Rehoboam consults two different groups of advisers. The structural parallels between the two consultations are evident; by them the narrator invites us to compare the two and take note of their differences. The first group is, literally, "old men." The term can also connote the wisdom that comes with age and experience. In this case it probably means both, since these people belong to the previous generation of royal advisers. The second group is, literally, "boys" (NRSV, "young men," but the Hebrew term is more commonly used for children than adults). The narrator's sympathy is clearly for the old men; his emphasis here is on the youth and inexperience of the "boys," who belong to Rehoboam's own generation. Perhaps the terms "elders" and "youngsters" best capture the nuances of the contrast.

Rehoboam asks the elders "how" to respond to the Israelites, a question of manner, not of content; and this is the way the elders answer him. Of the youngsters Rehoboam asks "what" to say, and the youngsters write his speech for him. A second difference in Rehoboam's questions is that when speaking to the youngsters, he includes a paraphrase of the Israelites' demands. (We will discuss this in a moment.)

The elders' advice is crafted and crafty. A literal rendering of the Hebrew shows the verbal artistry of the elders:

A. "If TODAY *you will be servant* to this people,
  B. and serve them,
    C. and answer them,
  B'. then say good things to them,
A'. and *they will serve* you ALL DAYS."

Their recommendation is to dissemble. If Rehoboam pretends to appease the Israelites now ("be servant *today,* and say good things to them"), they will make him king. He will then have their allegiance for "all days." The unspoken implication, of course, is that once they accept him officially as their king, he will be free to ignore the promises he made under pressure. The unspoken implication is hidden in an ambiguity in the Hebrew text, in the very center of the speech: "and answer them." Despite all the dialogue in this section, with two conversations between Rehoboam and the Israelites and two conversations between Rehoboam and his advisers, the usual Hebrew verb "to answer" (*'ānāh*) occurs only twice: here and in verse 13a. Elsewhere another common idiom, "to return word," is used. The two places where *'ānāh* occurs both allow for a powerful ambiguity with another verb whose consonants are the same, the verb *'innāh*, "to afflict." In the form used here, the differences are minimal: *ʿănîtām* ("answer them") and *ʿinnîtām* ("afflict them"). (In ancient Hebrew, vowels were not written, and doubled consonants were not indicated; to the ancient reader, therefore, the forms would have been identical and could have been read either way.) Alongside the reading given above, the ancient reader would be able to hear:

A. "If today you will be servant to this people,
  B. and serve them,
    C. (and afflict them),
  B'. then say good things to them,
A'. and they will serve you all days."

The youngsters' advice, by contrast, is crass and crude. They begin by paraphrasing, as Rehoboam also did, the Israelites' request, then continue with a detailed script they urge upon Rehoboam.

One of the means Hebrew narrative uses to convey characterization is to have one person repeat someone else's speech in a new context. The way the person modifies what he or she heard reveals much about character. Here we have the Israelites' original complaint (v. 4), Rehoboam's paraphrase of their speech to his younger advisers (v. 9), and the youngsters' version of it (v. 10). The original complaint is, as we have said, respectful but firm and straightforward. It uses a wordplay that will recur in all three versions of the speech but is impossible to capture in English. The word for "yoke" (*ʿōl*) and the preposition "on" (*ʿal*) are very similar. The Israelites' phrase, "his heavy yoke (*ʿullô*) that he placed on us (*ʿālênû*)" plays on these words. Rehoboam's version of their complaint uses the same wordplay, "the yoke (*hāʿōl*) that your father put on us (*ʿālênû*)." But otherwise it modifies the Israelites' words in significant ways. No longer is that yoke "heavy," nor is there any mention of the "hard service" of which the Israelites also complained. Words like "hard" and "heavy" are entirely absent from Rehoboam's paraphrase; it is as if he has not heard them at all. More striking, he gives no indication that the Israelites' speech is an attempt to negotiate. He transforms it into a simple demand. The impression we get is that Rehoboam thinks of the Israelites as subjects complaining to their king, not as independent agents who have not yet given him their allegiance. The younger advisers' version of the speech becomes a parody. They turn the complaint into a bit of rhyming doggerel:

"Your father made heavy our yoke (*ʿullēnû*),
Now you make it lighter upon us (*mēʿālênû*)."

Like Rehoboam, they treat the complaint as a simple demand and do not seem to realize that the kingdom's survival hangs in the balance. Unlike Rehoboam, they use the word "heavy"; they realize that the Israelites consider themselves oppressed. Their mockery, however, merely makes fun of the victims. We will not be surprised to see the same insensitivity in the response they advise Rehoboam to give.

The speech they draft for Rehoboam begins with a boast that may well be obscene. The meaning of "my little one" (NRSV, "my little finger") is uncertain. If, as some scholars suspect, it is gutter language for the male organ, Rehoboam's young advisers are coarse as well as crude. The rest of their speech (v. 11) is also in verse. It comprises two couplets, each of which contrasts what Solomon did ("my father") with what Rehoboam will do ("*I*"—emphatic pronoun in both contrasts). In both cases Solomon's oppression is not just admitted but celebrated, and Rehoboam pledges to exceed his father's mark. (The strange final image of disciplining with scorpions is to be explained as a metaphor. A "scorpion" was a particularly vicious and sadistic type of whip. Compare the use of "cat" in English for "cat-o'-nine-tails.")

THE SECOND INTERVIEW WITH REHOBOAM: 12:12-17

After three days Jeroboam and the Israelite leaders approach Rehoboam again. The narrator's point in recalling Rehoboam's speech from verse 5 is to emphasize that Jeroboam and the Israelites are cooperating fully with Rehoboam: he required a three-day delay, and they waited three days, "as the king had said." The narrator's next words are redolent with irony. "The king *answered*"—the Hebrew word is '*nh*, the ambiguous verb we discussed above in connection with the elders' advice to Jeroboam. "The king answered the people *harshly*"—though the NRSV obscures the link, this is the same word (*qāšâ*) used to describe the *hard* service the Israelites complained of in verse 4. The narrator's statement, then, says, "The king answered (*ya'an*) the people hard things," but it hints at, "The king afflicted (*yĕ'anneh*) the people in the same hard way that Solomon did."

Rehoboam's speech is an almost verbatim delivery of what his younger advisers coached him on. There are two changes. First, he eliminates completely the coarse boast with which they began. This slightly alleviates an otherwise dismal picture. Rehoboam is obviously a fool. He ignores the advice of experience and sides with his callow cronies. His response can only alienate the northern tribes, who approached him with a reasonable case. But even his foolishness has limits: he knows better than to indulge in petty pomposity. The second change is that he modifies the next line slightly. This results in an improvement of the poetic quality of the speech without changing its meaning. Fool he may be, but he is also apparently a reasonably skilled rhetorician.

The narrator injects an evaluative aside to us, the readers. He comments that Rehoboam's refusal to heed the Israelites is actually part of Yahweh's plan. This is not to excuse Rehoboam. He is culpably stiffnecked to the point of rupturing the kingdom. But the rupture itself is not to be regretted, since Yahweh purposed it. The explicit reference back to Ahijah's oracle in chapter 11 is one of the narrator's means of connecting the sections of the Jeroboam story.

The Israelites reply to poetry with poetry. Like Rehoboam's rebuff, their response is two couplets. The first couplet repudiates the alliance between Israel and the house of David. The terms are familial: "share" and "inheritance" refer to the portions brothers receive from their father. The Israelites deny that they have any such inheritance; in other words, they deny that the Davidic monarch is any longer their brother. (This goes beyond Yahweh's intentions, as we will see in 12:24.) The second couplet is similarly divisive: Israel and David (that is, the tribe of Judah) have no common dwelling. The poem may have been a traditional northern rallying cry, since the first three lines were heard also during the revolt of Sheba against David in 2 Samuel 20:1. Here the Israelites add a new line: "Look now to your own house, O David." Is there a hint of menace in this line that goes beyond separation to threaten aggression?

The scene ends with two narrative remarks. The first recounts that Israel carried out its cry literally and dispersed to their tents. The second is a parenthetical aside by the narrator explaining that Israelites living in Judahite territory remained Rehoboam's subjects. This is more than an academic detail. It indicates that as far as the narrator is concerned, the division that has occurred is only territorial. Israel and Judah remain one people, because they are the people of Yahweh. Because of Solomon's malfeasance (compounded, of course, by Rehoboam's stupidity), Yahweh has divided administration of the people's territory between two monarchs. But this is only a temporary situation (recall 11:39). The unity of the people under the Davidic house will one day be restored, and the presence of Israelite subjects in Rehoboam's kingdom is the gage of that future.

Narrative Conclusion: 12:18-20

The narrative conclusion begins with verse 18. The NRSV's paragraphing does not recognize this, but the unnecessarily repeated subject in verse 18 indicates this division: "Rehoboam reigned (v. 17) . . . . and King Rehoboam sent (v. 18) . . . ." This is one of the ways Hebrew narrative signals that a new paragraph is beginning.

If Rehoboam sends Adoram as negotiator at this point in an attempt to conciliate the rebellious Israelites, it is a singularly inept choice. Since the time of Solomon, Adoram has been in charge of the conscripted labor to which the Israelites were subject (see 4:6 and 5:14; the name "Adoniram" is simply a variation of "Adoram").[2] He is the last person the Israelites would listen to. But the text does not specify Rehoboam's motivation. It is equally possible—and entirely consistent with the insensitivity the king has already demonstrated—that he is trying to quell the Israelites with fear. Unfortunately, a riot ensues and Adoram is killed by stoning (the usual form of capital punishment in ancient Israel). King Rehoboam flees the scene, but the NRSV overlooks a nuance of the Hebrew. He does not flee *after* Adoram has been killed (as the NRSV's "then" would suggest) but *while* the riot is going on. (The Hebrew verb form implies that Rehoboam's mounting his chariot is simultaneous with Adoram's stoning.) In other words, Rehoboam abandons his envoy to his fate in order to save his own skin.

The narrator "breaks frame," that is, steps out of the time and place of the narrative to address his readers directly. The Israelite actions constitute a "rebellion"—which is more than Yahweh has sanctioned. God authorized a division of the territory but not a complete repudiation of the Davidic house, much less a sealing of that repudiation with human blood. Paradoxically, the narrator's observation that the rebellion has lasted "to this day" is a sign of hope. The story is not necessarily over: what holds today may not hold forever. And thus the narrator signals again his conviction that the schism is only temporary (see above on v. 17).

Verse 20a seems to be in some tension with verses 2-3. How can it be that all Israel only hears of Jeroboam's return and calls him to the assembly in verse 20 when he has been part of the negotiations at Shechem all along (vv. 3, 12)? The tensions are much worse in the NRSV rendering than in the Hebrew, however. First, by following the Greek in verse 2 (Jeroboam "returned" instead of "lived"; see the discussion above), the NRSV introduces an apparent contradiction that is not in the Hebrew text. Second, the "assembly" of verse 3 and that of verse 20 are different words in Hebrew. This suggests that two different gatherings, for two different purposes, may be in view. It is possible,

[2]The overseer of conscripted labor in David's time was also an Adoram (2 Sam 20:24). If this is the same man, he must have been quite elderly by the time of Rehoboam.

as some scholars conjecture, that an earlier version of the story did not introduce Jeroboam until this point. But we can read the verse quite satisfactorily in the present context. "When all Israel (that is, the populace as a whole, not simply the representatives who participated in the assembly at Shechem) heard that Jeroboam had returned (from the assembly at Shechem), they sent and called him to a (different) convocation, where they made him king over all Israel." Thus the narrative reaches its ironic conclusion. All Israel sent and called Jeroboam to one assembly to make Rehoboam king, but they eventually send and call Jeroboam again to another gathering and make him king instead.

In verse 20b the narrator expands parenthetically on the "all Israel" that has sworn allegiance to Jeroboam. Only the tribe of Judah—one piece of Ahijah of Shiloh's garment (see 11:29-32)—remains in the hands of the house of David.

Narrative Effect

There are two intertwined strands of narrative tension in this section. The first is Rehoboam's status as king of the northern tribes. The first verse introduces this theme, and the complication arises when the Israelite leaders present their ultimatum. The second is the unresolved status of Jeroboam, who at the beginning of this story still remains a fugitive, as verse 2 reminds us, but who appears in verse 3 as an Israelite leader. Both strands are rooted in Ahijah's oracle in chapter 11, where Jeroboam was promised a kingdom at the expense of Solomon's son.

Both subplots unfold through a series of dialogues. Narratively speaking, direct speech is one of the slowest moving forms of storytelling. The narrator can telescope hours, days, even years of information in a few words. But direct speech takes approximately as long to read as it does to occur. (Only descriptive passages or lengthy narrator's asides, where the movement of the action comes to a complete halt, are markedly slower than direct speech.) The effect of building a story predominately out of dialogue is to slow the development and create considerable tension.

Rehoboam's elder advisers propose a sort of diplomatic chicanery that, however dishonestly, might preserve the integrity of the kingdom. This would resolve the first narrative strand positively but complicate the second by frustrating the accomplishment of Yahweh's oracle. In the exact center of the story's structure, we learn that this avenue of plot resolution is closed: "he disregarded the advice that the older men gave him" (v. 8). There is momentary hope, however unlikely, that younger advisers may produce a happier solution. That hope lasts while

Rehoboam not only poses his question but paraphrases the Israelites' complaint. It lasts still more when the youngsters also cite the complaint and in so doing reveal their awareness of the Israelites' sense of oppression. But they soon crush hope beneath the callous response they prepare for Rehoboam. The final poetic exchange—Rehoboam's repetition of his young advisers' speech and the Israelites' repudiation of the house of David—resolves the first subplot: Rehoboam will not become king of the northern tribes. The narrative conclusion resolves the second subplot: Jeroboam does become king. Thus Yahweh's words through Ahijah come to tragic fulfillment.

The Characterization of Rehoboam

It is clear from the preceding discussion that the narrator has little respect for Rehoboam. He presents him as foolish, arrogant, insensitive, self-serving, and politically obtuse. There are also indications that his diplomatic gaffe is not due to simple bad judgment but to a much more fundamental weakness of character. The narrator's depiction of Rehoboam suggests that, far from weighing the two sides' advice and choosing between them on some rational basis, no matter how misguided, the king has no intention of taking the elders' advice seriously. The narrator's contrast between the "elders" and the "youngsters" whom Rehoboam consults makes evident where the narrator's sympathies lie. He identifies the two groups, however, not only by their generation but by their personal association with Solomon (the elders "had attended his father Solomon") or with Rehoboam (the youngsters "had grown up with him and now attended him"). He hints thereby that the elders no longer attend Rehoboam. Rehoboam's contemporaries have supplanted them at court, and Rehoboam will be predisposed to listen to those closest to him. This impression is strengthened when Rehoboam addresses himself to the youngsters and says, "What do you advise that *we* answer this people?" (v. 9). Even before hearing their advice, he identifies with these advisers, as he did not with the elders. (This is not a royal "we"; Hebrew did not have such a usage.)

The narrator, too, tells us in his own words of Rehoboam's bias. Even before the king consults with the youngsters, the narrator already asserts that "he disregarded the advice that the older men gave him" (v. 8). He repeats the sentence later (v. 13), like a sad refrain, just before Rehoboam almost slavishly parrots the contemptuous poetry the youngsters put in his mouth. The culmination of this theme of Rehoboam's refusal to listen to good advice is the statement that he "did not listen to the people" (v. 15). How far we are from a King Solomon, whose only request of Yahweh was for "a listening mind to judge your people, to discern between good and evil" (3:9)!

Aftermath of Schism: 12:21-25

The NRSV reads this unit as verses 21-24 and places a major paragraph break before verse 25. But this overlooks an unnecessarily repeated subject in verse 26 that indicates the beginning of a new paragraph at that point. The major paragraph break should come after verse 25. The literary unit is verses 21-25, and it has a concentric structure:

A. Rehoboam's offensive military preparations (12:21)
  B. Shemaiah's oracle (12:22-24)
A'. Jeroboam's defensive military preparations (12:25)

The first words make a link with the preceding section. Rehoboam's attempt to flee to Jerusalem (v. 18b) succeeds. Once home, the king assembles a mighty army to recapture the rebellious territory of Israel. Two details are notable here. First, Rehoboam draws his army not only from the house of Judah but from the tribe of Benjamin as well. Benjamin was traditionally reckoned one of the northern tribes; King Saul was a Benjaminite, and some of the staunchest opponents of the house of David were of that tribe (for example, Shimei, son of Gera; see 2:8-9). But Jerusalem is very near the Judah-Benjamin border. For security, therefore, Rehoboam has to consolidate his control over as much Benjaminite territory as he can. This resolves the loose end left over from Ahijah's oracle in chapter 11: the twelfth piece of Ahijah's garment is Benjamin, whose loyalties are probably with the north while its territory belongs in large part to Rehoboam.

The second detail is the size of the army Rehoboam musters. In historical terms, the figure 180,000 is utterly unrealistic. But it is not a random exaggeration. It recalls Solomon's labor force in 5:13-15, which also totaled 180,000. We are invited to compare Solomon's use of conscripted manpower for construction to Rehoboam's destructive intent. We also realize that Rehoboam is now visiting upon Judah the oppression Israel complained about under Solomon.

The narrator calls Shemaiah a "man of God"; the phrase is a synonym for "prophet." (Both terms occur frequently in 1 Kings, although they are rarely applied to the same person. If there is a nuance of difference, it is lost to us.) Yahweh addresses his words universally: to the king, to his Judahite and Benjaminite subjects, and to "the rest of the people." Now that Israel has formally chosen Jeroboam as its king, Yahweh demotes Rehoboam to "King of Judah," a title we have not seen before. Since the "house of Judah and Benjamin" includes all of Rehoboam's subjects, the "rest of the people" must be the people of Yahweh now living in the secessionist northern territories. The idea that northerners would hear of Shemaiah's proclamation is probably infeasible, but the fictive address has a literary purpose: it evokes once again the indivisible nature of the people, despite the territorial rupture. All God's people are to hear God's word as delivered by God's prophet.

In the oracle Yahweh forbids the military action Rehoboam plans against Israel, whom Yahweh calls "your brothers" (NRSV, "kindred"). The use of family language here contradicts the rejection of brotherhood in Israel's renunciation of Rehoboam (v. 16). For Yahweh, the *people* are not sundered; they remain one even though Yahweh has divided the kingdoms. The oracle also makes public knowledge what only Solomon, now dead, and Ahijah and Jeroboam have previously been told: that the division of the kingdom is Yahweh's doing. The response to Yahweh's command is obedience: "they heeded . . . and went home." That is, the army Rehoboam gathered disbands. The narrator's generalization of the obedience to a plural "they" enables him to avoid attributing expressly to Rehoboam anything that might elicit our admiration. Whether the oracle has any impact on Rehoboam or not we cannot tell, but the army went home.

While Rehoboam is making preparations to invade Jeroboam's territory, his rival is preparing his defense. He builds (that is, fortifies) Shechem and takes it as his headquarters for a time. Eventually, however, he moves to Penuel, across the Jordan River.

Chapter 11
THE SIN OF JEROBOAM
1 Kings 12:26–13:10

The next two sections of the Jeroboam story turn from the political developments that sundered the united kingdom of David and Solomon to the religious changes instituted by Jeroboam once he assumed the throne of Israel. The two sections are closely connected. Only the unnecessarily repeated subject in verse 32 marks the division between them; otherwise the narrative flows more or less smoothly from 12:26 to 13:10. The NRSV does not recognize the indicator of discontinuity at 12:32 and puts the major break between 12:33 and 13:1.

Jeroboam's Cultic Innovations: 12:26-31

The report of Jeroboam's cultic innovations begins with a brief scene. Jeroboam deliberates about a problem, then acts to solve it (vv. 26-29). There is a minimum of narrative tension in the scene. Then follows an even briefer narrative addendum about other cultic innovations Jeroboam undertakes (vv. 30-31).

JEROBOAM'S GOLDEN CALVES: 12:26-29

The scene has a loose structure: Jeroboam speaks to himself, then performs two actions; he speaks to the people, then performs two more actions.

Jeroboam is worried about the stability of his kingship. Solomon's magnificent Temple in Jerusalem, just a few short miles across the border, will attract northerners to participate in the splendor of its ceremonies. The Israelites may easily compromise their loyalty to Jeroboam if they continue to frequent Rehoboam's capital and to participate in rites that no doubt include prayer for the reigning monarch and in which he may even act as officiating priest (Solomon, after all, offered sacrifice on more than one occasion; see 3:4; 3:15; 8:62-64).

But Jeroboam reveals much about himself in the way he words his worries. A prophet of Yahweh assured him, in a solemn divine oracle, that he would become king, and despite his fugitive status in Egypt, the promise came true. But Jeroboam betrays an inner doubt: he calls Rehoboam by the restrictive title "King of Judah" twice, yet speaks of him as the "master" of Jeroboam's own people! Jeroboam seems to lack confidence not in himself but in God's word. His next words, "they will kill me," hardly ring true either. The narrator has shown us no grounds to suppose such a danger. Indeed, everything points to the high regard Israel has for Jeroboam: they kept in contact with him in his exile, recalled him as soon as possible, made him part of the team that negotiated with Rehoboam, and finally chose him as their king. Jeroboam's fears strike us as unrealistic and reinforce our impression that he does not trust in Yahweh's continuing favor.

To avert what he sees as impending disaster, Jeroboam makes two golden calves, which he presents to the people as gods. At this point we must pause to gain some historical and literary perspective. There are two issues we must consider: first, whether or not the golden calves are really idols; second, the echoes between this story and that of the golden calf in Exodus 32.

Historians are convinced that Jeroboam did not intend his calves to be representations of a god, that is, idols. It was standard practice in Ancient Near Eastern religions to depict deities as standing or sitting on animals. Even Yahweh in the Jerusalem Temple was thought of as invisibly enthroned on the cherubim atop the ark of the covenant. (Cherubim were some sort of mythological, composite creature, perhaps represented as winged lions.) It is likely that Jeroboam set up the calves as pedestals for the same deity, Yahweh, the recognized God of Israel. Jeroboam's innovation, then, would not have been the introduction of the worship of other gods but the establishment of Yahweh worship at new sanctuaries. (And in fact even this was not such an innovation, since Bethel and probably Dan as well were traditional sites for Yahweh worship long before Solomon's Temple in Jerusalem displaced them.) Accordingly, the portrayal of Jeroboam here is historically unreliable and is probably due to the author's pro-Judahite bias or, perhaps, to a generalized Judahite misunderstanding of the Israelite cult. Be that as it may, a literary analysis is different from a historical investigation and must deal with the text we have. The Jeroboam we meet in 1 Kings is an idolater and calls his golden calves "gods," even if that depiction defames the historical king.

The relationship between 1 Kings 12:26-31 and Exodus 32 is a matter of debate among scholars. If, as many experts speculate, the story of Aaron and the golden calf in Exodus 32 was composed *after* Jeroboam's schism as a way of heaping added scorn on the Israelite "heresy," then the original readers of the Jeroboam narrative may not have known the story we have in Exodus. But once both tales become widespread, and certainly when they both occupy a place in a collection of canonical literature, there are inevitable resonances between them.[1] A later reader can no more read of Jeroboam's golden calves without thinking of Aaron's than a modern moviegoer can hear Dukas's *The Sorcerer's Apprentice* without imagining Mickey Mouse. A literary analysis, therefore, cannot ignore those resonances, though it must recognize that they may not have been part of the original literary context of the story.

Jeroboam presents the golden calves to his people as the gods "who brought you up out of the land of Egypt" (compare Aaron's words in Exodus 32:4). This compounds Jeroboam's sin of idolatry by attempting to steal from Yahweh the very title on which Yahweh's relationship to the people was founded. The offense to Yahweh is extreme, and when one realizes that Jeroboam has just received his royal status through Yahweh's favor, the king's ingratitude is unspeakable. For the reader who knows the story in Exodus 32, the horror is greater. In Exodus the people's idolatry was followed by a violent slaughter in which three thousand people died (Exod 32:25-28). What might this portend for the future of Jeroboam's nation? Will they too fall into idolatry? And will disaster overtake them as well?

Jeroboam sets up the two calves in Dan and Bethel. The narrator does not tell us why Jeroboam chooses these two sites, though the king may intend to mark the boundaries of his kingdom: Dan is at the northern extremity of his territory, and Bethel is near his southern border with Judah. (Although the narrator does not allude to it, Bethel also had ancient roots in Israelite religious tradition: Jacob set up an altar to Yahweh there. See Gen 28:10-22 and 35:1-7.)

---

[1]One of the subtler resonances is found in the names of Aaron's and Jeroboam's sons. Aaron's oldest sons were Nadab and Abihu (*'ăbîhû'* means "He is my father"). Both died childless because of cultic improprieties (see Lev 10:1-2 and Num 3:4). Jeroboam's sons were Abijah (*'ăbîyāh* means "Yahweh is my father") and Nadab. Both died prematurely, the first by illness while Jeroboam was still alive (14:1-18), the second by assassination two years after succeeding Jeroboam on the throne (15:25-31); both deaths were due to Jeroboam's cultic sins (14:7-10).

OTHER INNOVATIONS: 12:30-31

The addendum begins with an evaluative comment by the narrator. He tells us that Jeroboam's establishment of idols at Dan and Bethel "became a sin" (v. 30a). The wording is important. He does not say that it "was" a sin, as if Jeroboam's personal idolatry is the principal issue. It "became" a sin, in that Jeroboam's actions lead the people of Israel into a practice of idolatrous worship. (We shall see later that this will develop into a major theme in the remainder of 1 and 2 Kings. The fullest term for it is "the sins of Jeroboam which he sinned and which he caused Israel to sin.") The rest of verse 30 explains how Jeroboam's misdeed "became" sin. Unfortunately, the Hebrew text may be corrupted at this point; it reads simply "and the people went before the one as far as Dan." The NRSV plausibly reconstructs the text by adding the clause about worshiping at Bethel on the basis of the ancient Greek. However the original Hebrew read, it is clear that the people followed Jeroboam into the idolatrous worship of the golden calves.

Jeroboam perpetrated two other cultic irregularities. He established high places, and he elevated to cultic office people who did not belong to Levi, the traditional priestly tribe of Israel.

Jeroboam Holds a Festival at Bethel: 12:32–13:10

The next section includes a long narrative introduction (12:32-33) and a dramatic scene of confrontation between Jeroboam and an anonymous man of God from Judah (13:1-10).

NARRATIVE INTRODUCTION: 12:32-33

The following literal rendering of the Hebrew shows the chiastic structure of the passage. It differs in several respects from the translation in the NRSV:

> A. Jeroboam made a festival
>   B. on the fifteenth day of the eighth month . . .
>   C. And he went up on the altar—thus he made in Bethel.
>   D. To sacrifice to the calves that he made,
>   D'. he set up at Bethel the priests of the high places that he made.
>   C'. And he went up on the altar which he made in Bethel

B'. on the fifteenth day of the eighth month . . .
A'. and he made a festival for the sons of Israel.
C". And he went up on the altar to offer incense.

The phrase "went up on the altar" is not as odd as it sounds in English. Ancient altars often incorporated large raised platforms that the officiating priest could ascend either by steps or by a ramp. The priest would then offer the sacrifice on top of the platform. The phrase is also ambiguous in Hebrew, since the verb form used can mean "he went up" (that is, he climbed) or "he made (something else) go up" (that is, he offered up a sacrifice). In C" it almost certainly means the former, but in the other two instances (C and C') it may mean either.

It is unusual in Hebrew narrative to find an introductory paragraph of such length, detail, and complex structure. These qualities focus a reader's attention on the introduction itself and warrant inquiring into its narrative effects. The first effect is to unify the description of Jeroboam's cultic innovations in 12:26-31 with the scene of confrontation that follows in 13:1-10. The establishment of a new festival is one more item in the list of Jeroboam's cultic inventions;[2] the Hebrew text strengthens this link by the repetition of a single verb, *'śh* ("to make, to do"), which the NRSV translates in a variety of ways: "he made *('śh)* houses on high places and appointed *('śh)* priests . . . and appointed *('śh)* a festival" (12:31-32). The festival itself becomes the link to the following scene, which takes place at Bethel on the festival day Jeroboam established. The final element of the introduction (C") forges an additional link by incorporating words from the introduction ("he went up on the altar") and from the following scene ("to offer incense"; see 13:1).

The second effect, closely related to the first, is to bring all Jeroboam's cultic deviations together in preparation for the scene of confrontation. The new festival forms the outer frame of the introduction; an altar at Bethel, which we have not heard about before, forms the inner frame; and the calves, priests, and high places he made occupy the center of the picture. The wealth of detail enhances our image of the situation. We envision Jeroboam traveling to Bethel in the middle of the eighth month and standing on a raised hilltop platform, surrounded by his non-levitical priests, to burn incense on an altar before a shining golden calf.

---

[2] The corresponding major festival in Judah was in the seventh month (see 8:2). Jeroboam's decision to celebrate in the eighth month is another of his illegitimate innovations; note how verse 33 emphasizes that this was a month "that he alone had devised." He celebrates at the wrong time, in the wrong place, on the wrong altar, in honor of the wrong gods.

A third effect is to awaken some echoes with the Solomon story. The narrator's attention to dates recalls a similar concern in the account of Solomon's Temple (6:1; 6:37-38; 8:2). This hints at a parallel between the stories of Solomon and of Jeroboam that we will explore later.

A fourth effect is to suggest the nature of the celebration described in 13:1-10. The festival is, presumably, an annual affair, since it is "like the festival that was in Judah." But this particular celebration is unusual: Jeroboam himself is officiating rather than the priests he placed in Bethel to offer sacrifice. The implied parallel with the Solomon story invites us to understand this ceremony as Jeroboam's dedication of the new calf-sanctuary in Bethel.

THE MAN OF GOD CONDEMNS JEROBOAM: 13:1-10

During Jeroboam's dedication ceremony, an anonymous man of God from the southern kingdom unexpectedly appears and delivers a dramatic oracle condemning the idolatrous altar at Bethel. The narrator arranged the scene chiastically, although the NRSV's translation is misleading in places and obscures the structure.

    A. Introduction (13:1)
       B. Oracle (13:2)
          C1. Parenthesis: sign given (13:3)
          C2. King's reaction and punishment (13:4)
          C1'. Parenthesis: sign fulfilled (13:5)
          C2'. King's reaction and healing (13:6)
       B'. Invitation and oracle (13:7-9)
    A'. Conclusion (13:10)

Grammatical forms in verses 3 and 5 mark those verses as parenthetical asides by the narrator to the reader. See the discussions of these two verses below.

The first verse is very vivid. The Hebrew has the force of making the scene immediately present: "Look! a man of God is coming from Judah by the word of Yahweh to Bethel, and Jeroboam is standing on the altar to offer incense!" (The NRSV reverses the order of the clauses for the sake of better English style.) The vividness and the use of comparable verb forms (both are participles) for the man of God and for Jeroboam initiates a thematic pattern of contrast between the two figures that will run through the story. The man of God is "coming"—in motion, active; Jeroboam is "standing"—passive and still. The verse also introduces a motif phrase, "by the word of Yahweh," that will come to dominate the chapter. It occurs frequently in 1 Kings 13—more often than in the rest of the Hebrew Bible. This phrase is one of the links that help unify the two stories in chapter 13; we will look at this in more detail later.

The prophet addresses his oracle to the altar itself. This would have struck the ancient reader very strongly. Nowhere else in Hebrew narrative does someone address words to an inanimate object.[3] This tactic (technically called "apostrophe") adds a dimension of opposition to the theme of contrast between man of God and king. We must picture the king standing on the altar platform in full ceremonial regalia and the man of God ignoring him completely to speak to the stones on which the king is standing. Even before the man of God delivers his oracle, his snub to the royal presence heralds Yahweh's anger at Jeroboam.

The oracle is unusually detailed, naming both Josiah, the king who will carry out the prophesied destruction, and the specific acts of desecration he will perform. The precision of the data is almost unique in prophetic oracles. Historians suspect that the author may in fact have composed our story *after* Josiah's time some three hundred years later; the details seem to enjoy the clarity of hindsight. But in this literary context the man of God's oracle is a true and unusually specific prophecy. The specificity of the prophecy points forward to the story of a much later time. The account of Josiah's campaign against Bethel appears in 2 Kings 23:15-20 and agrees closely with this oracle. The present oracle, then, is one end of a link that contributes to unifying all of 1–2 Kings. We will look briefly at the question of this larger unity at the very end of our study.

The divine words begin with the same vivid construction we saw in verse 1: "Look! a son is born to the house of David; his name is Josiah." The vividness intensifies the link with the fulfillment of the prophecy in 2 Kings 23: when evoked by the word of God, even the distant future is immediately present. This very oracle unleashes the divine power that makes the future inevitable. The identification of Josiah as a son of the house of David keeps alive the theme of a Davidic future and the hope of a Davidic restoration that we remarked previously (11:39; 12:19). Perhaps the Davidic scion who will undo Jeroboam's religious deviations will also be able to repair the political division in which his reign began.

---

[3]Hebrew poetry and prophecy will often address natural phenomena: earth, heavens, sea, mountains, sun, moon, stars, rain, hail, and the like. But even in poetry and prophecy, direct speech to a concrete object is rare, and it never occurs elsewhere in narrative.

The primary focus of the oracle is, of course, the condemnation of the altar and, by implication, of the entire cult associated with it. To sacrifice the priests upon their own idolatrous altar would be a fitting way of punishing them: they would be executed, as the law required, and the fashion of their execution—as human sacrifices—would provide an ironic commentary on their abominable crime of idolatry. Josiah's second action, burning human bones on the altar, would desecrate it irreparably, thus rendering it forever unfit for religious use. There is one chilling detail. The oracle refers to "the priests of the high places who offer incense upon you." To this point the only person spoken of as undertaking this particular priestly function, offering incense, is Jeroboam himself (12:33; 13:1). Since the ceremony apparently celebrates the dedication of the Bethel sanctuary, Jeroboam is likely the only one who has yet done so. In this way the oracle that so pointedly ignores the king by addressing the altar nevertheless implicates him obliquely in the prophesied destruction.

In verse 3 the narrator breaks frame to direct a parenthetical remark to the reader. Both the Hebrew grammatical form and the unnecessary introductory words show that we are not to read this statement as a continuation of the oracle in verse 2. Although the NRSV allows for this understanding, its phrasing is not completely clear. Translate (including the parentheses): "(He also gave a sign that day, saying, "This is the sign Yahweh has spoken: 'Look! the altar is torn down, and the ashes on it shall spill out!'")." In other words, this parenthetical sign is not part of the scene; we hear it but Jeroboam does not. The sign begins with the same vivid construction we saw in verses 1 and 2. In our mind's eye we see the altar split open and its sacred ashes pour onto the ground. The "ashes" are the remains of burnt offerings saturated with the melted fat that was the deity's choice portion of the animal. Because they were sacred to the deity, the priest had to dispose of them carefully, in a consecrated place (see, for instance, Lev 6:8-11). For the ashes to spill out onto the ground would be a desecration, in this case a dese-cration caused by Yahweh himself. We are not told when this will occur, or whether it will be associated with Josiah's purge. We infer that it will not happen earlier, since in that case the altar would already be desecrated and unusable, and Josiah's actions would be pointless.

Jeroboam reacts with a gesture and a word that transform the theme of contrast into a direct confrontation between king and man of God, and behind them between the king's gods and Yahweh. The man of God has spoken an oracle against the altar (literally, "upon the altar"), and Jeroboam lifts his hand from the altar (literally, "from upon the altar") to order the man of God's arrest. "Seize him!"—the king pits his own authority, bolstered by that of the gods he serves and upon whose altar he stands, against that of the man of God, who has claimed Yahweh as his master. Immediately the hand Jeroboam dares to raise against God's servant is paralyzed. Royal authority and the gods behind it are powerless before one who comes "by the word of Yahweh."

Dramatic tension is at its maximum. Will this singular demonstration of Yahweh's power suffice to bring Jeroboam to repentance? With exquisite timing, the narrator forces us to wait for resolution by breaking frame again to address a second parenthesis to the reader. The NRSV translation of verse 5 is misleading, since it includes the verse in the series of events that occurred at the king's ceremony. It is rather the narrator's affirmation to us that the man of God's prophecy in verse 3 was fulfilled by the time of the narrator. Translate (including the parentheses): "(And the altar *has been* torn down and the ashes on it spilled out, according to the sign that the man of God gave by the word of Yahweh.)" In addition to prolonging the suspense, this parenthesis has other effects on a reader. It confirms the reliability of God's word and draws an immediate connection from the scene of the story to the reader's own world. "Go to Bethel," says the narrator to us, "and look for yourselves. The shattered altar is there for all to see, just as the man of God said would happen." Even for us, readers for whom the altar's ruins themselves have long since disappeared, the message is clear: "This is real. God's word and its fulfillment work powerfully in our world."

Finally, if our surmise was correct that the altar's destruction could not take place earlier than Josiah's desecration of the altar, then the narrator also places himself in time as recounting the story sometime after Josiah's deeds. This has two implications, both of which go beyond the bounds of this study. First, it is evidence from within the story itself to support the historians' suspicion that the narrative of the prophecy was composed after its fulfillment had taken place. Second, it leads us to expect that when 2 Kings 23 recounts the fulfillment, it will match the prediction in all details. Any variations in the fulfillment will call for special attention.

After the parenthesis we return to the scene at Bethel, where Jeroboam is standing on the altar with his paralyzed arm outstretched against the man of God. His reaction is an implicit acknowledgment of the power of Yahweh and of the intercessory role of the man of God. His words are polite (the first word, "Entreat," carries an attached suffix that softens the imperative to a request), and simply request healing. Yet there is an ambiguity. Jeroboam calls Yahweh *"your* God." Certainly this is a confession that Jeroboam has abandoned Yahweh, but it contains no indication of return. To signal a change of heart plainly, Jeroboam would have to speak of "Yahweh *our* God." Jeroboam recognizes Yahweh's mastery but does not call him master. With no more prompting, the man of God intercedes for the king, and the king's arm is restored to health. This resolves the dramatic inner sub-plot of Jeroboam's paralysis, but the more fundamental issue remains open. Yahweh has decreed destruction for Bethel. Will Jeroboam repent of his idolatry? And if he does, will Yahweh reverse his decree?

Unexpectedly, Jeroboam invites the man of God to a meal and promises him a gift. On the surface this appears to be nothing more than royal hospitality and largesse. The man of God has just healed Jeroboam; the king is grateful. Beneath the surface, however, the invi-tation involves much more. First, the meal itself is ambiguous. Jeroboam says, literally, "Come with me to the house" (NRSV, "Come home with me"). But "house" can mean either "palace" or "temple," as we saw in the Solomon story, which spoke of the "house" of Yahweh as well as the "house" of the king. Does Jeroboam have a palace in this border town as well as in his capital? Or is Jeroboam inviting the man of God to join in a cultic meal at the sanctuary itself? The narrator does not tell us. Nor does he give us any indication of the king's motivation (as he did, for example, in 12:26).

We must speculate. Eating together, in the ancient world as in the modern, is a sign of solidarity. Jeroboam's invitation is an offer to join him in an expression of communion. The king either assumes that the healing of his arm has restored him wholly to Yahweh's good graces or, perhaps more likely, that the man of God's willingness to share fel-lowship with him will neutralize the divine rejection implicit in the oracle against the altar. Just as the man of God's oracle was thought of as word of power, so too a symbolic act like sharing a meal would unleash power to counter the oracle. If the "house" is the temple, the reversal would be even more startling: the man of God would join Jeroboam in the very cult Yahweh sent him to condemn.

Whatever Jeroboam's motivation, the man of God declines the invi-tation. This is the final transformation of the theme of contrast between the man of God and the king: invitation and refusal. The refusal is emphatic; its intensity makes it much less polite than the king's invi-tation and suggests that the man of God may harbor suspicions about Jeroboam's motivations too. He first rejects the king's offer of a gift, even if it were as much as half the kingdom (literally, "half your house"—playing on the "house" to which Jeroboam invited him). Then he turns down the invitation to a meal in graphic terms. He adds one telling phrase: he will not eat or drink "in this place." Jeroboam is not the problem—Bethel is. Though there can be no fellowship as long as the king persists in his idolatry, he can still repent and return to Yahweh. But the "house" of the golden calf, with its altar and its priests, is irrevocably doomed.

The man of God explains his refusal by repeating a personal command he received from Yahweh. God prohibited him in advance from just such behavior. In other words, part of his prophetic mission is to give a public sign, by not accepting hospitality, of the irrevocability of Yahweh's decree. (The significance of the third part of the prohibition is unclear. Some scholars think that returning by a different route has the same meaning: just as the man of God does not "backtrack," so too the word of God will not be reversed.) The conclusion of the story assures us that the man of God kept this third prohibition as scrupulously as he did the prohibitions against eating and drinking. There is, however, a very slight, almost unnoticeable indication that the story is not over. God's warning was simply "do not return by the road on which you go." The narrator, however, describes the man of God's compliance with two phrases. One corresponds to Yahweh's command: the man of God "does not return by the road on which he came." The other is that he "goes by another road." But this phrase does not use the word "return"; in other words, it tells us that the man of God sets out on a different road, but not that he comes all the way back to Judah. As we shall see in the next story, a tragic thing happens to him en route.

Chapter 12

THE WAGES OF SIN

1 Kings 13:11–14:20

The last two sections of the Jeroboam story are painted in darker colors. Both introduce death, and in neither case is the person who dies the principal evildoer. Both sections, then, evoke in us an uneasy sense that evil and its effects are more far-reaching and infectious than it first appears. In 13:11-32 the narrator leaves Jeroboam out of the picture and tells what befalls the man of God on his way home to Judah from Bethel. In the final section of the Jeroboam story (14:1-20), we meet Ahijah of Shiloh again, whose message to Jeroboam is that Yahweh rejects him and all his line. Between the two sections is a brief remark by the narrator that focuses on Jeroboam's continued sinfulness (13:33-34).

The Man of God and the Bethel Prophet: 13:11-32

The story of the betrayal of the man of God by the prophet of Bethel is haunting and mysterious. Both characters are nameless and both are enigmatic. The narrator gives us no insight into their motivations, yet we cannot help wondering why the prophet lies to the man of God and why the man of God succumbs to the deception. Above all, we wonder why such a tale is told and why it is told here, in the middle of the story of Jeroboam. (We will address the last question in our discussion of 13:33-34.)

The story consists of two parallel series of events, the second sequence lacking the final element. (The NRSV obscures the structure by putting a paragraph break after verse 25 instead of before it.)

    A. The prophet hears news of the man of God (13:11)
      B. He speaks in reaction to the news (13:12)

    C. He has his sons saddle his donkey (13:13)
      D. He journeys and finds the man of God (13:14-18)
        E. The man of God comes back and eats with him (13:19)
          F. The prophet speaks the word of Yahweh (13:20-22)
            G. The word is fulfilled (13:23-24)
A'. The prophet hears news of the man of God (13:25)
  B'. He speaks in reaction to the news (13:26)
    C'. He has his sons saddle his donkey (13:27)
      D'. He journeys and finds the man of God's corpse (13:28)
        E'. He brings back the man of God, and honors him (13:29-30)
          F'. He confirms the word of Yahweh (13:31-32)
            G'. . . .

This sort of structure is more developmental than contrastive. It focuses our attention on three dimensions of progression in the narrative: from element to element (A to B to C, etc.), from parallel element to parallel element (from A to A', etc.), and from sequence to sequence (from A through G to A' through G'). Not all these comparisons are equally significant; our discussion will attempt to highlight those that are.

THE FIRST SEQUENCE: 13:11-24

The story begins by introducing an old prophet from Bethel. The terms "man of God" and "prophet" are approximately synonymous (see, for example, the prophet's words to the man of God in verse 18). The narrator's care to distinguish the Bethel "prophet" from the "man of God" from Judah is not intended to convey a difference either in their professions or in their legitimacy. It is a practical matter. Since both figures are anonymous throughout the tale, the two terms are our primary means of identifying them. The narrator must keep them from becoming confused if we are to follow the story. (We will look at the reason for their anonymity when we consider the Jeroboam story as a single literary unit in the next chapter.)

The prophet is "old." The term here does not seem to imply either feebleness (as it did in David's case, 1:1) or wisdom (as it did in the case of Rehoboam's advisers, 12:6). Its importance is its literal meaning. If the prophet is old, he has presumably been a prophet for quite some time. He was probably a prophet of Yahweh before the days of the secession of the northern tribes and Jeroboam's cultic innovations. Yet he lives in the city where Jeroboam has set up one of his idolatrous calves. What is his allegiance now? Does he, like the man of God, still serve the word of Yahweh? Or has he, like Jeroboam, abandoned Yahweh for idolatry? He lives *in* Bethel, but has he also become a prophet *for* Bethel?

The prophet hears about the man of God's deeds and words in Bethel.[1] The deeds would include the oracle he delivered and the miracle of healing the king's arm. The words, since they are the words he spoke "to the king," would include information about the divine prohibition he is under against eating and drinking in Bethel and against retracing his steps. The prophet inquires about the man of God's present whereabouts and goes out after him. He says nothing to his sons (or to us) of his reasons. We can only follow him and try to discern what he is about from what he does.

The prophet finds the man of God sitting under a shade tree and begins a conversation. The prophet's first question and the man of God's response establish that the prophet has found the man he sought. When the prophet invites the man of God to join him at his home for a meal, we learn the reason for the prophet's journey; yet what we learn only raises more questions. The prophet knows of the man of God's claim that Yahweh has forbidden him to eat and drink in Bethel. Why would he incite the man of God to disobey Yahweh's command? If the prophet has become a servant of Jeroboam's calf-gods, then his reason could be similar to Jeroboam's: he is attempting to neutralize the man of God's oracle against the Bethel sanctuary. On the other hand, if the prophet is still faithful to Yahweh, he could be testing the man of God's bona fides: if the prophet can easily persuade the man of God to accept hospitality, it is unlikely that the man of God is an authentic bearer of Yahweh's word.

The narrator delays resolving the dilemma by having the man of God repeat fully the oracle we heard in verse 9. Yahweh's three prohibitions supply the framework for verses 16-19. First, the man of God refuses to return, to eat, or to drink; then he cites Yahweh's words forbidding him to eat, to drink, or to return. The prophet replies with his own oracle that the man of God should return (the NRSV's "bring him

---

[1]There is a strange shift in the Hebrew text of verse 2. "His son" tells him of the man of God's deeds, then "they" (his sons, apparently) tell him of the man of God's words. The shift from singular to plural is abrupt; the NRSV smooths the awkwardness by changing "his son" to "one of his sons." From here on the prophet's sons are always spoken of in the plural, and the singular in verse 2 seems to have no importance in the narrative.

back" is, literally, "make him return") and eat and drink. As a result, the man of God returns (NRSV, "went back"), eats, and drinks.

The prophet's claim to a contrary oracle is surprising; we have heard nothing of it before. That does not mean, of course, that it is false. It adds a third possibility to those we have already seen: the prophet may be a true servant of Yahweh who has received instructions to show his colleague hospitality as a sign of Yahweh's favor for a dangerous mission faithfully performed. We are, in effect, in the same position as the man of God, faced with the impossible dilemma of determining whether or not the old prophet is telling the truth.

The narrator, however, does not leave us in our uncertainty. He has to this point in this tale given us no glimpses at all into the inner life of his characters. Now he tells us bluntly, "He lied to him" (v. 18b). The narrative effect of this aside is strong. Our point of view abruptly changes. From an identification with the man of God based on shared uncertainty about the prophet, we suddenly move to a more objective, distanced perspective based on privileged information the narrator has shared with us. From this point on we will watch the man of God's tragic destiny unfold cushioned by this distance. Our sensitivity to his impossible dilemma (and therefore to the ultimate unfairness of his punishment) recedes; and our awareness of his disobedience is heightened with each repetition of the triad "return, eat, and drink." Our attitude toward the prophet changes too. We see him as evil, and perhaps our antipathy is the stronger because we have for so long entertained the possibility that he is good.

The man of God, however, succumbs to the prophet's deception and "returns, eats, and drinks." The narrator does not tell us what changed the man of God's mind nor whether he had any suspicion that the prophet was lying. This is consistent with the narrator's strategy. If he were to allow us too close an understanding of and sympathy with the man of God, the tale would focus too much on him as an individual and on the complex question of the justice of punishing unintentional sin. Since, as we shall see, both the prophet and the man of God are emblems of larger realities, and since the thrust of the tale is the inexorability of the divine word, the narrator centers our attention on the issues of obedience and disobedience to the word.

No sooner have we come to see the Bethel prophet as evil than the story takes an unexpected turn. He turns out to be an authentic prophet who receives a word from Yahweh! (We are entitled to wonder whether the event might not have surprised the old prophet as much as it does us.) The narrator intensifies the irony by dubbing him "the prophet who made him return"—that is, identifying him by his false prophecy in the very moment that he receives a true one. The prophet introduces the oracle he delivers to the man of God with the traditional prophetic formula "Thus says Yahweh," although in this case the oracle itself comes only after a long description of the man of God's wrongdoing. (Third-person references to "the word of Yahweh" and "the commandment that Yahweh your God commanded you" make it much more likely that verses 21-22a are the prophet's own words.) The description increases narrative tension by delaying the divine decree of punishment to the very end of verse 22. It is verbose ("you have disobeyed . . . and you have not kept the command-ment"), and it repeats the triad "return, eat, drink" almost twice more ("return" is left out the last time). Finally the doom falls: the man of God will not be buried in his ancestral tomb. There is something omi-nous but inconclusive about that punishment. It is ominous because lack of burial in one's family tomb usually results from death at a dis-tance from home; and this in turn hints at death from captivity, or vio-lence, or when traveling (and thus not in old age, when one would generally remain at home). It is inconclusive because it is not in itself a threat of imminent death; the man of God could return home safely and live many more years without escaping the fate decreed for him. But it introduces the specter of death when traveling, and the man of God is far from home. . . .

The opening words of verse 23 do not mean that the meal continued for a while; the prophet's oracle no doubt put an end to the festivities. The prophet himself saddles one of his own donkeys for the man of God. (The Hebrew has a singular where the NRSV reads a plural, "they saddled.") This is a further act of hospitality, since the prophet's sons usually do this for him (vv. 13, 27). The narrator reminds us that the prophet is the one who "made him return," perhaps to suggest that this act of hospitality is the prophet's attempt to apologize to the man of God for his earlier deception.

The man of God sets out, and, in an ironic echo of verse 14, where the prophet "found" him sitting under the tree, a lion[2] "finds" (NRSV, "met") him on the road and kills him. His body lies in the road. Then comes the wonder that makes possible the second half of the tale. Instead of devouring its kill or attacking the donkey, the lion simply stands next to the body. And instead of fleeing the predator, the don-key too stands next to the body. It is as if, in death, the man of God acquires an honor guard to watch over his remains. Such behavior clearly signals that the hand of God is directing events, and ends the first part of the tale with a sense that there is more to come.

[2]Although there are no lions in the Holy Land nowadays, they were a hazard in ancient times. See, for example, Judges 14:5-9 and 1 Samuel 17:31-37.

THE SECOND SEQUENCE: 13:25-32

In examining the second part of the story, we will look both at the events as they unfold and at the significant observations that emerge when we compare each element with its parallel in the first part.

The second part of the story begins with the vivid present construction we have seen before: "And here come people passing by!" They see both the body and the wonder of the lion's passivity, and bring the report to the old prophet's town. (The parallel of elements A and A' is emphasized by the echo of verse 11a, "there lived an old prophet in Bethel," in verse 25b, "the town where the old prophet lived.")

The prophet recognizes (probably because of the lion's odd behavior) that this must be the man of God and deduces what happened, and that it is in fulfillment of Yahweh's oracle. (His deduction is not entirely accurate: the lion does not "tear" the man of God.) There is an interesting contrast between elements B and B'. In the first, the prophet must ask his sons for basic information; in the second, he has been transformed into a bearer of Yahweh's word, and he can interpret hearsay with uncanny insight and accuracy.

As in the first part, the prophet sets out after the man of God with no word of explanation either to his sons or to us. He again "finds" the man of God (or rather, this time, his body). In the first half there ensues a conversational exchange between the prophet and the man of God; in the second half this is transformed into the shared silence of the two animals standing by the body. The dialogue makes element D much longer than the parallel D'. As discussed above, the narrator uses this greater length to increase narrative tension and to highlight the motivic triad of "return, eat, and drink." There is a further ironic contrast. The conversation in the first half repeatedly speaks of Yahweh's command that the man of God not eat. In the second half the narrator points out to us that the lion does not eat the body. The beast, unlike the man, is obedient to Yahweh.

Again the Bethel prophet finally reveals his intentions through his actions. He has come to fetch the body and give it burial, thereby fulfilling the letter of Yahweh's oracle that the man of God would not be buried in his own ancestral tomb. In another ironic echo of the first sequence, where the man of God "returned with him" (v. 19), now the prophet "makes him return" (NRSV, "brought it back"; but the pronoun in Hebrew refers to "the man," not to "the body"). In the first half the man of God's return leads to a celebration of hospitality. Sharing a meal usually symbolizes communion in life. Unknown to the man of God, however, this meal conceals betrayal and will lead in fact to his death. In the second half the man of God's return leads to a ceremony of burial and mourning. The ceremony reveals an ironic renewal of sincere communion (they[3] mourn him as "my brother," and prophet and man of God will share a tomb) and points forward to a miraculous salvation the man of God will achieve for his betrayer (see below). An even deeper irony hides in the term "my brother." By this phrase the prophet, so to speak, adopts the man of God into his own family. The man is buried, then, not in his ancestors' tomb but in a tomb nonetheless belonging to his "family."

The prophet's speech to his sons parallels the oracle he delivered in the first half of the tale. His speech has two parts: instructions to his sons to bury him in the same tomb as the man of God (v. 31b) and a confirmation that the man of God's disobedience has not neutralized his original oracle (v. 32).

Mention of the tomb creates a link with element F, where Yahweh's word decreed that the man of God would not come to his ancestral tomb. The description of the tomb as the one "in which the man of God is buried" instead of "my tomb" indicates that what is important for the prophet is not that the tomb is his own (presumably ancestral) tomb, but that he be in proximity to the man of God's body. His next words, that his bones should lie alongside the man of God's bones, stress the same idea. As usual, the prophet gives no reason for his instructions. Since his next words will affirm the continuing validity of the man of God's oracle, we may surmise that the prophet's desire reflects his new solidarity with the man of God in service to the word of God. (In fact, the instructions will bear unexpected fruit in 2 Kings 23:16-18, when Josiah, the prophesied destroyer of Bethel's idolatrous sanctuary, spares the tomb where the man of God is buried, thereby sparing the old prophet's bones from desecration as well.)

The prophet's confirmation of the man of God's oracle is emphatic; the NRSV's "shall surely come to pass" paraphrases an untranslatable Hebrew idiom that adds strong stress to the sentence. But the prophet does not simply repeat what the man of God announced; he adds to it a significant clause: "and against all the houses of the high places that are in the cities of Samaria." The prophesied destruction will extend far beyond the confines of Bethel to idolatrous sanctuaries throughout much of the northern kingdom. The prophet, in other words, is not simply commenting on the continuing validity of the man of God's words; he is himself delivering a prophecy, one that incorporates and

---

[3]The unexpected plural here is puzzling, especially in view of the immediate return to the singular in "Alas, *my* brother," which can only be the words of the old prophet. Presumably the other mourners are the prophet's sons (the "sons" of a prophet, in Hebrew, are sometimes his disciples rather than his offspring).

exceeds the original one. This explains why the man of God's disobedience and death do not neutralize his oracle: the very prophet who tricked him into deviating from Yahweh's road picks up the burden the man of God laid down and carries it onward.

The most significant difference between the first and second parts of the story is the absence of element G' in the second half. This deprives the story of a sense of closure on two levels: the structure cries out for resolution like a musical scale that stops with the subtonic; and the contents, a divine oracle, look forward to future fulfillment to complete them. In this way the story begins to build a bridge that will span large sections of time and text and reach all the way to 2 Kings 23. In 2 Kings 23:16-18 Josiah spares the common tomb of the man of God and the Bethel prophet; in 2 Kings 23:19 he destroys "all the houses of the high places that are in the cities of Samaria" (the words in 1 Kings 13:32 and 2 Kings 23:19 are identical in Hebrew, though the NRSV varies them); and in 2 Kings 23:20 he desecrates the altars in exactly the ways the man of God prophesied against the Bethel altar in 1 Kings 13:2.

THE WHOLE STORY

Now that we have looked at the entire passage, we can examine more closely the third level on which the story develops, namely, the progression from the first sequence to the second. Each sequence represents a separate stage of development for each of the two main characters.

In the first sequence the Bethel prophet begins by trying to nullify the word of Yahweh (although this does not become clear to us until the narrator informs us that "he lied to him"). Whether or not he was a prophet of Yahweh in his younger days, his loyalties now belong to Bethel and Jeroboam's new religion. By the end of the first sequence, the Bethel prophet undergoes an ironic transformation: he becomes, willy-nilly, the bearer of an authentic word of Yahweh. The man of God, on the other hand, moves tragically in the course of the first sequence. From a faithful and obedient servant of Yahweh he becomes unwittingly disobedient and finally dies for his error. Behind both transformations stands the inexorable word of Yahweh. When one bearer proves deficient, it casts him aside and seizes another.

In the second sequence the Bethel prophet is different. He has become, however unwilling and unworthy, a bearer of Yahweh's word, and therefore a "brother" to the man of God. He risks the lion to retrieve and honor the body of his brother with burial and mourning, and thus offsets his earlier deception and betrayal. Ultimately he makes his own the very oracle he tried to neutralize. His ironic movement thus culminates in his becoming witness against his own king and cult in service to the word he once betrayed. By contrast, the man of God's tragic movement is reversed. Slain, he is honored by the lion who slew him, by the donkey who carried him, and by the prophet who betrayed him. He is mourned, buried with reverence, and his memory is commended to the next generation. In 2 Kings 23 he is revealed at the last as a salvific figure whose reputation protects the Bethel prophet's bones from violation.

These patterns are reflected in the very language of the text. One key word is the verb *šwb* ("to return, turn back"), which occurs in its various forms nine times in verses 11-32. It gives the whole story a feeling of repeated reversals in both physical and moral direction, and thus emblematizes the various twists that transmute the prophet's Bethelite patriotism into Yahwistic piety and transform the man of God from prophet of destruction to victim to agent of salvation. A second key word, Hebrew *yšb* (which means both "to dwell" and "to sit"), reflects the original separation and ultimate communion of the two prophetic figures. We learn in verse 11 that the old prophet lived *(yōšēb)* in Bethel. In verse 14, at the other end of his journey, the prophet finds the man of God sitting *(yōšēb)* under a tree. In verse 20 they are sitting (plural, *yōšĕbîm*) together at table, foreshadowing their eventual resting together in a common tomb.

Jeroboam Is Intransigent: 13:33-34

Between the stories of 13:11-32 and 14:1-20 the narrator inserts a two-verse evaluation of Jeroboam. The wording recalls 12:30-31; indeed, the two passages are almost mirror images:

A. "This thing became sin" (12:30)
    B. houses on high places (12:31a)
        C. "he made priests from among all the people" (12:31b)
        C'. "he made from among all the people priests" (13:33b)
    B'. priests for the high places (13:33c)
A'. "This thing became sin" (13:34)

This lengthy series of verbal links builds a complex inclusion around the two stories in chapter 13 and invites us to look at them together as a single unit.

THE TWO STORIES

Several links connect the two stories. Most obvious, of course, is the figure of the man of God from Judah, who is prominent in both. The two oracles he pronounces in the first story, one against the altar and the other concerning his own behavior, both reappear in the second story. The unusual phrase "by the word of Yahweh" is a leitmotif in chapter 13; it occurs seven times here and only five times in the rest of the Hebrew Bible. Finally, both stories find their explicit completion and the fulfillment of their prophecies in the account of Josiah in 2 Kings 23.

As the man of God's single story, chapter 13 shows him in three confrontational situations: before the king, before an opposing prophet, and before God. These three situations are almost paradigmatic for the complexities of the prophetic vocation, and will recur repeatedly not only in the Books of Kings but in the prophetic literature as well. We shall see Elijah, for example, confronting King Ahab (1 Kgs 17, 18, and 21), opposing the prophets of Baal (1 Kgs 18), and even challenging Yahweh himself (1 Kgs 19). We will also see other prophets confronting both kings and contrary prophets of Yahweh (1 Kgs 20 and 22).

Insofar as 1 Kings 13 is an exemplar of what it means to be a "man of God," it is really at its deepest level a story of the word of God itself. The motivic phrase "by the word of Yahweh" (the Hebrew is, literally, "*in* the word of Yahweh") means something like "in the power of/by the authority of the word of Yahweh." The word is not simply something passive, entrusted by Yahweh to the man of God and delivered by the man of God like an inert message. It is active; it is power and authority. The man of God speaks and acts "in the word of Yahweh" as in a cloud of divine energy. And nothing succeeds in derailing the momentum of that power. Before it the royal arm shrivels, and the Bethel prophet's lie rebounds on his own head: he takes up the office left vacant by the man of God's defection. And nothing will succeed in derailing it in the future, neither the unbroken history of Israelite infidelity nor the equally unbroken history of Judahite compromise, both of which constitute the story of the divided kingdoms in 1–2 Kings. For, centuries later, "a son will be born to the house of David, Josiah by name."

THE INCLUSIVE FRAME

The frame (12:30-31 and 13:33-34) adds another dimension to the unity of chapter 13. It incorporates the whole chapter into the story of Jeroboam, despite the fact that Jeroboam does not figure at all in 13:11-32. The opening words of 13:33 insist on the connection. It explicitly sets the narrator's editorial remark "after this event," that is, after the dramatic death and burial of the man of God. And it picks up the key word "return, turn back" and even the image of the man of God "returning from the road" by accusing Jeroboam of "not turning (Hebrew, *šwb*) from his evil road (NRSV, "way")." The contrast is ironic: the man of God, who was on the right road, turned back; Jeroboam, whose road is evil, does not.

By repeating after the events of chapter 13 the same information and almost the same words about Jeroboam's cultic evils, the narrator implies that the intervening events make no lasting impression on the king. He has heard the man of God's condemnation of the altar and felt the power of that condemnation in his own flesh, withered and then restored. He has heard, surely, of the man of God's violent death and miraculous honor guard, and of the Bethel prophet's confirmation of the original oracle. Yet he perseveres, apparently unperturbed, in his evil ways. To the offenses of idolatrous sanctuaries and illicit priests, Jeroboam adds obduracy.

There is one small but telling variation in 13:34 that is not reflected in the NRSV. In 12:30 we read, "This thing *(haddābār)* came to be a sin"; 13:34 begins "*In* this thing *(baddābār)* came to be the sin of the house of Jeroboam." What is the king's sin in the first case becomes in the second the starting point for a whole dynasty's wickedness. The variation also awakens a bitter echo with the key phrase "by the word *(baddābār)* of Yahweh." The king's evildoing, his *dābār*, encroaches on the realm proper to Yahweh's word, the divine *dābār*. God's word has shown itself invincible, however, and the inevitable result will be the downfall of the house of Jeroboam, "to cut it off and destroy it from the face of the earth."

Ahijah of Shiloh Condemns Jeroboam: 14:1-20[4]

The last section of the Jeroboam story is not a fully developed narrative. It is a long speech of Ahijah the prophet set in a relatively sketchy narrative setting. There is, nonetheless, a skillful manipulation of narrative tension to achieve strong emotional effects. Grammatical indicators divide the story into three unequal sections: a scene between Jeroboam and his wife (vv. 1-4a); a scene between Ahijah and Jeroboam's wife (vv. 4b-17a); and a very brief conclusion (vv. 17b-18). The two scenes have similar structures:

---

[4]I have profited a great deal in my reading of this passage from the commentary of Richard D. Nelson, *First and Second Kings* (Interpretation; Atlanta: John Knox, 1987), pp. 90–97.

A. Background information (14:1)
   B. Jeroboam's speech to his wife (14:2-3)
      C. Jeroboam's wife "arose" (NRSV, "set out"), "went," and "came" (14:4a)
A'. Background information (14:4b-5)
   B'. Ahijah's speech to Jeroboam's wife (14:6-16)
      C'. Jeroboam's wife "arose," "went," and "came" (14:17a)
Conclusion (14:17b-18)

The last verses of the section are a formulaic notice of Jeroboam's death and burial and the succession of his son (vv. 19-20). There are, unfortunately, a number of places in the story where the Hebrew text poses severe difficulties. We will comment on them below.

JEROBOAM SENDS HIS WIFE TO CONSULT AHIJAH: 14:1-4a

The opening words are misleading in English. The Hebrew idiom does not mean to set this story at the same time as the preceding chapter. On the contrary, Ahijah's advanced age and the evidence of strained relations between him and the king suggest that quite some time has elapsed since Jeroboam's defection from the worship of Yahweh. A better rendering than "At that time" would be a paraphrase, "There came a time when." The reason for the phrase is to establish a small verbal link with the scene in chapter 11 where Ahijah announced Jeroboam's kingship; see 11:29, where "about that time" translates the same Hebrew phrase as we find here.

We know nothing of Jeroboam's son except his name. Even his age is unclear. Jeroboam will call him a "lad" in verse 3, as will the narrator in verse 17 (Hebrew, *na'ar*; NRSV, "child" in both places), while Ahijah calls him a "child" (Hebrew, *yeled*) in verse 12. These two terms can cover a wide range of ages from toddler to a fully mature young man. Nor do we know whether he is Jeroboam's eldest and presumed successor. We know that he is sick (this is the premise of the plot) and, unnecessarily, his name. What's in a name? In this case, several things. First, knowing Abijah's name enables us to identify more closely with him. The illness of Abijah, whom we know by name, has greater immediacy than that of some anonymous son. The name is, furthermore, a strikingly inappropriate one for the son of an idolatrous king. It means, "Yahweh is my father"! The narrator offers no explanation of why Jeroboam would give his son a Yahwistic name. Perhaps Abijah was born before the king fell into idolatry, or perhaps the name was an oblique homage to Ahijah ("Yahweh is my brother"), the prophet who named Jeroboam to the throne. Whatever Jeroboam's intentions in the naming, the name itself relates Abijah directly to both Yahweh and to Ahijah and implicitly distances him from Jeroboam's gods and cult. In the ancient world everyone understood that "the sins of the fathers were visited upon the children"; but in Abijah's case his name hints at reasons to hope that he may escape his father's punishment.

Jeroboam sends his wife, in disguise, to consult Ahijah at Shiloh about his son's illness. That the king does not go himself suggests that he is no longer on good terms with the prophet. That he tells his wife to conceal her identity suggests more: the breach is not merely personal between Ahijah and Jeroboam but involves the king's whole family. Jeroboam recalls Ahijah's oracle that named him king of Israel (11:29-39). His phrasing is nuanced. What the NRSV translates as a simple relative clause ("Ahijah is there, who said of me . . .") involves in Hebrew two emphatic words ("*Look,* Ahijah is there. *He* said of me . . ."). The emphasis is on why Jeroboam wishes to consult Ahijah rather than some other prophet who might be more favorable to Jeroboam. Since Ahijah is, so to speak, the divinely appointed godfather of Jeroboam's dynasty, his intercession for the king's son would be particularly appropriate and perhaps particularly effective.

Prophets earned their livelihood from their ministry, so it is quite in order for Jeroboam's wife to take him food (compare, for example, 1 Samuel 9:6-10). Her offering is reasonable for an ordinary citizen with a comparable request; to take gifts appropriate to her royal status would defeat the purpose of her disguise. (The word rendered "cakes" in the NRSV is uncertain. It literally means "dots" and may refer to some sort of baked goods covered with seeds or raisins.) Jeroboam's statement that "*he* (emphatic pronoun) will tell you what shall happen" does not merely expect information. The pronoun emphasizes the prophet. Just as he once foretold Jeroboam's kingship with a word of power that ultimately proved true, Jeroboam hopes that he will now speak another word of power both announcing and effecting Abijah's recovery.

Jeroboam's wife carries out her husband's instructions. The narrator abbreviates, leaving out the disguise and the gift. This both speeds the tale along and also allows the narrator to use the wife's actions structurally to end each of the two scenes with the triad "arose, went, came" (vv. 4a, 17a).

AHIJAH OF SHILOH'S SPEECH: 14:4b-17a

The second scene also begins with background information. We learn first that Ahijah is blind; then we learn that Yahweh has informed him of the impending visit from Jeroboam's wife.

It is not clear whether Ahijah's eyesight is merely failing (as the NRSV would have it) or whether he is completely blind. The Hebrew idiom is not specific. But the narrator assures us that the affliction is due to old age, lest we suspect that Ahijah may be under divine displeasure. The prophet's disability is a crucial part of the plot development. It heightens the miraculous character of the moment when Ahijah recognizes Jeroboam's wife: there is no chance that the sightless old man could penetrate her disguise without divine help. We know from verse 5 that Yahweh has told Ahijah everything. But the miracle demonstrates to Jeroboam's wife as well that the word this prophet speaks is divinely guaranteed.

Yahweh forewarns Ahijah of the woman's identity and the reason behind her visit. The NRSV overlooks the vivid present construction in the Hebrew that situates Yahweh's speech at the moment Jeroboam's wife arrives. The Lord says, "Here comes the wife of Jeroboam to inquire of you . . . ." The next words, "Thus and thus you shall say to her," are an example of a narrative technique that translates awkwardly into English. It does not mean that God said "thus and thus"; it means that the narrator is abbreviating the divine speech. The technique can be used to avoid repeating information the reader already knows (as in 2:30); here it is used to keep the reader in suspense about what will happen.

The last words of verse 5 are a very odd construction in Hebrew. The NRSV follows the ancient translations and makes a very slight change to the text; the result is that these words become part of the narrative rather than part of Yahweh's speech. As the Hebrew text stands, the words must be understood as belonging to Yahweh, though they are still very awkward grammatically. A tentative translation would be: "And as she is coming, she is in disguise." Narratively this reading is more likely than the NRSV's. If the words are not Yahweh's to Ahijah, the prophet has no way of knowing that Jeroboam's wife is in disguise (or, as the NRSV puts it, "pretending to be another woman"); yet his first words to her when she arrives are "why do you pretend to be another?"

Though Ahijah cannot see, he can hear her footsteps at his door. He invites her in and unmasks her immediately: "Come in, wife of Jeroboam; why are you in disguise?" Blind eyes, illumined by Yahweh's word, see through every human pretense. Ahijah's next words forewarn her that his news will not be good. This is the first inkling we get of the divine message the narrator withheld from us. But we have not begun to suspect just how devastating the news will be. The rest of Ahijah's speech falls into two parts. The first is an oracle to Jeroboam, which the king's wife is to deliver to him (vv. 7-11). It begins and ends with traditional prophetic formulas, "Thus says Yahweh" and "for Yahweh has spoken." Yahweh speaks in the first person ("I") and addresses Jeroboam in the second person ("you"). In the second part of the speech Ahijah speaks in his own name to Jeroboam's wife; Yahweh and Jeroboam are both spoken of in the third person (vv. 12-16). The second part, therefore, is somewhat less formal, though it still presumably derives from the message Yahweh gave to Ahijah. The formulation simply allows us to understand it as Ahijah's paraphrase of the message, where the oracle is presented as Yahweh's own words.

The oracle to Jeroboam is shocking in two respects. The narrator has primed us to expect an oracle about Abijah's illness. What we get is a wholesale condemnation of Jeroboam and his entire line. Second, Yahweh's language is violent and extremely crude. God does not merely condemn Jeroboam's house; he damns it in gutter language. The oracle is couched in terms that sound like a formal indictment. First comes a list of Yahweh's deeds in Jeroboam's favor (vv. 7-8a), then a list of Jeroboam's sins against Yahweh (vv. 8b-9), followed by the punishment Yahweh will impose (v. 10). The oracle ends with a devastating poetic couplet (v. 11).

The lists of Yahweh's deeds and Jeroboam's sins contain several explicit quotations from Ahijah's oracle in chapter 11. They are concentrated in verse 8. "Tore the kingdom away from the house of David" parallels 11:31; "and gave it to you" parallels 11:35; "my servant David, who kept my commandments" parallels 11:34; and "doing only that which was right in my sight" parallels 11:33. These and other allusions to the earlier oracle emphasize the contrast between Yahweh's approval of Jeroboarn there and the condemnation here. We will see in our next chapter how the parallel of the two oracles serves the structure of the whole Jeroboam story.

Yahweh's deeds are four (the NRSV obscures the impression of a list by rephrasing some of the elements to subordinate clauses): "I exalted you, I gave you as leader, I tore the kingdom away, I gave it to you." The repeated verb "gave" emphasizes the gratuity of Yahweh's favors to Jeroboam. Jeroboam's crimes demonstrate that he has failed to keep the condition imposed on him in Ahijah's earlier oracle, that he "walk in my ways, and do what is right in my sight by keeping my statutes and my commandments as David my servant did" (11:38). In contrast to David, who "did what was right," Jeroboam has "done evil," and his evil is greater than that of anyone before him. Jeroboam's offense is threefold. He made other gods (in violation of the first commandment of the Decalogue); he cast images (in violation of the second commandment); and he turned his back on Yahweh. (This last means that he did not merely worship other gods *alongside* Yahweh but *instead of* Yahweh.)

The punishment begins with a vivid present: "Therefore, here I come bringing evil upon the house of Jeroboam!" (v. 10). The sentence is a generalization that evokes the law of talion. ("Talion" is the law that assures that the punishment fits the crime. It is usually cited as "An eye for an eye, a tooth for a tooth.") Jeroboam has done "evil" against Yahweh; Yahweh will bring "evil" upon Jeroboam.

The next sentences describe the punishment in gross and graphic metaphors. The general sense is clear; unfortunately several individual words are not. The first statement is bowdlerized by the NRSV to "I will cut off from Jeroboam every male, both bond and free in Israel." For "every male" the Hebrew reads a vulgarity: "one who urinates against a wall." (The meaning of the Hebrew phrase translated "bond and free" is completely unsure. It is likely intended to be inclusive of every male in Jeroboam's house as English phrases like "man and boy" or "old and young" would be.) The second statement is also unsure. The verb, which the NRSV translates "consume" once and "burn up" once, may also mean "sweep out." Another word (which the NRSV leaves out completely) is either the preposition "after, behind" or a noun meaning "descendants." Here are two possible translations for the sentence: "I shall burn up the descendants of the house of Jeroboam as one burns up dung until it is all gone." (The very poor used dried dung for fuel. Food cooked on dung fires was apparently considered unclean; see Ezek 4:9-15.) Or, "I shall sweep up behind the house of Jeroboam as one sweeps out dung until it is all gone." Whatever the exact meaning, it is clear that Yahweh's vulgarity continues, and that he is comparing the house of Jeroboam to a pile of dung.

The oracle ends with two bitter poetic lines announcing that none of Jeroboam's descendants will receive proper burial. Whether they die in the city or die in the country, their bodies will be food for scavengers (v. 11).

The second part of Ahijah's speech is directed personally to Jeroboam's wife. (The NRSV leaves out an emphatic pronoun; verse 12 actually begins, "But *you*, arise, go to your house.") It begins with the triad "arise, go, come" that characterizes Jeroboam's wife throughout this chapter. At last we learn that Abijah will not survive his illness, but how cruel the news is! The woman herself becomes the walking herald of his death. The feet that announced her arrival to Ahijah will announce the arrival of death for Abijah.

The oracle to Jeroboam declared that none of Jeroboam's descendants would receive proper burial. Here an exception is made for Abijah. The people will mourn him and bury him fittingly, since "in him is found something pleasing to Yahweh." As his name led us to hope, Abijah has a special relationship to Yahweh; sadly, it is not enough to preserve him from the fate his father's infidelity merits for his whole house. The next step of the speech (v. 14) broadens the view from Abijah to Jeroboam's dynasty. The narrator has already told us that Yahweh intends to destroy it; here we learn how. Yahweh will do to Jeroboam as he did to Solomon: he will "raise up" a foe (cf. 11:14, 23), a new king who will "cut off" (a Hebrew idiom for destroy) the house of Jeroboam.

The last words of verse 14 (NRSV, "today, even right now!") are, quite simply, hopeless. They are barely translatable: "This is the day; and what? even now." They may reflect an ancient textual corruption or perhaps a marginal annotation that some subsequent copyist incorporated into the text. The only way we can make even minimal sense of them at this point in the narrative is to read them as an alien voice (for even the narrator's interruptions are more smoothly accomplished than this) speaking to us from the days of the downfall of Jeroboam or perhaps of the northern kingdom: "This is happening! Now, what next?"

Ahijah's speech broadens still further. Its purview grows to include the whole of the northern kingdom, not just the house of Jeroboam. Israel itself shall undergo punishment. A new set of images drawn from the plant world depicts Israel as a river reed aswirl in the current or as a crop plant uprooted from arable soil. Both images foreshadow the exile of the northern tribes "across the River" (that is, across the Euphrates, as the NRSV paraphrases it). Once more we have the opening of a link to a much later story in 2 Kings; Israel's conquest by Assyria and subsequent exile are recounted in 2 Kings 17. Israel's sin, like Jeroboam's, is idolatry. Where Jeroboam made golden calf-idols, the people of Israel make *'ăšērîm* (NRSV, "sacred poles"), or cult objects representing the goddess Asherah. Like Jeroboam's, Israel's idolatry "provokes Yahweh to anger" (v. 15; cf. v. 9). These parallels point to a deeper connection between Jeroboam's sin and Israel's that the last words of Ahijah's speech bring out. Jeroboam's sin also *caused* Israel to sin. The "sin" of Jeroboam (a thematic phrase that will recur frequently in 1–2 Kings) has come to term. It was first simply "sin" (12:30), then "the sin of the house of Jeroboam" (13:34), and finally "the sin which he sinned and which he caused Israel to sin" (14:16).

As we have seen in several other passages, the narrator hides a double meaning beneath ambiguous wording and syntax. The NRSV translation is correct, but the word translated "because of" *(bgll)* evokes an echo with the word "dung" *(gll)* from verse 10. The sentence could also be translated, "Yahweh will give Israel up for the dung of the sins of Jeroboam . . . ." God's opinion of Israel's sin is no less insulting than it is of Jeroboam's.

The scene ends with Jeroboam's wife returning home with the triad of "arose, went, came." The narrator has not mentioned the city of Tirzah before in 1 Kings, but later remarks that four of the next five kings of Israel reigned from there suggest that Jeroboam may have moved his capital there from Shechem or Penuel (12:25). If so, this is a further indication that this last Jeroboam story occurs relatively late in Jeroboam's reign.

Conclusion: 14:17b-18

The conclusion recounts in almost the same words the fulfillment of Ahijah's prophecy to Jeroboam's wife about Abijah. He dies at the moment Jeroboam's wife arrives home, and all Israel buries and mourns him. The narrator's remark that all this occurred "according to the word of Yahweh" does not merely remind us of the prophecy and call our attention to its accuracy. Since Ahijah's speech also included the oracle to Jeroboam and prophecies about a new king over Israel, the destruction of Jeroboam's whole house, and the eventual exile of Israel, the meticulous precision of the first fulfillment is a guarantee that the rest of what Ahijah foretold will come to pass with equal accuracy.

In the light of the exactitude with which the fulfillment matches the prediction, it is worthwhile examining the narrative effect of the one noticeable deviation. Ahijah said that Abijah would die when Jeroboam's wife entered the city; the narrator tells us that he died when she came to the threshold of the house. The sentence is, first of all, not in the narrative past, as the NRSV translates it, but in something closer to the English historical present: "She comes to the threshold of the house, and the child dies." This vividness, along with the realization that she almost, but not quite, reached her son's side before his death, increases enormously the poignancy of her mission and the bitterness of her bereavement. Finally, the phrase allows the narrator to suggest another subtle wordplay: the phrases "threshold of the house" (*sap habbayit*) and "ending of the house" (*sôp habbayit*) differ by only a vowel. The death of Abijah is the beginning of the end for the house of Jeroboam.

Narrative Effect and Characterization

The principal narrative effect of this passage is to draw tightly together threads from the rest of the Jeroboam story. The most obvious link, of course, is with chapter 11, Ahijah's first speech to Jeroboam. Not only does the oracle of doom contrast with the earlier oracle of promise, but also the theme of the condition imposed on Jeroboam that he act according to the model of David (11:38) comes to closure here (14:8). The narrative connects with the rest of the Jeroboam story as well. Yahweh's words to Jeroboam in verse 7 that "I exalted you from among the people and made you leader over my people Israel" recall Jeroboam's leadership of the people at Shechem and his eventual choice as king in 12:1-20. The accusation that he made other gods and cast images (v. 9) is a reference to the cultic innovations of 12:26-31. In addition, this narrative shares with all of chapter 13 the dominant theme of the power of the word of God.

There is little characterization of either Jeroboam or Ahijah in the passage. We infer Jeroboam's alienation from Ahijah; and we learn of the prophet's continued faithfulness to Yahweh—and therefore of his relative independence from his king's religious policies. His word of forewarning to Jeroboam's wife at the end of verse 6 may indicate a compassion for her plight in view of the painful news he must give her. On the other hand, the narrator draws a most poignant portrait of Jeroboam's wife, whose name we never learn and whose voice we never hear. The narrative characterizes her with three verbs of motion: she arises, she goes, she comes (vv. 2-3, 4, 12, 17; the NRSV does not reflect the verbs accurately in every case). She is a shuttlecock sent back and forth between stiff-necked king (who seeks a word but will not bend enough even to ask for healing for his son) and hostile prophet (who returns a word, but it is crude and cruel). She is reduced to a passive function, a speechless messenger. As Abijah's mother, she must be filled with maternal concern (the word for compassion in Hebrew derives from the word "womb"). Her feelings, however, remain unspoken and unconsidered until, in the unkindest cut of all, she herself becomes the sign and, in a certain sense, the agent of her son's death.

THE DEATH OF JEROBOAM: 14:19-20

The last two verses are a standard "regnal formula" concluding the account of the reign of Jeroboam. (See the discussion on p. 206.) This is the way the narrator will end his treatment of almost every king from this point on. The narrator makes it clear that much more could be said about Jeroboam: "how he warred and how he reigned." The purpose of the present chapters, then, is not to give a complete account of Jeroboam's reign. By this admission the narrator implies that we should approach his text as something different from a chronicle. He has selected, omitted, and arranged material according to his own agenda. When we examine the shape of the Jeroboam story as a single creation, as we will in the next chapter, we must keep this in mind.

The "Book of the Annals of the Kings of Israel" to which the narrator refers the interested reader (and to which he will make several references in later chapters) was, presumably, a more detailed chronicle of the northern kingdom. Some scholars think it may even have been an official court history. Unfortunately we will never know, since the work is long since lost. The regnal formula conventionally tells how long the king reigned, something about his death and burial, and the name of his successor. Jeroboam himself was buried in his ancestral tomb (that is what "slept with his ancestors" means); Ahijah's oracle did not apply to him but to his descendants (except for Abijah, of course). His son Nadab succeeds him. The dynasty goes on, but we await the "new king" who Ahijah prophesied would one day overthrow it.

Chapter 13

THE WHOLE JEROBOAM STORY

1 Kings 11:26–14:20

Like the Solomon story, the Jeroboam story is not a simple collection of episodes. It has an overall symmetrical structure that charts the course of Jeroboam's career around the turning point of his religious policies:

A1. Ahijah of Shiloh announces Jeroboam's kingship (11:26-40)
A2. Closing formula for Solomon's reign (11:41-43)
  B. Political disunity: the rejection of Rehoboam (12:1-20)
    C. A Judahite man of God's approval (12:21-25)
      D. Jeroboam's cultic innovations (12:26-31)
    C'. A Judahite man of God's condemnation (12:32–13:10)
  B'. Prophetic disunity: the prophet and the man of God (13:11-32)
A1'. Ahijah of Shiloh announces Jeroboam's downfall (14:1-18)
A2'. Closing formula for Jeroboam's reign (14:19-20)

The Jeroboam Story Itself

The concentric structure asks us to compare the parallel elements before and after the center. The contrast between Ahijah's oracle of election in chapter 11 and his oracle of rejection in chapter 14 is evident. What becomes clear in this larger structure is that approval and disapproval of Jeroboam come not only from Ahijah, a prophet of Shiloh in the northern kingdom, but also from men of God from the southern kingdom. In 12:22-24 Shemaiah, a man of God at Rehoboam's court in Jerusalem, forbids Judah to war against secessionist Israel because, he says, the secession is Yahweh's will. In 13:1-10 the man of God who condemns the altar at Bethel is also said to be from Judah—a detail that was of little consequence in our earlier consideration of the story but becomes crucial when we read the text in this larger context. Political divisions are immaterial; Israelite and Judahite servants of Yahweh's word are unanimous in their attitudes toward Jeroboam. Even the old prophet of Bethel cannot withstand the power of Yahweh's word.

These parallels invite us to compare the less similar stories of the secession at Shechem and the conflict between prophet and man of God (elements B and B'). We observe first that the two nations in conflict at Shechem are represented by the two prophetic figures in conflict at Bethel; again the man of God's Judahite provenance emerges as a salient detail. Prophetic oracles that voice Yahweh's approval of and agency in the political disunity surround the story of its inception. The secession begins with bloodshed (the stoning of Adoram, 12:18), but because these things are according to God's will, Shemaiah's prophetic word averts further violence. By contrast, oracles that voice Yahweh's disapproval of Jeroboam surround the story of prophetic conflict, and the story shows Yahweh himself using violence to resolve the conflict: he commandeers the Bethel prophet and sends a lion against the disobedient Judahite man of God. The political separation of Judah and Israel is acceptable; religious schism between the two territories is not. The impression the narrator gives us is that God does not intend the political division of territories to affect the religious unity of Yahweh's people. The latter is fundamental and inalterable; the former is only temporary (11:39). As we shall see in the next chapter, this commitment to the unity of the people of Israel and Judah explains the way the narrator will organize his subsequent history of the kingdoms.

There is more. The prophet is "old," and therefore was likely a prophet of Yahweh before Jeroboam's cultic innovations. But he is "of Bethel," and his behavior demonstrates that his loyalties now lie with Jeroboam's calf sanctuary in his city. The Bethelite puts patriotism ahead of truth to such a degree that he is willing not only to counter Yahweh's word but even to counterfeit it. In other words, the prophetic conflict we see in 13:11-32 is the direct result of Jeroboam's idolatrous cultic innovations. The one whom God chose to be king of Israel infects the religious life of Yahweh's people with the separation Yahweh intends only for the political realm. Jeroboam sets Bethel against Jerusalem, cult against cult, feast against feast, and prophet against man of God.

The center of the story of Jeroboam and its literary pivot is therefore the account of his cultic innovations, particularly the establishment of calf-idols at Bethel and Dan. This is the heart of Jeroboam's sin and the cause of his downfall.

The Larger Canvas

The concentric structure above reveals two important connections with the Solomon story. First, the overall shape of the two stories is similar. Both move from a dominantly positive evaluation of the central figure to a dominantly negative one. And both pivot on the founding of a sanctuary. The sanctuaries, however, form a contrast. Solomon's Temple is the "house of Yahweh" and Solomon's greatest glory. Jeroboam's sanctuary is a "house of the high places," and his greatest sin. Second, the two stories share one passage: 11:26-43. The last element of the symmetrical organization of Solomon's story is the first element of Jeroboam's. This means that while we can consider each story as a literary unity in itself, the two stories together also form a larger indivisible whole. We begin to realize that our narrator's canvas is vaster and his project more ambitious than we suspected.

There are thematic connections with the Solomon story as well. The story of the secession of Israel and Jeroboam's accession to the throne brings closure to the motif of Solomon's "servant" that first appeared in 11:11. It leaves unfulfilled, however, Yahweh's quest for a king who will live up to the model of David. The prediction of a new king over Israel (14:14) means that the quest continues. Another theme already present in the Solomon story undergoes significant modifications: the theme of the "word of Yahweh." In 1 Kings 1:1–11:25, Yahweh speaks four times to Solomon. The divine word does not dominate or direct the story but acts more as a commentary on preceding events and a warning about the future. With the appearance of Jeroboam in 11:26, however, the word of Yahweh takes on a much greater role. It is central to five of the seven major sections of the Jeroboam story, and its power directs the plot at each step. In contrast to Solomon, though, Yahweh never addresses Jeroboam directly. The word comes to him through prophetic figures. This points forward to the major role that prophets and men of God will play in the subsequent stories of the kings. In fact, the next significant block of narratives in 1 Kings will feature the prophet Elijah as the principal character rather than Ahab, the king Elijah confronts.

Prophetism is a complex theme, and subsequent stories will ring the changes on all its aspects. The Jeroboam story already sets the tone by highlighting several of them: the opposition of prophet to king, of prophet to prophet, and even of prophet to Yahweh himself. The introduction of the theme of prophetism also clears the way for the narrator to use one of his most powerful narrative techniques for forging literary unity: the correlation of prophecy and fulfillment. By bridging large sections of time and text with prophecy at one end and fulfillment at the other, the narrator creates a network of links that connect the sprawling histories of the kings of Israel and Judah into a coherent whole. In the course of the Jeroboam story, the narrator lays the first abutments of several bridges: the restoration of the Davidic house (11:36, 39); Josiah's desecration of the altar at Bethel (13:2) and of the high places of Samaria (13:32); the downfall of the house of Jeroboam (14:14); and the exile of Israel (14:15). The other ends of these diverse spans will be found throughout 1–2 Kings, as early as 1 Kings 15 and as late as 2 Kings 23. The correlation of prophecy and fulfillment is not simply a narrative technique; behind it lies a profound theological understanding of Israel's history and Yahweh's role in it. The narrator believes that events are caused by human behavior: for instance, Rehoboam's diplomatic heavy-handedness precipitated the secession of the northern tribes. But they are also, and more primally, Yahweh's doing (see 12:15). Prophecy and fulfillment do not merely reveal the interconnectedness of history. The word of Yahweh itself, with or without human cooperation, drives history and brings it into being. Israel's history—which is that of the narrator and of his intended readers as well—is *co-created* by Yahweh and Yahweh's people.

There is one further transformation of the prophetic word. In the context of the history that will be the subject of the rest of 1–2 Kings, the story of the prophet of Bethel and the man of God from Judah is itself prophetic. The future will see the northern tribes, because of their infidelity to Yahweh, conquered by the Assyrians and driven into exile, never to return. Judah will maintain its political and religious traditions longer, but eventually they too will succumb to idolatrous practices, fall prey to the Babylonians, and go into exile. In that light, we can see that the prophet of Bethel and the man of God from Judah mirror their respective kingdoms. (This representative function is easier because the figures are both unnamed; we tend to think of them as types rather than as individuals.) Their tragedy foreshadows what awaits Israel and Judah. Israel has become unfaithful. Judah can still speak the word that Israel needs to hear, but if Judah follows Israel's lead and compromises its worship, then Judah will be banished from its homeland and the only reunion of the two will be in the tomb of exile.

Chapter 14
KINGS OF JUDAH AND ISRAEL
1 Kings 14:21–16:34

The tone and pace of 1 Kings change suddenly. Instead of long, narratively rich treatments like the stories of Solomon and Jeroboam, we get short, almost staccato accounts of reign after reign. Moreover, the formulaic introductions and conclusions that mark each account give the whole passage the feel of a dry chronicle rather than a story with dramatic movement.

Formal Considerations

Before we examine the text itself, there are two issues we must consider concerning the way the narrator organizes the material. The first is the pattern according to which he structures the account of each reign. The second is the order in which he arranges the accounts.

Each account follows a constant outline. (There are individual exceptions to most of the details that follow, but in general this is the pattern.) It begins with set information: (1) The year the king takes the throne is synchronized with the regnal year of the king of the other kingdom.[1] (Naturally, after the end of the northern kingdom in 2 Kings 17, this correlation no longer appears.) (2) For kings of Judah, but not for kings of Israel, the narrator gives the age of the king at his accession

---

[1] This information, along with the length of reign of each king, ought to enable us to reconstruct the chronological framework of the two kingdoms with precision. Unfortunately, what ought to work in theory proves impossible in practice. The chronology of the kings is one of the most vexed questions in the history of Judah and Israel. However, although it is a historical issue of first importance, it does not have a significant effect on the narrative character of the stories of the kings. For a recent discussion of the question, see the article "Chronology" in *The Anchor Bible Dictionary* (New York: Doubleday, 1992), vol. 1, pp. 1005–1010.

to the throne. (3) Next comes the number of years the king reigned and, usually, his capital. (For kings of Judah, the capital is Jerusalem; for kings of Israel, it is Tirzah for the first few reigns, then Samaria.) (4) For kings of Judah, but not for kings of Israel, the narrator notes the name of the king's mother. This reflects the high status she holds in the court of Jerusalem as *gĕbîrâ*. The neglect of this element in accounts of the kings of Israel may indicate that the position of queen mother is less influential in the north.

A theological evaluation of the king usually follows the introductory data. This is much less formulaic than the introduction, although there are several recurrent motifs that form the basis for many of the evaluations. Kings of Judah often receive qualified approval, but their failure to "eliminate the high places" almost always counts against them. Kings of Israel are condemned without exception, usually for following the "sin of Jeroboam."

After the evaluation (or sometimes before it) there is a brief account of some event in the king's reign. For kings of Judah this often involves events touching the Temple or the treasuries of the Temple and palace. Other topics are wars, conspiracies, and assassinations, particularly in Israel, where the throne often changes hands by violence.

Finally, there is usually a formulaic conclusion with the following elements: (1) The narrator refers the reader to other sources, the "Book of the Annals of the Kings of Judah" or the "Book of the Annals of the Kings of Israel," for further information about the king under consideration. (2) The death and burial of the king are noted, and the name of his successor is given. The narrator will omit part or all of this last element if he has already presented the information, for example, in recounting an assassination or a coup d'état.

The account of each reign runs uninterrupted from the formulaic introduction to the formulaic conclusion, and the accounts are then connected to one another like links in a chain. Very little material appears between the formulaic conclusion of one account and the formulaic introduction of the next; when it does, there is usually a narrative reason for it. Since, however, reigns in Judah and reigns in Israel usually overlap, the account of one reign will often extend chronologically past the accession of a king in the other kingdom. Nevertheless, the narrator completes the tale of the one king before backtracking to pick up the story of the other. In other words, he tells the stories in the order in which each king came to the throne, regardless of whether the king reigned in Judah or Israel. The effect of this is to make the book (as its title indicates) a history of the *kings* rather than a history of the *kingdoms*.

This arrangement confirms something we learned in the Jeroboam story about the narrator's attitudes. The political division of the territory of David into Judah and Israel, each ruled by its own king, is legitimate. But that division is no more significant than the unity of the people of Yahweh. To tell the history of Judah and the history of Israel as separate histories would belie the unity of the people. To tell the history of Judah and Israel as one history would belie the political separation Yahweh has decreed. In the narrator's view, Yahweh's people is one, but by God's will it lives under the rule of two kings. He arranges his material to do justice to both realities.

Kings of Judah and Israel

Since much of the material in this section is formulaic, we will concentrate on places where the narrator deviates from the standard formulas and on the material that is more variable, that is, the evaluations of each king and the events specific to each reign. After briefly considering each account, we will inquire about the narrative effect of this section on our reading of 1 Kings.

REHOBOAM OF JUDAH: 14:21-31

There is no correlation with a northern king, of course, because Rehoboam begins his reign before the secession that makes Jeroboam the first king of Israel. Rehoboam's age means that he was born before Solomon came to the throne (see 11:42). The narrator reminds us of Yahweh's choice of Jerusalem to be his own; this remark prepares the way for the theological evaluation, which cites Yahweh's jealousy when Judah embraces idolatrous shrines and practices. Finally, Rehoboam's mother is identified as an Ammonite. Given Rehoboam's age, it is clear that Solomon's fascination with foreign women began while Adonijah was still the heir apparent.

The theological evaluation does not conform to what will become the standard pattern; it refers to Judah rather than to the king. The accusation is parallel to the cultic evils perpetrated in the north: Jeroboam made high places (12:31), and Israel set up symbols of the goddess Asherah (NRSV, "sacred poles"; cf. 13:15). Judah does the same. In addition, Judah makes "pillars," which were standing stones with various religious functions, some idolatrous; they were sometimes symbols of the god Baal. Judah builds shrines on top of hills and beneath trees—probably an accurate description of the high places and sacred groves favored by pagan cults. But the words also form a merism (a figure of speech in which a complete range of things is suggested by naming the extremes, like "young and old"). Judah builds shrines "high and low," that is, everywhere.

Judah also engages in rites that were blatantly part of the Canaanite cult. It is common opinion that these rites involved sexual intercourse with sanctuary personnel, both female and male (perhaps eunuchs); this is the basis for the usual translation "cult prostitutes" or, as here, "male temple prostitutes." (The underlying Hebrew words are simply *qādēš* or *qĕdēšâ*, literally, "holy man" and "holy woman.") In recent years, however, this view has come under challenge. All we can say for sure is that the *qādēš* and *qĕdēšâ* were cultic personnel who did not belong to the worship practices of Yahwism and whom Yahwistic orthodoxy found particularly abhorrent.

The narrator summarizes: Judah fell into complete paganism (v. 24b). Such a situation goes far beyond the evils for which Yahweh condemned Solomon. Solomon indulged his foreign wives by permitting the worship of their foreign gods on a hilltop near Jerusalem and by participating in that worship himself. Now all of Judah has apparently joined in wholesale idolatry, not just with foreign gods, but with the much more insidious cults of the local Canaanite deities, Baal and Asherah.

The event of Rehoboam's reign that the narrator singles out is an invasion by Pharaoh Shishak of Egypt. Since Shishak was Jeroboam's patron during his self-imposed exile in Egypt (see 11:40), the implication is that Shishak is coming to Jeroboam's aid by attacking his rival.[2] Shishak departs with the entire contents of Temple and palace treasuries; the narrator emphasizes by repeating, "he took everything." He also takes the golden shields Solomon made to hang in the palace (10:16-17). Rehoboam replaces the golden shields with bronze—a fitting emblem of the downturn in Judah's fortunes since Solomon's day and of Judah's religious sin of replacing the worship of Yahweh with that of other gods. The narrator does not say explicitly that Shishak's invasion is a punishment for Judah's idolatry, but the inference is inescapable.

The formulaic conclusion notes continual war between Jeroboam and Rehoboam, which seemingly contradicts 12:24. We are probably to

---

[2]Egyptian records from Shishak's reign make it clear that, as a historical conclusion, this inference is completely wrong. They reveal that Shishak's invasion was as devastating to Israel as to Judah. In fact, those records do not even name Jerusalem among the 150 cities Shishak claims to have conquered on his campaign. External controls like this enable us rare glimpses of how uninterested the narrator is in reporting historical information accurately, and how readily he selects and manipulates the data he has for his own narrative purposes.

understand this as referring to recurrent border skirmishes, not the full-scale invasion of the north initiated by Rehoboam until Shemaiah forbade it. The narrator repeats the name of Rehoboam's mother as if to reemphasize her foreign origins and to remind us that foreign women, including Naamah herself, were Solomon's downfall as well.[3]

ABIJAM OF JUDAH: 15:1-8

The introduction has two points of interest. First, Abijam's reign is short, even shorter than the text might suggest. Each regnal year is reckoned from New Year's day, and any part of the reign preceding the king's first New Year or following his last one is counted as a "year." Abijam's reign, therefore, may be as short as one full year plus an extra month or two at each end.

Second, the queen mother's father is named; "Abishalom" is a variant form of the name "Absalom." Is Maacah the daughter of David's son Absalom, who rebelled against his father and drove him temporarily from Jerusalem? (If so, she was much older than her husband Rehoboam, who was born long after Absalom's death.) The narrator says no more, but the name itself is enough to conjure up memories of earlier troubles in the house of David and of the sin David committed that brought Absalom's rebellion as punishment upon him (see 2 Sam 12:10-12).

The theological evaluation (vv. 3-5) begins with a camouflaged genealogy: "He committed all the sins that his father [that is, Rehoboam] did before him; his heart was not true [Hebrew, *šlm*, playing on the name Solomon, *šlmh*] to Yahweh his God, like the heart of his father David." The genealogy not only evokes the continuity of the Davidic line but also retraces the degeneration of their fidelity. Rehoboam was Abijam's model in sin. Solomon was not entirely *šlm* (see 11:4). David was the paradigm of uprightness.

The theological evaluation continues in verses 4-5. Two themes converge to the enrichment of both. First is the theme of hope for a restoration of the Davidic house, and particularly the image of leaving a *nîr* (NRSV, "lamp," but see the comments on 11:36) in Jerusalem. Second is the theme of David as a paradigm of obedience. This is the only time when the "David as paradigm" theme is qualified by a reference to his sin of murdering Uriah (2 Sam 11:14-27). The name "Abishalom" in

[3]The sentence is lacking at this point in the ancient translations. Its presence in the Hebrew text may be, as many scholars speculate, the result of a scribal error. Nevertheless, in the Hebrew text the repetition has the narrative effect of emphasis.

verse 2 foreshadowed this reminder, since Absalom's rebellion was God's punishment on David for this crime. The point is not that David was a flawed paradigm but that he was a paradigm nonetheless. His fidelity was not without sin but in spite of it (see David's humble repentance and acceptance of Yahweh's judgments in 2 Samuel 12:13-23). Sin does not preclude repentance, return, and restoration. Despite all the sins of Rehoboam, despite Abijam's continuation in evil, there is still hope. God will raise up another scion to David in Jerusalem, one who, as we shall see, will return to David's ways.

The only event cited from Abijam's brief reign is the continuing war between Israel and Judah (v. 6).[4] The conclusion includes a repetition of the same information, specifying that Abijam, too, is involved in the war. Otherwise, the formulas of the conclusion are standard.

Asa of Judah: 15:9-24

The introduction to Asa's reign is standard. The only surprising note is that his "mother" is the same as Abijam's. Since Abijam reigned such a short time, the most likely explanation for this is that Maacah, Abijam's mother, continues in the position of *gĕbîrâ* when her grandson comes to the throne. Perhaps "mother of the king" was another title for the *gĕbîrâ* (compare the narrator's somewhat formal use of the phrase in 2:19), even in the rare cases where the office was held by someone other than the king's biological mother.

The theological evaluation begins on a positive note: Asa followed the model of David his "father" (the term in Hebrew can refer, as here, to a more remote ancestor). The narrator spells out what this entails. Asa removes the Canaanite cultic personnel (see above on 14:24) and gets rid of his predecessors' idols; the word for idols here is an insulting one, *gllym*, reminiscent of the *gll*, "dung," of 14:10. He deposes his grandmother from her office of *gĕbîrâ* for idolatry: she made something for the goddess Asherah. The NRSV's "abominable image" is a guess; we have no idea what the Hebrew term means. Since Asa cuts it down and burns it, perhaps it is an image made of wood. The next verse reveals that Asa's reforms do not go so far as to destroy the high places, although

---

[4]The NRSV's paraphrase smooths over an awkwardness in the Hebrew text. The sentence is almost an exact repetition of 14:30: "There was war between Rehoboam and Jeroboam all his life." Scholars speculate on whether or not the repetition is a copyist's error. In light of the brevity of Abijam's reign, perhaps the continual border skirmishes were known to later generations simply as "the war between Rehoboam and Jeroboam."

Asa's own loyalties to Yahweh are undivided. Thus the narrator qualifies his original positive evaluation: everything Asa does is right; he just does not do everything he should. Asa's "votive gifts" echo the offerings Solomon brought into his new Temple (7:51b; the sentences are much more similar in Hebrew than in the NRSV). Solomon deposited his offerings in the Temple treasuries; presumably Asa does the same, to replace the things that were lost to Shishak during Rehoboam's reign.

Like the theological evaluation, the event selected for Asa's reign is a mixture of positive and negative. It begins with a negative note, that the warfare between Israel and Judah continues throughout his reign. As the tale of that war unfolds, however, we see that Asa manages a significant victory in the matter of fixing the border, though it is won at a heavy price. The places mentioned reveal that Baasha, king of Israel, is encroaching more and more on Asa's territory; Ramah is south of the Israelite border sanctuary of Bethel, and only a few miles north of Jerusalem itself. To break Baasha's threatened blockade, Asa takes everything in the Temple treasuries (which he just deposited there in verse 15!) and offers it to the king of Aram in exchange for a treaty. When Aram's subsequent pressure on the northern part of Israel forces Baasha to withdraw from Ramah, Asa dismantles Baasha's fortifications and pushes the border farther to the north.

The appearance of Aram on the stage of 1 Kings introduces a new player into the drama of Israel and Judah. For the next two centuries (in textual terms, up to 2 Kings 17), the power politics of the region will be driven by the shifting alliances among these three kingdoms. The future uncertainty of those alliances is reflected in the murkiness of the present text. Asa's words to Ben-hadad of Aram are, "An alliance between me and you, an alliance between my father and your father" (v. 19). Is this a request, as the NRSV paraphrases it, to reestablish an alliance that has existed but is no longer in force? Or is it a claim that such an alliance currently exists, and has existed for a generation? If Aram and Jerusalem are already allied, what is the nature of Aram's alliance with Israel that Asa asks Ben-hadad to break? We have no evidence, textual or historical, to resolve any of these questions.

The formulaic conclusion continues the mixture of positive and negative. The narrator sends the reader to other sources to learn of Asa's many admirable accomplishments. "However," he says, "in his old age, Asa suffered a disease of the feet." The key word is "however," which marks Asa's disease (regularly understood in the ancient world as a sign of divine disapproval) as in some way qualifying the preceding positive picture.

NADAB OF ISRAEL: 15:25-32

During the long reign of Asa of Judah, Jeroboam of Israel dies and a series of successors comes to the throne. The first is the only descendant of Jeroboam to rule Israel, his short-lived son Nadab. The formulaic introduction to his reign is entirely standard.

The theological evaluation is couched in generalities (as it will usually be in the accounts of the kings of Israel). Nadab "did evil," he "followed the way of his father," he "sinned," and he "caused Israel to commit sin" (v. 26). The language is similar to that used of Jeroboam in 14:9, 16; in other words, Nadab is no different from his father Jeroboam in his religious infidelities.

The event singled out for this reign is Nadab's assassination by Baasha. Baasha's father, Ahijah, is of the house of Issachar, and therefore not the same as the prophet Ahijah of Shiloh. The name, however, awakens reminders of the last appearance of the prophet, when he announced the doom that would befall Jeroboam's family at the hands of a new king Yahweh would raise up (14:14). Ahijah of Issachar may have sired Baasha, but Ahijah of Shiloh is his father in the spirit. Baasha kills Nadab while the king is on military campaign. The implication is that, as Ahijah of Shiloh prophesied, this son of Jeroboam does not receive burial in the family tomb. Baasha then claims the crown and goes on to exterminate Jeroboam's whole line, also according to Ahijah's oracle. The narrator's wordiness in 15:30 is an explicit reference to Ahijah's speech (14:15-16) and hammers home the theological reason for the downfall of the house of Jeroboam.[5]

The conclusion repeats verse 16 exactly, establishing a strong unifying link between the regnal accounts of Asa and Nadab (even though the sentence does not even mention Nadab!). It omits the elements of Nadab's death, burial, and successor because the story of his assassination (and presumed lack of burial as a result) makes them unnecessary.

BAASHA OF ISRAEL: 15:33–16:7

The account of Baasha's reign begins with the standard introduction and the generalized negative theological evaluation typically given to kings of Israel. The event of Baasha's reign that the narrator

---

[5]Historically, extermination of the previous ruling family was an inevitable political deed, lest there be a survivor around whom later opposition to the new king could crystallize. For our narrator, however, this brutal fact of political realism is negligible; the *real* cause of events is Yahweh's word.

describes is an oracle delivered to Baasha by the prophet Jehu. The oracle is based on the condemnation of Jeroboam by Ahijah in chapter 14. It has the same three parts—Yahweh's deeds in Baasha's favor, Baasha's sins, and Yahweh's decree of punishment—and its wording is an abbreviation of Ahijah's: compare 16:2a with 14:7b, 16:2b with 14:16b, and 16:3a with 14:10b. The reference to Jeroboam's house in 16:3b explicitly directs the reader's attention to the parallels. Jehu's oracle does not use the gutter language of Ahijah's, but it does end with the same devastating couplet; compare 16:4 with 14:11. The links between the two passages are part of a larger series of parallels between the house of Jeroboam and the house of Baasha that we shall look at more closely below.

The conclusion contains the standard formulas, but the narrator expands it by referring back to Jehu's oracle. As usual, this sort of repetition affords emphasis and invites us to pay special attention to variations. Jehu's oracle was directed to Baasha, though it concerned both him and his house. The narrator, however, says the oracle was "to Baasha and to his house" (not "against," as the NRSV has it in 16:7). For the narrator, the validity of the prophetic word transcends the single moment of its delivery; it remains effective and immediate through the generations. (The placement of this verse between reigns, after the formulaic conclusion to Baasha's regnal account and before the introduction to Elah's, underscores the relevance of the oracle to the whole house of Baasha.) Of the three parts of Jehu's oracle, the narrator only refers to that concerning Baasha's sins. The emphasis is on Baasha himself: the narrator changes Jehu's "with their sins" to "with the work of his hands" and eliminates the accusation that Baasha caused the people to sin.

The last phrase of 16:7 is difficult (NRSV, "because he destroyed it"). The conjunction translated "because" can also mean "concerning" or, in rare instances, "although." And the antecedents of the pronouns are anything but clear. While the NRSV translation is as likely as any, we must in the last analysis concede that we are not sure what the phrase means. If we use the NRSV's rendering as an admittedly tentative basis, the phrase has the shocking effect of finding Baasha blameworthy for actions that in fact fulfilled a prophecy. The idea that God can use people to accomplish the divine will and then punish them for it is uncomfortable, to say the least. But there is perhaps some precedent in the story of the man of God in chapter 13, and, as we shall see in chapter 22, Yahweh is not above lying to bring about the death of an unfaithful king.

ELAH OF ISRAEL: 16:8-14

The introduction to Elah's reign is standard. The theological evaluation is missing, but an equivalent evaluation will follow the account of the chosen event from Elah's reign, in this case his assassination at the hands of Zimri.

Assassination reports in these brief regnal accounts usually follow a pattern almost as fixed as the formulaic introductions and conclusions. (1) There is a conspiracy, and the name of the assassin is given. (2) The assassin strikes down the king and kills him. (3) The assassin takes the throne in the murdered king's place. In this case we learn a few more details. Zimri is a military commander; as we will discover in the next regnal account, the troops are on campaign against Gibbethon, as they were also at the time of Nadab's assassination. Unlike Nadab, however, Elah is not in the field with his armies; he is back in the capital carousing. The narrator ensures that we have no sympathy whatsoever for the drunken king and shows his contempt even further in verse 11, where he uses the same crude language as Yahweh used in 14:10, "one who urinates against a wall" (NRSV, "a single male"), to refer to the male descendants of Elah.

Zimri follows his coup, as Baasha did, by exterminating the entire line of his predecessor. He goes far beyond Baasha's purge, however. He wipes out the males not only of Baasha's entire house but of all his kin and friends as well. The narrator presents Zimri's destruction of the house of Baasha and Elah as the fulfillment of Jehu's prophecy, just as Baasha's destruction of the house of Jeroboam and Nadab was the fulfillment of Ahijah of Shiloh's (compare 16:12-13 with 15:29-30). The reason for the destruction is the evil of which these kings are guilty. Somewhat surprisingly, the "sin of Jeroboam" is not cited as the paradigm of evil; Baasha and Elah themselves fill that role.

As with Nadab, who also was assassinated, the narrator omits the notices of Elah's death, burial, and successor.

ZIMRI OF ISRAEL: 16:15-20

Despite the extreme brevity of Zimri's reign, the narrator gives him the full royal treatment: formulaic introduction, an event from the reign, formulaic conclusion. (As in the account of Elah, the narrator omits the theological evaluation in favor of a theological rationale following the account of Zimri's violent death.) The formulaic introduction is standard, though the fact that Zimri reigns only seven days insinuates much about his lack of support from Yahweh as well as from the people.

As the selected event from Zimri's reign, the narrator recounts the rise of another military commander, Omri, and Zimri's resultant suicide. According to the narrator, at the news of Elah's assassination "all Israel" chooses Omri as king. The term is clearly an exaggeration, since Omri is on military campaign near the southwestern border of Israel and since, as we shall see, there is enough opposition to Omri's kingship to plunge the country into civil war for years. We are to envisage a spontaneous expression of support by Omri's troops "in the camp" (v. 16), which encourages his ambition and convinces him to attempt the throne; note how "all Israel" means Omri's troops in the next verse as well. The narrator's language is more than a mere exaggeration, however; it is a portent. Omri is the first king of Israel since Jeroboam to have any expression of popular support, and he will be the first king of Israel to found a dynasty that lasts more than two years beyond his own death. The stories of the Omrid dynasty, in fact, will occupy the next seventeen chapters of 1–2 Kings. Despite his ultimately very negative religious evaluation of Omri, the narrator grudgingly allows a few small indications that there was political greatness in the man.

Zimri's suicide keeps Omri's hands clean of blood, and the brevity of the reign would prevent Zimri's family from developing any dynastic hopes or pretensions. Zimri himself has already exterminated the preceding dynasty.[6] Omri therefore does not have to kill anyone in his bid for the throne, and he can begin his reign free of the stain of murder. The narrator attributes Zimri's death, as he did Nadab's and Elah's, to the sin he committed and caused Israel to commit.

The conclusion is standard, though with the omission of notices of death, burial, and successor, just as in the preceding cases of violent death.

INTERREGNUM: 16:21-22

These two verses fall between the formulaic conclusion of Zimri's reign and the formulaic introduction to Omri's. That unusual placement reflects their content: they recount a four-year struggle between Tibni and Omri for possession of the throne of Israel. Between Zimri's death in Asa's twenty-seventh year (16:15) and Omri's accession in Asa's thirty-first year (16:23), there is no single recognized king. The civil war is an interregnum.

[6]This is another indication of the narrator's willingness to play fast and loose with historical realism for the sake of his theological agenda. It is hard to believe that Zimri could have tracked down all the males of Elah's line as well as "his kindred and his friends" (16:11) in seven days!

The narrator describes the situation with language that reflects long-drawn-out turmoil and division: "were divided," into "halves" (NRSV, "two parts"), "half followed Tibni," "half followed Omri," "the people following Omri," "the people following Tibni." By contrast, the four-word resolution is abrupt and definitive: "Tibni died. Omri reigned."

OMRI OF ISRAEL: 16:23-28

The introduction to Omri's reign is standard. One note of interest is that though his accession is not reckoned until Asa's thirty-first year and his son succeeds him seven years later (16:29), Omri's reign is calculated as lasting twelve years. That means that the narrator credits the years of the interregnum to Omri. This is another subtle sign of the narrator's mixed feelings about Omri. His victory over Tibni allows him to assume the kingship uncontested, but in fact he has been king all along, ever since "all Israel" chose him (16:16).

The mention of the capital is more complex than usual. Since Omri reigns in Tirzah for only six years, the question naturally arises about his capital for the remainder of his reign. This prepares the way for the selected event from Omri's reign, the establishment of a new capital city, Samaria. In order to smooth the transition between the two, the narrator defers the theological evaluation until after the report about Samaria, following the precedent set in the regnal accounts of Elah and Zimri.

The Shemer (Hebrew, *šmr*) from whom Omri bought Samaria (*šmrwn*; the ending *-wn* often marks the names of mountains) is probably not an individual but a clan: the Hebrew text calls Shemer "the owners of the hill" (NRSV, "owner"). The site is newly acquired crown land, suitable for a centrally located capital, strategically situated and easily defended. It apparently has no tribal ties, since Shemer is given no tribal affiliations (and no Israelite clan of that name is known from external evidence either). This is a double-edged freedom. Like David's Jerusalem, Omri's Samaria will be free from pressures of tribal favoritism. But it will also be free of the tribal traditions that form Israel's Yahwistic roots.

It is noteworthy that Omri is the only Israelite king in this section of the text whose regnal account contains nothing of violent death, either actual or prophesied. This is another indication that the narrator acknowledges the success of Omri's political policies. After this relatively positive regnal account, the negativity of the narrator's theological evaluation comes as a surprise. He not only condemns Omri as he has every preceding Israelite king; he also claims that Omri "did more evil than all who were before him." Yet he couches the evaluation in the generalizations typical of the accounts of kings of Israel, and we are left to wonder precisely what sins of Omri the narrator finds so superlatively heinous.

The conclusion to Omri's regnal account is entirely standard.

AHAB OF ISRAEL: 16:29-34

The introduction to Ahab's reign is standard. The theological evaluation is brief and pointed. Ahab is more evil than all who were before him (presumably including his father). The repetition of "Ahab son of Omri" in 16:29-30 is noteworthy; past regnal accounts have not insisted so strongly on the reigning king's patronymic. This is another indication of the narrator's recognition of Omri's significance in the history of Israel.[7]

In the accounts of other kings of Israel, the theological evaluation was a simple generalization. In Ahab's case, the narrator elaborates the generalization (v. 30) with a list of specifics (vv. 31-33a), followed by an even more emphatic repetition of the initial generalization (v. 33b). The NRSV's translation of verse 31 captures the sense adequately but smooths out considerably the oddness of the unusual Hebrew. A more literal rendering shows the narrator's intense feelings: "And then— was it a light thing that he walked in the sins of Jeroboam son of Nebat?—he took as his wife . . . ."

Ahab's first crime is marriage to the daughter of the king of Sidon. Foreign marriages, as we saw in the Solomon story, are always considered dangerous. But this marriage is particularly pernicious. The names tell the tale. Ethbaal, Ahab's father-in-law, is named for the Canaanite god Baal (the Phoenician form of his name, Ittobaal, means "Baal exists"). Baal will be Yahweh's chief rival for Israel's worship throughout the centuries of the monarchy. Here, the first time the god's name appears in 1 Kings, it sneaks into the text under cover of Ahab's foreign marriage. Furthermore, Ahab's wife, Jezebel *('yzbl)*, is also named for Baal. The element *zbl* means "Prince" and was one of the divine titles of Baal.[8] Both names, therefore, foreshadow the entry of Baal

---

[7]There is external evidence that this recognition was widespread. Several decades later, Assyrian records still speak of the "house of Omri," even when referring to Jehu, the king who displaced the Omrid dynasty from the throne.

[8]There may be even more to the name Jezebel. It may involve an insulting deformation of Baal's title. The word *zbl*, "Prince," was probably pronounced *zābūl* or *zĕbūl*, as in the name Baalzebul or Beelzebul, "Baal is Prince"(which itself is usually deformed in the Bible to Baalzebub or Beelzebub, "Baal of Flies"). Pronounced *zebel*, the element resembles a word in other Semitic languages for "excrement" that may well have existed also in Hebrew, though it is not attested in the Hebrew Bible.

onto the stage of Israel's religious life and the ensuing struggle between Yahweh and Baal for dominance. The struggle begins immediately, with Baal winning the first throw: Ahab serves Baal, worships him, and builds an altar and a temple to Baal in the newly founded capital city. Ahab also makes an Asherah (NRSV, "sacred pole"), either a symbol or an image of the Canaanite goddess Asherah. By all of this, the narrator insists, Ahab angers Yahweh more than all the idolatrous kings that preceded him.

The event singled out from Ahab's reign is the reestablishment of Jericho by Hiel of Bethel. The notice is strange, since it does not mention Ahab at all. We can safely infer, however, that the reoccupation of such an important site (a rich oasis in the arid Jordan valley) could only occur under royal patronage. Thus the narrator's "in his days" is an oblique way of suggesting "under his aegis." The narrator is equally unclear about the deaths of Hiel's two sons and how they are related to the building of Jericho. "At the cost of" is the NRSV's vague rendering of an even vaguer Hebrew turn of phrase. We are left uncertain whether Hiel sacrifices his sons (if so, it is presumably to Baal, who was worshiped with human sacrifice in some Ancient Near Eastern cultures) to win divine blessings on his project, or whether his sons die by chance during the rebuilding and their deaths are taken as a sign of Yahweh's displeasure. In either case, the verse has two important narrative effects. First, it puts the account of Ahab's reign under a shadow of death. Second, it completes a prophecy-and-fulfillment connection that stretches all the way back to Joshua 6:26, where Joshua imposes exactly this curse upon whoever would in the future attempt to rebuild Jericho.

According to the standard outline for regnal accounts, the next element should be the formulaic conclusion. However, the narrator defers the conclusion to 22:39-40 and inserts at this point two large narrative blocks set during the reign of Ahab. The first is a series of stories of the prophet Elijah (chs. 17–19); Ahab appears in some of the stories, but he is only a supporting character. The second is a series of stories of Ahab (chs. 20–22), all of them involving confrontations with hostile prophets, and most of them set during wars between Israel and Aram.

Narrative Effect

The most obvious narrative effect of this series of regnal accounts is an enormous increase in the pace of the narrative. More than thirteen chapters are dedicated to the reigns of Solomon and Jeroboam, which cover a period of approximately sixty years. Here in less than three chapters the narrator covers nine reigns and another sixty years or so. We feel as if we are skimming over the surface of events, touching down only briefly in each reign to make contact with one incident that is particularly revealing of the period or particularly momentous for the future. By comparison, the stories of Solomon and Jeroboam take on new portent because of the expansive treatment the narrator gives them. When the rapid recital of reigns suddenly stops and we spend the next six chapters on events of Ahab's reign, those stories too become charged with significance.

Segmenting the narrative into discrete regnal accounts runs the risk of making the material piecemeal and disjointed. To counter this, the narrator uses a series of unifying themes to link several reigns together. The theme of "war between Judah and Israel" occurs in 14:30; 15:6, 7, 16-22, and 32 and links the first four accounts (Rehoboam, Abijam, Asa, and Nadab). The figure of Baasha is prominent in the regnal accounts of Asa and Nadab as well as his own and his son Elah's. Zimri links Elah's account with his own, and Omri is prominent in Zimri's account and the interregnum as well as his own and Ahab's.

There is also a series of parallels between Jeroboam and Baasha that extends to their sons. Jeroboam reigns twenty-two years, Baasha twenty-four. Both receive very similar prophetic oracles of condemnation, and Jeroboam's oracle is cited as the model of Baasha's. Their sons, Nadab and Elah, both reign for two years, and are assassinated during a military campaign against the Philistines at Gibbethon (though Elah is not actually on campaign himself, and the campaign is not mentioned until Zimri's regnal account). Each assassin then proceeds to obliterate the preceding royal line in fulfillment of a divine oracle. These parallels establish a pattern for the first two dynastic families of Israel. As we begin the stories of Omri and his descendants, we cannot help but wonder whether the third dynasty will escape the fate of the others. (It will not. Elijah will use almost the same prophetic words to announce the same fate for Ahab in 1 Kings 21, and in 2 Kings 9–10 Jehu will drown the Omrids in a tidal wave of blood.)

Other motifs link the successive regnal accounts of each kingdom. In Judah, the accounts of Rehoboam and Asa mention high places, idols, and Canaanite cultic personnel (*qādēš*); both also show a concern for the contents of the Temple and palace treasuries. In Israel, the "sin" (or "way") of Jeroboam is mentioned in almost every account.

We explained at the beginning of this chapter that the narrator arranges the regnal accounts according to the chronological order of each king's accession, regardless of whether the king reigned in Judah or in Israel. In this section, because of the long reign of Asa of Judah and the rapid turnover of the Israelite throne, that arrangement produces a neat separation between the Judahite and Israelite kings. The first three kings are of Judah; the last six are of Israel. Each series of accounts has a different pattern; we might speak of "trajectories," since it becomes clear in 2 Kings that the patterns continue true after the reign of Ahab. The Judahite trajectory is infidelity (Rehoboam and Abijam) followed by reform (Asa). The stories of Judahite monarchs in 2 Kings will reveal a regular alternation between idolaters (Jehoram and Athaliah, Ahaz, Manasseh and Amon) and reformers (Joash, Hezekiah, Josiah). At each swing of the pendulum the apostasy grows more outrageous and the reform more aggressive. The Israelite trajectory, on the other hand, is an unbroken downward spiral. Jeroboam is adjudged the paradigm of evil. Baasha's dynasty is condemned in the same terms, but the campaign against the Philistines at Gibbethon suggests the deteriorating state of northern political affairs.[9] It was going on when Nadab was assassinated (15:27), and it was going on (again? still?) when Elah was assassinated twenty-four years later (16:15). Omri's dynasty represents new depths of evil. Both he and his son Ahab "did more evil than all who were before him." One of the purposes of the next six chapters will be to support this evaluation of Ahab.

[9] If the NRSV translation is correct, the phrase at the end of 16:7 may also suggest religious deterioration, in that Baasha's sin exceeded Jeroboam's.

Part Three

THE STORY OF ELIJAH
1 Kings 17–19

Chapter 15

ELIJAH ANNOUNCES A DROUGHT

1 Kings 17

The account of Ahab's reign is expanded by the insertion of two large narrative complexes. The first of these, 1 Kings 17–19, features Elijah the Tishbite in a series of stories. Unlike the earlier narrative complexes about Solomon and Jeroboam, where the successive stories formed a single, all-encompassing larger narrative, the stories about Elijah form larger units embedded in each other like a series of Chinese boxes. The organization of chapters 17–19 might be schematized as in *Figure 2* on page 226.

As this diagram suggests, narrative development goes on simultaneously on several levels throughout these chapters. Our approach will be to study the individual episodes in a chapter, and then to look at the larger narrative units that encompass those episodes. We shall begin with the stories of chapter 17.

Elijah Confronts Ahab: 17:1

The first verse of the Elijah story is not itself a narrative, nor does it directly connect to any of the three stories that follow it in chapter 17. Nevertheless, it is the anchor point for several bands of narrative tension that stretch across various expanses of the Elijah materials. This warrants a close examination of its details, in anticipation of their function in unifying the larger structures within these three chapters. Elijah appears here for the first time in the Hebrew Bible, abruptly and with minimal background information. He is identified as "a Tishbite," a word of quite uncertain meaning. Its form in Hebrew as in English marks it as describing Elijah's origins, but whether it refers to a place (an otherwise unknown "Tishbe") or to a societal category (for example,

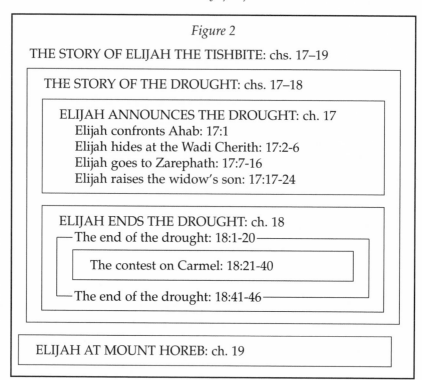

Figure 2

THE STORY OF ELIJAH THE TISHBITE: chs. 17–19

THE STORY OF THE DROUGHT: chs. 17–18

ELIJAH ANNOUNCES THE DROUGHT: ch. 17
Elijah confronts Ahab: 17:1
Elijah hides at the Wadi Cherith: 17:2-6
Elijah goes to Zarephath: 17:7-16
Elijah raises the widow's son: 17:17-24

ELIJAH ENDS THE DROUGHT: ch. 18
The end of the drought: 18:1-20
The contest on Carmel: 18:21-40
The end of the drought: 18:41-46

ELIJAH AT MOUNT HOREB: ch. 19

a clan, family, or social class) is unclear. The next words do not resolve the problem. The NRSV's translation, "of Tishbe in Gilead," is based on ancient attempts to clarify an obscure Hebrew phrase that is more likely to mean something like "one of the settlers in Gilead." In short, while these opening words may have been more intelligible to the ancient reader than they are to us, they give us today little information about Elijah: he is from Gilead, an Israelite region east of the Jordan River, but whether he is a native of the region or an immigrant is not clear.

What we do *not* learn about Elijah is as important as what we do learn. The narrator does not call him a prophet or tell us anything about his relationship to Yahweh. Elijah's name is suggestive (it means "Yahweh is my God"), but in view of the bold claims Elijah makes in this verse, the narrator's silence about his religious authority is striking. Elijah himself is not so reticent. He appears before Ahab, claims to be a faithful servant of Yahweh (this is the meaning of the Hebrew idiom "before whom I stand"), and decrees on the strength of that claim a drought that will last "these years." Since all we know of Ahab is the narrator's catalogue of Ahab's sins in 16:29-34, we naturally interpret the drought as a punishment from God. Yet neither the narrator nor, surprisingly, Elijah himself confirms that interpretation. Indeed, Elijah seems to arrogate to himself the authority to unleash or restrain the drought: "except by my word." (Thus the NRSV paraphrases a Hebrew idiom that is more literally translated "except at the mouth of my word." The NRSV captures the sense accurately, but the literal wording will be important when we hear it echoed in verse 24.)

The narrative effects of this opening verse are manifold. First, it immediately links the ensuing story of Elijah to the account of the reign of Ahab, despite the fact that Ahab does not appear again in chapter 17. In this way it begins a narrative thread that will not be complete until the end of Ahab's reign in 22:40: the condemnation and punishment of the sinful king. Second, Elijah's claim to be a servant of Yahweh ("before whom I stand") opens the question of his relationship to God: Is his claim justified? And what are the contours of his servanthood? The narrator will address these questions in the course of chapters 17–19. Third, the drought he proclaims creates a crisis for the kingdom. The story of the drought continues through chapters 17–18 and ends only in 18:45 with the return of rain. Finally, the source of the authority Elijah claims for his own word will be gradually revealed through chapter 17, culminating in the widow's confession in 17:24. The first verse thus begins the narrative development on most of the levels indicated in the diagram above.

Elijah Hides at the Wadi Cherith: 17:2-6

Ahab now disappears from the scene. The remainder of chapter 17 is a succession of three brief narratives that follow Elijah during the drought and subsequent famine (vv. 2-6, 8-16, 18-24). Each narrative reaches a situation of temporary stability, but the intervening short lines (vv. 7, 17) introduce further complications and move the story on to new stages.

The first episode is short and plain: Yahweh commands Elijah and Elijah obeys. Though the scene lacks significant narrative tension, it contains several notable elements. First, Yahweh's command is that Elijah "hide." The inference is that Elijah's announcement to Ahab has put him in danger; presumably the king holds Elijah responsible for the drought and seeks to nullify the decree by acting against its author.

Second, Elijah's refuge is a wadi in the Jordan valley. A "wadi" is a stream that flows only during the wet season—hardly an auspicious hiding place during a drought! In this way the narrator foreshadows two elements of the subsequent tale: Yahweh will sustain Elijah miraculously, but the wadi will eventually dry up nonetheless. The location of the Wadi Cherith is unknown today. If it is "east of the Jordan," as the NRSV translates, we are probably to think of Gilead, Elijah's home territory; however, the Hebrew phrase may mean no more than "near the Jordan." More significant than its location is its name (Wadi Cherith = "Cut Off Creek"), since the term will be echoed in chapter 18.

Third, the narrator recounts Yahweh's command and Elijah's obedience in almost identical words. This "command and compliance" pattern is common not only in the Elijah stories but elsewhere in the Hebrew Bible as well. The effect of the verbatim repetition is to emphasize that the obedience is absolute and complete: Elijah fulfills Yahweh's commands to the letter. Wherever such a pattern occurs, variations in wording between the command and the compliance are noteworthy. In this case there are two deviations from the standard pattern. First, the account of the compliance usually follows directly upon the command. Here there is an added line between the two: "So he went and did according to the word of Yahweh" (v. 5a). This line highlights the motif of "the word," which we shall discuss below. Second, Yahweh's statement that the ravens will "feed" Elijah is expanded to the detailed notice in verse 6a. This too points forward to an overarching theme, the comparison of Elijah and Moses, that we will examine when we consider the Elijah story as a whole (see p. 284).

Elijah Goes to Zarephath: 17:7-16

The first episode closes with verse 6: Elijah has obeyed Yahweh's word and receives the sustenance that Yahweh promised. Verse 7 leaps forward in time ("after a while") to a new complication. The Wadi Cherith dries up because of the lack of rain, and so Yahweh must make new provisions for his obedient servant. This effects a transition to the next scene.

The second episode begins in the same way as the first: Yahweh's word comes to Elijah with a command and an explanation, and Elijah obeys immediately. In this scene, however, the command-and-compliance pattern gives way to a much fuller dramatic development than in the first episode. Yahweh's command is twofold: "go" and "live there." Elijah goes, but his obedience to the second command is not explicitly reported; instead, it is narrated in the subsequent interaction with the widow.

The dramatic action begins with Elijah's obedience: he goes to Zarephath, a town in Phoenician territory north of Israel, on the coast between Sidon and Tyre. He comes to the city gates and sees a widow there gathering kindling. The Hebrew of verse 10 is vivid, showing us the widow through Elijah's eyes: "He came to the gate of the town, and there's a widow there gathering sticks!" Elijah initiates a dialogue with two polite requests. (The Hebrew is less brusque than the NRSV's rendering might suggest. The tone is closer to "Would you bring me. . . .") First, he asks for drink; then, as the widow prepares to comply, he adds a request for food. In each case his words emphasize the modesty of the request: he seeks only "a little water"—a drinking-vessel full; and he wishes only "a morsel of bread"—a mere handful. (The word translated "morsel" may even mean "crumb"—it is used as a metaphor for hailstones in Psalm 147:17.)

The widow's instant readiness to fetch water for Elijah contrasts with her refusal of his request for food. Serious as the drought is, she can cope with it; but its more severe consequence, famine, is beyond her means. The widow's response reveals her plight: she and her son are starving. Just as in the episode of the Wadi Cherith, Yahweh has sent Elijah into a situation where only a miracle can supply him with sustenance.

The widow's words begin with an oath taken in the name of Elijah's god. This is not surprising in a polytheistic culture; the widow is simply acknowledging that Elijah is a devotee of Yahweh rather than of one of the deities of Sidon. (Compare Hiram of Tyre's praise of Yahweh in 5:7.) The oath shows the widow to be observant (she recognizes Elijah's Israelite origins), respectful of his foreign ways, and deferential toward Yahweh even though she is not a worshiper. It thus evokes in us a positive attitude toward her, to obviate any negative judgment based on her subsequent inability to honor Elijah's request for food. The rest of her speech is graphic. She has "nothing baked" (literally, she has no "baked-thing"). What she has corresponds, ironically, with what Elijah requested. He asked for a morsel of bread in her hand; she has only a scant handful of meal (literally, a "palmful"). He asked for a bit of water in a vessel; she has only a bit of oil in a juglet. She intends to use up her remaining provisions in a last meager meal for herself and her son: "we shall eat it, and we shall die." Her speech moves from life (the first word of her oath is "alive"; literally, "Alive is Yahweh your God!") to death (her last word is "we will die"), symbolizing the only destiny she can foresee for herself.

Elijah's response to the widow's hopeless declaration takes the same form as Yahweh's original speech to Elijah at the beginning of the episode, a command followed by an explanation promising hope. The command begins with a reassurance but adds a challenging proviso. Elijah approves the widow's proposed course of action but insists that before preparing anything for herself and her son, she must use some of her meal and oil to bake something for Elijah and bring it to him. The position of the words "first" and "afterwards" emphasizes their contrast and points up the extreme sacrifice to which Elijah calls the widow. The explanation takes the form of a classic prophetic utterance. The formula "Thus says Yahweh" is one of the standard ways in which a prophet introduces a divine oracle, whether of promise or of condemnation. In this case the oracle is a short poem that promises the widow continuing sustenance as long as the drought lasts. The wording of Elijah's response corresponds point for point with the widow's speech. She intends to "go and do" a cake (NRSV, "go home and prepare"; Elijah tells her to "go and do" what she has proposed. She protested that she has no "baked-thing" (Hebrew, *māʿôg*); he tells her to make him a small cake of baked dough (*ʿūgâ*, from the same root, meaning "to bake"). She speaks of a palmful of meal in a jar and a bit of oil in a juglet; he promises in Yahweh's name that the jar of meal and juglet of oil will be inexhaustible.

The widow's compliance echoes Elijah's command with one significant variation, which we shall discuss later: his words were, "go and do as *you* have said"; in response, she "went and did as *Elijah* had said." Verse 15b even echoes the order in which Elijah says the principals are to be fed: the best ancient Hebrew manuscripts read, "he and she and her household,[1] for many days." (The NRSV word order, "she as well as he and her household," follows an alternate manuscript tradition.) The echo of Elijah's words continues in the narrator's assurance that the prophetic promise was fulfilled (v. 16a). With the last words of verse 16 the narrator confirms that Elijah's claim to speak for Yahweh is authentic.

Elijah Raises the Widow's Son: 17:17-24

Like verse 7, verse 17 leaps forward in time ("after this") to introduce a new complication: the widow's son falls seriously ill and dies. This effects a transition to the final episode in the chapter. The narrative is structured in a detailed concentric pattern:

A. speech by the widow (17:18; "man of God")
    B. speech by Elijah (17:19a; "give me your son")

[1]The mention of "her household" where we would expect "her son" may be a scribal slip of the pen; the words are very similar in Hebrew (*byth* and *bnh*). But it fits the context, since it points forward to the next episode, where we will learn that the widow is the owner of a house (*byt*, v. 17a).

  C. Elijah takes the boy from his mother (17:19b)
   D. He brings him up to his own room
    E. He puts him on the bed
     F. Elijah raises the child (17:20-22)
    E'. Elijah picks the child up (17:23a)
   D'. He brings him down from his own room
  C'. He returns him to his mother (17:23a)
 B'. speech by Elijah (17:23b; "your son is alive")
A'. speech by the widow (17:24; "man of God")

The pattern focuses attention on the climactic scene of the story, verses 20-22, where Elijah prays and the child is miraculously restored to life.

In verse 18 the widow addresses Elijah as a "man of God," a title approximately equivalent to "prophet" in the Hebrew Bible. There is some irony in the usage here. In the preceding scene Elijah demonstrated by a life-sustaining miracle that he speaks authentically as a prophet, but neither the widow nor the narrator referred to him by such a title. Here the widow acknowledges his office but connects that acknowledgment with the accusation that Elijah has indirectly brought death to her son. In her grief she lashes out at Elijah, claiming that his presence in her house has drawn unwanted divine attention to her. The "sin" of which she speaks is nothing specific, but the inevitable unworthiness of any human life in a deity's eyes (compare Solomon's sentiments in 8:46).

Elijah's speeches and actions represent a transfer of the widow's son from one realm to another and back again. The narrator contrasts "the house," that is, the family's ordinary space, with "the upper chamber," that is, a place of power where the prophet resides and encounters God. Elijah takes the child from intimate proximity to his mother in the house, to intimate contact with the prophet himself in his room (v. 21), and finally returns him to his mother in the house. The central scene has its own structure: two parallel prayers by Elijah, each followed by narrative lines:

  A. He cried out to Yahweh, "O Yahweh my God . . ." (17:20)
   B. Narrative (17:21a)
  A'. He cried out to Yahweh, "O Yahweh my God . . ." (17:21b)
   B'. Narrative (17:22)

Elijah's first prayer is accusatory. Explicitly he simply attributes the child's death to Yahweh. But implicitly he reminds Yahweh of the widow's hospitality—a hospitality Yahweh himself mandated (v. 8)—and therefore of the unfairness of using her obedience as an occasion to cause her ill. Elijah's words echo the widow's in verse 18: not only is the tone of both speeches resentful, but they end in almost identical phrases ("to kill my/her son"; the NRSV obscures the similarity). In the preceding episode (v. 13), Elijah addressed the widow with command and explanation, just as Yahweh had addressed him. Here Elijah addresses Yahweh with accusation, as the widow has addressed him. In this way the narrator positions the prophet in an intermediary role: as Yahweh to him, so he to the widow, and vice versa. Prophetic mediation is a two-way street: the prophet speaks the divine word to human beings and speaks the human word to God as well.

Elijah's action of stretching himself out upon the child is an act of symbolic communication of the prophet's vitality to the boy. (Compare the attempt to reinvigorate the aged David by physical contact with a nubile bed-partner in 1:2.) It also marks the turning point in the child's journey from death to life. Dead, he has been carried from physical intimacy with his mother ("from her bosom," v. 19b) to this physical intimacy with Elijah. Under the prophet's hand he will be restored to life and returned to his mother.

Elijah's second prayer is much more respectful in tone than his first. It does not even directly ask Yahweh to restore the child but merely expresses a wish that the child's life return to him. (The NRSV's "Let this child's life come into him again" is a slight paraphrase, since "let" is an imperative verb directed to Yahweh. A closer rendering would be "May this child's life please come into him again.") The narrator is equally circumspect. He acknowledges that Yahweh heeds Elijah's prayer, but the actual restoration of the child is phrased in the same impersonal terms Elijah used: "The child's life came into him again, and he lived" (NRSV, "revived"). The effect of this indirection will be discussed below, under the motif of "word and obedience."

The widow's final speech (v. 24) is striking. We would expect profuse expressions of gratitude; instead we hear a profound profession of faith in Elijah and the word he bears. The narrator unexpectedly transforms a tale of family tragedy and prophetic wonders into an exemplum of Yahwistic faith. The words also establish a strong inclusion with verse 1. There Elijah claimed that rain would be withheld "except at the *mouth* of my *word*" (thus the Hebrew idiom; NRSV, "except by my word"); here the widow proclaims that "the *word* of Yahweh in your *mouth* is truth." The inclusion alerts us to the structural unity of the whole chapter and to the importance throughout it of the theme of the word, which we shall examine below.

The Whole Chapter

Two sets of themes pervade the chapter. The first involves motifs of food and drink, famine and drought, and life and death. The second involves the motifs of word and obedience and the frequent occurrence of the command-and-compliance pattern.

FOOD AND FAMINE, LIFE AND DEATH

The context of the drought makes this complex of motifs central to the plot of chapters 17–18. Drought results in famine and is thus a matter of life and death for an essentially agricultural society. Of particular note, however, is the unusual way in which the narrator uses these motifs to unify and develop the dramatic action. The first episode has an ironic, almost farcical quality. Yahweh's care for Elijah is not only miraculous but lavish. Few of the prophet's contemporaries would have enjoyed "bread and meat in the morning, and bread and meat in the evening." Yet the God who delivers these delicacies by air express does not keep the Wadi Cherith from drying up. Even stranger is the fact that Elijah does not seek water from the nearby Jordan River, whose spring-fed flow is permanent. It is as if the question of Elijah's sustenance is merely a pretext, allowing the narrator to demonstrate the prophet's absolute obedience to Yahweh's commands.

The second episode has something of the same character. Yahweh claims to have commanded the widow to feed Elijah; but she seems to know nothing of it, and her desperate straits bode ill for her ability to do so. The ironic development of the motif is most striking at the end of the widow's speech, which paradoxically juxtaposes the motif of food and famine to that of life and death: "we shall eat it, and we shall die." The famine's severity will not be averted by a bit of bread. Even when Yahweh miraculously multiplies the widow's meal and oil, Elijah is reduced to much more meager fare than he enjoyed at the Wadi Cherith. The situation induces a development in the character of Elijah. From a completely passive recipient of divine bounty he becomes an active collaborator, conveying to the widow both his own need and the miraculous promise of Yahweh.

The motifs of food and famine do not appear in the third episode, but the irony continues. Despite the life-sustaining miracle of inexhaustible supplies, the widow's son dies. This brings the plot to a new intensity. It is no longer merely a question of finding water and food; it is not even a matter of averting possible death from starvation. It is now a matter of overcoming actual death. Moreover, responsibility for the boy's death falls upon the one who has been sustaining life: the widow blames Elijah, and Elijah blames Yahweh. As a result, Elijah's character undergoes a further development. He takes the initiative to confront Yahweh and ask that the boy be restored. When Elijah's prayer is answered, the development of these motifs reaches its fulfillment. Food and drink are assured, even in the midst of drought and famine, and life is victorious over death.

WORD AND OBEDIENCE

The inclusion in verses 1 and 24 alerts us to the importance of the motif "word" in the chapter, but many of the occurrences of the motif are obscured in the NRSV translation. Besides the inclusion, the motif occurs in verses 2, 5, 8, 13, 15, and 16. In addition, Elijah identifies his promise to the widow in verse 14 as a divine utterance, even though the word "word" does not appear. The development of the motif progressively enriches the characterization of Elijah. In verse 1 he claims to be a servant of Yahweh ("before whom I stand") but offers no support for the claim. He announces the drought on his own authority rather than on Yahweh's ("except by my word"), and even the narrator does not call him "prophet" or the like.

The first episode demonstrates that Elijah does indeed hear and obey Yahweh's word. The command-and-compliance pattern of the episode emphasizes Elijah's obedience in two ways: the unconventional line between the command and the compliance elements, "he went and did according to the word of Yahweh," suggests the alacrity of his response, and verbatim repetition highlights its completeness and exactitude. But obedient servanthood is not enough to underwrite the word of power Elijah claimed for himself in verse 1.

In the second episode the motif of "word" shows Elijah taking the initiative in a way that demonstrates his authority. To his approval of the widow's word (v. 13, "go and do according to your word"; NRSV, "as you have said") he adds his own condition, to which he attaches a divine pledge (v. 14). When the widow acts in conformity with Elijah's word (v. 15, "she went and did according to *Elijah's* word"; NRSV, "as Elijah said"), the divine promise is fulfilled "according to the word of Yahweh that he spoke by Elijah" (v. 16). Elijah is more than an obedient servant; this episode makes clear that he speaks a divine word of power with full authorization, and that obedience to *Elijah*—spotlighted by the variation in the command-and-compliance pattern from "your word" (v. 13) to "Elijah's word" (v. 15)—is equivalent to obedience to Yahweh. The reader and, as verse 16 makes clear, the narrator recognize the source of Elijah's authority.

All that remains is to have that recognition articulated within the story by a character. This occurs in the third episode, where the widow twice addresses Elijah as a "man of God." But within that episode the theme of word and obedience takes a further, unexpected twist. Elijah's second prayer begins a command-and-compliance pattern. Although the prophet's prayer is expressed as a wish rather than a command ("may this child's life come into him again"), it is echoed perfectly in the miraculous restoration ("the child's life came into him again"). Between the command and the compliance elements falls the line "Yahweh listened to the voice of Elijah." The phrase "to listen to the voice" of someone is the usual idiom in the Hebrew Bible for "to obey," and it is often translated that way when the subject is a human being (for example, 1 Kgs 20:36). In cases where Yahweh is the subject, it is treated as having weaker force: "to heed," "to grant a prayer," or the like. There is one passage, however, that betrays some discomfort in using the phrase of Yahweh, as if it could be construed that Yahweh were actually obeying a human being: Joshua 10:14 tells us that "there has been no day like it before or since, when Yahweh heeded a human voice." Both the command-and-compliance pattern and the use of the phrase "listen to the voice" thus hint at another dimension of the relationship between Yahweh and Elijah. In ordinary usage both would point toward obedience, as if Yahweh were obeying Elijah. Here both are slightly weakened—the pattern by the use of a request instead of a command, and the phrase by the impersonal wording of both elements ("the child's life came into him again")—so that Yahweh does not appear in any way submissive or constrained. Nevertheless, just as Elijah receives and acts upon Yahweh's word, so Yahweh in turn is responsive to Elijah's. This complements the insight mentioned earlier about Elijah's prophetic mediation being a two-way street (see above on v. 20): when human beings obey the divine word Elijah speaks, they obey Yahweh; and when Elijah addresses a human word to Yahweh, it is heeded.

Chapter 16

ELIJAH ENDS THE DROUGHT

1 Kings 18

Chapter 18 comprises two stories, both longer and more complex than the brief, almost anecdotal narratives in the preceding chapter. The first story recounts the ending of the drought (18:1-20, 41-46). The second, embedded within the first, tells of a contest on Mount Carmel between Yahweh and Baal for supremacy in Israel (18:21-40). The two stories are so different in theme and in characters (only Elijah appears in both stories) that many scholars believe them to have been originally independent of one another and only combined by later tradition. While there may be some truth to this view, in the present text the two stories form episodes in a single continuous narrative. Our approach will be to examine the two stories in relative isolation from one another, then to look at the entire chapter as a literary unity, and finally to consider the whole story of the drought (chs. 17–18).

The End of the Drought: 18:1-20

One of the literary conventions of the ancient world was the restriction of scenes to two principal actors ("actor" being understood broadly enough to include a group acting more or less in concert). While biblical Hebrew narrative does not universally observe this limitation, exceptions are rare (1 Kings 3:23-27 is notable in this regard). The narrator makes imaginative use of this convention in structuring the story of the end of the drought. After a word of Yahweh that starts the dramatic movement, the narrator dedicates three scenes to the three possible combinations of his main characters, Elijah, Obadiah, and Ahab. The first and third of these scenes are relatively short (Ahab and Obadiah, vv. 2b-6; Elijah and Ahab, vv. 17-20). This focuses attention on the longer central scene of Obadiah and Elijah, vv. 7-16.

236

INTRODUCTION: 18:1-2a

As in 17:2 and 17:8, a word of Yahweh sends Elijah on a journey and thus sets both the prophet and the plot in motion. The word comes to Elijah "in the third year"—in other words, the drought and consequent famine have reached disastrous proportions. In Israelite reckoning, "three years" may mean no more than one full year, plus small portions of the preceding and following years. But in the rain-dependent climate of Palestine, the absence of rain for even this amount of time is catastrophic.

Yahweh's word to Elijah follows the same pattern as in 17:2 and 17:8, a command accompanied by an explanation. Though the NRSV translation does not reflect it, Yahweh's words express a sense of purpose: "Go, present yourself to Ahab, *so that* I may send rain on the earth." Elijah's audience with the king is not simply to inform him of the impending end of the drought. It is somehow a necessary step toward accomplishing that result, though why that should be the case is not made clear. Although it is a minor element in the text, resolving this unclarity will take the rest of the chapter (see the discussion of the whole chapter below).

The divine word begins a command-and-compliance pattern that Elijah's subsequent actions only partially echo. The first divergence is that where Yahweh says "go, present yourself," Elijah "went *to* present himself." Substituting an infinitive of purpose for the imperative of command affords the narrator an opening for dramatic development (compare the similar strategy in verses 41-42 below). Instead of simply telling us that Elijah "went and presented himself," the narrator can present a whole series of scenes that accomplish the same result dramatically. These scenes extend through to verses 17-20, where Elijah finally encounters Ahab. The second divergence is the lack of anything corresponding to the explanation. In this case, too, rather than simply stating that "Yahweh sent rain on the earth," the narrator shows how this was accomplished. In the second half of the chapter, the assembly on Carmel, the contest, and Yahweh's victory prepare the way for the return of rain in verses 41-46.

AHAB AND OBADIAH: 18:2b-6

The first scene begins very slowly. The narrator tells us of the severity of the famine that results from the drought. This is not, however, merely a descriptive bit of background; we already know that the drought is in its third year and can easily surmise about the famine.

The words "in Samaria" indicate that the narrator is showing us the situation from Ahab's point of view: the famine is no doubt severe everywhere, but its severity in Ahab's Baalist capital (see 16:32) will be the king's first concern. Ahab calls upon one of his retainers, Obadiah, to help deal with the crisis. In view of the fact that after 18:16 Obadiah never appears again, the narrator tells us a surprising amount about him. This alerts us already to the importance he will have in the short time he does appear. His dialogue with Elijah (vv. 7-16) forms the centerpiece of this part of the story and contains links to chapters 17 and 19 that help to unify the Elijah narratives on several levels. (We will discuss these links later, when we consider the larger narrative units.) The first thing we learn about Obadiah is his name. Like Elijah's, it is significant, particularly for the chief servant of a king who worships Baal: "Obadiah" means "servant of Yahweh." In a moment the narrator will spell out in detail the depth of Obadiah's Yahwistic fidelity and the dangers such fidelity entails for him. The second thing we learn is that he is "in charge of the palace." The Hebrew phrase is a technical term, referring to a chief officer of the royal court, sometimes called the "chief steward" or "majordomo." Under David and Solomon, the responsibilities of this office were apparently limited to overseeing the running of the palace and the royal estates. But the office grew in importance and eventually became second only to the king (see, for instance, Isa 22:15-24 and 2 Kgs 15:5). Obadiah certainly has primary responsibility for the royal estates; that is why he alone joins the king's search for provisions for the royal animals. Whether his duties include anything beyond that is not said, though the next verse will make clear that the real second-in-command in the kingdom is the queen, Jezebel.

The narrator interrupts the action with a lengthy descriptive parenthesis about Obadiah. The keynote is straightforward: "Obadiah revered Yahweh greatly." The rest of the parenthesis illustrates his reverence. We learn that Jezebel has been persecuting (literally, "cutting off"; NRSV, "killing off") prophets of Yahweh, and that in the face of such persecution Obadiah takes the risk of rescuing a hundred of them, hiding them in caves, and keeping them supplied with bread and water (the verb form in Hebrew indicates that he supplies them regularly over a period of time). The parenthesis establishes Jezebel and Obadiah as antithetic characters, the one killing Yahweh's prophets and the other sustaining their lives. The contrast will deepen in verse 19, where we learn that Jezebel, too, supplies food and drink for prophets, but her bounty goes to prophets of Baal and Asherah.

Narrative action begins again with Ahab's speech directing Obadiah to a desperate search for any overlooked sources of water near which vegetation may be growing. The problem is fodder for the royal stables. On the surface of it, the king's concern is admirable: literally, "that we may keep horse and mule alive and not cut off some of the animals." (Mules were particularly valuable animals; see the remarks on 1:33.) But by inserting the immediately preceding parenthesis about Obadiah, the narrator creates a context that puts Ahab in a very bad light. While Jezebel is "cutting off" the prophets of Yahweh with impunity, Ahab worries about "cutting off" some of his animals. Ahab's speech also reveals a contrast between himself and Obadiah: because of the drought, Ahab is unable to provide sustenance for his animals; despite the drought, Obadiah is able to provide bread and water for the prophets of Yahweh.

This brief scene, therefore, contributes significantly to the characterization of Ahab and especially to that of Obadiah. The king is callous, more concerned with animals than people, and apparently indifferent to the depredations of his queen against the prophets of Yahweh. Obadiah is ambivalent. By position and duties he is a trusted servant of the king; but by name and clandestine deeds he is servant of Yahweh, set in opposition to Ahab and Jezebel. The last verse of the scene aptly symbolizes Obadiah's ambiguous position. In obedient cooperation with Ahab, he does his share of the search for fodder; yet, as the last words show, king and steward are moving separately and in opposite directions.

OBADIAH AND ELIJAH: 18:7-16

The scene of Obadiah's encounter with Elijah begins with narrative lines and a brief dialogue between Obadiah and Elijah (vv. 7-8). The narrative lines use vivid forms to present Elijah's appearance through Obadiah's eyes: "As Obadiah was on the way, there's Elijah coming to meet him!" Obadiah immediately recognizes Elijah and reverences him ("fell on his face" is a Hebrew idiom for greeting someone with a profound, respectful obeisance). Since the narrator has already told us that Obadiah recognizes Elijah, we realize that Obadiah's question is not seeking information so much as expressing surprise. It is not "Sir, are you really Elijah?" but "After all these years, Elijah, is it really you?"

Three elements of Elijah's response are noteworthy. First, it is very terse. In Hebrew, Elijah answers Obadiah's question with one word, then, with five more, commands him to carry the news of Elijah's return to Ahab. The prophet offers no explanations: not where he has been hiding, or how he has survived, or why he now intends to confront the king. Compared with Obadiah's attitude toward him, Elijah's attitude toward Obadiah seems highhanded. While Elijah does not owe Obadiah any explanations, our sympathy for the steward's faithful, if clandestine, service of Yahweh makes us feel that he deserves more understanding from Elijah.

The second point of note reveals the reason for Elijah's attitude. Even though Obadiah has already addressed Elijah as "my lord," Elijah retorts that Ahab is actually Obadiah's "lord" (using a slightly more solemn form of the same word). Elijah apparently will not countenance the ambivalence of Obadiah's position. Obadiah's "lord" is either Elijah and the God he represents, or Ahab and the god he follows; it cannot be both.

The third point makes the uncompromising character of Elijah's position clear. Obadiah is to announce to Ahab, *hinnēh ᵓēlîyāhû*, "Elijah is here." But because of the meaning of Elijah's name, those same words also mean "Behold, Yahweh is my God"! To carry out Elijah's command, Obadiah must profess his Yahwistic faith to the Baalist king.

Obadiah's reaction to this command is a long speech of protest. The structure of the speech is not completely symmetrical:

> A. Protest; sentence of death ("to kill me"; 18:9)
> > B. First argument (18:10)
> > > C. Elijah's command quoted (18:11)
> > B. First argument continued (18:12a)
> A'. Sentence of death ("he will kill me"; 18:12a)
> > B'. Second argument (18:12b-13)
> > > C'. Elijah's command quoted (18:14a)
> A". Sentence of death ("he will surely kill me"; 18:14b)

Twice Obadiah repeats Elijah's command verbatim; three times he says the command is tantamount to a death sentence. Interspersed among the repetitions are two arguments to support his unwillingness to do what Elijah wants. The loose organization and frequent repetitions give the speech an air of terrified desperation that exactly fits Obadiah's situation.

The first words of Obadiah's speech are a rhetorical question that reproves Elijah for endangering Obadiah's life. This sets the tone for the rest of the speech, since both arguments that Obadiah makes against Elijah's command focus on the mortal danger it entails for Obadiah and Elijah alike.

The first argument is in two parts. Obadiah tells Elijah of Ahab's sedulous search for the prophet not only in Israel but in surrounding countries as well. Obadiah does not say precisely why Ahab has been seeking Elijah. Violence against the prophet is not the only possibility, but Ahab's acquiescence in Jezebel's pogrom makes it the most likely one. Ahab's failure to find Elijah has no doubt done nothing to improve the king's feelings toward the prophet. And now Elijah wants

Obadiah to tell Ahab that he knows where Elijah is! The frustrated king's reaction is readily imaginable. But beyond this, if Ahab comes to suspect, however wrongly, that Obadiah has been sheltering Elijah, it could lead the king to discover Obadiah's true secret—that he has been secretly hiding other Yahweh prophets all along. The second part of the argument (v. 12a) raises a further issue. Elijah apparently has a reputation for mysterious appearances and disappearances, perhaps in part because of Ahab's failure to locate him. Obadiah protests that if he tells Ahab of Elijah's whereabouts and Elijah meanwhile disappears again, Obadiah's life is certainly forfeit.

The second argument, beginning with the final clause of verse 12, repeats very closely information the narrator gave us in the parenthetical aside in verses 3b-4. For this reason it is probably better to connect the clause with what follows rather than with what precedes, as the NRSV does:

> As soon as I have gone from you, the spirit of Yahweh will carry you I know not where; so, when I come and tell Ahab and he cannot find you, he will kill me.
> But I your servant have revered Yahweh from my youth. Has it not been told my lord what I did . . . ?

With this argument Obadiah informs Elijah of things we already know: Jezebel's persecution of the prophets of Yahweh and Obadiah's secret work to save them. By reappearing in public, Elijah risks running afoul of Jezebel; and, by public profession of Yahwism (*hinnēh 'ēlîyāhû* = "Behold, Yahweh is my God"), Obadiah may be liable to the same persecution. At the very least, he would jeopardize his position in the royal court, and therefore his opportunity to wield some influence on the prophets' behalf.

In reporting Obadiah's words, the narrator makes a few small but effective changes from the wording he used in verses 3b-4. The narrator said, "Obadiah revered . . ."; Obadiah says, "I your servant have revered . . . ." The echo is stronger in Hebrew than in English, since "Obadiah" means "servant of Yahweh." Obadiah, servant of Yahweh, acknowledges himself as Elijah's servant (and Elijah as his "lord": see v. 13). To serve Yahweh is to serve Elijah. Implicit in Obadiah's admission is a commitment to obey Elijah's command if Obadiah is unable to convince the prophet that it is too dangerous. The narrator said that Obadiah revered Yahweh "greatly"; Obadiah says, "from my youth." The narrator generalizes about the degree of Obadiah's fidelity to Yahweh; Obadiah specifies its duration. His efforts on behalf of the prophets of Yahweh are the fruit of lifelong adherence to the God of

Israel. Despite his position in the court of Ahab, he has remained true to Yahweh. The narrator told us that Jezebel was "cutting off" (*hakrît;* NRSV, "killing off") the prophets; Obadiah speaks of her "killing" them (*hărōg*). The narrator's verb is echoed in Ahab's speech in verse 5 about "cutting off" some of the animals (*nakrît;* NRSV, "lose"); in this way the narrator evokes a negative impression of Ahab, as we discussed above. Obadiah's verb, on the other hand, is echoed in his claims that Ahab "will kill me" (*hărāgānî,* vv. 12, 14); in this way Obadiah parallels his own likely fate at Ahab's hands to the persecution of other faithful Yahwists perpetrated by Jezebel.

Elijah's reply to Obadiah's frantic monologue is almost as laconic as his original command. He begins with a solemn oath, asserts his own calling as a servant of Yahweh, and unbends enough to assure Obadiah that he truly will appear before Ahab. This responds to Obadiah's least pressing concern, namely, that Elijah will vanish before Ahab catches up with him; but it offers the steward no reassurance about the other risks he has adduced. Obadiah may perhaps take some solace from the fact that Elijah no longer refers to Ahab as Obadiah's "lord," but this is weak consolation indeed. Elijah uses the same verb (NRSV, "show myself") as that used in verses 1 and 2 (NRSV, "present yourself/himself"): his intention to obey Yahweh's command exactly bears out his claim to be Yahweh's servant. The scene ends with another set of identical descriptions of Obadiah and Ahab moving in opposite directions (cf. v. 6b).

The ambivalent characterization of Obadiah that we saw in verses 2b-6 continues in this scene. At the beginning, Elijah considers Obadiah to be a servant of the king ("your lord," v. 8); at the end, however, he is at least neutral. In fact, since his oath in verse 15 is intended to reassure Obadiah, Elijah probably assumes at least some Yahwistic faith on Obadiah's part; he certainly presumes Obadiah's obedience. Obadiah considers himself a faithful follower of Yahweh but inadvertently betrays the ambivalence of his position by using "my lord" once of Ahab (v. 10) and once of Elijah (v. 13). Since Obadiah does not appear again anywhere in the stories of Elijah or Ahab, the narrator's careful efforts to characterize him as ambivalent may seem overdone. As we shall see below, however, they form part of the narrator's strategy for unifying the two stories in the chapter.

ELIJAH AND AHAB: 18:17-20

This scene begins like the preceding one, with a narrative line describing the encounter between Elijah and another character, and a question of identity addressed by that character to Elijah. There are significant differences between the two scenes, however. In verse 7 the narrator showed us Obadiah's encounter with Elijah through Obadiah's eyes; this contributed to the narrator's overall strategy of presenting Obadiah as an at least ambivalently sympathetic character. Here the narrator presents Ahab's encounter with Elijah neutrally. We are not invited to share the king's point of view or to develop any rapport with him at all. Similarly, his question to Elijah contrasts with Obadiah's. The questions are identical in structure but opposite in tone. Where Obadiah called Elijah "my lord," the king calls him "troubler of Israel." The word is easily misunderstood in English. The term generally describes people whose behavior causes difficulties *indirectly* rather than directly. Here, for example, it does not mean that Elijah himself is directly troubling Israel by causing the drought, as if Ahab recognizes and admits that Elijah has the power he claims over rainfall. It means rather that something Elijah has done has indirectly resulted in the drought; presumably, in the mouth of the Baalist king it means that Elijah's intransigent championing of Yahweh as sole God of Israel has aroused the wrath of Baal and caused him to withhold Israel's rain. (Baal was the Canaanite god of rain and storms; see the discussion below of "The Whole Drought Story: Baal vs. Yahweh.")

Elijah's reply is in two parts. First he turns Ahab's accusation back against him. It is Ahab, and indeed the whole house of Omri, whose behavior bears responsibility for the drought. Then he issues a command to which Ahab accedes. Both parts merit further comment.

Most translations, including the NRSV, do not represent the first part of Elijah's reply accurately. A closer rendering would be:

> I have not troubled Israel, but you have, and your father's house, because (all of) you have forsaken the commandments of Yahweh. And you yourself have followed the Baals.

Elijah accuses Ahab and the whole house of Omri of disobedience to Yahweh. To this sin he attributes the "troubling" of Israel, that is, the drought. But Ahab himself is guilty of an even greater sin. He has not only disobeyed Yahweh; he has also taken up with Baal.[1] These claims are in harmony with the information in 16:25-33, which decried Omri's

[1]Although Elijah uses the plural "Baals," Baal was a single god, the chief deity of the Canaanite religious system. (The word *baʿal* means "master" or "lord" in several Semitic languages; the god Baal's personal name was apparently Hadad.) The plural may be an allusion to the fact that Baal was worshiped under different titles at different places. For example, at Ekron he was known as Baal-Zebul, "Prince Baal" (deformed in Hebrew writing to Baal-Zebub, "Lord of a Fly"; see 2 Kgs 1:2-3).

evil as following Jeroboam's calf-idols (16:25-26) and identified Ahab's greater evil as Baal worship (16:31-33).[2]

The second part of Elijah's reply is a command. However, the description of Ahab's compliance that follows does not conform to a standard command-and-compliance pattern. The vocabulary of the command is echoed in the compliance, but the construction is quite different.

> "And now, send, gather all Israel to me at Mount Carmel, and the four hundred fifty prophets of Baal and the four hundred prophets of Asherah, who eat at Jezebel's table." And Ahab sent to all the Israelites, and he gathered the prophets at Mount Carmel.

The command-and-compliance pattern usually uses verbatim repetition to indicate the careful and detailed obedience of the respondent. Here, despite the fact that Ahab in the last analysis carries out Elijah's orders, the narrator apparently *avoids* verbatim repetition. He sends to all Israel, but the text does not say that he gathers them; he gathers "the prophets," but does he gather all the prophets Elijah demanded? The effect is to depict Ahab as not submitting to Elijah's authority but as voluntarily (and perhaps only grudgingly and imperfectly) cooperating with his wishes. The introduction of the people of Israel and the prophets of Baal affords a transition to the other main component of chapter 18, the story of the contest on Mount Carmel.

The Contest on Mount Carmel: 18:21-40

Neither Obadiah nor Ahab appears in the story of the contest on Mount Carmel. Elijah's dialogue partners are the people of Israel and the prophets of Baal. Elijah, representing Yahweh, and the prophets of Baal, representing their deity, contend for the loyalties of the people of Israel. There is no explicit reference to the drought or its ending, to famine, or to royal persecution of followers of Yahweh. The story does not have the symmetrical structure we have often seen in other narratives, but it can be conveniently subdivided according to Elijah's dialogue partners.

---

[2]The reference to Omri alerts us to the possibility that the system of stories embedded within stories may be more extensive than we suspected (see the remarks above on p. 225). The story of Elijah in chapters 17–19 forms part of the story of Ahab in 16:29–22:40. But this in turn forms part of the story of the dynasty of Omri that begins in 1 Kings 16:23 and continues until the cataclysmic violence of 2 Kings 9–11 that wipes out the entire family.

ELIJAH AND THE PEOPLE: 18:21-24

The story opens with a narrative line, "Elijah came near to all the people." The verb "to come near" is an important leitmotif in this story; we shall examine it later. Elijah's dialogue with the people is in two unequal parts:

A. Elijah speaks to the people (18:21a)
B. The people do not answer (18:21b)
A'. Elijah speaks to the people (18:22-24a)
B'. The people answer (18:24b)

Verbal echoes in B and B' highlight the parallel structure, but they are not all reflected in the NRSV. In verse 21b, "the *people* did not *answer* him a *word*." In verse 24b, literally, "all the *people answered* and said, 'The *word* is good!'"

Elijah's first speech is a direct challenge to the people, accusing them of wavering between deities. Elijah's verb, *psḥ* (NRSV, "limping"), is of uncertain meaning. It refers to some sort of uneven or ungainly gait, perhaps limping, hobbling, skipping, or even leaping. In the present context it seems to refer to hobbling along on two uneven crutches. (The NRSV's "with two different opinions" translates a Hebrew phrase that means literally "on two tree branches.") The grotesque image is hardly flattering to the people, but awkwardness is not the only point of Elijah's metaphor. In ancient Israel, crippling illness or injury was in itself a sign of divine disfavor. For this reason, one who was so afflicted was excluded from functioning as a priest (see Lev 21:18, where *psḥ* is listed among the disqualifying defects). As long, then, as the people continue to *psḥ*, they will be unfit for membership in Yahweh's cultic community. And so Elijah insists on a clear, exclusive choice between Yahweh and Baal.

From a modern perspective, we can appreciate Elijah's position. We are accustomed to thinking of religions in either/or categories: either Yahweh or Baal. It is perhaps harder for us to understand the Baalist view. Ancient paganisms were not generally exclusivistic. A belief in many deities, each with his or her own proper sphere of influence, entails an openness to worshiping whichever god is appropriate in a given situation. For a Baalist, then, there would be no need to choose between Yahweh and Baal; a person could reverence both deities as long as they did not become rivals for the same sphere of influence. Hidden, then, behind the choice Elijah offers the people is a prior choice: exclusive or inclusive worship. Since Yahweh is on the side of exclusivism and Baal is not, even a willingness to consider choosing moves one toward Yahweh. The people, however, are not willing to choose. They "did not answer him a word."

Elijah's second speech is much longer. If the people are not willing to choose between Yahweh and Baal, it must be that they do not see the two gods as rivals. Elijah therefore proposes a contest that will pit them against one another. He begins by identifying the representatives of each side: himself for Yahweh, and the prophets of Baal for their deity. His words emphasize strongly the inequality of numbers: Yahweh's one ("I, even I alone,") against Baal's four hundred fifty. The advantage the Baal prophets have in the contest will become a recurrent motif in the following verses.

Elijah then defines rules for the contest. First, he allows the Baal prophets complete control over the sacrificial animals (v. 23a). They supply them, and they have first choice. (The NRSV translates "let two bulls be given us," as if the bulls were to be supplied by a third party, but this is misleading. A more accurate translation is "let them give us two bulls"—the Baal prophets themselves furnish the animals.) This arrangement favors the Baal prophets, of course, because there is nothing to prevent them from providing one worthy and one unworthy animal and leaving the imperfect one to Elijah.

Second, Elijah details the preparations both sides will make. Here he balances the terms: both will prepare the sacrifice and arrange it on the wood, but not light it (v. 23b).

Third, both sides will invoke their respective deities (v. 24a). At this point, however, Elijah unexpectedly changes pronouns. Instead of talking about the Baal prophets, "they will call on the name of their god," he says to the people themselves, "you call on the name of your god." Since Yahweh demands choice, as long as the people are unwilling to make a choice between Yahweh and Baal, they are in effect siding with Baal.

Finally, the contest will be decided by divine response. (The assumption that only one god will answer, like the issue of choice itself, is a Yahwist presupposition. If both gods send fire, then there will be no need to choose, and Baalist theology will be victorious.) This time the people respond. Their approval of the proposed contest implies a willingness to consider choosing between gods. They begin, without realizing it, to adopt a Yahwistic point of view. In this way the narrator foreshadows Yahweh's imminent victory over Baal and his prophets.

ELIJAH AND THE PROPHETS OF BAAL: 18:25-29

Like Elijah's dialogue with the people, his dialogue with the prophets of Baal is in two parts that end with parallel lines: "no voice, and no answer" (v. 26a); "no voice, no answer, and no response" (v. 29). Each part includes a speech by Elijah and a description of how the prophets of Baal act in response to Elijah's words.

Elijah's first speech instructs the prophets on the rules of the contest that he spelled out in verses 23-24. The only thing Elijah adds is that because of their greater numbers, the Baal prophets can go first. The remark is practical, since they will be able to complete their preparations before he will. But it also deepens the impression given earlier that the Baal prophets have a definite advantage in the contest, since it gives Baal the chance for a preemptive strike, so to speak. The Baal prophets follow Elijah's instructions in almost identical terms. The effect of the similar vocabulary is to establish a command-and-compliance pattern with an ironic twist: the Yahweh prophet commands, and the Baal prophets obey without objection, as if they acknowledge his authority. This is the first in a series of sardonic insults aimed at the Baal prophets, sometimes by Elijah, sometimes by the narrator himself.

There are three new elements in the description of the Baal prophets' actions. The bull is one "that he gave them" (NRSV, "that was given them"); the invocation of Baal lasts "from morning until noon"; and the prophets' words are, "O Baal, answer us!" The first of these elements is difficult to explain, since it directly contradicts verse 23, which in Hebrew specifies that the Baal prophets themselves supply the bulls (see above), and verse 25, where Elijah grants them first choice of animal. The NRSV's passive translation lessens the contradiction but does not eliminate it entirely. The second element begins a series of time references that organize and unify the two parts of Elijah's dialogue with the prophets: the first part occurs during the morning "until noon" (v. 26), the second part begins "at noon" (v. 27) and continues "as noon passed" (v. 29; NRSV, "midday") "until the time of the offering of the oblation" (v. 29; see also v. 36).[3] The third element, the invocation of Baal, is the first and only time the prophets of Baal speak in the entire story. Their prayer is a simple demand (only two words in Hebrew). To a Hebrew ear such a prayer, unaccompanied by motivation clauses or appeals to the deity's previous gracious deeds, would likely sound abrupt and even rude; contrast Elijah's parallel prayer in verses 36-37.

Baal's prophets encounter silence. "There is no voice. There is no answerer." This is closer to the Hebrew than the NRSV's rendering,

---

[3]The "time of the offering of the oblation" is mid to late afternoon, no earlier than three o'clock in the afternoon, and perhaps as late as twilight. The exact hour is difficult to determine, and may have varied through the centuries in ancient Israel.

and it reveals several noteworthy elements that are obscured by the NRSV. All of them point to a profound theological judgment about Baal. First, the narrator does not say, "Baal did not answer," as if Baal exists and can answer but for some reason remains silent. By phrasing the sentence in terms of absence ("There is no") rather than presence, the narrator hints at Baal's nonentity. Second, the terms express a present, not a past tense. Besides making the scene vivid for the reader, this too suggests an absolute judgment of nonexistence, not a mere observation about the nonoccurrence of an event. Finally, the sequence "no voice, no answerer" (not "no voice, no answer," as in the NRSV) implies a causal relationship: there is no voice *because* there is no one to answer when Baal is invoked.

Between the two parts of Elijah's dialogue with the prophets of Baal is an isolated narrative line (v. 26b): the prophets "limped about the altar they had made."[4] The line's isolated position draws attention to it. It is generally held to refer to a ceremonial dance around the Baalist altar (or perhaps on it; ancient altars were often large platforms onto which the officiant priest would climb to offer the sacrifice). The significance of the line is that it describes the Baal prophets as "limping," the same word that Elijah used of the people of Israel (Hebrew, *psḥ;* see the remarks above on v. 21). The effect is twofold. It satirizes the Baal prophets: their dance is ungainly and reveals them as unfit to offer sacrifice to Yahweh. It also creates a subtle link between the people of Israel and the Baal prophets, underscoring that the people's "limping with two different opinions" is in effect a Baalist stance.

The order of events in the text presents this picture. All morning the Baal prophets prepare their sacrifice and invoke Baal's name. As midday approaches and the unresponsiveness of Baal becomes more evident, they intensify their efforts by dancing about (or upon) the altar. Elijah, meanwhile, watches their carryings-on with growing amusement. "At noon, Elijah mocked them" (v. 27). His second speech is biting sarcasm; unfortunately it is also beyond our resources to understand in detail. The middle of the speech, for example, *ky śyh wky śyg* (NRSV, "either he is meditating, or he has wandered away"), uses two similar-sounding words, one of which occurs nowhere else in the Hebrew Bible.[5] There is some evidence that the two terms together may mean "to be busy"; there are even some commentators who think

---

[4]The best Hebrew manuscripts actually read, "the altar *he* had made," but this seems likely to be a slip of the scribal pen.

[5]An alternate form of the first word, *śwḥ,* occurs in Genesis 24:63, where its meaning is equally uncertain (NRSV, "to walk").

the idiom is bathroom humor ("he's doing his business"). It may be, however, that the second word is simply a sound-play whose meaning is unrelated to anything else in the lexicon (compare "helter-skelter" in English, for example). The references to Baal's being on a journey and being asleep may allude to commonly known mythological stories of the god, including his temporary imprisonment in the underworld by the god Death. The entire taunt, however, is as pungent in its form as it probably was in its unrecoverable content. The following loose paraphrase tries to capture something of the tone:

> At noon Elijah mocked them, saying: "Cry louder! After all, he's a god: he's busy, in a tizzy, he's off on the road! Or perhaps he's asleep, and you can wake him! "

The Baal prophets do exactly what Elijah tells them: they cry louder, as if they agree with his sarcastic comments about Baal's being too preoccupied to pay attention. In this way the narrator turns Elijah's insults against Baal into insults against Baal's prophets as well. The derision of the prophets takes a brutal turn when the narrator describes the ritual self-mutilation they indulge in to attract Baal's notice. (Such rites are not an exaggeration. We have ancient testimony of similar self-mutilation in the pagan cults of the same part of the world centuries later. In Israel, too, some practiced self-laceration as a mourning rite, though it was generally forbidden. See, for example, Jer 41:5; Deut 14:1; Lev 19:28.) The prophets' bloodletting injects an ominous note and points forward to verse 40, where the silence of Baal will cost his prophets their lives.

The prophets continue in their frantic prophetic activity well into the afternoon. The word translated "raved on" by the NRSV is a derived form of the ordinary verb "to act as a prophet." It usually refers to the more uncontrolled aspects of prophetic behavior, such as frenzies and trances (see 1 Sam 10:1-13; 19:18-24), while the basic form refers to the more rational and controlled aspects, such as delivering oracles. The contrast is striking: as the day wears on, the prophets of Baal become progressively wilder in their desperation to elicit a response. Elijah, meanwhile, calmly goes about his preparations. Despite all their efforts, however, the Baal prophets are met with silence. "There is no voice. There is no answerer. There is no attention." To the devastating negatives of verse 26, the narrator adds a third, "no attention" (the NRSV's "no response" misses the Hebrew nuance). The absence of a voice reveals not only the absence of an answerer but even the absence of anyone paying heed to the Baal prophets at all.

ELIJAH 'S SACRIFICE: 18:30-39

Like the preceding dialogues, the description of Elijah's sacrifice is in two parts, the preparations (vv. 30-35) and the sacrifice proper (vv. 36-39). Each part begins with movement, using the motif word "come near" (Hebrew, *ngš*): in verse 30 Elijah calls the people to "come near" him (NRSV, "come closer"); in verse 36 Elijah himself "comes near." Time indicators show that Elijah prepares his sacrifice while the Baal prophets are still carrying on: they "raved on until the time of the offering of the oblation" (v. 29), and Elijah will have completed his preparations and will be ready to offer his prayer when that moment arrives (v. 36).

Elijah's preparations begin with a command to the people to approach him and their compliance. The image is pregnant: at Elijah's words the people, who have been watching the fascinating but futile to-do of the Baal prophets, turn from them to attend the prophet of Yahweh. This "coming near" foreshadows their ultimate re-turning from Baal to Yahweh.

Elijah next prepares an altar upon which to offer his sacrifice. The fact that he repairs a destroyed altar informs us of two things: Carmel was previously a site for the worship of Yahweh, and royal persecution of Yahwism was systematic, involving worship sites as well as cultic personnel. Dramatic movement comes to a halt as the narrator gives us a lengthy aside about the stones Elijah uses to construct the altar (v. 31). The grammatical complexity of the sentence as well as the pause in the action draws attention to the aside and points up its importance. It recalls Israelite traditions about the patriarch Jacob: that he had twelve sons, from whom descended the twelve tribes of Israel; that he built an altar to God in the presence of "all the people" (Gen 35:5-7); and that his uniquely intimate relationship with Yahweh was reflected in the name "Israel," which God bestowed on him (see the stories in Genesis 32:22-32 and 35:9-15). The blessing that makes Israel a people and indeed their very name are gifts to them from Yahweh through their ancestor Jacob/Israel! By offering the reader this aside as a comment on Elijah's twelve stones instead of having Elijah interpret the twelve stones to his audience, the narrator implies that the prophet's audience needed no such interpretation. The simple fact of *twelve* stones, he suggests, would evoke the Jacob traditions for Elijah's spectators. Their Baalism, then, is not so deep-rooted as to have choked out Yahwism altogether. This is consistent with the picture the narrator has already given us. The people have no difficulty worshiping both gods simultaneously; only Elijah considers Baalism and Yahwism mutually exclusive. The narrator is able to represent both points of view, though his sympathies lie with Elijah.

Elijah builds the altar "in the name of Yahweh." Since this whole story hinges on invoking names of the deities, the motif of the divine name appears several times. But introducing it here is both unexpected (in verse 30 the same altar was simply "the altar of Yahweh") and significant. The immediately preceding words were the divine decree "Israel shall be your name." The patriarch's name—which now belongs to all the people—and the divine name are a pair. Yahweh gave Israel its name: Israel is Yahweh's people. Israel must now proclaim Yahweh's name: Yahweh must be their God.

Elijah continues his preparations for the sacrifice. He digs a trench around the altar,[6] arranges the wood, dresses the sacrificial animal, and places it on the wood. All conforms to the rules laid down in verse 23, except for the mysterious trench. The word usually refers in Hebrew to an artificial channel for water, but it never occurs in conjunction with a religious sacrifice or an altar. The trench would puzzle the people watching Elijah dig it, just as it puzzles the reader until the narrator reveals its purpose in verses 34-35.[7] Elijah has the people drench the sacrifice—bull, wood, altar, and all—with gallons upon gallons of water. The amount of water is indeterminate, since the jars used are not of a standard size. But the Hebrew word refers to a large, portable jar used to carry household water from a well or cistern, and therefore each jar will hold at least a few gallons. The trench would catch any runoff; in addition, Elijah himself fills the trench with water (v. 35; read "and he filled" for the NRSV's "and filled"), perhaps to mark the limits of the sacred area.

What is the point of this drenching? The amount of time and detail the narrator spends on it alerts us to its importance. Within the narrow context of the contest story, at least three things are clear. First, Elijah directs the people to empty twelve jars onto the sacrifice (four jars three times). Verse 31 already evoked the peculiar Israelite significance of the number twelve. Second, the people comply with Elijah's commands.

---

[6]The size of the trench is difficult to determine. The Hebrew phrase "capacity of two measures of seed" may mean large enough to hold two measures of seed, as the NRSV takes it; but this seems unrealistically small for a trench surrounding a stone altar big enough to hold a sacrificial bull and wood to burn it. (Two *sĕʾâ*, or "measures," would be about three pecks or seven gallons.) On the other hand, the phrase is also used in Hebrew for a measure of area, the amount of land that could be sown using two measures of seed. In this case the trench presumably surrounds the area, which would be on the order of 1,500 square yards—unrealistically large for the situation.

[7]The NRSV follows an alternate tradition in numbering the verses at this point. In the standard Hebrew text, verse 34 begins with the sentence "He said, 'Fill the jars with water,'" not with the following sentence, "Then he said, 'Do it a second time.'"

Their obedience to his first command is implied; to the second and third it is explicit and exact. As it did in verse 30, the people's conformity with Elijah's commands foreshadows their eventual complete capitulation to his demand for exclusive worship of Yahweh. Finally, soaking everything with water heightens the impressiveness of the imminent miracle, since Yahweh's fire has to cope with wet materials. (We will see below that in the larger context of the whole chapter, the libation of water is even more meaningful.)

The sacrifice proper begins when Elijah "comes near," presumably to the altar and sacrifice he has prepared, and directs a prayer to Yahweh. His prayer comprises two invocations of Yahweh, each followed by specific and parallel requests:

> A. "Yahweh, God of Abraham, Isaac, and Israel"
> B. "Today, let it be known that you are God in Israel . . . ."
> A'. "Answer me, Yahweh, answer me."
> B'. "Let this people know that you are God . . . ."

The emphatic position of the word "today" adds urgency to Elijah's requests. To demonstrate his supremacy, Yahweh must act immediately: he must "answer by fire."

The first invocation addresses Yahweh under the rare patriarchal title "God of Abraham, Isaac, and Israel"; the normal phrase is "God of Abraham, Isaac, and Jacob." Substituting "Israel" for "Jacob" recalls the narrator's reference in verse 31 to the story of Jacob's name. It is as Israel's God—the God of the whole people descended from Jacob/Israel—that Elijah calls upon Yahweh. His requests will include that Yahweh show himself to be God "in Israel" and, after the second invocation, that "this people" come to know that Yahweh is God. He also requests public vindication for himself and his deeds (v. 36b), though always as embodying obedience to Yahweh: "your servant," "your bidding." In the context of the contest story, this means ratifying Elijah's demand for choice between Yahweh and Baal and justifying his call for a contest by winning it.

The second invocation corresponds to that of the Baal prophets in verse 26, a straightforward plea that the deity "answer." Elijah's final request is difficult to interpret. Literally, he asks that the people come to know that "*you* [emphatic pronoun] have turned their minds backwards." The NRSV takes it as meaning that Yahweh is responsible for the people's conversion back to him, but this is not the most likely reading of the text: the verb is past tense, though the people have not yet come back to Yahweh; and "turning backwards" is quite different in Hebrew from "turning back," in the sense of conversion. Furthermore, the emphatic pronoun suggests that without this revelation, the people will probably credit the turning of their minds to Baal rather than to Yahweh. Startling though it may be, Elijah seems to be attributing to Yahweh the popular confusion of Yahweh and Baal that the contest is intended to resolve. If the people of Israel have been turned away from Yahweh, only Yahweh himself could have done it.[8] In other words, Elijah does not even credit Baal with enough reality to be an effective rival to Yahweh. Yahweh's response is dramatic. Miraculous fire of some sort or other is a standard feature of divine appearances (see, for example, Exod 3:1-6), divine punishments (2 Kgs 1), and divinely consumed sacrifices (Judg 6:19-24). Here "the fire of Yahweh" is probably lightning, a most appropriate and impressive display of divine power, particularly in the larger context of the drought story, where the sky is still cloudless (see 18:41-44). The fire consumes everything inside the sacred area bounded by the trench. The Hebrew word order highlights the completeness of the destruction by surrounding the direct objects with the verbs "to eat" and "to lick up": "It ate the offering and the wood and the stones and the dust and the water in the trench it licked up." Nothing escapes the divine fire.

The people's reaction to Yahweh's fire is equally dramatic. When they witness Yahweh's power displayed, they fall on their faces in awe. (There is an ironic echo here: the people must see fire "fall" before they themselves will "fall.") And they acclaim Yahweh's victory in words that echo Elijah's when he set the contest rules. (See v. 24. The NRSV obscures the connection slightly by adding the word "indeed" to both verses 24 and 39, but adding it in a different place each time. A more literal translation would be: verse 24, "the god who answers by fire—he is God!"; and verse 39, "Yahweh—he is God! Yahweh—he is God!")

Elijah, the People, and the Prophets of Baal: 18:40

Elijah addresses the people once more, and once more they comply with his command. They seize the prophets of the silent Baal. Elijah takes the prophets down off Mount Carmel to the Wadi Kishon, which runs through the Jezreel Valley to the north of the Carmel ridge. There

---

[8]Although Elijah does not suggest any reason why Yahweh would do such a thing, the idea is not unusual in Hebrew thought. Yahweh can lead people into error to trap them (1 Kgs 22:19-23), to gain glory through their downfall (Exod 7:1-5), to chastise them (2 Sam 24), to test their faithfulness (Deut 13:1-3), and even for reasons unknown (Isa 63:17). The underlying theological principle is that since Yahweh is the only God of Israel, all that happens to Yahweh's people is ultimately his responsibility.

he slaughters (Hebrew, *šāhat;* NRSV, "killed") them. The narrator's choice of verb is subtle. It is not the same as those used of Jezebel's killing of the Yahweh prophets in verses 4 and 13 or of Obadiah's danger in verses 9, 12, and 14. The Hebrew Bible uses the verb *šāhat* primarily for the slaughtering of animals, usually for sacrifice, and for the wholesale killing of large numbers of people (for example, 2 Kgs 10:7, 14). In the case of human beings, the connotations tend to depersonalize the victims, treating their deaths as mass phenomena and reducing them to the same category as animal slaughter. These two usages of the verb, for animals and for groups of humans, set up an oblique resonance with the earlier uses of the verb "cut off." In verse 4, "cut off" was used of Jezebel's persecution of the prophets of Yahweh (NRSV, "killing off"), and in verse 5 it was used of slaughtering livestock (NRSV, "lose"). Elijah's massacre of the Baal prophets is the counterblow to Jezebel's pogrom.

THE WHOLE CONTEST STORY

Before we return to the story of the end of the drought, it is worth pausing to appreciate the literary quality of the contest story in itself. There are three interwoven strands of dramatic development: the contest of the gods, the rivalry of the prophets, and the conversion of the people. The narrator uses several devices, particularly keywords and motifs such as "answer" and "come near," to advance all three strands.

The contest of the gods is the most evident plot line. Here the keyword "answer" is particularly significant. Elijah originally proposes the contest in terms of a god's answering (v. 24). When Baal's prophets plead with him to answer them (v. 26), there is "no answerer" (vv. 26, 29). When Elijah calls upon Yahweh to answer (v. 37), Yahweh's response demonstrates his power beyond dispute. (The narrator does not use the word "answer" in describing Yahweh's response. Had he done so, it would have echoed Elijah's prayer too closely and established a command-and-compliance pattern, with Yahweh obediently doing exactly what Elijah asked. Compare the narrator's similar avoidance of this impression in 17:21-22; see above, p. 235.)

In the development of this plot line, the narrator skillfully manipulates the tempo of the story for maximum dramatic effect. The course of the action takes unexpected detours, slows, halts temporarily, always delaying the climax. After Elijah spells out the rules of the contest to the people and gains their agreement (v. 23), he repeats them in detail to the Baal prophets (v. 25). We watch them carry out Elijah's instructions one by one, hear their words addressed in vain to Baal, and reflect on their failure (in the present as well as the past: "There is no voice, there is no answerer," v. 26). Then we go through a whole second scene of Baalist activity: limping, listening to Elijah's mockery, mutilating themselves, raving on. This scene adds depth to the negative characterization of the prophets of Baal, but it does not advance the contest of the gods at all. At its end, as at its beginning, "there is no voice, there is no answerer" (v. 29).

The action takes a new step forward when we turn to Elijah's preparations for the sacrifice. But the piling up of detail and the unnecessary verbiage in the description are a further delaying tactic. The narrator tells us of the stones, of the trench and its size, of arranging the wood, of cutting up the bull, of disposing the offering on the wood, of filling water jars and drenching the offering once, twice, three times, of the runoff water and of Elijah's filling the trench himself. And as if that slowing of the narrative pace were not enough, the narrator stops the action completely in verse 31 by "breaking frame" (a technical term for the narrator's stepping outside the boundaries of the story to address the audience directly) to remind us of the Jacob traditions implied in the twelve stones. When Elijah eventually invokes Yahweh, he does so in two parallel prayers with much repetition in word and idea. Finally, after all the delay, the climax comes in two verses that strike like the lightning they describe: "Yahweh's fire fell . . . and the people said, 'Yahweh—he is God!'"

The second plot line in the contest story is the rivalry of the prophets. Elijah stages the entire scene; the Baal prophets do whatever he says. He proposes the contest to the people and they agree; he spells out the rules to the Baal prophets and they obey (vv. 25-26). On one occasion the Baal prophets even comply with Elijah's ironic command, satirizing themselves in the process (vv. 27-28). When they offer their sacrifice, their preparations begin calmly but become progressively more chaotic (they limp, cry loudly, cut themselves, rave) as Baal's failure to respond lasts throughout the day; Elijah's preparations are careful, systematic, and immediately effective. The Baal prophets' prayer is abrupt, a demand without a context; Elijah couches his prayer in terms that propose Yahweh's greater glory as the reason for his response. The most obvious embodiment of this rivalry is in the contrast between the beginning and the end of the story: Elijah complains that "I, even I only, am left a prophet of Yahweh; but Baal's prophets number four hundred fifty" (v. 22). Ultimately, however, Elijah slaughters all his rivals (v. 40).

The third plot line is the conversion of the people. At the beginning of the contest story, several things identify the people with the Baalist position. Like Baal's prophets they limp, and like Baal himself they do not answer (vv. 21 and 26). Their refusal to answer signals their initial unwillingness to accept the Yahwistic demand for exclusivism. This posture changes gradually, however, and the change develops in tandem with the motif word "come near" (*ngš;* vv. 21, 30, 36). At first Elijah "comes near" the people to challenge them (they do not answer) and to propose the contest (they answer and accept). As we noted above, willingness to consider choosing between deities is essentially a Yahwistic point of view. This first movement, therefore, already results in the people beginning to adopt a Yahwistic perspective. Next, after the futility of Baal becomes obvious, Elijah commands the people to "come near," and they do. This compliance is literally their first step away from Baal and back toward Yahweh. They will subsequently become actively involved in Elijah's preparations by complying with his commands to drench the offerings two and three times (v. 34). Finally, Elijah "comes near" to invoke Yahweh (v. 36), implicitly bringing the people along with him. Yahweh's spectacular acceptance of the offering brings the people to the choice they initially refused to make; their obeisance and acclamation (v. 39) reverses their original silence (v. 21). And their compliance with Elijah's final command to seize the prophets of Baal definitively breaks any ties between the people and Baal.

The last verses of the story, then, bring the three narrative strands to completion and link them causally: Yahweh's victory over Baal accomplishes the conversion of the people, who then assist Elijah to destroy his rivals.

THE END OF THE DROUGHT, CONTINUED: 18:41-46

The narrative returns to the story of the end of the drought. The people of Israel and the prophets of Baal disappear from the scene and Ahab reappears, along with a nameless and previously unmentioned servant of Elijah. The purpose of these verses is to resolve the remaining part of Yahweh's words to Elijah in 18:1, the promise to send rain on the earth.

The episode begins with a command-and-compliance pattern. Elijah gives three commands to Ahab: go up, eat, and drink. Ahab complies with the first, but the narrator replaces the others with infinitives of purpose: Ahab goes up *to* eat and *to* drink. As in 18:1-2, the substitution creates space for narrative development. Things must happen before Ahab can be shown eating and drinking. (As a matter of fact, the narrator never does tell us whether Ahab actually complied with these commands. The omission is significant, as we shall see when we examine the Mosaic allusions in the whole Elijah story; see below, p. 286.) The reason for the command is provocative: Elijah hears rain coming, despite the fact that the sky is still cloudless. Throughout this section Elijah will always be one step ahead of things. He will warn Ahab of the coming downpour before it happens, and he will precede the king all the way to Jezreel.

The Hebrew word order in verse 42 implies that after their encounter Ahab and Elijah climb Carmel at the same time, though to different places. A closer English paraphrase might be, "When Ahab went up . . . Elijah also went up . . . ." (The verb "go up" is a keyword throughout verses 41-44. This kind of remark, describing a double movement, often marks a scene break in Hebrew narrative; the same thing occurs, for instance, in 18:6b and 18:16b, and a similar technique will end the whole chapter in verses 45b-46.) Atop Carmel, Elijah crouches in an odd and presumably awkward posture. Since the verb is very rare in biblical Hebrew, exactly what Elijah is doing and why he is doing it are obscure. Some think it is a posture of prayer, others of extreme concentration. Whatever it is, Elijah is unable to scan the sky for the approach of rain and must send his servant to do so. His command to the servant, "Go up now," is identical to his word to Ahab in verse 41, except that with the servant Elijah uses a polite form that softens the command slightly (something like "Go up, would you"; the NRSV adds "now" to capture this nuance). Toward his servant, Elijah is courteous; toward the king, he is still confrontative.

The servant makes several trips up to a point overlooking the Mediterranean Sea, and finally descries a wisp of cloud on the horizon. The phrase "small as a person's palm" may be a standard metaphor indicating smallness (see 17:12, for instance: the widow had only "a palmful" of meal), or it may mean a cloud so small that the palm of a person's hand held at arm's length would cover it. In any case, it is enough for Elijah. Still acting through his servant, he warns Ahab to make his escape immediately, or else the rain will impede his chariot. The rain comes, though an unusual Hebrew phrase makes the timing uncertain; it may mean "meanwhile" or "between one moment and the next." The NRSV's translation, "in a little while," suggests some delay between Elijah's command and the beginning of the downpour. The point of the phrase, however, is almost certainly the immediacy of the rain. In other words, this is no natural rainstorm. From a wisp of cloud to a lowering sky with wind and heavy rain takes but an instant. Yahweh's purpose in 18:1 has been fulfilled.

The motif word "go up" in this section deserves comment. The word occurs seven times in four verses (the NRSV obscures the last two occurrences by translating them as "rising" and simply "go [say to Ahab]" in verse 44). The sequence is framed by two occurrences of the opposite verb, "go down," in verse 40 (Elijah "brought them down";

literally, he "made them go down") and verse 44. The words set up a contrast between high places and low. High places are the realm of the sacred: the meal Ahab goes up to eat and drink is a covenant ceremony, as we shall discuss below (see p. 286); Elijah goes up to await Yahweh's promised rain; the servant goes up to look for Yahweh's manifestation in the clouds; the cloud that will bring Yahweh's blessing goes up from the sea; Elijah's servant goes up to Ahab to announce the fulfillment of God's promise of rain. Low places are the realm of the everyday world: Elijah brings the prophets down to Wadi Kishon to slaughter them; Ahab descends the mountain to return to Jezreel, one of his centers of government.

The story closes with another description of double movement. Ahab rides off to the city of Jezreel (about seventeen miles from Mount Carmel); and Elijah, empowered by the hand of Yahweh, outpaces the king's chariot on foot. The implication of the image is twofold. On one level it puts Elijah in the position of king's herald and chief of his retinue (cf. 1 Kgs 1:5), but it also awards a kind of precedence to the divinely endowed prophet, who arrives at Jezreel before Ahab with the news of Yahweh's rain.

Whole Chapter

In the present text several elements link the story of the end of the drought and the story of the contest of the gods on Mount Carmel. The mention of the people of Israel and the prophets of Baal in verses 19-20 makes a transition from one story to the other. And the mention of Carmel in verse 42 places the end of the drought story in the same setting as the contest story. But the narrative connections between the two stories go much deeper than these details. Without the story of the contest and resultant conversion of the people to Yahweh, the ending of the drought would be unmotivated and gratuitous. Elijah shows himself to Ahab as commanded by Yahweh in 18:1, but there would be no explanation why this showing is necessary to Yahweh's intention to end the drought (18:1 reads, "Go, present yourself to Ahab, *so that* I may send rain on the earth"). As the story develops in the present text, Elijah's appearance before Ahab (vv. 17-20) leads to the contest on Carmel (vv. 21-38), which leads in turn to the people's decision for Yahweh and against Baal (vv. 39-40), which leads finally to the ending of the drought (vv. 41-46). On the other hand, without the drought story, the story of the contest loses an essential element of explanatory context. The contest story begins *in medias res:* the presence of people and prophets on Mount Carmel and the urgency of a decision for Yahweh are unexplained.

The context of the drought story also deepens the meaning of several elements of the contest story. Most obviously, after three years of drought, the emptying of twelve large jars of water is a priceless libation; water is as precious a fluid as the blood spilled by the Baal prophets, and much more acceptable in Yahwist worship. Moreover, in the context of drought, the appropriateness of a contest by fire becomes clear. Fire is the opposite of water and therefore a fit element to emblematize the divine power that can dry up the land. Yahweh's fire not only consumes the drenched sacrifice but also "licks up the water that is in the trench" (v. 38), demonstrating beyond doubt that it is Yahweh who holds and withholds the rain.

Finally, when considered apart from the drought story, Elijah's complaint that he is the only prophet of Yahweh left (v. 22) is not problematic, but in the larger context it becomes paradoxical, since Obadiah has told Yahweh of a hundred prophets of Yahweh hidden away in caves (v. 13). There are two possible explanations for Elijah's claim. Elijah could be concealing the existence of the other prophets in order to protect Obadiah or simply to heighten the contrast of his solitude with the Baal prophets' multitude. Or he could be implying a disdain for prophets of Yahweh who hide in caves instead of taking a public stand for Yahweh (see the remarks on 19:10 in the next chapter).

When we consider 1 Kings 18 as a whole, it appears to have a parallel structure surrounded by an introduction and a brief conclusion:

> A. Introduction (18:1-6): Elijah, Ahab, and Obadiah en route
> B. Elijah and Obadiah (18:7-16)
> C. Elijah shows himself to Ahab (18:17-20)
> B'. The contest on Carmel (18:21-40)
> C'. Yahweh sends rain on the earth (18:41-45a)
> A'. Conclusion (18:45b-46): Ahab and Elijah en route

The two "C" elements correspond to the two parts of Yahweh's command to Elijah in 18:1, "Go, present yourself to Ahab, so that I may send rain on the earth." The much longer "B" elements, however, are not foreseen in the introductory command, and thus both act to delay fulfillment of the command and to increase dramatic tension in the story considerably.

The length of the "B" elements focuses attention on them, and their parallel functions point to a deeper parallel between them. Elijah's dialogue partners in the two sections, Obadiah and the people of Israel, fill comparable roles. Both are Yahwist by name: Obadiah means "servant of Yahweh," and Yahweh himself bestowed the people's name, "Israel," on their ancestor Jacob. Both consider themselves faithful to Yahweh: Obadiah protests his own fidelity (vv. 12-13), and the people see no conflict between their worship of Baal and of Yahweh. Yet both are hesitant to announce publicly their adherence to Yahweh: Obadiah objects to Elijah's orders because he fears royal reprisals, and the people are silent when Elijah challenges them. Eventually, however, both comply with Elijah's commands and confess Yahweh as their deity. Obadiah "went to meet Ahab, and told him" (v. 16); presumably what he tells Ahab is what Elijah commands him to in verse 8, namely, *hinnēh ʾēlîyāhû:* "Elijah is here"/"Behold, Yahweh is my God." And the people proclaim that "Yahweh—he is God!" (v. 39). The narrator describes the obeisance of both with the same phrase: upon recognizing Elijah, Obadiah "fell on his face" (v. 7); the people of Israel do likewise in acknowledging Yahweh's victory (v. 39).

As a character, then, Obadiah is not significant as an individual (he appears nowhere else in the Hebrew Bible) but as an emblem of the whole people. His ambivalent status as servant of Yahweh and servant of Ahab mirrors the ambivalence of the Israelites, "limping on two branches" trying to follow Yahweh and Baal simultaneously. And Obadiah's eventual capitulation to the exigent demands of the prophet Elijah portends the eventual and total conversion of the people to the exclusivism of Yahwistic worship.

The Whole Drought Story: Baal vs. Yahweh

The story of the drought extends from 17:1, where Elijah announces it, to 18:45, where the rain returns. The widely varying materials in the two chapters all relate directly or indirectly to this plot line. Yahweh provides for Elijah, hiding in the Jordan Valley from Ahab's reprisals, until the drought dries up his water supply. In Zarephath the drought has caused famine, yet Yahweh miraculously sustains Elijah and the widow who houses him. The raising of the widow's son not only has the same characters as the preceding scene but also leads to the widow's confession of faith that acclaims the authority (the "word") by which Elijah imposed the drought. In chapter 18 the story of the contest of the gods and the people's conversion to Yahweh functions as a necessary step in the encompassing story of ending the drought.

The contest between Yahweh and Baal, however, is not limited to the story of Mount Carmel. It forms the theological backdrop for the entire narrative of the drought. To understand this, we must learn something of Canaanite belief. (The Canaanites were the people who lived in Palestine before the establishment there of the people of Israel and who remained a significant element of the population of the Israelite kingdoms; Baal was their principal deity.) Since Palestine has very few permanent rivers, and those irrigate only a minuscule percentage of the arable land, the country's agriculture is almost entirely dependent on springs, wells, cisterns, and the rainfall that replenishes them: in Palestine, the god who controls the rain controls life and death. According to the Canaanites this was Baal, the god of rain (one of Baal's titles was "Rider on the Clouds") and storms (he is often depicted wielding a thunderclub or a lightning bolt). In Palestine, rain falls from mid-October to mid-April. Biblical references to the "early rains" and the "late rains" refer to the beginning and end of the six-month rainy season. The six months of summer are dry. This is reflected in Baalist mythology as Baal being imprisoned in the underworld by the god Death for several months, until Anath, Baal's consort goddess, rescues him. Thus Baal's mythological cycle of death and resurrection becomes the paradigm for understanding the annual cycle of dry and wet as well as the annual growth cycle of crops.

To make the claim, as Elijah does in 17:1, that he, a servant of Yahweh, controls the rain is to blaspheme Baal. It is to claim for Elijah, and implicitly for Yahweh his master, territory that has traditionally been Baal's dominion. The conflict between Baal and Yahweh is joined from that instant, and there can be no quarter or compromise. In this light, everything related to the drought is seen to be part of the rivalry of the gods, and the contest on Carmel is simply the climactic moment in a lengthy narrative of struggle. Elijah's effective announcement of the beginning and ending of the drought shows that Yahweh, not Baal, controls the rain. The ability of Yahweh and Yahwists to secure food and water during the drought demonstrates Yahweh's command of those resources: Yahweh sustains Elijah at the Wadi Cherith with bread, meat, and water; Elijah assures the widow's meal and oil at Zarephath; Obadiah provides bread and water for the hundred hidden prophets; at Elijah's command the people of Israel on Carmel have access to a large quantity of water. In contrast, Ahab cannot find water to save his livestock, and Baal's prophets survive only by sharing in the royal dole (18:19).

There are several other threads that unify the two chapters of the drought story and enrich the theme of the rivalry of the gods. In 17:2-6, there are three links with chapter 18. First, Yahweh orders Elijah to hide at the Wadi Cherith and miraculously provides (Hebrew, *klkl*) him with bread, meat, and water. In chapter 18 we are told that Obadiah, "servant of Yahweh," hid a hundred prophets of Yahweh in caves and provided (klkl) them with bread and water. In both situations Yahweh protects his prophets from royal wrath as well as from starvation. Second, the "wadi" itself is a sign of the divine struggle. Wadi Cherith supplies the Yahwist prophet Elijah with water. The Baalist king Ahab seeks desperately, but in vain, for a wadi that still holds a trickle of water (18:5). Ultimately, however, the only flowing wadi to be found is the Wadi Kishon, brimming with Baalist blood (18:40). Finally, the very name of the Wadi Cherith (Hebrew, kĕrît, "Cut Off Creek") begins a significant echo. We have seen above that the narrator uses the verb "cut off" in 18:4 (hakrît; NRSV, "killing off") and 18:5 (nakrît; NRSV, "lose") to paint a damning picture of Jezebel's persecution of the prophets of Yahweh and Ahab's callous disregard of it, and to counterpose the figure of Obadiah to both Jezebel and Ahab. The presence of the same verbal root in 17:2-6 deepens the contrast between the Baalist royals and their Yahwist opposites, Obadiah and Elijah. At Cut Off Creek, Yahweh sustains Elijah and keeps him from being cut off by Ahab, just as Obadiah will sustain a hundred prophets and keep them from being cut off by Jezebel.

The remaining episodes in chapter 17 also have several links with chapter 18. Yahweh sends Elijah to "Zarephath, which belongs to Sidon." There is a double irony here. First, the region of Sidon was solidly Canaanite, acknowledged by all as properly Baal's domain. Yet famine has struck the land: Yahweh's drought devastates Baal's own territory. Second, Jezebel, Ahab's queen, is the daughter of the king of the Sidonians (16:34). In his search for Elijah, Ahab is not only unable to find the Yahweh prophet living in Baal's own territory; he also extracts an oath from his own father-in-law that Elijah is not there (18:10)! A further link is the repeated use of the images of high and low to distinguish places of divine manifestation from ordinary human space; at least to some degree high and low become identified as places of life and death. In 17:17-24 Elijah raises the widow's dead son to life in the upper chamber; the prophet takes his body from her and returns him to her alive in the lower part of the house. In chapter 18 Yahweh demonstrates his sovereignty first by fire, then by life-giving rain, on the top of Carmel; at its foot Elijah slaughters the prophets of Baal and sets out to return to the everyday political world of Jezreel (where, as we shall see in the next chapter, Jezebel immediately threatens him with death).

The figure of the widow of Zarephath sets up complex echoes with the figures of Obadiah and of Jezebel. Like Obadiah, the widow sustains (klkl: 17:9; 18:4, 13) Yahweh's prophet with the meager fare available to her. Like Obadiah, she uses the oath "As Yahweh your God lives" to preface objections to Elijah's command (17:12; 18:10); yet, like

Obadiah, she finally does all that Elijah wishes. Like Obadiah, she does not hesitate to reprove Elijah when she believes he brings tragedy upon her unfairly (compare the tone of the widow's question in 17:18 and Obadiah's in 18:9). Finally, like Obadiah, she begins as an ambivalent character: she is a Sidonian, therefore Baalist, who nevertheless shows great respect for the God of Israel; he is a Yahwist, who nevertheless is an important figure in the court of his Baalist "lord," King Ahab. But by the end of their respective stories both make explicit professions of faith in Yahweh: the widow acknowledges that the word of Yahweh in Elijah's mouth is truth; and Obadiah announces to Ahab, *hinnēh ʾēlîyāhû*, "Behold, Yahweh is my God." The comparison between the widow and Jezebel is an antithesis. Both are Sidonian women; this is the fundamental common element that invites us to compare them. Everything else is contrast. One is a widow, the other married. One is poverty-stricken, the other royally wealthy. One, living outside of Israel, respects Yahweh; the other, living in Israel, combats him. One provides food for the prophet of Yahweh, the other for prophets of Baal and Asherah. Elijah restores the one's favorite to life, and kills the favorites of the other.

The cumulative effect of these links is to set up character dynamics in the drought story as a whole different from those in the individual component stories. There are two sets of contrasting characters, aligned with Yahweh and Baal respectively:

for Yahweh	*for Baal*
the widow	Jezebel
Obadiah	Ahab
the people of Israel	the prophets of Baal

Behind Yahweh's partisans stands Elijah, as surrogate for Yahweh himself. Elijah acts on all these characters to move them from initial ambivalence to unambiguous faith in Yahweh. There is no counterpart to Elijah standing behind Baal's partisans in Baal's place; the god has no surrogate, because the god has no substance: "There is no voice. There is no answerer. There is no attention" (18:29).

Chapter 17

ELIJAH AT MOUNT HOREB

1 Kings 19

The final chapter of the Elijah story contains a single narrative of Elijah's flight in fear from Jezebel's threat, his journey to Horeb and his encounter there with Yahweh, and his return to the land of Israel. There are some indications that the narrative has a complex editorial history and draws on originally independent traditions, but the result is a literary unity possessing its own coherence. There are also signs of tension between this story and that of the drought in chapters 17–18, suggesting that the story of Elijah at Horeb may have existed apart from the preceding material before being incorporated into its present literary context. Our approach will be to examine the story as a coherent narrative, indicating how the current literary context of chapters 17–18 influences its interpretation. In the next section, we shall consider 1 Kings 17–19, that is, the entire story of Elijah, as a complex but unified narrative.

The story begins with a brief introductory section that makes the transition from the immediately preceding material in chapter 18. Three characters from chapter 18, Ahab, Jezebel, and Elijah's unnamed servant, all figure in the introduction, but none of them is mentioned thereafter in the story. Notices of movement (vv. 4, 8, 19, 21b) organize the rest of the story into a journey with three scenes of encounter: Elijah encounters a mysterious messenger in the desert, then he encounters Yahweh, and finally he encounters Elisha.

What is the main narrative line of the story? The first potential for dramatic development appears in the introduction: Jezebel threatens Elijah's life. But this plot line does not unfold any further. We do not have a tale of pursuit and escape. The focal point of the whole story is rather the encounter between Elijah and Yahweh at Horeb, including both dialogue and theophany. The precise meaning of that encounter, however, is a matter of debate among commentators. While Elijah's journey has traditionally been seen as a pilgrimage to the sources of Israel's covenant for the purpose of renewing his commitment to serve as Yahweh's prophet, more recently several commentators have argued that Elijah goes to Horeb to renounce his calling as a prophet.[1] There are, as we shall see, several elements in the story that support this reading. The dramatic line, then, is the question of what happens when a prophet attempts to resign from his office. How will Yahweh respond? And what will happen to the prophet?

Introduction: 19:1-4a

The story opens with a link to the end of chapter 18. On reaching Jezreel, Ahab immediately informs Jezebel what happened at Mount Carmel. The grammar of verse 1 is strangely overloaded. The NRSV captures the sense, but a more literal rendering of the Hebrew would run: "Then Ahab told Jezebel all that Elijah had done, and all that he had killed all the prophets with the sword." The triple repetition of "all" puts a great deal of emphasis on the detailed completeness of Ahab's report. Jezebel reacts quickly. She sends a messenger to threaten Elijah with the same fate he has inflicted upon her protégés. Jezebel's first words are a common Hebrew oath, modified slightly to accommodate Jezebel's belief in many gods instead of one. (Compare, for example, Solomon's use of the same oath in the singular in 2:23.) Her threat uses the Hebrew *nepeš*, which can mean "throat," "spirit," or "life." The word *nepeš* is a motif throughout this story (it occurs seven times), suggesting that beneath the surface drama of Elijah's attempt to resign his prophetic ministry lies a deeper issue of life and death.

It is worth pausing to note a possible weakness in the plot at this point. If Jezebel were really serious in her intention to do away with Elijah, she would hardly give him advance notice. Her warning may be nothing more than an awkward editorial attempt to connect the originally separate drought story with the story of Elijah at Horeb by supplying a motivation for Elijah's trek into the wilderness. This is a likely explanation of the process of composition, especially in view of the fact that Jezebel's threat does not furnish the plot line for the rest of the narrative. On the other hand, we can also make sense of Jezebel's

---

[1]The idea was proposed long ago by R. Breuil and has since been taken up by several other scholars, for example, E. von Nordheim, R. Cohn, R. Coote, S. DeVries, and R. Nelson among others. (See the list of works recommended for further reading at the end of this book.)

action in context. The warning suggests that Jezebel does not in fact seek Elijah's death but his departure, and that she is attempting to frighten him into exactly the sort of flight he undertakes. This in turn suggests that Elijah's victory on Carmel has fundamentally altered the earlier situation in the kingdom when Jezebel was free to kill other Yahweh prophets. Perhaps the people's conversion makes Jezebel's open persecution of Yahwism less prudent, or perhaps Ahab himself is less prone to overlook his queen's depredations.

Elijah's response is to flee. The Hebrew text reflects Elijah's panic in a rapid series of short clauses, beginning with three consecutive verbs: "he feared[2] and he arose and he fled for his life *(nepeš)*." With the fourth clause, the narrator slows the pace by adding the clause "which belongs to Judah." The effect is twofold. First, we realize that Elijah has fled the entire length of the divided kingdoms from the heart of the north, the Jezreel Valley in Israel, to the extreme southern boundary of the southern kingdom, Judah. Since this entire journey has taken only five words, we are left a bit breathless. Second, the slowed pace makes us anticipate a pause in Elijah's headlong flight, especially when we see in the next clause that he rested (NRSV, "left") his servant there. But it is not to be; Elijah keeps on going. The Hebrew verb forms require that the first clause of verse 4 be read together with the end of verse 3, not, as in the NRSV, as a new paragraph:

> He was afraid and he got up and he fled for his life and he came to Beer-sheba, which belongs to Judah. He left his servant there, while he himself went a day's journey into the wilderness.
> He came and sat down under a solitary broom tree and he asked that he might die. . . .

This reading better reflects the focus of the Hebrew text. The emphasis is not on the servant who is left in Beer-sheba but on Elijah's unbroken journey. In a series of abandonments, he gradually removes himself from his own kingdom, Israel, to enter Judah, then from settled land to enter the wilderness, and finally from all human companionship. As we shall see in the next scene, his renunciations culminate in a wish to die.

---

[2]The first Hebrew verb is ambiguous; the consonants *(wyr')* can be read two different ways. The medieval Hebrew tradition, from which our modern Hebrew Bibles with vowels derive, read the word "he saw" *(wayyar')*: that is, Elijah perceived the seriousness of Jezebel's threat, arose, and fled. The ancient translations into Greek, Latin, and Syriac read the word "he feared" *(wayyīrā')*. This is the choice of the NRSV as well. In the final analysis, the difference between the readings is not overly significant, except insofar as the standard Hebrew text, by not explicitly mentioning Elijah's fear, is a bit more subtle in its characterization of the prophet.

Elijah and the Mysterious Messenger: 19:4b-8

The scene has three parts, each containing a speech surrounded by narrative lines. In the first part Elijah expresses his despair. In the second and third parts an unnamed figure brings him food and drink. Narratively, the entire scene advances the plot hardly at all; at the end, as at the beginning, Elijah is making his way through the wilderness. Its power, however, is twofold: it reveals much about Elijah's state of mind, and it sets in place narrative elements whose importance will become clear only in the following scene.

Once he has gone a day's journey into the wilderness, Elijah sits under a desert bush. The "broom tree" is not really a tree but a shrub whose shade, while better than nothing, is not generous. Without as within, Elijah's burdens overwhelm him: he can escape neither his despair nor the desert sun. Even the solitariness of the broom tree is telling. The Hebrew counts it—"he sat under *one* broom tree"—even though this species of shrub is not necessarily a solitary growth. But in the case of the solitary prophet, who has just left his sole companion behind in Beer-sheba, the loneliness of *one* broom tree appropriately reflects his own isolation.

Elijah asks to die (literally, he asks that his *nepeš* might die). His prayer begins with an emphatic monosyllable, *rab*, "Enough!" (The NRSV turns the word into a phrase, "It is enough," but this weakens the interjectional force of the Hebrew.) This and the next word, "now," point up Elijah's insistent concentration on himself and on the present moment. He uses a simple imperative verb, "take my life *(nepeš)*," instead of the polite form and third-person circumlocution he used in 17:21; and the motivation clause he attaches to his request concerns not God's glory or Israel's future but himself (contrast his prayer in 18:36-37). He wants God to act here and now, not for God's own sake or for the people's, but simply for Elijah's: "I've had enough, and I want it to end. Now!"

The narrator's psychological insight is powerful. If this were a literal request, that is, if Elijah truly wished to die, then he would have had no reason to flee from Jezebel! Elijah's words reveal something much deeper about him: his sense of hopelessness, of disillusion and despair, of the futility of any further effort. We can appreciate the depth of Elijah's despond especially in the context of chapter 18. As far as he is concerned, his triumph on Mount Carmel and the conversion of the people have had little lasting effect: Jezebel's persecution of the prophets has become less overt, perhaps, but no less lethal, and Ahab seems not to have been affected by the Carmel display at all (see the remarks in the next chapter about the Mosaic references in 18:41-42).

To the height of Elijah's exaltation (measured by his miraculous run in 18:46) corresponds the depth of his despair.

There is more. The blunt form of the imperative verb and the motivation clause, "I am no better than my ancestors," constitute a sort of challenge to Yahweh. If Elijah has failed, it is because Yahweh demanded too much of him. Elijah is not superhuman, yet Yahweh expects him to convert the king and the whole people singlehandedly. By calling on Yahweh to take his life (instead of passively waiting for Jezebel to do it), Elijah puts the whole situation squarely before God. If Yahweh accepts Elijah's prayer and allows him to die, he releases the prophet from the task of Israel's conversion and implicitly admits that his demands on Elijah were excessive. If, on the other hand, Yahweh does not accede to Elijah's request, then he must address the underlying causes of the prophet's despair and act even more forcefully to bring Israel back. In either case, Elijah himself no longer bears responsibility for the outcome.

Having presented Yahweh with the dilemma, Elijah takes no further action. He lies down and goes to sleep. Oddly, the text does not say that he lay down "under the broom tree" and slept, as the NRSV translates, but that he lay down and slept "under a solitary broom tree," repeating the words of the previous verse almost exactly.[3] The repetition emphasizes the sense of isolation and solitude; this makes the next words, which announce the unexpected presence of a messenger, more startling.

To describe the messenger's approach, the narrator uses a Hebrew construction that makes the scene very vivid and also presents it from Elijah's point of view. (The same construction will recur several times in the story, giving the whole narrative a vitality and immediacy that most translations, including the NRSV, fail to capture.) A further translation problem is the Hebrew word *mal'āk*, "messenger." The term is used frequently of divine messengers—thus the NRSV's translation

---

[3]The situation is complicated by another oddity in the text. The broom tree in verse 4 is modified by a feminine adjective (*'ht*, "one, solitary"), that in verse 5 by the masculine form of the same adjective (*'hd*). The word for broom tree is rare enough in biblical Hebrew that its grammatical gender is unsure. The confusion could be a simple scribal error; alternatively, the word may be one of those in Hebrew that can be either masculine or feminine. In either case, however, the repetition of the indefinite phrase "a solitary broom tree" instead of "*the* broom tree" (that is, "the broom tree previously mentioned") is striking. Could it be that the narrator wants to *distinguish* two broom trees: Elijah prays sitting under the one but lies down under the other? The change from feminine to masculine adjectives could support this reading, but it is hard to see what significance Elijah's change of broom trees could have for the story line.

"angel"—but it is also used of human messengers; Jezebel's messenger in verse 2, for instance, is a *mal'āk*. In Hebrew, then, the scene is gripping: "Elijah lay down and slept under a solitary broom tree. And oh! there's a messenger touching him!" In the middle of the wilderness, far from human habitation, Elijah is startled out of a sound sleep (one from which he perhaps expected never to awaken) by a figure that he cannot at first distinguish from the messenger who brought him Jezebel's death threat.

This messenger, however, brings life, not death. He bids Elijah rise and eat. Elijah looks around and sees (again, the vivid present construction in Hebrew): "and next to his head there's a cake . . . !" The whole scene echoes elements of chapter 17. There, as here, Elijah receives miraculous sustenance in the wilderness (17:2-6). There, as here, he eats a "cake" (*'ūgâ*, 17:13). There, the widow kept her oil in a flat, round juglet called a *ṣappaḥat* (NRSV, "jug"); here, Elijah drinks water from a *ṣappaḥat* (NRSV, "jar"). The echo is unmistakable, since the word *ṣappaḥat* is quite rare in the Hebrew Bible, occurring elsewhere only in 1 Samuel 26. These links hint that the mysterious messenger who furnishes the food may be, like the ravens and the widow of chapter 17, another manifestation of Yahweh's providence toward his prophet. But that in turn implies that from Yahweh's point of view, Elijah is still active in his prophetic ministry and that Yahweh is not prepared to relieve him of his duties.

Except for the phrase describing the food, verse 6 consists entirely of one-word sentences describing Elijah's actions: he looked, he ate, he drank, he returned, he lay down. Except for the food, there is no description and no dialogue. Elijah does not question the messenger's provenance or largesse—after so many experiences of being fed by divine providence, he surely by this time recognizes Yahweh's sustaining hand. Nor does Elijah attempt to repeat his request. He has made his point already, and the food does not change his mind. He eats, he drinks, he returns to his withdrawal. He apparently does not fall asleep again. The narrator tells us that "he lay down" but not that "he slept," and when the messenger rouses Elijah again, it is without the vivid, startled present construction of verse 5. Moreover, when the messenger approaches the second time, there is no confusion about his identity: he is clearly "the messenger of Yahweh" (NRSV, "angel of the LORD").

The messenger's second approach contains an ironic echo of the immediately preceding phrase. When Elijah lay back down after the first miraculous meal, the Hebrew used an idiomatic phrase to express repeated action: "he returned and he lay down" (NRSV, "he lay down again"). In verse 7 the messenger of Yahweh "returns" (NRSV, "came") a second time. The repetition of the verb "return" is not innocent. The narrator implies that Yahweh (in the person of his messenger) is just as stubborn as Elijah. The prophet, fed by God's miraculous bounty, refuses to take up his office once more and instead "returns" to his inaction. In response, Yahweh's messenger "returns" again to urge Elijah to renewed effort. Once more the messenger touches him and directs him to rise and eat. This time, however, the messenger adds a motivation clause (v. 7b). The Hebrew construction is idiomatic. While the NRSV's paraphrase captures the sense correctly, it omits an important verbal echo. A slightly more literal rendering would be: "for the journey is more than enough for you." In Hebrew the first word after the conjunction "for" is *rab*, "enough"—the word with which Elijah began his prayer in verse 4. By this allusion to Elijah's earlier speech, the messenger of Yahweh makes it clear to the prophet that this is the divine answer to his request. God refuses Elijah's plea to die and sends him on a journey instead. Yahweh has little patience with a complaining prophet (compare the divine rebuke of Jeremiah in Jeremiah 12:5).

Elijah obeys the messenger, rises, eats, drinks, and sets out for "Horeb, the mountain of God," famous as the place where Moses and the people of Israel encountered Yahweh in their exodus from slavery in Egypt to the Promised Land. ("Horeb" is an alternative name for Mount Sinai in biblical tradition; see, for example, Exodus 3:1.) The narrator evokes the memory of Moses also in Elijah's forty days and nights of fasting before he encounters Yahweh at Horeb (compare Moses' stays atop Mount Sinai in Exodus 24:18 and 34:28). Allusions to the Moses traditions pervade this chapter, but, as we shall see, they are found subtly throughout chapters 17–18 as well. We shall call attention to them as we examine the rest of chapter 19, but we shall defer lengthy discussion of this major theme until we consider the three chapters of the Elijah story as a literary whole in our next chapter.

The narrator obliquely raises one question that is easy to overlook. Is Elijah's trek to Horeb the journey the messenger of Yahweh sends him on? Although this is the most apparent reading of the text, there is one signal that it may not be the case. Elijah's response to the messenger's second visit completes a command-and-compliance pattern: the messenger says "get up, eat," and Elijah "got up and ate." But where the messenger speaks of a "journey" (literally, a "way"; Hebrew, *derek*), Elijah is not said to set out on a *derek*. He simply "went to Horeb." The narrator's deviation from the command-and-compliance pattern here leaves room to question whether the road to Horeb is the "way" Elijah is supposed to be following. In the next scene we shall learn that it is not.

Elijah and Yahweh: 19:9-18

Elijah's encounter with Yahweh at Horeb is a well-known biblical scene. The evocative power of the numinous "still, small voice" has been the subject of innumerable attempts to describe the mysterious self-revelation of God. There is, however, much more (and, perhaps, somewhat less) to this scene than a teaching about the nature of the divine. There is, for example, the potential conflict set up in the preceding scene between a stubborn prophet who seeks to renounce his calling and an equally stubborn deity who refuses to accept the prophet's resignation. As befits a scene where the primary focus is a clash of wills, most of the passage consists of dialogue between Elijah and Yahweh (or, in verse 13, Yahweh's "voice"). There is very little action. Aside from the verb "he said" that introduces the various speeches, there are only five narrative verbs in the ten verses. (Compare verse 6, where there are five verbs in a single verse.) Even the theophany in verses 11-12 is described with participles and verbless clauses rather than with finite verbs.

The narrator organizes the scene in two parallel parts:

   A. Narrative: Elijah's actions (19:9a)
      B. Yahweh's word questions Elijah (19:9b)
         C. Elijah's answer (19:10)
            D. Yahweh's commands (19:11a)
               E. Description of Yahweh's theophany (19:11b-12)
   A'. Narrative: Elijah's actions (19:13a)
      B'. Yahweh's voice questions Elijah (19:13b)
         C'. Elijah's answer (19:14)
            D'. Yahweh's commands (19:15-16)
               E'. Description of Yahweh's victory (19:17-18)

Since the mention of Horeb in the previous scene already evoked the memory of Moses, awareness of traditions associated with him forms part of the background of this scene. Particularly germane is a passage that describes Yahweh's appearance to Moses. In Exodus 33:12-23, Moses complains to Yahweh about bearing sole responsibility for bringing the people of Israel up from Egypt and gives God an ultimatum: either assure us of your presence or abandon us. Yahweh responds to Moses by promising him a personal theophany, which he describes in detail (Exod 33:17-23). The narrator alludes frequently to this description in his account of Elijah's experience.[4]

---

[4]In Exodus 33 Yahweh describes a theophany that he promises to grant Moses. Exodus 34 describes a theophany that Moses experiences, presumably in fulfillment

The scene begins with Elijah's arrival at Horeb. The Hebrew reads, literally, "He came there, to the cave, and spent the night there." The repeated "there," first referring to Horeb and then to *"the* cave," alerts us to the importance physical location will have throughout this scene. Furthermore, the definite article in *"the* cave" (which the NRSV omits) implies that this cave at Horeb is well-known to the reader. The word conveys a double allusion. Against the background of Moses' theophany in Exodus 33, it recalls the "cleft of the rock" where Yahweh promised to shelter Moses to protect him from the overwhelming glory of the divine visage (Exod 33:22). In the context of 1 Kings 18, it recalls "the cave" (the word is the same) where Obadiah hid prophets of Yahweh (18:4, 13).

The vivid present construction that shows us the event from Elijah's point of view introduces Yahweh's question: the prophet overnights in the cave, "and look! Yahweh's word comes to him!" The question itself stresses the word "here," continuing the narrator's insistence on the importance of place: "What are you doing *here,* Elijah?" The emphasis means that Yahweh expects Elijah to be somewhere else, not at Horeb. This confirms our suspicion that the "journey" for which Yahweh's messenger fortified Elijah was not a pilgrimage to Horeb but a return to his "way," that is, to his work as a prophet in Israel. Elijah's decision to come to Horeb was his own, and therefore embodies a continuing refusal to take up once again his prophetic duties.

Elijah's answer is a long complaint about the Israelites' crimes against Yahweh and himself. He begins by insisting on his own fidelity. His "zeal" (Hebrew, *qn'*) is the same sentiment that biblical tradition ascribes to Yahweh as "jealousy" (see Exod 20:5 and 34:14). "Jealousy" is the better term, for *qn'* refers, not to a fervor to see Yahweh worshiped ahead of all other deities, but to a fanaticism to see Yahweh worshiped *instead* of all other deities. Elijah names Yahweh under the royal and militaristic title "God of hosts," that is, God of the heavenly armies. The current situation in Israel, Elijah implies, is a full-scale battle between Baal and Yahweh for divine kingship in Israel; no quarter can be asked, and none given.

The NRSV presents the Israelites' crimes against Yahweh as a series of three: they have forsaken the covenant, thrown down the altars, and killed the prophets. The Hebrew text, however, orders things differently. Elijah accuses the Israelites of abandoning Yahweh's covenant; the other two items are examples of what that fundamental defection entailed. Both allude to passages in chapter 18: the altar Elijah rebuilt

---

of the promise. Yet the two descriptions are very different in vocabulary and details. Most of the allusions in 1 Kings 19 are to the description in Exodus 33.

on Carmel had been "thrown down" (18:30), and Jezebel was said to have killed the prophets of Yahweh (18:4, 13). The fact that in this chapter Elijah imputes both crimes to the whole people reveals more about him than about them. Even if the Israelites cooperated in the desecration of Yahweh's altar and the murder of his prophets, they have since demonstrated their return to Yahweh by their libation of precious water over his restored altar on Mount Carmel and by assisting Elijah in executing the prophets of Baal. According to the timetable implied by 1 Kings 18:20–19:3, Elijah fled Israel almost immediately after his victory on Carmel and the people's conversion; he has therefore no reason to doubt the sincerity of their acclamation of Yahweh as God. Yet he ignores their conversion entirely and accuses them of crimes they have since abjured. Elijah thus betrays his own cynicism about the people's integrity and reveals that his reasons for despair and for renouncing his prophetic office are precipitate and potentially baseless.

Elijah goes on to claim, "I, I alone, am left." The words deserve several comments. First, Elijah's emphasis on himself is very strong: an emphatic pronoun, plus the word "alone." This deepens our impression that behind Elijah's complaints about the Israelites' crimes against Yahweh lies a more fundamental egoism: Elijah feels that he himself has been mistreated. Second, it is unclear whether Elijah means that he is the only Israelite left who has not forsaken the covenant or that he is the only prophet left whom the people have not killed. His next words support the second understanding, but Yahweh's assurance to Elijah in verse 18 that seven thousand faithful Yahwists yet remain in Israel argues that Yahweh takes Elijah's words in the first sense. Finally, the words echo Elijah's statement to the people of Israel in 18:22: "I, I alone, am left a prophet of Yahweh." Just as there, Elijah ignores the hundred prophets Obadiah has hidden in caves (see above, p. 259). It is as if Elijah does not consider people who hide from Jezebel in caves to be worthy of the name prophet. Yet, ironically, Elijah himself is hiding from Jezebel in a cave! And indeed he no longer calls himself, as he did in 18:22, "a prophet of Yahweh." The omission reflects his renunciation of his calling.

Elijah concludes, "they have sought my life *(nepeš)*, to take it away." (The NRSV translates the sentence in the present tense, but the Hebrew refers to the past here as it does in the earlier crimes for which Elijah indicts the people.) Elijah thus paints a picture at considerable variance with what seems to be the actual situation. He does not speak of royal opposition to Yahweh but of universal desertion of the covenant, and he presents himself as the last faithful Yahwist. If this were true, then his renunciation of the prophetic ministry would in effect deprive Yahweh of his sole remaining champion. This would raise the stakes considerably from the challenge of verse 4b. There, if Yahweh allows Elijah to die, he merely admits that he demanded too much of his prophet. Here, if he permits Elijah to resign, he concedes victory to Baal. Indeed, if Yahweh allows Elijah to die, he is furthering the projects of the Baalist populace who have sought Elijah's life! In effect, this would force Yahweh's hand: he must intervene in Elijah's favor in order to assure his own future as Israel's God. We know, however, that the circumstances are not as Elijah portrays them. One Israelite, Obadiah, has remained true to Yahweh, and where there is one there may be others; at least a hundred prophets of Yahweh remain alive while the prophets of Baal are dead, and the people of Israel have resoundingly declared for Yahweh. It remains to be seen how Yahweh will respond to Elijah's claims.

Yahweh gives Elijah a double command: "go out" and "stand" (cf. Exod 33:21). Two locational phrases make the second command more precise. Elijah is to stand "on the mountain" (compare "on the rock" in Exodus 33:21), and he is to stand "before Yahweh." The latter phrase is familiar: Elijah himself has used it twice to identify himself as a faithful servant of Yahweh ("Yahweh, before whom I stand," 17:1; 18:15). Yahweh, then, is not calling Elijah merely to witness a theophany but to witness it precisely as a faithful servant—in other words, to take up once again his prophetic ministry. The divine directive begins a command-and-compliance pattern that will be completed in verse 13, but, as we shall see, although Elijah obeys the two commands, he disregards both locational precisions.

The description of the theophany begins with the statement about Yahweh "passing by" (compare Exodus 33:22 and 34:6, where the same verb is used) and extends through verse 12. It is in the vivid present construction that occurs so often in this chapter:

> Look! Yahweh is passing by! And a wind, great and strong, splits mountains and breaks rocks in pieces before Yahweh! But Yahweh is not in the wind. And after the wind, an earthquake! But Yahweh is not in the earthquake. And after the earthquake, a fire! But Yahweh is not in the fire. And after the fire, a sound of sheer silence!

This powerful and evocative picture calls for several comments. The first concerns a crucial grammatical ambiguity. Since Hebrew lacks punctuation comparable to quotation marks, we must determine from context where direct discourse begins and ends. Usually this is clear, but in the present case it is possible to read Yahweh's speech that begins in v. 11a as including part or all of the description of theophany. There are several alternatives. (1) Treat the whole description as

Yahweh's words. God graphically describes to Elijah the theophany that is about to unfold. Elijah responds to the description by going to the mouth of the cave (v. 13) and preparing himself to experience Yahweh's passing by. (2) Treat the whole description as narrative. Yahweh's brief command to Elijah is followed by awesome manifestations of wind, earthquake, and fire, after which Elijah hears the "sound of sheer silence." Recognizing this as a sign of the divine presence, he goes to the mouth of the cave. (3) Treat part of the description as Yahweh's words and the rest as narrative. This is the choice of the NRSV and a few other modern translations, which include the first phrase of the description within Yahweh's speech. The difficulty with this option is that the entire description is unified by the vivid present construction, and it seems arbitrary and contrary to the sense of the text to divide it between Yahweh and the narrator.

Hebrew grammar does not resolve the issue. Some arguments from the larger literary context support the first possibility. In the structure of the whole scene, the description of the theophany parallels the description of Yahweh's victory, which is clearly part of a divine speech. And the density of allusions to Exodus 33 argues that this passage, too, might be read as Yahweh's announcement of an imminent theophany rather than as a narrative of its actual occurrence.

Other arguments favor the second possibility. The frequent third-person references to Yahweh in the passage sound odd as Yahweh's own words, and the lack of any reference to wind, earthquake, and fire after Elijah goes to the mouth of the cave in verse 13 argues that he is responding to the "sound" of verse 12 rather than preparing to witness the whole series of phenomena.

These conflicting signals point to a compromise possibility. The description may fulfill a double function: it contains Yahweh's words anticipating the theophany; but it also serves as an implicit description of the events as they unfold, in order to avoid a repetition of details that would no doubt weaken the power of the images. (For a comparable use of this technique, see Exodus 9:13-21, where Yahweh's speech to Moses imperceptibly becomes Moses' repetition of the speech before Pharaoh and his court.) Based on this reading, verses 11-13a would run:

> [The word of Yahweh] said, "Go out and stand on the mountain before Yahweh. Look! Yahweh is passing by! And a wind, great and strong, splits mountains and breaks rocks in pieces before Yahweh! But Yahweh is not in the wind. And after the wind, an earthquake! But Yahweh is not in the earthquake. And after the earthquake, a fire! But Yahweh is not in the fire. And after the fire, a sound of sheer silence!" And when Elijah heard it, he wrapped his face in his mantle and went out and stood at the entrance of the cave.

A second comment on the theophany concerns the natural phenomena listed: wind, earthquake, fire. These are traditional accompaniments to Yahweh's appearance; compare, for example, the theophanies at Sinai in Exodus 3:2 (fire) and Exodus 19:16-18 (thunder, lightning, cloud, smoke, fire, and "the whole mountain shook violently"). Two of the three have already appeared in the story of Elijah as manifestations of the divine—fire (18:38) and wind (18:45). The repeated denial of Yahweh's presence in these phenomena is not, therefore, a denial that they point to the divine presence but that they *contain* the divine presence. Yahweh's appearance is heralded by natural upheavals, but it is ineffably more: it is a "sound of sheer silence."

What is this mysterious sound of silence (Hebrew, *qôl děmāmâ daqqâ*)? The phrase is rich in sound (note the chiastic series of consonants, *q-d-m / m-d-q*) and paradoxical in sense. It is a "sound," perhaps intelligible, perhaps not (Hebrew *qôl* means "voice" as well as "sound"). Yet it is a sound of "silence" *(děmāmâ)*. (The same oxymoron is central to Eliphaz's description of his mysterious night vision in Job 4:12-16: "it stands, but I discern not its looks/a shape before my eyes/I hear silence and sound," v. 16.) Finally, as if to confound us even more, the narrator follows two aural words with a tactile one: *daqqâ* (NRSV, "sheer") describes something that is "fine" like powder or dust. The numinous power of the image lies precisely in our inability to grasp it—a quality utterly lost by translations that render it "a thin, whispering sound" or the like; the NRSV's "sound of sheer silence" captures the sense perfectly without losing any of its mysterious paradox. As climax to the theophanic procession, it puts the divine not only beyond all natural phenomena but also beyond all human ability to comprehend it.

Hearing the mysterious silent sound, Elijah veils his eyes (compare Exodus 33:20-23, where Yahweh promises to shield Moses from the lethal sight of Yahweh's face) and obeys Yahweh's two commands to "go out" and "stand." But the command-and-compliance pattern is imperfect. Where Yahweh told Elijah to stand "on the mountain before Yahweh," Elijah goes only to the mouth of the cave. He assumes neither the place (fully exposed to Yahweh's passing) nor the position (the posture of renewed service "before Yahweh") that God commanded.

A *qôl*, a voice, speaks. As in the parallel question in verse 9b, the construction is vivid: Elijah stands at the entrance of the cave, "and look! a voice comes to him!" This *qôl* is not the *qôl* of silence that drew Elijah to the mouth of his refuge (if it were, the narrator would have said "the voice," not "a voice"); nevertheless, the echo of verse 9b makes it clear that this is Yahweh's voice. It addresses Elijah with the same question about his presence "here" that Yahweh's word posed in verse 9b, but the sense has changed. In verse 9b Yahweh asked what Elijah is doing "here," that is, at Horeb instead of in Israel. The continuing emphasis on location throughout this scene makes us conscious that in verse 13b the prophet is not standing where Yahweh told him to. "What are you doing *here*, Elijah?" means "Why are you still hiding in the cave, Elijah? Why are you not standing on the mountain before me as my servant?"

Elijah's response to the question is identical to his speech in verse 10, but, as is the case with Yahweh's repeated question, intervening events give the speech a new dimension of meaning. In verse 10 Elijah used an implied threat of resignation in an attempt to force Yahweh to intervene on behalf of his prophet. Since then Yahweh has called Elijah back to service and granted him an impressive theophany, but this is apparently not enough to satisfy the stubborn prophet. He refuses to "stand before Yahweh," he continues to plead his own isolation, and he continues to avoid calling himself a prophet. Elijah's verbatim repetition of his earlier speech demonstrates that neither the divine commands nor the majesty and mystery of the divine self-revelation have had the slightest effect on his purposes.

Yahweh's commands offer a rebuke and a compromise. The rebuke is that instead of accepting Elijah's resignation, Yahweh assigns him new duties to perform; the compromise is that one of those duties is the installation of someone to succeed him as prophet. Yahweh tells Elijah to "return on your way *(derek)*." Yahweh's messenger used the same word in verse 7 (NRSV, "journey"); as we have seen, it meant there not Elijah's subsequent journey to Horeb but his prophetic duties back in Israel. Here, too, it means Elijah's prophetic duties but, surprisingly, not just in Israel. He is to travel to the "wilderness of Damascus"; the phrase is unique in the Hebrew Bible but probably refers to the desert region bordering the large oasis of Damascus, capital of Aram.

The new duties Yahweh gives Elijah are three: to anoint a new king of Aram, to anoint a new king of Israel, and to anoint a new prophet to take Elijah's own place. The Hebrew verb forms make it clear that though Yahweh expects Elijah to carry out all three commissions, they need not be carried out in the order listed. Several comments are in order. First, sending Elijah to involve himself in the politics of Aram is unexpected; generally speaking, Israelite prophets respected the autonomy of other realms. This is reminiscent of chapter 17, where Yahweh demonstrated his power within Baal's own territory around Sidon by causing drought, miraculously sustaining Elijah and the widow, returning the widow's son to life, and protecting his prophet from pursuit. Beneath the surface story of struggle between Baal and Yahweh for divine supremacy in Israel lies the seed of a more universalist claim: Yahweh is supreme in all the earth. Yahweh's meddling in the politics of Aram also points forward to the remaining chapters of 1 Kings, which will have as a major theme wars between Aram and Israel during the reign of Ahab.

Second, the verb "anoint" is unexpected, at least in regard to the installation of Elisha as Elijah's successor. We have no evidence that anointing played a part in the commissioning of a prophet in Israel. The narrator may be using the word loosely as a synonym for "install in office," but it will also give him the opportunity to show Elijah acting at odds with Yahweh's command by designating Elisha as prophet without anointing him.

Finally, as the stories of 1 and 2 Kings unfold, Elijah will carry out only one of these commissions, and that only in terms that differ from Yahweh's command. Elisha, not Elijah, will visit Damascus and nominate Hazael to the throne (2 Kgs 8:7-15); Elisha, not Elijah, will send a disciple to anoint Jehu king of Israel (2 Kgs 9:1-13). Elijah will choose Elisha as his servant (1 Kgs 19:19-21) and eventual successor (2 Kgs 2:1-14), but both events involve investing Elisha with Elijah's mantle rather than anointing him.

Yahweh's speech continues by describing the results of these anointings in terms that respond to Elijah's complaints in verses 10 and 14. Where Elijah complained of the Israelites' defection from Yahweh and in particular of their killing the prophets with the sword, Yahweh responds that Hazael and Jehu will both wield swords against Israel's wrongdoers, and that Elisha the prophet too will encompass their death. (The stories of Hazael and Jehu are in 2 Kings; there are also many stories of Elisha, but none of him killing anyone.) Where Elijah complained of being the sole remaining worshiper of Yahweh, Yahweh informs him that there remain several thousand faithful Israelites. (The word "seven" is a standard biblical term for a generally adequate or ample quantity.) In this way Yahweh gives the lie to Elijah's claims about the people's universal apostasy and tells him in effect that if he insists on renouncing his prophetic office, Yahweh has a successor lined up to take his place. If, on the other hand, Elijah is willing to continue as a prophet, he has work to do.

Elijah and Elisha: 19:19-21

Elijah leaves Horeb and finds Elisha. The narrator interrupts with a brief parenthetical description of the scene: Elisha is plowing, guiding the last of twelve yoke of oxen. The number of oxen is very large for a single family and hints that Elisha comes from wealth. Without a word, Elijah passes Elisha, flings his mantle over him, and keeps on going (the last is clear from the fact that Elisha must run after him to catch up). Nothing in the story so far has prepared us for the symbolic significance of Elijah's mantle (it appeared only in 19:13, where Elijah used it to protect himself from Yahweh's glory), but we are probably dealing with a cultural convention familiar to ancient audiences concerning the prophet's mantle as a distinctive badge of office.[5] Elijah's action literally "invests" Elisha into prophetic service.

Elisha leaves the cattle behind and runs after Elijah. As narrative actions these statements paint a graphic picture. Elijah strides across the tilled fields away from the startled young man he has just accosted, and Elisha dashes in pursuit. But the statements are more than narrative description. They foreshadow the outcome of the scene: Elisha will leave behind the farming life to follow his new master. Elisha's request to bid his parents goodbye is understandable; Elijah's response is less so. Literally Elijah says, "Go, return, for what have I done to you?" Is this a refusal of Elisha's request ("Go back again," as the NRSV translates it)? Or is it permission ("Go, then return")? In either case, the question "what have I done to you" cannot be merely rhetorical, as if Elijah were saying, "After all, I haven't done anything to you." Investment into Yahweh's prophetic service, as Elijah well knows, is no light thing. It is more likely that Elijah intends the question literally. What does Elisha think this investiture means? (We, the readers, think we know: Elijah has taken Elisha for his successor, as Yahweh told him to. But we are wrong, as we shall learn at the end of the next verse.)

There is a brief moment of suspense: Elisha "returns from following him." Has Elisha understood Elijah's words as a refusal and turned, perhaps sadly, back to his twelve yoke of oxen and his old life? The narrator quickly dispels the suspense. Elisha slaughters one yoke of oxen, cooks the meat, and prepares a meal for "the people"—presumably his coworkers. Clearly the destruction of beasts and their tackle represents a break with his past, and the meal is a farewell feast. But two clues hidden in the Hebrew text reveal a deeper meaning of the meal. First, the verb *zbḥ* (NRSV, "slaughtered") generally means to

---

[5]See, for example, 2 Kings 1:8, where Elijah is identified by the phrase "a man who possesses hair" (NRSV, "a hairy man"; but the phrase probably means "a man with a hairy garment"); Zechariah 13:4, where false prophets put on hairy mantles in order to pass as true prophets; and the New Testament descriptions of John the Baptist's camel's-hair garment (Mark 1:6; Matt 3:4). See especially 2 Kings 2:7-14, where Elijah's mantle is both a badge of office and a talisman of power.

kill an animal *as a sacrifice*. Second, the sentence about boiling the animal's flesh is oddly worded and strongly poetic in Hebrew; this calls
attention to the phrase. One word in it is particularly unusual, *bšlm*,
"he boiled them"; the formation evokes the notion of a *šlm*, or communion sacrifice, in which a person offers an animal to Yahweh in
thanksgiving for divine blessings and uses the sacrificial meat to host
a meal for family and friends. Elisha's action, therefore, combines elements of separation from his old life, cultic thanksgiving upon undertaking the new, and ritual solidarity with "the people" among whom
he will pursue his prophetic service.

Finally Elisha goes off with Elijah. But where we expect something
like "and became prophet in Elijah's place," corresponding to Yahweh's
command in verse 16, we learn that Elisha follows Elijah as a servant.
The term here is different from that used in verse 3 of the servant Elijah
left behind in Beer-sheba; Elisha's service is that of a chief assistant (the
same word is used of Joshua's position in Moses' service; see Exod
33:11). Such a position of responsibility may point ahead to successor-
ship, but Elijah has certainly not ceded his place to Elisha just yet.

What does this scene reveal about Elijah's response to Yahweh? In
verse 15 Yahweh gave Elijah a double command: "go, return on your
way." In verse 19 Elijah obeys the first command: he "goes" (NRSV,
"set out"). But does he "return on his way"? That is, does he take up
once more his prophetic ministry? The narrator carefully leaves the
question open. Elijah finds Elisha, presumably in Abel-meholah, which
Yahweh mentioned as Elisha's home town in verse 16. Abel-meholah,
as far as we can tell from 4:12, was in the Jordan Valley, which would
put it not too distant from the most convenient route from Horeb to
Damascus. The narrator thus offers us the possibility that Elijah is en
route to Damascus to anoint Hazael. And since Elijah does not anoint
Elisha as his successor, as Yahweh commanded, but invests him as his
chief servant, it is reasonable to infer that Elijah has decided not to resign his prophetic ministry immediately. (In the larger context of 1 and
2 Kings, this leaves narrative space for further Elijah stories such as
those in 1 Kings 21 and 2 Kings 1. Elisha will finally succeed to Elijah's
office in 2 Kings 2.)

The Whole Chapter

The whole narrative has a certain thematic symmetry: Elijah leaves
behind companionship (v. 3) and food (v. 8) on his journey to Horeb.
On his return he regains both (v. 21). His pilgrimage takes him away

from the things of ordinary life to a place of sacred power (compare the narrator's careful distinction in 17:19-23 between the ordinary house and the upper room as a place of miraculous power), from which he returns to ordinary life with a renewed series of responsibilities. The ironic counterpoint to this thematic structure is the contest of wills between Elijah and Yahweh. The pilgrimage is an act of defiance, not devotion; the prophet does not seek renewal, he demands release; and the deity seems indifferent to Elijah's ultimatum.

The irony continues into the last scene. As we have seen, the narrator leaves open the possibility that Elijah decided to defer his own resignation for an indefinite period of time by enlisting Elisha as a servant rather than a successor. Yet there are subtle echoes of the theophany scene in the final verses that set up a peculiar analogy: Elijah begins to act toward Elisha as Yahweh acted toward Elijah. Yahweh "passed by" Elijah on Horeb (v. 11); Elijah "passes by" Elisha in the fields (v. 19b). Elijah wrapped his face in his mantle (v. 13); he now covers Elisha with the same mantle (v. 19b). Yahweh's commands to Elijah began, "Go, return" *(lēk šûb);* Elijah's first words to Elisha are identical (v. 20b, *lēk šûb;* NRSV, "Go back again"). We can infer that Elisha's encounter with Elijah is parallel to Elijah's encounter with Yahweh, and is therefore more of a prophetic empowerment than Elijah either realizes or intends.

The characterization of Elijah in this chapter adds depth and complexity to his personality as we saw it in earlier chapters. Traits found there develop in new and unexpected directions here. In chapter 18 we saw signs of Elijah's fanaticism for Yahweh. He was unwilling to countenance Obadiah's clandestine Yahwism, and he was intolerant of the people's readiness to worship both Baal and Yahweh equably. He forced the contest on Carmel and, once the people declared for Yahweh, turned the scene into a bloodbath by executing all the prophets of Baal. In chapter 19 his extremism betrays him. The overwhelming victory on Carmel, the mass conversion of the people and destruction of his rivals, the return of rain at his word—all this is forgotten in the face of Jezebel's menace. Just as he allows no middle ground between Baalism and exclusive Yahwism, so too he sees no middle ground between defeat and total victory. If Yahwism (in the person of Elijah) has not swept the field, if opposition (in the person of Jezebel) remains, then Elijah gives up in despair. He proclaims his zeal ("I have been very jealous for Yahweh," vv. 10, 14), but he speaks in the past tense and acknowledges no result of that zeal besides his own danger.

A second trait in the previous chapters is Elijah's frequent focus on himself as unique servant of Yahweh. Twice he identifies himself as one who "stands before Yahweh" (17:1; 18:15). He emphasizes his solitary fidelity (18:22), tacitly denying that of Obadiah's hundred hidden prophets, and he considers his own public vindication on a par with the demonstration of Yahweh's supremacy (18:36). There is even one point where Elijah seems to arrogate to himself the power that is properly Yahweh's ("except by *my* word," 17:1). In chapter 19 this trait deepens to the point where Elijah seems to confuse his role as prophet with Yahweh's role as deity. He describes his own zeal for Yahweh with a term traditionally used of Yahweh's jealousy (*qn'*, 19:10, 14), and for him the crowning evil result of the people's abandonment of Yahweh's covenant is their death threat against him. This confusion of roles means that when Yahweh reminds Elijah with a powerful theophany of the ineffable distance between God and prophet, it only strengthens Elijah's resolve to renounce his prophetic role.

Connected with Elijah's increasing preoccupation with himself is a change in his way of responding to Yahweh. In chapters 17–18 Elijah addressed Yahweh with respect and deference (17:20-21; 18:36-37), and he complied quickly and scrupulously with Yahweh's commands. In chapter 19, however, his words to Yahweh are stubborn and defiant, his obedience is imperfect (compare 19:11 with 19:13, and the order to anoint Elisha as his successor with the action of investing him as a servant), and some of Yahweh's commands Elijah does not carry out in the story at all (the anointings of Hazael and Jehu). In short, the narrator paints Elijah larger than life: bearer of the divine word and wielder of divine power, swinging from ecstatic exaltation (18:46) to deepest despair (19:4), fanatic in his Yahwism yet focused on himself, scrupulously obedient and stubbornly resistant, heroic and heroically flawed.

Chapter 18
THE WHOLE ELIJAH STORY
1 Kings 17–19

Both structural and thematic elements forge the various stories of 1 Kings 17–19 into a literary unity. The figure of Elijah is, of course, the principal unifying factor. A secondary factor is the drought; chapter 17 describes its beginning, chapter 18 its ending, and chapter 19 the aftermath of the events that ended it. The motif of supplying food and drink pervades the three chapters: ravens, the widow, Obadiah, Jezebel, the messenger of Yahweh, perhaps even Elisha—all provide food and drink for prophets. Each chapter, furthermore, has as its climax a miraculous divine manifestation in a sacred, elevated place: the widow's son is raised from death in the prophet's upper room; Yahweh demonstrates his sovereignty first by fire, then by rain, atop Mount Carmel; Yahweh reveals himself to Elijah on Horeb. We shall examine first the structural elements that support a unified reading, then turn to one major, pervasive theme that we have to this point considered only briefly: the use of the Moses traditions.

Structural Unity

There is a significant structural element that organizes the three chapters into a tight unit: Elijah's journey. Throughout the whole story Elijah is on the move, and his journey takes a symmetrical form:

A. Elijah in the Jordan Valley (17:2-7)
  B. Elijah outside of Israel, to the north (17:8-24)
    C. Yahweh's word; Elijah returns to Israel (18:1)
      D. Ahab and Elijah on the road to meet (18:2-20)
        E. Elijah on Mount Carmel (18:21-45)
      D'. Ahab and Elijah on the road to Jezreel (18:46)

C'. Jezebel's word; Elijah flees Israel (19:1-3)
B'. Elijah outside of Israel, to the south (19:4-18)
A'. Elijah in the Jordan Valley (19:19-21)

Beginning and ending in the Jordan Valley, Elijah's journey comes full circle. This gives the entire story a sense of closure and completeness. It is noteworthy, too, that territory *across* the Jordan is even more definitively Elijah's place of beginning and ending. He originates in Gilead (17:1), and he departs from the world across the Jordan from Jericho (2 Kgs 2:1-18).

On this geographical framework hangs a triptych about the prophet. In chapter 17 we see him in a private setting, dealing with ordinary people in daily life; in chapter 18 we see him immersed in the public, political life of Israel; in chapter 19 we see him face to face with God. In this way the story of Elijah presents a comprehensive view of the prophetic life. In private life he can bear a divine word of promise for the faithful (17:14) or a human word of entreaty for the suffering (17:20). Publicly, he is Yahweh's representative before king and people, condemning and punishing unfaithfulness, calling to conversion and offering hope, finally praying for and receiving the display of divine power in fire and rain. Before God he is one to whom God speaks directly and to whom God is willing to appear in the fullness of divine majesty and mystery. The prophet, moreover, is one whom God protects and provides for, whether in the wilderness (17:2-6; 19:5-8), in private society (17:8-16), or in public danger (18:10). The structure centers attention, however, on Elijah's involvement in the public sphere of politics and religious practice. His confrontation with Ahab and the contest of the gods on Mount Carmel are the focus of the whole story. In addition, the three chapters begin (17:1) and end (19:15-18) with Elijah involved in, or commissioned to involvement in, national and international politics. In this way the example of Elijah locates the essence of prophetism in the public realm. Private ministry and wilderness pilgrimages have their place, but the proper place for the prophet is to "stand before Yahweh" in the sight of the king and the people. Prophets hiding in caves are, as Elijah himself implies, unworthy of the name.

Elijah and the Moses Traditions

There is a further theme that we must consider, namely, references to Moses and the Exodus that are found in all three chapters of the Elijah story. The allusions are not drawn randomly from throughout the Moses story; rather, each chapter of the Elijah narrative echoes specific passages of the Moses traditions. We have touched on the issue in mentioning the frequent allusions in chapter 19 to the theophany Yahweh promised Moses in Exodus 33. We shall examine how other parts of the Elijah narrative also use Moses traditions, then draw some general conclusions about them.

1 KINGS 17

The two stories of manna and quail in Exodus 16 and Numbers 11 furnish the principal parallels. The thematic link, miraculous feeding in the wilderness, is evident. The first explicit verbal allusion is also very clear. The account of Elijah's compliance diverges in verse 6 from the wording of Yahweh's command in verse 4 by describing in detail the ravens' feeding of Elijah: "the ravens brought him bread and meat in the morning, and bread and meat in the evening." This echoes Moses' words to the Israelites in Exodus 16:8, "When Yahweh gives you meat to eat in the evening and your fill of bread in the morning," and Yahweh's words to Moses in Exodus 16:12, "Between the evenings (NRSV, "at twilight") you shall eat meat and in the morning you shall have your fill of bread."

There are other less obvious verbal allusions that connect the stories of manna with the second episode in 1 Kings 17 as well. The words *'ūgâ* ("cake") and *šemen* ("oil") occur in the dialogue of Elijah and the widow in 17:12-13. Both words occur also in Numbers 11:8, in the description of manna: the people made cakes of it, and it tasted like it was baked in oil. An even more striking though more subtle verbal link connects the "jug" *(sappaḥat)* in which the widow kept her oil (1 Kgs 17:12; the word refers to the flat, round shape of the vessel and is rare in biblical Hebrew; see the remarks on 19:6) and the description of manna as "wafers" *(sappîḥit,* Exod 16:31; this word, also referring to a flat, round shape, is unique in the Hebrew Bible).

Finally, Numbers 11:10-12, immediately following the manna passage, has verbal and thematic links with the third episode in 1 Kings 17. In both the prophet accuses Yahweh of mistreating someone who deserves better; the prophet's complaint in both cases is *hărē'ôtā,* literally, "have you done evil?" Moses compares the Israelites to a child carried in the bosom; Elijah takes the child from his mother's bosom.

1 KINGS 18

The story of the establishment of the Sinai covenant in Exodus 24 furnishes the primary parallel. The clearest link, including several verbal correspondences, is the construction of an altar out of twelve elements (stones in 1 Kings, pillars in Exodus), and the explicit explanation of the number as corresponding to the twelve tribes of Israel (Exod 24:4; 1 Kgs 18:31). After building the altar, the prophet pours a libation over it. In Exodus, Moses splashes the altar with sacrificial blood; in 1 Kings, Elijah drenches altar and sacrifice with precious water. In both cases the liquid symbolizes life: blood is the fluid of life, and after a three-year drought water is no less so. In both contexts the prophet "comes near" to Yahweh as intermediary between God and the people (Exod 24:2; 1 Kgs 18:36). In both passages Yahweh's glory is displayed in a fire that "eats" (Exod 24:17; 1 Kgs 18:38). Finally, in both passages the scene of sacrifice is followed by a meal on top of the mountain. In Exodus, Moses, Aaron and his sons, and seventy elders of Israel go up Mount Sinai, where they see God and eat and drink; the ritual is intended to seal a covenant between Yahweh and the people of Israel, represented by their leaders (Exod 24:9-11). In 1 Kings, Elijah commands Ahab, "Go up, eat and drink." In other words, the king is to join in a meal on the top of Mount Carmel, where Yahweh has just demonstrated his divine sovereignty and been acclaimed God by the assembled people (1 Kgs 18:41-42). The parallel with Exodus 24 makes it clear that the meal to which Ahab is bidden is also a covenant meal; Elijah expects the leader of the people to confirm the people's decision. In this light the narrator's slight deviation from a command-and-compliance structure is portentous. Elijah says, "Go up, eat and drink." In describing Ahab's response, the narrator does not say "Ahab went up, ate and drank," but "Ahab went up *to* eat and drink." Ahab is invited to renew the covenant with Yahweh, but whether he actually partakes of God's bounty is left unsaid.

A secondary parallel to 1 Kings 18 is Exodus 32, where Moses pleads with Yahweh to have mercy on the unfaithful Israelites who have just committed the apostasy of worshiping the golden calf. He argues that Yahweh will ruin his own reputation among the Egyptians if he now destroys the people he brought out of Egypt with such wonders and power (Exod 32:11-13). Elijah's prayer to Yahweh on Carmel asks him to demonstrate his supremacy for his own glory's sake and implies that the people's unfaithfulness may have been Yahweh's doing in the first place (see the discussion of 18:37). A clear verbal link between the passages is the very unusual phrase "Abraham, Isaac, and Israel." Except for these two prayers and two very late passages in Chronicles, the patriarchs are always named as "Abraham, Isaac, and Jacob." Finally, both prayers are followed by a bloody scene in which the prophet, with the help of faithful Israelites, executes a large number of sinners. Moses enlists the Levites and together they kill three thousand unfaithful Israelites (Exod 32:25-29); Elijah enlists the people of Israel and slaughters the prophets of Baal.

THE GEOGRAPHICAL FRAMEWORK

The journeys of Moses and Elijah are not identical, of course, but they share enough common elements to establish an echo between them. Both prophets flee eastward to escape a king's wrath (Exod 2:15; 1 Kgs 17:2-6). Both lodge with a family in a foreign land (Exod 2:16-22; 1 Kgs 17:8-24). At Yahweh's word both return to their homeland to face and challenge the king and to awaken faith among the people of Israel (Exod 3–4; 1 Kgs 18). Both journey to Sinai/Horeb, where they experience a personal revelatory theophany. Both then depart for the land of Israel via Transjordan.

ELIJAH: A PROPHET LIKE MOSES?

The extent and detail of the parallels between Moses and Elijah invite a comparison of the two prophets. The journey framework, allowing of course for the fact that Moses must start from Egypt and Elijah from Israel, is congruent from beginning to end. The parallel is even stronger when we advert to Moses' failure to enter the Promised Land (Deut 34:48-52): in 1 Kings 19 Elijah's journey also ends before he has returned to his active ministry in Israel, and indeed he never will carry out the commissions to anoint Hazael and Jehu that Yahweh gave him.[1] The congruence of the frameworks shows that we are to compare the whole Elijah story with the whole Moses story, not simply the isolated episodes alluded to in the individual narratives about Elijah. In other words, Moses is the paradigm by which Elijah is to be measured. Is Elijah, in the words of Deuteronomy 18:15-19, the "prophet like Moses" whom Yahweh promised to raise up?

The Mosaic allusions in 1 Kings 17:2-16 show Elijah and the widow, like Moses and the Israelites, miraculously provisioned by Yahweh; those in 1 Kings 17:17-24 show Elijah, like Moses, rebuking Yahweh and interceding for others. The allusions in 1 Kings 18 show Elijah, like

---

[1]Moreover, in 2 Kings 2, Elijah departs from earth in a region not far from the place of Moses' death. It is notable that the Elijah stories in 1 Kings 21 (Naboth's vineyard) and 2 Kings 1 (Elijah and Ahaziah) lack any significant Mosaic allusions, while the story of Elijah's departure from earth has strong thematic links with the account of Moses' death in Deuteronomy 34.

Moses, leading the people to a powerful theophany on a mountain. The theophany becomes the basis of a covenant to be sealed by a meal shared by God and the leaders of the people on top of the same mountain. In 1 Kings 18:36-37 Elijah, like Moses in Exodus 32, is an intercessor, this time not simply for an individual but for the whole people. In these chapters, therefore, Elijah corresponds quite closely to the Mosaic paradigm.

It is in 1 Kings 19 that the parallels between Moses and Elijah become contrasts. In Exodus 33, Moses complains of solitude (33:12), but all his references to himself are in function of his leadership of the people. Moses reminds Yahweh that if he does not support him, it is ultimately Yahweh's people who will suffer. By contrast, in 1 Kings 19 Elijah's preoccupation with himself overshadows, or at least equals, his concern for God's own glory; moreover, all Elijah's references to the people are accusatory and, as we saw, unfairly so. In Exodus 33, Moses begs a theophany, which Yahweh grants as a reward ("for you have found favor in my sight," Exod 33:17). Elijah makes no such request, and is unmoved when Yahweh freely grants him a theophany. Moses risks being overwhelmed by the divine glory, so Yahweh pledges to protect him from the sight of the divine face. Elijah needs no such protection, since "Yahweh is not in" the impressive natural phenomena, and Elijah does not go out of the cave to watch them anyway. When he does go to the mouth of the cave, he himself wraps his face in his mantle, as if unwilling to watch the sights Yahweh is providing for him. If we read the event in Exodus 34 as the theophany announced in Exodus 33, Moses obeys Yahweh: he "went up on Mount Sinai, as Yahweh had commanded him" (34:4), and Yahweh "stood with him there" (34:5). Elijah, as we saw, does not obey Yahweh: he does not stand "on the mountain," nor does he stand "before Yahweh," as Yahweh commanded him. After Moses' theophany, he repeats in more or less the same words the request he made previously (compare Exodus 34:9 with 33:15-16), a request for Yahweh's assistance in carrying out the task of leading the people. The entire scene is one of harmony and cooperation between Moses and Yahweh. Elijah, too, repeats his request before and after his theophany, but his intention is to abandon his prophetic ministry. The entire scene is one of stubborn resistance between deity and prophet. In this chapter, therefore, Elijah fails to live up to the Mosaic paradigm.

The effect of the pervasive allusions to the Moses traditions, then, is to depict Elijah as almost the equal of Moses, but as ultimately failing to meet the standards Moses set. This redounds to the glory of Moses, in that he remains the unquestioned paradigm of prophecy in Israel. Ironically, it redounds to the qualified glory of Elijah as well, since he is in many ways, though not all, a Moses *redivivus*. Finally, it enables us to see precisely what constituted Elijah's failure. Where Moses continued in his dedication to the people and considered his own unique closeness to Yahweh primarily as a function of Yahweh's devotion to his people, Elijah became more self-absorbed and finally came to see himself in opposition to the people Yahweh expected him to serve as a prophet.

Part Four

THE STORY OF AHAB
1 Kings 20:1–22:40

Chapter 19

WAR WITH ARAM: AHAB'S VICTORIES

1 Kings 20

The story of Ahab's reign continues with a series of three narratives that focus much more on Ahab himself than the previous Elijah stories did. Chapters 20 and 22 recount military hostilities between Israel and Aram. Between them chapter 21 tells of a domestic affair: how the royal couple encompassed the judicial murder of an Israelite landowner and seized his property. Each chapter includes a scene of prophetic condemnation of Ahab.

The narratives, particularly the stories of Ahab and the Aramean wars, contain serious historical problems. Many historians of Israel, for instance, are convinced that the incidents recounted in chapters 20 and 22 reflect relations between Israel and Aram not during Ahab's reign but several decades later. If that is the case, stories originally told of some subsequent king have been transferred to Ahab for literary rather than historical purposes. In other words, the likelihood that these stories do not recount historical events from the reign of Ahab makes them all the more significant as narrative characterizations of him.

The narratives likewise contain puzzling literary features. There are indications of a complex history of composition in each chapter, particularly in the story of Naboth's vineyard in chapter 21. Since our focus is the final form of the text, we shall not try to reconstruct the history of composition. However, one stage in that history is reflected in an unusual element in the text as we now have it: in each chapter the story of Ahab is symmetrically structured and narratively complete *without* the scene of prophetic condemnation, and the latter presents a characterization of Ahab at considerable variance from the former. It is likely that this reflects the original independence of the Ahab stories and their subsequent expansion within prophetic circles. The result, however, is a literary complex filled with narrative tension, particularly in its characterization of the king of Israel.

Ahab and the War with Aram: 20:1-34

The narrator organizes the story of Ahab's victories in the Aramean war symmetrically, putting as much emphasis on the surrounding scenes of negotiation as on the accounts of the battles. The scene of prophetic condemnation follows the story of Ahab's victories.

> A. Ben-hadad demands tribute (20:1-12)
> B. The battle of Samaria (20:13-21)
> B'. The battle of Aphek (20:22-30)
> A'. Ben-hadad begs for his life (20:31-34)
> -. Prophetic condemnation (20:35-43)

Dialogue dominates the scenes of negotiation (A and A'). The internal structures of these scenes are parallel: in each there are three exchanges between Ben-hadad and Ahab, usually through intermediaries. The context of hostile negotiations alerts us to be attentive to unspoken nuances in the diplomatic language used. The battle accounts (B and B') are more concerned with preparations and results than with describing the battles themselves. They too have similar structures: dialogue with advisers, mustering of forces, battle preliminaries, brief description of battle, aftermath.

BEN-HADAD DEMANDS TRIBUTE: 20:1-12

The scene is concentric, centering on Ahab's consultation of the elders of the land:

> A. NARRATIVE INTRODUCTION (20:1)
> B. FIRST EXCHANGE OF MESSAGES
> i. Ben-hadad to Ahab (20:2-3)
> ii. Ahab's reply (20:4)
> B'. SECOND EXCHANGE OF MESSAGES
> i. Ben-hadad to Ahab (20:5-6)
> C. AHAB CONSULTS THE ELDERS (20:7-8)
> ii. Ahab's reply (20:9)
> B''. THIRD EXCHANGE OF MESSAGES
> i. Ben-hadad to Ahab (20:10)
> ii. Ahab's reply (20:11)
> A'. NARRATIVE CONCLUSION (20:12)

The tone of the messages deteriorates gradually from pseudo-polite formalities to outright insults.

The narrative introduction depicts Ben-hadad of Aram preparing for war. He assembles his own forces and those of his vassals. Given the political realities of the day, "thirty-two kings" can only be a pretentious term for desert chieftains bound to Aram by treaty. The verse reads, in Hebrew and in English, as if Ben-hadad besieged and attacked Samaria prior to opening negotiations and being rebuffed by Ahab. However unrealistic this may be historically, it is narratively revealing. Ben-hadad plans military attack from the first. His diplomatic exchanges with Ahab are not intended to win Ahab's capitulation but to provide an excuse for armed aggression. This will become still clearer as the negotiations develop.

The kings do not parley face to face but through messengers. (Notice how in verse 2 Ben-hadad is the subject of the verb "said" even though the messengers actually deliver his words.) The military situation makes this necessary, but the distance between the kings is also emblematic of the larger situation. Ben-hadad sits in his siege camp sending messages like arrows at Ahab; only at the conclusion of the story, when Ahab's victory has ended the conflict, will the kings meet face to face. The verb "to send" (Hebrew, *šālaḥ*) is a leitmotif in the story and reflects the changing fortunes of the two kings. In Hebrew it occurs six times in verses 1-12, always with Ben-hadad, the aggressor, as subject; at the end of the story it occurs twice, in an intensified form (Hebrew, *šillaḥ*, "to send away, dismiss"; NRSV, "let go," v. 34), with the victorious Ahab as the subject.

The first exchange is stilted and formal. Ben-hadad's opening words, "Thus says Ben-hadad," identify the message as an official regal decree. (Prophets regularly use a similar formula to identify an oracle as coming from Yahweh; see, for example, verses 13, 14, 42.) Ben-hadad's first message is peremptory, but in fact it demands nothing but a declaration of submission and fealty. He requires that Ahab acknowledge Ben-hadad's rights to all Ahab's wealth (silver and gold) and household (wives and children); the latter, in cases of a vassal's disloyalty, could be taken and held as hostages to guarantee good behavior. Ahab's reply is equally formal but polite. He addresses Ben-hadad as "my lord the king," thereby admitting his status as Ben-hadad's vassal; and he agrees to his overlord's rights over himself and all his possessions. All the diplomatic proprieties are satisfied.

The second exchange unexpectedly deepens the conflict and exposes Ben-hadad's real agenda. Unfortunately, there are two translation difficulties that touch not the content but the emotional coloring of Ben-hadad's words. His message is in two parts, each introduced by a similar conjunction. The NRSV omits the first *(kî)* and renders the second *(kî 'im)* by "nevertheless." Both decisions are debatable. The first is probably emphatic: *"See here!* I sent to you, saying, 'Deliver to me your silver and gold, your wives and children . . . .'" The second conjunction is more difficult, but it is unlikely to mean "nevertheless." It may also be emphatic ("I will *surely* send my servants to you . . ."), or it may be conditional *("for if* I send my servants to you . . ."). The ambiguity may be due simply to our limited grasp of ancient Hebrew today, or it may be part of the ancient language itself.

The first part of Ben-hadad's message cites his earlier demand with one significant change. Originally he only required Ahab's assent to his declaration of rights over Ahab's wealth and household ("they are mine," v. 3). Now he claims that he told Ahab to "deliver" his wealth and household to him. The claim is false, of course, but the besieged Ahab is in no position to say so. More seriously, the new demand flouts the proprieties between vassal and suzerain. Unless Ahab is guilty of rebellion against his overlord, Ben-hadad should be content with the formal declaration Ahab has already expressed. By the standards of the day, Ben-hadad's insistence is unwarranted and excessive, and we begin to suspect intentional provocation.

The second part of the message, despite the ambiguity of the conjunction, is clear intimidation. Whether Ben-hadad's words are an announcement ("I will send my servants") or an implied threat ("If I send my servants . . ."), they intend to push Ahab to an impossible choice. Either he must give up everything, wealth and family, without protest, or he must surrender his city to the Arameans' plundering. Ben-hadad's words are even more malicious than the NRSV allows. According to the Hebrew text, Ben-hadad's servants will "lay hands on whatever pleases *you* (NRSV, following the ancient translations, reads "them"). In other words, Ben-hadad threatens not merely plunder, but plunder expressly calculated to punish Ahab by seizing things he prizes most.

Before answering Ben-hadad's ultimatum, Ahab consults "the elders of the land." The term probably refers to local officials (as distinct from royal appointees) of the towns and villages surrounding the capital city, perhaps of settlements throughout the whole country.[1] He submits to them his analysis of the situation as well as his dilemma. Ahab says that Ben-hadad is "seeking evil" (NRSV, "trouble"); in other words, Ahab knows that Ben-hadad is simply looking for a pretext to attack. Resistance will provide such an excuse, and not only Samaria but the whole country will suffer as a result. Ahab has already agreed

---

[1]Note the narrative flaw here. If Ben-hadad has Samaria besieged, how can Ahab summon elders from outside the city? It is a credit to the author that we overlook the inconsistency so easily and that even when it is pointed out, we tend to dismiss it as a cavil.

to the formalities of vassalage ("I did not refuse him"); should he now draw the line and risk full-scale war?

Of course, if Ben-hadad is set on attack, neither resistance nor appeasement will avail; war is inevitable, and Ahab's consultation of the elders will not avert it. Paradoxically, therefore, the narrator has centered and thus highlighted in the section a scene that does not advance plot development. What is its point? It is characterization: Ahab is the kind of king who is aware of his subjects and attentive to their voice. Contrast Ben-hadad, who never consults but only commands, even though his subjects are themselves "kings"—thirty-two of them in his army as well as Ahab himself. There is a further touching characterization of Ahab. In his demands, Ben-hadad places wealth before people. When Ahab recounts those demands to the elders, he cites his family before his silver and gold. The difference implies much about the respective value systems of the two kings.

The elders urge Ahab not to capitulate to Ben-hadad. The narrator associates "all the people" with the elders in this response, suggesting either that the elders brought others with them in answer to Ahab's summons or that the elders' advice genuinely reflects popular opinion.[2] There is a nuance in the Hebrew that is difficult to capture in English: the second command is slightly more emphatic than the first. "Do not listen; above all do not consent" comes close to the feeling of the Hebrew. The point here, too, is characterization. Ahab has the confidence of his people; they are willing to stand by him even in the face of Aram's overwhelming menace.

With his people's support, Ahab returns a polite refusal to Ben-hadad. He still calls him his overlord ("my lord the king," v. 9),[3] and he repeats his willingness to offer formal testimony of vassalage. Perhaps the "first" demand Ahab refers to even includes the first part of Ben-hadad's second speech: Ahab may be willing to go beyond formal testimony and give up his own wealth and family. But Ben-hadad's threat of unrestrained pillage, which Ahab apparently understands as an announcement, not merely as a warning, Ahab cannot allow. Even here, however, his language is calculated to placate Ben-hadad rather than

[2]Alternatively, the narrator may be using the phrase in the more restricted sense of military forces: Ahab has the support not only of the elders of the land but of the army as well. See verse 15 for the same usage, and compare the use of "all Israel" in 16:16-17.

[3]The NRSV misses a very slight nuance in the Hebrew text of verse 9. Ahab's words to the messengers are not: "Tell my lord the king: 'All that you first demanded . . . .'" They are: "Say: 'To my lord the king: all that you first demanded. . . .'" In other words, the phrase "my lord the king" is direct address to Ben-hadad, which the messengers are to repeat as part of Ahab's message to him. Ahab remains polite and subservient.

enrage him: "I cannot" is less defiant than "I will not." Ben-hadad's messengers carry Ahab's reply to their master. (The NRSV adds an unnecessary "again" in verse 9 that makes the translation misleading. The "him" to whom the messengers bring word is Ben-hadad.)

The third exchange is not so polite. Ben-hadad utters bombast, sealed with a conventional oath (compare Jezebel's identical oath in 19:2). He claims that when his troops are through with Samaria, there will not be enough left of it for each of them to carry away a handful of dust. The threat is twofold: it vaunts the size of Ben-hadad's army, and it forebodes total destruction of Ahab's capital. Ahab's reply is more restrained, though no less insulting. He no longer calls Ben-hadad "my lord the king" or even refers to him at all; he simply tells the messengers to "speak!" (the NRSV paraphrases, "tell him"). His message is a pithy proverb, only four words in Hebrew, whose literal translation is "Let one who girds not brag like one who loosens." The reference is to putting on and taking off clothing. Reasoning from the military context of the story, the NRSV thinks of armor, but the proverb probably means simply dressing in the morning and undressing in the evening. A satisfactory paraphrase in English might be: "Boast of the day at bedtime, not at dawn!" or in rather less elegant English folk idiom, "Don't count your chickens before they hatch."

The narrative conclusion recounts Ben-hadad's reaction to Ahab's jibe, but the narrator interrupts it with a descriptive aside about Ben-hadad. Because the remark breaks the narrative flow, it calls attention to itself. It has a double function. First, it adds a further dimension to the already uncomplimentary characterization of Ben-hadad. In the midst of what are, on the surface, tense diplomatic negotiations, the king of Aram is carousing with his vassals.[4] This behavior strengthens our suspicion that the outcome of the negotiations is irrelevant to Ben-hadad's plans. Second, it adumbrates the motif of Ben-hadad's drunkenness, which the narrator will develop in the next section.

Ben-hadad's command is a single word, literally, "Put!" The NRSV's "Take your positions" is an attempt to unpack its meaning; perhaps

---

[4]We may have here a vestige of historical detail. The standard, vocalized Hebrew text reads that Ben-hadad was drinking "in the booths." The term "booths" (*sukkôt*) refers to temporary shelters like those constructed to celebrate the Feast of Booths. We are probably to think of the army's field tents, though the word is not generally applied to tents. But the more ancient Hebrew text, which did not indicate the vowels, could also be read "in Booths," that is, "in Succoth," a town just east of the Jordan River, less than thirty miles from Samaria (see, for example, 1 Kings 7:46); the modern site is called Tell Deir 'Alla. This would have been a logical stopping place for an Aramean army invading Israel, though it is rather remote for the commander of a siege already in progress.

"Set to!" would capture the laconic quality even better. Precisely this laconic quality confirms beyond question that Ben-hadad has his battle plans laid all along and is simply waiting for a sufficient excuse to put them in action.

THE BATTLE OF SAMARIA: 20:13-21

This section of the text has five sections, alternating between longer and shorter:

1. dialogue between Ahab and one of his prophet-advisers (20:13-14)
2. mustering of Israel's forces (20:15)
3. battle preliminaries (20:16-19)
4. battle (20:20a)
5. aftermath of battle (20:20b-21)

(The parallel section on the battle of Aphek, verses 22-30, will have a very similar structure.)

The dialogue between Ahab and the unnamed prophet begins with a vivid construction: "And see! a prophet approached Ahab . . . ."[5] Royal courts in the Ancient Near East included prophets among the advisers of the king; their role was to interpret current affairs from the point of view of the gods. When they spoke, they often purported to deliver the deity's own words: thus the so-called messenger formula, "Thus says Yahweh," and the use of "I" and other first-person forms to mean Yahweh. The fact that a prophet can approach Ahab with a message delivered in Yahweh's name does not reveal much about the king; throughout Israel's history prophets spoke the divine word to kings good and bad, whether they wanted to hear it or not. More revealing is the fact that the message includes a promise of victory: Ahab enjoys Yahweh's favor.

The divine message begins with a rhetorical question: "Have you seen all this great tumult?" The NRSV translates with "multitude," but the Hebrew term refers to the crowd in terms of its noise and commotion, not just its numbers. The term is not itself disparaging, but in this context, where Yahweh announces the imminent defeat of Aram's army, it takes on a wry overtone: Ben-hadad's troops (like Ben-hadad himself) are noisy, but it is all bluster. The only sound that counts is the

[5]In our standard Hebrew text, the construction is slightly weaker than the "vivid present" we have seen so often in 1 Kings. The difference, however, is a matter of a single vowel (*niggaš* instead of *niggāš*); the ancient Hebrew consonantal text may well have been read otherwise: "and here comes a prophet approaching Ahab . . . ."

word Yahweh speaks: victory for Ahab. Yahweh continues with a vivid present construction, "Look! I am giving it into your hand today!" and follows the promise with his reason. Yahweh acts for his own glory and renown, and specifically in order that Ahab himself acknowledge Yahweh: "and you [singular] shall know that I am Yahweh." This is the first indication we have in the chapter that Ahab's adherence to Yahweh may be less than perfect. It does not become a major issue in the story; even in verses 35-43 the prophet will condemn Ahab for disobeying, not for being untrue to Yahweh. Rather the words recall the theme of chapters 17–19, the struggle between Yahweh and Baal for the loyalties both of the people and of Ahab. In this way the narrator keeps before our eyes the larger context, namely, the whole story of the reign of Ahab (see below, page 363).

Ahab does not doubt the prophet's promise. His question is not to be understood as skeptical but as a straightforward concern for strategy: "By whom?" means "By whose hands will this deliverance occur? How does Yahweh want me to deploy my forces?" The prophet's response is also introduced by the messenger formula: Yahweh actually deigns to detail Ahab's tactics! "Young men who serve the district governors" seems to be a technical term, though we are no longer sure of its exact meaning; perhaps it was a select group of commandos. The king's next question is difficult. Literally he asks, "Who shall bind the battle?" The NRSV takes this in the sense of beginning the fighting (compare the English "to join battle"), but others more plausibly take it in the sense of ending it (compare the English "to wrap up the battle"). A single verse describes the mustering of Israel's troops. The small commando force leads, as the prophet directed. Then follows the rest of the army (literally, "all the people of Israel"; see 16:16-17 for a similar use of "all Israel" in the sense of military troops).

The description of battle preliminaries is a brilliant example of literary art. One of the most challenging tasks in any linear medium, such as prose narrative, is to express simultaneity, since inevitably one description must precede the other. Our narrator has come very close to achieving the impossible. He has created a sort of verbal split screen that allows us to watch two simultaneous processes at the same time: the progress of the Israelite army toward battle, and the descent of Ben-hadad into his cups. It is worth reproducing verses 16-19 to show this split-screen technique:

[The Israelite army] went out at noon.	Ben-hadad was drinking himself drunk in the booths, he and the
The young men who served the district governors	thirty-two kings allied with him. Ben-hadad sent, and they told him

went out first.

These came out from the city:
the young men
who served the district governors,
and the army that followed them.

"Men have come out from Samaria."
And he said,
"If they have come out for peace,
take them alive;
and if they have come out for war
take them alive."

The Israelite army sets out from Samaria in the bright noonday—hardly a prudent strategy for a surprise attack against an overwhelmingly superior force. Ahab is not relying on surprise but on Yahweh's promise. As Yahweh directed through his prophet, the commandos lead the attack: they go out first, and the army follows them. Meanwhile, Ben-hadad is drinking in his tent. He has been drinking since verse 12, and now he is drunk, even though it is only noon. He has enough presence of mind to "send," but the verb has no direct object. (The NRSV supplies "scouts" in verse 17 to smooth over the awkward gap in the Hebrew.) The vague construction suggests an equally vague situation. Ben-hadad, dulled by wine, is not thinking tactically; that is, he is not sending out scouts. He is simply "sending" someone, anyone, to report back to him whether anything is happening. When word arrives that the Israelite army is on the move, Ben-hadad's speech is strange. The contrast of "if they have come out for peace" and "if they have come out for war" leads us to expect contrasting commands: "take them alive" versus "kill them." If the commands are to be the same, we expect something like "Whether they have come out for peace or for war, take them alive." Ben-hadad's reply has that borderline incoherence that betrays slow, muddled thought processes.

By this time, however, it is too late. Battle is joined and over in three words: "Each-man killed his-man." There is a starkness in this line that merits our attention. In what precedes and follows, Israel and Aram are clearly distinguished. They are enemies, Yahweh is on Israel's side, Aram flees and falls before Israel and its king. But in the moment of battle the sides are indistinguishable: ultimately war comes down to one human being killing another human being.

In the wake of battle the Arameans flee, with the Israelites in pursuit. Ben-hadad too flees, literally, "on horse and steeds." The NRSV's "on a horse with the cavalry" is an attempt to interpret the odd Hebrew phrase; there is actually no indication in the text that the Arameans used mounted cavalry in this engagement.[6] Finally the king

---

[6]Could this be an erudite historical note by the author? We know that prior to this time Israelites did not use horses as mounts but only as chariot horses. In the battle of Qarqar, during Ahab's reign, for example, Hadadezer of Aram fielded twelve hundred chariots and twelve hundred cavalry, while Ahab fielded two

of Israel "goes out." The narrator used the same verb four times in verses 16-19 to describe the march of Israel's armies. The king, in obedience to the prophet's advice that he should "wrap up" the battle (see above on verse 14b), goes out last to join the pursuit of the fleeing Arameans. He attacks the "horses and chariots" of the Arameans. The verb is the same as that used in verse 20a and translated "killed" there (Hebrew, *hkh*); in that light, it should probably be understood equally strongly here and translated "destroyed." The phrase "horses and chariots" forms an inclusion with the beginning of the story in verse 1: Ben-hadad began the hostilities by amassing horses and chariots; Ahab ends the hostilities by destroying them.

The story ends with a summary line (v. 21b). The NRSV treats it as part of the preceding sentence, but its character as a summary means that it should be independent: "Thus he defeated Aram with a great defeat" (the verb is *hkh* again, and the noun is from the same root).

THE BATTLE OF APHEK: 20:22-30

The story could end with verse 21. Ahab's unexpected victory over Ben-hadad's superior forces has secured peace for Israel. The only unresolved element is the person of Ben-hadad, Ahab's erstwhile overlord. He has escaped, and the relationship between him and Ahab—and therefore between Aram and Israel—is unsettled: the vassal has fought and defeated the master. This becomes the springboard for the next part of the story, Ben-hadad's second campaign against Israel. The story of the battle of Aphek has the same five components as the preceding parallel story of the battle of Samaria:

1. dialogue between kings and advisers (20:22-25)
2. mustering of troops (20:26-27)
3. battle preliminaries (20:28-29a)
4. battle (20:29b)
5. aftermath of battle (20:30)

As in the account of the battle of Samaria, most of the emphasis lies on what precedes the battle rather than on the battle itself.

---

thousand chariots but no cavalry. (We have an Assyrian record that itemizes the forces of the coalition that opposed Shalmaneser at this battle in 853 B.C.E.) Is this odd remark about Ben-hadad escaping "on a horse" the author's way of calling our attention to a startling Aramean innovation of riding horses instead of using them only for pulling vehicles?

The NRSV separates the first two scenes, the prophet's advice to Ahab and the servants' advice to Ben-hadad, with a section heading as well as a paragraph break. This runs counter to the syntax of the Hebrew text, which uses a special construction to suggest a comparison of the scenes. The advice to Ahab will be restrained and prudent; the advice to Ben-hadad will be blasphemous and pretentious.

"The" prophet approached Ahab. The definite article indicates that this is the same prophet as in verses 13-14; the use of the same verb strengthens the impression (although the NRSV translates the verb differently in each place: "came up to" in verse 13 and "approached" in verse 22). This time the prophet offers judicious military advice but not a divine oracle. He simply warns Ahab to get ready for another battle. The advice consists of a blunt series of commands (in Hebrew the prophet's first four words are imperative verbs) followed by the reason for the advice: Ben-hadad will attack again at the next battle season. (The Hebrew phrase "at the turn of the year" may simply mean "next year about this time" rather than "in the spring," as the NRSV renders it.)

The king of Aram, too, has advisers, but they are called "the king's servants," not prophets. Nevertheless, they presume to make an overweening theological judgment: "their gods are mountain gods." (A translation in the singular is equally possible, "their god is a mountain god.") This, they explain, is why Israel defeated Aram in the hilly country around Samaria. All Ben-hadad has to do is choose level terrain for the next engagement and he is sure to win.

To this confident claim they add two specific suggestions. First, Ben-hadad should replace the allied kings with "governors" (NRSV, "commanders"); the Hebrew word is vague but seems to denote political more than exclusively military office. In other words, Ben-hadad is to depose the kings and reduce their semi-autonomous kingdoms to mere districts within his empire. Such severe measures would mean that he blames his defeat on his allies, perhaps for their carousing during the battle, though they were, after all, only keeping their drunken lord company. This is entirely compatible with the character of Ben-hadad as we have already seen it: highhanded and arbitrary to the point of cruelty, bent on conquest and acquisition of goods and territory, and now revealed as unwilling to take responsibility for his own failure. And his advisers are ready to give him the kind of advice they know he wants to hear; they are "the king's servants" indeed!

Their second suggestion is that Ben-hadad himself amass another army comparable to the one lost at Samaria. The emphatic pronoun ("and *you* muster an army," not reflected in the NRSV) suggests that the former army was at least in part amassed by someone else—probably the "thirty-two kings"—and was thus not as reliable as one that Ben-hadad himself will muster. Again, Ben-hadad's vassals become scapegoats for his defeat. The advisers conclude by repeating verbatim their blithe guarantee of success, and Ben-hadad follows their sycophancies without hesitation.

Just as verses 22-25 contrast the advice received by the kings of Israel and Aram, so verses 26-27 contrast the muster of the armies of Aram and Israel. The muster takes place "at the turn of the year" (NRSV, "in the spring"), as the prophet told Ahab it would. The hostilities begin as they did in verse 1: Ben-hadad gathers his forces and "goes up" against a city to "fight against" it. (The Hebrew uses the same verbs, *ʿlh*, "to go up," and *nlhm*, "to fight," in both places. The NRSV translates them differently: "marched . . . and attacked," v. 1; "went up . . . to fight," v. 26.) The echoes of verse 1 in verse 26 portend that the second campaign may end like the first, with the defeat of Ben-hadad.

There is a difference, however, that raises the stakes considerably. In verse 1 Ben-hadad mustered "his army" to fight against a single city, Samaria. In verse 26 he musters "Aram" to fight against "Israel" at Aphek. This is no longer a contest of overlord against vassal, or a battle for plunder of a capital city. This is nation against nation. Israel itself is at stake, and all Aram is ranged against it. Since the site of Aphek is uncertain, its choice as the battleground is difficult to interpret. No doubt it was on level ground, in accordance with the tactics suggested by Ben-hadad's advisers. Most scholars locate it on or near the border between Aram and Israel. If that is the case, then the situation has changed markedly in the intervening year: Ben-hadad is no longer so quick to invade Israelite territory, and Ahab is ready to protect the integrity of his land. In other words, both Ben-hadad and Ahab recognize that Israel's vassalage is over; this war will determine what will take its place.

The NRSV misses a nuance of the word order in verse 27. The syntax invites comparison of the Israelites' muster with that of the Arameans. A better translation would treat verses 26-27 as a single sentence: "In the spring Ben-hadad mustered the Arameans and went up to Aphek to fight against Israel, while the Israelites were mustered and provisioned and went out to engage them." In Hebrew the verbs "were mustered and provisioned" are very unusual passive forms. Because they are unusual they draw attention to themselves, and because they are passive they enable the narrator to describe the scene without naming Ahab. This has two effects. First, by emphasizing the Israelites instead of the king, verse 27 reinforces the impression already established in verse 8 that Ahab's military resistance to Aram enjoys popular support. Second, the passive voice often carries theological significance in Hebrew: it is a way of indirectly ascribing actions to Yahweh. The implication here is that Israel's troops are being assembled and supplied at God's initiative.

In verse 27b the narrator describes the two camps with the same grammatical construction of comparison that he used twice already, in verses 23 and 27a (the NRSV preserves the nuance this time). The Israelites' camp is pathetically small: "like two little flocks of goats." The translation is standard but conjectural; the word translated "little flocks" occurs nowhere else in biblical Hebrew, and its meaning is entirely uncertain. Whatever the word means, the point of the image is clear: the Israelites' vulnerability is in contrast to the overwhelming size of the Aramean army, which "filled the country."

Between two mentions of the opposing camps (vv. 27b and 29) comes an oracle of victory for Israel. Since the phrase "man of God" is another way of designating a prophet, this may be the same individual who approached the king of Israel in verses 13 and 22. The phrase could just as correctly be translated "the man of God" as "a man of God," and the verb "approached" is the same as in the other two verses as well. If it is the same person, the narrator's reasons for using a different term to describe him are lost to us.[7]

The oracle begins with the messenger formula (see above on 20:13) and repeats much of the wording of the oracle of victory in verse 13: Yahweh promises Ahab to "give into your hand" "all this great multitude," so that "you shall know that I am Yahweh." The verbal echoes undergird the message: it is not simply that Yahweh promises victory here as there; he promises it in the same words. Both form and content point to a like outcome.

There are three slight divergencies between the two oracles. First, in verse 13 Yahweh promises victory "today"; in verse 28 that element is missing, since the armies will not fight for another seven days (v. 29). Second, in verse 28 Yahweh explains his reason for defeating the Arameans: they have insulted him by calling him "a god of the hills and not a god of the valleys." In other words, just as in verse 13, Yahweh's principal concern is his own renown. Third, in verse 13 the phrase "you shall know that I am Yahweh" is singular: Israel's victory will reveal Yahweh to Ahab. In verse 28 the phrase is plural: Ahab and others—presumably the Israelites as well as the blasphemous Arameans, who have so underestimated Yahweh—will come to realize Yahweh's power.

---

[7]At this point in the Hebrew text there is a minor scribal error. The text reads, literally, "a man of God drew near and said to the king of Israel and said." Evidently either the first "and said" was inserted by a copyist who did not read far enough ahead to see the second one, or the second one was miscopied from the very similar form "saying," which is often used to introduce direct discourse.

The armies face one another for several days ("seven" is a conventional number) before engaging in battle. Dramatically, this is the calm before the storm; narratively, the line delays the climax and thus builds suspense. Here, as in verse 20a, the narrator chooses stark language. Despite the disparity in size, the camps are not distinguished: literally, "these camped over against these for seven days." When war finally comes, it is personified: "On the seventh day, war drew close." There is something about war that depersonalizes Israelite and Aramean alike but reveals war itself as having an inexorable power of its own. Once battle arrives, the narrator describes it in few words: the Israelites kill (the verb is *hkh*, as in verses 20 and 21) a hundred thousand Aramean infantry, and the collapse of Aphek's city wall fells twenty-seven thousand more.[8] The similarity to the collapse of Jericho's city walls (Josh 6) implies that this, too, is a divine stroke. Ben-hadad escapes the falling wall by taking refuge within the city. The NRSV's "entered into the city to hide" is a considerable paraphrase. The Hebrew says "entered into the city room by room," that is, furtively sneaking deeper and deeper into the maze of buildings. The picture is of a king leaving his remaining troops behind to defend the city walls while he scurries to find a safe hiding place.

BEN-HADAD BEGS FOR HIS LIFE: 20:31-34

The next section parallels the first: it contains negotiations between Ben-hadad and Ahab through intermediaries. In this section, however, the final round of negotiations is face to face. As in verses 1-12, there are three speeches by each party, although in this section the Hebrew text does not clearly mark Ahab's third speech. The section begins with an introductory scene, in which Ben-hadad's "servants" give him more advice.

The servants' speech has a slightly apologetic tone. Twice they use a polite Hebrew particle that they did not use at all in their advice in verse 23. The particle, *nā'*, is sometimes translated "please," though often that is a bit too strong. In verse 31 the NRSV omits it entirely. To capture the precise degree of politeness of the Hebrew here requires a paraphrase, something like: "Look, *m'lord*, we have heard . . . ; let us, *if you will*, put sackcloth . . . ." (For comparison, see verse 32, where

---

[8]The Hebrew could also mean that there are only twenty-seven thousand survivors of the battlefield, and that they are all felled by the wall. The numbers are clearly unrealistic, no doubt exaggerated for the sake of the story. Compare the number of troops fielded by Aram in the battle of Qarqar (see note 6 above).

the NRSV renders the same particle with "please.") The servants are perhaps unsure of how Ben-hadad will respond after the disaster that resulted from their earlier counsel. They have heard "that the kings of the house of Israel are merciful kings," according to the NRSV. The Hebrew is more nuanced than that:

> *kî malkê bêt yiśrā'ēl*
> *kî malkê ḥesed hēm*

The sentence merits several comments. First, the identical introductions invite us to read the two phrases as parallel, even though *kî* must be translated differently in each phrase. In the first phrase it is "that," introducing the object of the verb "hear" ("we have heard *that* the kings . . ."); in the second phrase it is emphatic ("are *indeed* merciful kings"; the NRSV omits this). The parallel structure implies an identity: to be a "king of the house of Israel" is to be a "king of *ḥesed*" (NRSV, "merciful king") and vice versa.

Second, the word *ḥesed* is a quintessentially untranslatable word. It is, first and foremost, a covenant term and expresses the faithful and loyal devotion of one covenant partner for the other. On this basis it takes on in biblical Hebrew rich theological overtones. It is the faithfulness of Yahweh to the covenant with Israel—a faithfulness that transcends the strict obligations of the covenant and includes Yahweh's forgiving mercy toward Israel even when Israel has through sin forfeited any claim to the covenantal promises. Correlatively it is the faithful, loyal devotion to Yahweh that God expects from the covenanted people and, further, the faithful loyalty that Yahweh's covenant demands on the part of one Israelite for another, especially those who are most in need of mercy. All the following nuances, therefore, are potentially present in the phrase: Israel's covenanted loyalty to Yahweh and the king's responsibility for that relationship; Ahab's erstwhile covenanted vassal relationship with Ben-hadad; the mercy needed by the now helpless Ben-hadad in the face of Ahab's victory.

Ben-hadad's advisers propose to appeal to the renowned *ḥesed* of Israelite kings. They will appear before Ahab as suppliants: sackcloth around the waist is penitential garb to implore mercy and forgiveness; ropes on the head apparently have a similar meaning, though our ancient texts do not give us enough evidence to be more precise. The servants' hope for Ahab's clemency sounds an ironic echo with their earlier advice to Ben-hadad in verses 23-25. There they insisted on the certainty of victory with the adverb "surely" (*'ûlām*); here their diffidence expresses itself with the very similar sounding "perhaps" (*'ûlay*). Ben-hadad does not reply to their proposal. Perhaps unexpected defeat has made him indecisive. His advisers go ahead and carry out their plans.

The first exchange of speeches begins with Ben-hadad's servants' words to Ahab: "your servant, Ben-hadad, says"—ironic counterpoint both to Ben-hadad's regal formality in verse 2 ("Thus says Ben-hadad") and to Ahab's reply to Ben-hadad in verse 4, "my lord the king." Roles are reversed. Where Ahab acknowledged vassalage, Ben-hadad is now prepared to submit. (Or at least Ben-hadad's servants are prepared to make submission for him! We do not really know how Ben-hadad feels about this, nor will we find out until verse 34. This is a minor element in the whole narrative, but it adds its own fillip of suspense.) In verse 32 the servants rephrase the plea for mercy. To Ben-hadad they said, "Perhaps he will let you live" (NRSV, "spare your life"); they made Ahab the subject of the sentence. To Ahab himself they say, in Ben-hadad's name, "May I please live" (NRSV, "Please let me live"). Their phrasing avoids any suggestion of determining Ahab's action. (Compare Elijah's use of the same roundabout phrasing in 17:21 to avoid seeming to command Yahweh.) Ahab's response corresponds to both parts of the servants' message, in reverse order:

> A.   *"Your servant* Ben-hadad says,
>   B.   'May I please *live.'"*
>   B'. "Is he still *alive?*
> A'. He is *my brother."*

Ahab's first words are neutral. His surprise that Ben-hadad survived the carnage of battle and the collapse of the city wall could give way to vengeance as easily as to mercy. His second sentence, however, is determinative. He declines Ben-hadad's concession of vassalage ("your servant") and offers to treat him as an equal ("my brother").

The first two exchanges are separated by a narrative line (v. 33a) whose meaning is obscure. The word "took it up" occurs nowhere else in the Hebrew Bible, and its translation is conjectural; the NRSV's understanding is reasonable. Like good diplomats, Ben-hadad's servants are attentive to every nuance of the conversation; Ahab's use of "my brother" does not escape their notice, and they are quick to capitalize on it. The line is a vivid narrative detail, but it does not seem to contribute anything essential to the plot development. What is its point? It focuses our attention forcefully on Ahab's readiness to extend not only clemency but even parity to Ben-hadad. The servants' immediate reaction plants a niggling suspicion that perhaps the decision is hasty and will have unforeseen repercussions.

The second exchange is brief. The servants quickly ratify Ahab's offer of parity—a better outcome than they could have hoped for—and

Ahab sends them to fetch Ben-hadad. Preliminary negotiations through intermediaries have determined the relative positions of the two kings; now they can meet face to face to work out the terms of a new treaty.

A narrative line separates the second and third exchanges. Ben-hadad emerges from hiding to appear before Ahab, who has him "come up" into his own royal chariot, thus demonstrating by deed the parity he promised. The gesture contains an ironic echo too. The verb is a causative form of *'lh*, "to go up" (literally, Ahab causes Ben-hadad to go up into his chariot), the same verb used of Ben-hadad's advances on Samaria (v. 1; NRSV, "marched") and Aphek (v. 26). Ben-hadad's attempts to "go up" against Israel both failed; in the end, however, Ahab enables Ben-hadad to successfully "go up" from likely subservience to Israel to equality.

The speakers in the third exchange are not clearly marked in Hebrew. The NRSV adds "Ben-hadad" (the Hebrew has "he said to him") and "The king of Israel responded" (the Hebrew has nothing corresponding to this phrase) to indicate (correctly) who is saying what. But the absence of these indicators in Hebrew has certain effects. Until we reach the word "Damascus," we cannot be sure whether Ahab or Ben-hadad is making these major concessions. Logic tells us that it is Ben-hadad: the loser forfeits to the winner, not the other way around. Yet we have already seen Ahab's unexpected degree of magnanimity to Ben-hadad, and the narrator has hinted that Ahab's merciful treatment may be ill-considered. In view of Ahab's eagerness to establish a parity treaty with Ben-hadad, it is not entirely inconceivable that he might offer to restore any territory Israel has previously seized from Aram. The concessions are of two sorts, territorial and commercial, and both sorts aim at reestablishing balance between Aram and Israel: territorial boundaries will return to those of earlier generations, and one-sided commercial advantages will become reciprocal. Only with the details of the commercial arrangements does it become clear that Ben-hadad is the one making the concessions.

Only an emphatic pronoun marks Ahab's reply in Hebrew: "And *I*, I will let you go in that treaty" (NRSV, "on those terms"). If Ben-hadad were still speaking, the emphatic pronoun would have nothing to contrast with; only if we read these words as Ahab's does it make sense: "You have offered acceptable terms; I for my part will make such a treaty with you." As the words, so the deeds: "he" makes a treaty with "him" and lets him go. Again the actors' identities are obscured by a fog of vague pronouns. It is as if Ahab's decision to treat Ben-hadad as a peer has eroded any distinguishing features of the two monarchs and robbed Ahab's victory of its decisiveness. If war is "each-man killed his-man" (v. 20a), this peace is "he made a treaty with him." There is, however, one subtle and ironic verbal indicator of Ahab's victory. Early in the story Ben-hadad "sent" (Hebrew, *šālaḥ*) imperious messengers and messages to Ahab (vv. 2, 5, 6, 7, 9, 10). Now it is Ahab who sends Ben-hadad away (Hebrew, *šillaḥ,* the intensive form of *šālaḥ;* NRSV, "let him go").

Prophetic Condemnation: 20:35-43

The balanced symmetry and narrative completeness of the preceding stories give a sense of closure to verse 34: Ahab's status as vassal has been reversed, Ben-hadad's arrogance has been decisively crushed, Yahweh's good name has been vindicated. Ahab has shown himself courageous in danger, attentive to his people, obedient to his God, and generous in victory. The story, it seems, is over. The next section begins as something entirely new and independent: new characters, a new setting, and a situation that shows no immediate connection with what has preceded.

The story begins with an unnamed member of a prophetic company accosting one of his colleagues with an odd command. The prophet politely (he uses the particle *nā'*; see on verse 31 above) tells his fellow to strike him a severe blow. (The verb is *hkh,* which has had very strong translations throughout chapter 20—"kill," "destroy," "defeat" and the like.) He gives his companion no explanation for this strange request and no indication that this is a divine command, though the narrator tells *us* that the prophet acts "at the command of Yahweh." When his colleague refuses, the first prophet condemns him to a violent death for disobedience to Yahweh, and the death takes place as foretold. (The lion's action, too, is *hkh;* NRSV, "killed.")

Narratively, this strange episode leads nowhere, since after the victim's death the plot line goes back to the starting point and begins again. What is its purpose? In fact, it has an effect on two levels. We will examine one level, that of the interpretation of the whole of chapter 20, in the next section. Here we will consider the effects within the confines of verses 35-43. The episode foreshadows, both thematically and dramatically, the remainder of the section. Themes of disobedience to Yahweh, punishment, violence, and death set a somber tone in sharp contrast to the obedience, victory, and mercy that characterize verses 1-34. Even more discomfiting is the sense that the victim's disobedience is unwitting: the prophet does not indicate in any way to his colleague that the request to strike him is a command from Yahweh. As a result, we respond to the story with mixed feelings for both figures:

the prophet at best misleads the victim by silence, and the victim's disobedience is due to invincible ignorance. Dramatically, the sequence of a compassionate act, identification of the act as disobedience to Yahweh, and condemnation for the disobedience presages the structure of the prophet's subsequent encounter with the king.

The prophet's second attempt to get a colleague to hit him succeeds. "Striking and wounding him" makes it clear that the blow is not a sham but a real wound: a prophet's "oracle" is not just words; it incorporates the prophet's own person into its message. The wounded prophet goes to stand in wait for "the king." The definite article assumes that we know which king is meant. This is the first indication we have that this story is connected to the preceding story of Ahab. The prophet awaits the king along the route of his return from his victory at Aphek, and the prophet's message, we assume, will be a comment on the victory. He covers his eyes with a "bandage" (or some sort of covering; except for this story, the word is unknown in biblical Hebrew), presumably to bind up his wound. He has another purpose, too, but the narrator conceals this from us until verse 41.

While the king is passing by, the prophet calls upon him for a judgment, as any citizen had the right to do (compare, for example, 1 Kings 3:16-28 and 2 Kings 8:3). He presents himself as a soldier. His bandage adds credibility and sympathy to his case by suggesting to the king that he was wounded in battle. The "soldier," however, makes no explicit reference to his wound, not even to excuse his subsequent behavior. He paints a vivid picture of the circumstances: "And here comes a fellow turning aside, and he brought a fellow to me, and he said . . . ." The scenario the king is to envision is that of a soldier withdrawn from battle, probably because he has been wounded, who has been assigned guard duty over a prisoner by his captor. The captor no doubt intends to keep or sell the prisoner as a slave after the battle. The indemnity the captor specifies is revealing. If the prisoner escapes, the guard must take his place as the captor's slave (this is the meaning of "your life shall be given for his life"; it is not a threat of capital punishment) or else pay an enormous sum of money. A talent of silver is roughly one hundred times the value of an ordinary slave (see Exod 21:32). Since a common citizen was unlikely to have such wealth, slavery would be the only possibility for the guard, and perhaps for his entire family as well. We, the audience, know that the whole tale is false, but this unrealistic detail is the only clue the king will get that he is being set up. The "soldier" offers a lame excuse for his dereliction of duty. This leaves the king free to decide the case either way. Ahab has shown himself to be a king of *hesed* toward Ben-hadad; he can exercise similar mercy toward a soldier wounded in his service. Or he can judge that the soldier's inattentiveness is blameworthy and hold him fully responsible.

The king's judgment is lapidary. He settles the case in a pointed four-word sentence, including an unnecessary emphatic pronoun: "Thus your judgment: *you* have decided." The NRSV's paraphrase captures the sense but loses the chiseled quality of the words.

The narrator emphasizes the speed of the prophet's reaction to the king's words. He "quickly" removes the bandage; the literal Hebrew idiom is "he hurried and removed . . . ." The identical construction described the reaction of Ben-hadad's servants to Ahab's words in verse 33. The echo links these two scenes and hints that once more Ahab's unconsidered words may have gotten him into difficulty unawares. The prophet rips the bandage from his eyes, and the king identifies him "as one of the prophets." The phrase suggests that the king does not know this individual prophet personally but only recognizes his prophetic status. How? Did prophets perhaps wear some characteristic identifying mark such as a tattoo? The answer was probably clear to the original audience; it no longer is to us. At this moment we realize that the prophet's bandage had a double purpose of disguise: it presented him as a wounded soldier, and it also concealed his prophetic identity from the king.

The prophet pronounces an oracle of condemnation on the king, using the messenger formula. Ahab's crime is that he has "sent away" (Hebrew, *šillaḥ*, as twice in verse 34; NRSV, "let go") Ben-hadad, whom Yahweh refers to as "the man I had devoted to destruction." Despite the NRSV's rendering, the Hebrew term does not focus on the idea of destruction as much as on the idea that Yahweh retained for himself the right to decide Ben-hadad's fate; a better translation might be "the man I had reserved for myself." Yahweh's claim is that Ahab had no right to make a treaty with Ben-hadad and release him; the Aramean king was Yahweh's personal possession entrusted to Ahab for temporary safekeeping. (In the next section we must ask whether there is any support in verses 1-34 for Yahweh's claim.) Since Ahab has let Ben-hadad go, his own life is forfeit and his people's as well. The details of the case the prophet put before Ahab now fall into place. The exaggerated indemnity should have been Ahab's clue that the prisoner was no ordinary soldier but a person of utmost importance. Just as the "soldier" faced slavery for himself and his family as a result of his negligence, so too the consequences of Ahab's leniency toward Ben-hadad will fall not only upon Ahab but also upon his people. The condemnation is not explicit about what these consequences will be. Will Ahab die as punishment? Will he be captured in battle? Will Israel fall under the control of enemies? Nothing is spelled out. We are left simply with the vague notion that Yahweh is severely displeased with Ahab and will punish the king and his people accordingly.

The king says nothing. He continues on to his palace in Samaria "resentful and sullen"; both words are highly nuanced. The first, *sar,* indicates not only resentment but willfulness that clings obstinately to its position in the face of pressure to change. The second, *zāʿēp,* refers to a hotter emotion than "sullen" indicates; it is the stormy rage that characterizes balked kings (see, for example, Proverbs 19:12). Ahab, chastised for what he must have considered appropriate and legitimate behavior, refuses to accept the rebuke and burns with anger at what he perceives as an affront to his royal authority. The picture of Ahab stalking off to Samaria in angry silence ends the story on a note of considerable tension. God and king are at odds; such a situation cannot endure without drama. The next chapter will connect to this narrative tension by verbal echoes: when Naboth turns down Ahab's request, the king goes home "resentful and sullen." The final chapter of 1 Kings will pick up much more directly on the hostility between Ahab and Yahweh and carry it to its ultimate, and ultimately tragic, conclusion.

The Whole Chapter

When we appreciate chapter 20 as a single narrative, we must take seriously the considerable tensions, in both structure and content, between verses 1-34 and verses 35-43. Structurally, verses 1-34 have a unified, closed symmetry. The narrator does not integrate verses 35-43 into the symmetry but presents them as a separate unit. In content, verses 1-34 portray Ahab quite positively, not only as king and military leader but as favored of Yahweh and on good terms with Yahweh's prophets. Verses 35-43 voice Yahweh's condemnation of Ahab through a prophet. We have seen two-sided portrayals before. The Solomon and Jeroboam stories both contain positive and negative characterizations of their respective kings. But in each case the narrator integrates the double characterization into a single symmetrical structure and thereby presents the evaluation as a single, complex assessment that needs both sides to be complete and accurate. Here the structural isolation of verses 35-43 gives the negative characterization of Ahab the flavor of revisionist history. By presenting the positive picture of Ahab with its own literary integrity, the narrator admits its legitimacy as an evaluation of the king. The negative view in verses 35-43 is juxtaposed as an alternative rather than a corrective. Its position as the last word indicates that it is the narrator's preferred view, but it does not disqualify the preceding positive portrayal. It is as if the narrator is telling us, "It is true that Ahab was a

political and military success. From the religious point of view, however, he failed to obey Yahweh, and this is more important."

The tensions between verses 1-34 and verses 35-43 thus pose a challenge to any attempt to understand chapter 20 as a unified narrative.
Yahweh's motives for giving Ahab the victory in both battles offer
some slight continuity between the two parts of the chapter. In the battle of Samaria, Yahweh promises Ahab the victory so that Ahab "shall
know that I am Yahweh." In other words, Ahab's devotion to Yahweh
needs some bolstering. In the battle of Aphek, Yahweh announces that
he will defeat Ben-hadad because of the Arameans' insulting claim
that Yahweh's power is limited to the hill country. In other words, this
is not a military engagement of king against king. It is a matter of
honor: Yahweh against Ben-hadad to avenge Yahweh's reputation.
Ahab is merely Yahweh's lieutenant and therefore has no right to negotiate independently with his captured foe. But these minor details
do not outweigh the fundamental differences between the positive picture of Ahab in verses 1-34 and the condemnation in verses 35-43.

There is, however, a pointer to an avenue of approach. The strange
episode in 20:35-36 has striking similarities to the story in 1 Kings
13:11-32. In both, prophetic figures are in conflict with one another; one
prophet occasions another's unwitting disobedience to Yahweh, then
condemns him for disobeying; the condemnation involves a lion attacking the disobedient prophet, and the attack takes place. There is a
verbal link between the passages as well. The phrase "at the command
of Yahweh" (20:35) occurs seven times in 1 Kings 13 (where the NRSV
translates it "at the word of the LORD") and nowhere else in 1 Kings.

These links invite us to read chapter 20 with one eye on chapter 13
and its context, the whole story of Jeroboam. The similarities are suggestive. Both stories recount events in the kingdom of Israel, where the
king is embroiled in military hostilities with a neighboring kingdom—
Judah in the case of Jeroboam and Aram in the case of Ahab. Both stories report how prophets voice Yahweh's approval of the king's military and political actions. Both kings make a further decision that
seems politically wise: Jeroboam establishes sanctuaries at Bethel and
Dan to assure that his people's loyalties do not revert to Jerusalem
(12:26-27), and Ahab establishes a parity treaty with Ben-hadad in return for significant territorial and commercial concessions. In each case
the decision has religious dimensions that make it unacceptable to
Yahweh, and he voices his condemnation of both decision and king
through prophets. Both kings respond to the condemnation with in-
transigence (13:33-34; 20:43).

These parallels between Ahab and Jeroboam afford new insight
into a verbal leitmotif that runs through all the regnal accounts of

kings of Israel. Even in the briefest and most formulaic accounts, Israelite kings are condemned for continuing in the "sin of Jeroboam." Ahab is no exception (16:31). Usually that phrase is understood quite specifically: Israelite kings maintained the calf-shrines Jeroboam established at Bethel and Dan. Here, however, the theme undergoes a literary transmutation that reveals hidden depths. In Jeroboam's case, the sanctuaries were the surface manifestation of a deeper deviance: the subordination of Yahwistic religious demands to political expediency by a king who owed his political successes to Yahweh in the first place. Ahab is guilty of the same evil.

Chapter 20

NABOTH'S VINEYARD

1 Kings 21

The two chapters that tell of Ahab's wars with Aram are set three years apart (see 22:1). Between them the narrator recounts the story of Ahab's acquisition of Naboth's vineyard and Elijah's condemnation of Ahab for his sins.[1] As in chapters 20 and 22, the story of Ahab is narratively complete in itself, without the episode of prophetic condemnation. The prophetic story, however, presumes the associated Ahab story and introduces a dimension of religious judgment.

Ahab Obtains Naboth's Vineyard: 21:1-16

The story of Ahab's successful attempt to gain possession of a vineyard belonging to an Israelite landowner includes six symmetrically arranged scenes:

    A. Ahab tries to buy Naboth's vineyard (21:1-4a)
    B. Ahab and Jezebel in Ahab's chambers (21:4b-7)
    C. Jezebel's letter details a plot (21:8-10)

---

[1] In the Greek textual tradition, the story of Naboth's vineyard precedes the stories of the Aramean wars. In other words, the material comprising chapters 20, 21, and 22 in the Hebrew text is in the order 21, 20, 22 in the Greek text. This puts the story of Naboth's vineyard immediately after the other Elijah stories in chapters 17–19 (Elijah appears in 21:17-29), and it puts the two chapters about the Aramean wars side by side. While this is superficially neater, it significantly changes the focus of the stories. In the Greek text we have four chapters about Elijah followed by two about the Aramean wars. In the Hebrew text we have three chapters about a paradigmatic prophet like Moses followed by three about a paradigmatic conflict between the monarchy and the prophetic movement.

C'. Jezebel's plot succeeds (21:11-14)
B'. Ahab and Jezebel in Ahab's chambers (21:15)
A'. Ahab takes possession of Naboth's vineyard (21:16)

Parallel scenes share locations (for example, A and A' are set in the vineyard), styles (for example, B and B' are both dialogue following a single narrative line), and characters (for example, C features Jezebel and mentions the elders, the conspirators, and Naboth; C' mentions Jezebel and features the elders, the conspirators, and Naboth). In addition, there is extensive verbal repetition, particularly between scenes C and C'.

AHAB TRIES TO BUY NABOTH'S VINEYARD: 21:1-4a

The first scene features a dialogue between Ahab and Naboth the Jezreelite (vv. 2-3) set between a narrative introduction (v. 1) and a narrative of Ahab's angry reaction to Naboth's speech (v. 4a). The dialogue is a particularly noteworthy literary device. It functions like the statement of theme in a musical theme and variations. Three times in the course of the story Ahab or Jezebel will cite elements of the opening dialogue (vv. 4a, 6, and 15), in each case modulated and transposed in a way that reveals new facets of their characters.

The scene begins with a vague temporal introduction (NRSV, "Later"), which sets the events after Ahab's victories in chapter 21 and before his death in chapter 22. The NRSV accurately reflects the slight awkwardness of the Hebrew, which has, in effect, two successive introductions—the temporal one and a circumstantial one about Naboth's vineyard.[2] The narrator describes the location of Naboth's vineyard in detail. It is "in Jezreel"—this is important for two reasons, both of which have to do with Naboth's later claim that this vineyard is his ancestral inheritance (we shall discuss this technical term below). First, since Naboth is a Jezreelite, his "ancestral inheritance" has to be located there; land Naboth may own elsewhere cannot be his patrimony. Second, Ahab's main capital is Samaria, to which he went at the end of the last chapter (see 16:29 and 20:43). That city was established only one generation previously (16:24) and therefore had no tradition of Israelite ancestral inheritance. Since the narrator is about to locate the vineyard

---

[2]One can suspect here the hand of an editor who used the temporal introduction ("Later the following events took place:") to insert an originally independent story ("Naboth the Jezreelite had a vineyard . . .") between the stories about the Aramean wars.

next to Ahab's palace, he must specify that this palace is *not* in Samaria but in some place where Israelite traditions are deeply rooted.[3] The second detail is that the vineyard lies beside Ahab's palace. This makes Ahab's desire to purchase the land reasonable. Finally, the narrator identifies Ahab as "king of Samaria," a very unusual title in the Hebrew Bible (found elsewhere only in 2 Kings 1:3). The title subtly points up Ahab's connection with his father's new city and thereby hints at his alienation from Israelite land and land traditions.

Ahab makes a proposal to Naboth. Its tone is moderate and its terms are generous. The king does not use the polite particle *nā'* (see the remarks on 20:31) but he gives a reason for his request and offers Naboth a choice of either better land or a fair price in return. He puts the offer of a better vineyard first, since that is more likely than money to appeal to one who lives from the land's produce.

Naboth's response implies that he does not accept Ahab's proposal. Two phrases deserve comment. The first is the opening exclamation, which the NRSV renders "The LORD forbid that . . . ." This accurately captures both the strength and the religious dimension of Naboth's words, which mean literally, "It would be a profanation for me to . . . ." The second phrase is "ancestral inheritance." The Israelites' fundamental understanding of their relationship to the land was that the land belonged to Yahweh, who entrusted it to their ancestors. God assigned certain portions of the land to each family; this was the patrimony, or "ancestral inheritance," and it was subject to special laws for purchase and ownership. For example, a family could sell their "ancestral inheritance" only if they were so impoverished that they could not otherwise survive; and then they could sell it only temporarily, namely, until the next jubilee year, when it returned to their possession.[4] (Not all land was so designated. Land that did not qualify as "ancestral inheritance" could be bought and sold normally.) With these two phrases Naboth reveals that his rejection of Ahab's offer is not a willful refusal but a matter of conscience, and he establishes both a religious and a legal basis for his inability to accede to Ahab's request. Naboth is not rebuking the king for knowingly proposing a religious profanation—the king, after all, is a native of Samaria and cannot be

---

[3]The narrator does not tell us why Ahab would have a palace in Jezreel in addition to his palace in the capital. Historians speculate that there might have been two capitals, for Israelite vs. Canaanite affairs, or that Jezreel might have been a seasonal residence.

[4]Laws incorporating these traditions are found in Leviticus 25:23-28. It is uncertain whether these specific laws were in effect in Ahab's time, but the traditions behind them were surely familiar to the author and audience of the Naboth story.

expected to know under what aegis each piece of property in Jezreel is held. But Naboth's reply makes it clear that he is not simply holding out for a better price; his decision is definitive.

Ahab recognizes the finality of Naboth's words and goes home[5] "resentful and sullen." On the nuances of these words, see the comments above on 20:34.[6] They imply that Ahab does not resign himself to Naboth's decision but continues to desire the vineyard. Since the purpose for which he wants it, a vegetable garden, is rather trivial, Ahab's strong emotional response suggests that he is taking Naboth's decision as a personal rebuff.

There is a subtlety in the Hebrew text of verse 4a that is missed by the NRSV. In the phrase "for he had said," the NRSV takes "he" as meaning Naboth. The phrase thus becomes the narrator's statement to us, explaining Ahab's foul mood by citing the speech of Naboth that caused it. In fact, however, the phrase is literally "and he said," with "he" meaning Ahab. The subsequent citation of Naboth's speech is thus not the narrator's but Ahab's, as he angrily broods over Naboth's words. Translate verse 4a:

> Resentful and sullen over what Naboth the Jezreelite had said to him, Ahab went home, muttering, "'I will not give you my ancestral inheritance.'"

This is the first variation on the original dialogue. It is instructive to note how Ahab remembers—or misremembers—Naboth's words. He understands the landowner's response as an outright refusal ("I will not give") rather than as a statement of the impossibility of the sale. And though he recalls the legal term Naboth used, "ancestral inheritance," he leaves out the religious exclamation by which Naboth characterized selling his property as a profanation. Ahab, in other words, focuses on the fact that Naboth is balking him and on the Israelite legal tradition Naboth uses to do so rather than on the divine will enshrined in that tradition.

---

[5]The narrative is not explicit, but we are probably to understand Ahab's destination as Samaria, not his palace in Jezreel. In verse 8 Jezebel will send her letter "to the elders and the nobles who lived with Naboth in his city"—a rather roundabout phrasing if Jezebel and Ahab are in residence in the same city as Naboth. If the whole story were set in Jezreel, we would expect simply "to the elders and the nobles of the city" or the like.

[6]In the larger context, the echo with 20:34 points up that in both passages the words that anger Ahab are rooted in Yahweh's will, whether expressed by the anonymous prophet of 20:41 or by Naboth's appeal to the law of patrimony.

AHAB AND JEZEBEL IN AHAB'S CHAMBERS: 21:4b-7

Ahab's anger becomes petulance, and perhaps despondency. (The phrase "turned his face" seems to indicate despair in 2 Kings 20:2, where King Hezekiah, on hearing that he was about to die, "turned his face to the wall.") Whatever his mood, Ahab refuses to eat. We shall have reason below to ask whether Ahab's motives here are as simple as they seem. Jezebel's question is that of any concerned spouse: What's the matter? Why won't you eat?

Ahab reports the whole affair to Jezebel—his own offer as well as Naboth's response. This is the second variation on the original dialogue. Here too the differences are significant. In recounting the offer, Ahab makes several changes: he omits the reason why he desired the vineyard, he places his offer of money before his offer of another vineyard, and he does not describe the vineyard he offers in exchange as better than Naboth's. In each case the difference reflects that Ahab is speaking to Jezebel rather than to Naboth and reveals something about the queen's character. Omitting the reason for wanting the vineyard can suggest either of two things. Perhaps for Jezebel the desire to possess more land requires no explanation, or Ahab may not want to admit to his queen that he stooped to justifying himself to a mere commoner. Reversing the order of things that Ahab offers in exchange for the vineyard reflects Jezebel's priorities: offering land for land would make sense to the landowner Naboth; offering money for land would make more sense to the queen. Finally, leaving out the better quality of the land he offered in exchange may also reflect an unwillingness to admit to Jezebel how openhanded Ahab was willing to be. All these variations point to an imperious queen whose attitudes toward royal prerogative are quite different from those envisaged in Israelite law and tradition. Jezebel was, after all, the daughter of the royal house of Sidon (16:31), a society with alien religious and political understandings of the relationship of king and people.

In recounting Naboth's reply, Ahab omits Naboth's religious exclamation, as he did in verse 4a; but now he also omits the legal term "ancestral inheritance." This, too, probably reflects Ahab's surmise that the niceties of Israelite law will not impress his Baalist queen. Ahab continues to recall Naboth's words as an overt refusal ("I will not give") rather than as a religiously grounded objection.

Jezebel's reply opens with a statement introduced by an emphatic pronoun. The NRSV takes the sentence as a rhetorical question. This is possible, but since there is no interrogative marker in the Hebrew sentence, it is probably better to take it as a statement: "Now, *you* hold kingship over Israel!" The emphatic pronoun reminds Ahab that he, not Naboth, is king; in the mouth of the Sidonian queen, this means that the king has the right to take any property he wants and therefore should not brook Naboth's refusal.[7] Whether we take the words as a statement or a rhetorical question, their full freight of irony will become obvious as the story progresses: the one who acts as king is Jezebel herself! She continues with encouragement and a promise: "*I* [emphatic pronoun] will give you the vineyard." Again the emphatic pronoun adds rich irony. It contrasts Naboth, who will not give Ahab the vineyard, with Jezebel, who will. But since Jezebel just used an emphatic pronoun to refer to Ahab, it implies a contrast there too: Ahab may hold kingship in Israel, but it is Jezebel who will act. She does not tell Ahab her plans, and so we are left with the king to wonder what she will do to fulfill her promise.

This brief scene, so simple on the surface, is suggestive of complex relationships between Jezebel and Ahab. Although it is sometimes difficult for a modern reader to draw the line between appreciating the narrator's subtleties of characterization and over-psychologizing the characters, Hebrew narrative is clearly capable of deep psychological insight. (See, for example, the stories of Saul's paranoid disintegration in 1 Samuel.) In this passage Jezebel's attitudes toward Ahab include the compassionate support of a spouse, but at the same time the kind of simplistic consolation she gives him has a parent-to-child tone about it ("Don't cry. Mommy will make everything all right."). This suggests that Ahab is passive and acquiescent before the more assertive character of his queen, or at least that this is Jezebel's opinion of him. Ahab's behavior—pouting in his room, not eating, and editing his account of the interview with Naboth to make a favorable impression on Jezebel—can support this understanding of things. On the other hand, the bottom line is that Ahab now has someone else, less heedful than he of Israelite traditions, working to achieve his purposes. His behavior first awakens Jezebel's concern, then her chagrin, and finally her resolve. Is the king merely passive or is he cleverly manipulating Jezebel into doing his dirty work? The narrator will tantalize us with this question again.

[7]If we read the statement in the larger context of chapter 20, the meaning is slightly different, though the ultimate effect is similar. The emphatic pronoun reminds Ahab both that he is now independent of Ben-hadad and that, as his vassalage to Ben-hadad demonstrated, the rights of kings include the seizure of anything belonging to their subjects (see 20:3-4).

JEZEBEL'S LETTER DETAILS A PLOT: 21:8-10

Jezebel initiates her plan by writing a letter to the local leaders and officials in Jezreel. The narrator emphasizes her assumption of royal authority by repetition: she writes in Ahab's name, and she seals the letter with his seal. Immediately following Jezebel's words, "Now, *you* hold kingship in Israel," the ironic force of the narrator's emphasis is unmistakable. The "elders and nobles" to whom she sends her letter do not seem to be two different groups (though our knowledge of ancient Israelite social structures is far from complete) but two different terms for leading citizens. The last words of verse 8 are awkward: "who were in his city, the ones living with Naboth." (The NRSV smooths out the phrase considerably, basing the translation on the much smoother word order in verse 11.) The strained word order in verse 8 puts the emphasis on Naboth (the last word of the phrase) and highlights that those whom Jezebel is about to enlist in her conspiracy are Naboth's own fellow citizens, bound to him in the web of covenantal obligations that constituted Israel as Yahweh's people. Naboth will not be the only victim of this crime; it will also tear apart the weave of Israelite social order.

In the first part of her letter (v. 9), Jezebel calls for a public assembly and fast. Such fasts were usually proclaimed as acts of public penance in times of distress—war, plague, or similar disasters. Jezebel offers no pretext for the fast; presumably she expected the elders and nobles to supply a plausible one. She directs that they are to place Naboth "at the head of the assembly"—probably a place of honor, though some scholars think it might be the place reserved for the one accused of the crime that precipitated the disaster. The second part of Jezebel's letter (v. 10) details the conspiracy itself. The elders and nobles are to engage two "scoundrels" (NRSV; the Hebrew literally means "sons of worthlessness" or "good-for-nothings") and place them in a position to accuse Naboth before the assembly of blasphemy and *lèse majesté*. They (that is, the elders and nobles) are then to take Naboth out of the city and execute him by stoning. Jezebel leaves nothing to chance. She supplies the stage directions, stipulates the crime, scripts the accusation, and specifies the required outcome.

Jezebel's letter requires two sets of comments, the first regarding the legalities envisioned in her plans, and the second concerning the narrative effect the letter has on the flow of the story. We shall consider the first issue here but defer the second set of comments until we have examined verses 11-14, which recount the success of Jezebel's plans. As to the legalities, Jezebel specifies two scoundrels, because Israelite law required the testimony of at least two witnesses in capital cases (see, for example, Deuteronomy 17:6). To blaspheme the name of God was a capital crime, punishable by stoning outside the settlement (see Lev 24:10-23). And cursing the king was comparable in seriousness to blaspheming God (Exod 22:28).[8] Clearly Jezebel is more aware of the ins and outs of Israelite law than Ahab gives her credit for (see the remarks above on verse 6) and has no scruples about using its letter to pervert its spirit.

JEZEBEL'S PLOT SUCCEEDS: 21:11-14

The narrative of the success of Jezebel's plot begins with an introductory sentence whose striking verbosity is somewhat subdued in the NRSV. The verse comprises two parts, each of which involves a simple statement followed by a more detailed repetition of the same statement:

> And the men of his city,
> > the elders and nobles who were the ones living in his city,
> did just as Jezebel had sent to them,
> > just as was written in the letter she had sent to them.

The patterned reiteration emphasizes two things: Jezebel's co-conspirators are from "his city"—that is, they are Naboth's own neighbors; and their compliance with Jezebel's orders was exact, "just as she had sent to them." Together these point up the misplaced loyalties of the elders and nobles, who are meticulous in cooperating with the conniving queen against their innocent fellow Jezreelite.

The letter-perfect character of the leaders' obedience is reflected in the next verse as well. Not only does it correspond word for word with Jezebel's commands in verse 9b; it actually violates the standard syntax of Hebrew narrative in order to correspond almost letter for letter!

> v. 9b: *qīrĕʾû sômu wĕhôšîbû ʾet-nābôt bĕrōʾš hāʿām*
> v. 12: *qārĕʾû sômu wĕhōšîbû ʾet-nābôt bĕrōʾš hāʿām*

Standard Hebrew narrative would use *wayyōšîbû*, "and seated," to correspond to Jezebel's imperative verb *wĕhôšîbû*, "and seat." By using a non-standard narrative form, *wĕhōšîbû*, verse 12 can repeat even the exact letters of verse 9b.

Variations begin in verse 13. The elders and nobles disappear from the picture: the two scoundrels enter on their own, take their own

---

[8]Hebrew linguistic usage reflects Israel's horror of the crime. Instead of using the phrase "curse God," the Hebrew Bible uses a euphemism, "bless God." This is the case not only here and in verse 13 but wherever the phrase "curse God" would appear (Job 1:5, 11; 2:5, 9; Ps 10:3).

seats, and speak against Naboth. (The narrator emphasizes by unnecessary repetition that they are scoundrels.) When they accuse Naboth
they address the assembly ("Naboth cursed . . .") instead of Naboth
himself, as the queen directed ("You have cursed . . . ," v. 10). These
variations allow the narrator to shift to a more vivid presentation:
where verse 12 is a report of the elders' actions, verse 13 depicts the actual assembly and places us among the people. We watch the scoundrels
enter and hear their accusation. (If the scoundrels used the second person, "You cursed . . . ," we would hear the accusation from the perspective of Naboth. But the narrator consistently avoids showing us
things from Naboth's viewpoint. Once he speaks his piece in verse 3,
he becomes the passive object of others' actions.)

The variations also produce a significant change in the grammar
from verse 10. Now the scoundrels are the subjects of the verbs "took
him outside the city and stoned him to death." This, too, is in conformity with Israelite law, where the accusers in a capital crime were required to begin the execution by casting the first stones (see Deut 17:7).
The scoundrels then report back to Jezebel on the success of the plot.
There are two surprises here. One would expect the elders and nobles
to report back, not the scoundrels, since the original letter came to them
and did not indicate that the scoundrels were Jezebel's direct agents.
And in fact that is how readers often understand verses 13b-14, probably under the influence of verse 10: as if the elders and nobles take
Naboth out, stone him, and report back to Jezebel. But the grammar is
clear: the scoundrels are the subjects of the verbs.[9] A second surprise is
that the report is sent to Jezebel, even though the original letter was "in
Ahab's name and sealed with his seal." Both of these details reveal the
closeness of Jezebel and the scoundrels. They are not merely tools of the
elders and nobles; they are, in fact, direct agents of the Baalist queen.

Here we must pause a moment to consider the narrative effect of
these central scenes. The main issue we must address is their apparent
narrative weakness. Compare, for instance, a hypothetical version of
the story *without* verse 10. Jezebel sends to the leaders of Jezreel a
straightforward request for a fast and public assembly (v. 9). The leaders comply, but the assembly is suddenly disrupted when two
scoundrels unexpectedly accuse a leading citizen, Naboth, of capital
crimes. Their testimony holds, and the community, led by the accusers,
executes the alleged blasphemer. Only when the scoundrels report

---

[9]It is also possible to read "the people" (v. 13) as the subject of the verbs "took
him out" and "stoned him." But the verb in verse 14, "sent to Jezebel," is coordinate
to those in verse 13b, and it is difficult to imagine the whole people sending the report back to Jezebel.

back to Jezebel does all become clear to us: the queen was behind the plot all along. Dramatically, such a story would be far superior—more concise, yet with greater tension. Instead we get verbose repetition (vv. 10 and 13) and an unlikely letter in which the queen not only spells out in writing to a large number of people all the details of her murderous plot but even refers to her own personal agents as scoundrels!

What are we to make of this? Or, better stated, what other effects are realized at the expense of this dramatic weakening? The first effect is to broaden the circle of responsibility. Without verse 10 the elders and nobles are not part of Jezebel's conspiracy; verse 10 implicates them and allows us to infer that they knowingly misjudge Naboth and join in executing him. A second effect is distance. By lessening the dramatic tension, the narrator distances us from the action: we are less intent on what will happen next, since Jezebel's letter has already told us. (The narrator's technique of not showing us things from Naboth's point of view contributes to this same effect of distance. The accusation presumably surprises Naboth; it does not surprise us.) A third effect is to use that distance to make room for an element of judgment. When Jezebel refers to the false witnesses as "scoundrels," the effect is both sarcasm (she does not have much respect for her own agents) and irony (if her collaborators are so contemptible, what of the elders and nobles? And what of the queen herself?). A fourth effect, related to this, arises when in verse 13 we discover that "scoundrels" is actually the narrator's word for the false witnesses. This confers narrative authority on Jezebel's use of the term (and on the sarcasm and irony it effects). It also hints that the narrator may have infiltrated Jezebel's words in verse 10, so that we hear both voices at once. (This last effect will be significant when we see a similar narrative technique at work in verses 20-26.) In short, the overall effect of verse 10 in the narrative is to transform it from a poignant tale of individual tragedy to an ethical exemplum that invites the reader to make moral judgments about widespread responsibility for an act of judicial murder.

Ahab and Jezebel in Ahab's Chambers: 21:15

Jezebel keeps her promise and tells Ahab that the vineyard is now his for the taking. Her speech is the third variation on the theme of the original dialogue between Ahab and Naboth. Her version, filtered through Ahab's version to her in verse 6, recalls Ahab's offer of money for the vineyard but omits his alternative offer of land, and understands Naboth's decision as an outright refusal, just as Ahab had depicted it. When she announces Naboth's death as the justification for

Ahab's seizure of the vineyard,[10] she emphasizes it by repetition ("Naboth is not alive, but dead") but does not explain to Ahab how it came about. Nor does the king ask, as we might expect him to. This may be another indication of Ahab's passivity, or it may be that Ahab is fully aware of the deeds Jezebel is capable of but prefers blissful ignorance of the facts. The narrator leaves Ahab's motives to our imagination, but none of the possibilities puts the king in a good light.

Ahab Takes Possession of Naboth's Vineyard: 21:16

The last verse begins with the same words as verse 15: "As soon as Jezebel/Ahab heard that . . . ." The echo highlights the subsequent divergence of the sentences: Jezebel hears that Naboth has been stoned, but Ahab hears only that Naboth is dead. This points up once again Ahab's failure to inquire how Naboth's death came about. A command-and-compliance pattern reflects the king's obedience to Jezebel: Jezebel tells Ahab, "Get up, take possession . . ."; in response, Ahab "got up . . . to take possession." (The NRSV obscures the pattern by translating the verb "get up" as "go" in verse 15 and "set out" in verse 16.) The scene has a feeling of closure, but the use of an infinitive of purpose ("to take possession") instead of a finite verb ("and took possession") hints at the possibility that the story may continue.

The Whole Story: 21:1-16

When we consider the overall sweep of this story, at least two questions merit our attention. What is the fundamental evil the story portrays? And who is really the main character? On the surface the narrative recounts the judicial murder of an Israelite landowner so that the crown can obtain his property. That is certainly one level of the story, but there are numerous indications of deeper issues. One of those issues is the royal couple's assault on the legal and religious principles that guarantee the structure of Israelite society. The narrator evokes those principles in several ways. First, Naboth's insistence that the vineyard is his ancestral inheritance and that to sell it would be a profanation points to Israelite law and its religious foundation as the basis

---

[10]Our limited knowledge of Israelite law does not explain whether Ahab has legal basis for taking possession of the vineyard. Perhaps the property of convicted felons reverts to the crown, at least in cases of *lèse majesté*. Or perhaps the seizure is simply illegal. Presumably the original audience knew the answer.

for the opening situation of stability in the story. Second, the narrator's insistence that the elders and nobles are Naboth's fellow citizens implicates in the events the mutuality of covenant obligations that constituted Israel as the people of Yahweh. Third, Jezebel's call for a public assembly and fast highlights religious observances as the means by which a new situation of stability—Naboth's death and Ahab's acquisition of the vineyard—is achieved. In each instance, however, these mechanisms of social order are under attack. Whether Ahab intends it or not, his desire for Naboth's vineyard runs counter to the Yahwistic traditions enshrined in the laws concerning the ancestral inheritance. When Jezebel enlists the elders and nobles in her conspiracy against Naboth, she thereby rends the very fabric of Israelite covenantal identity. Finally, the assembly is hypocritical and perverts ritual by using it as an occasion for perjury. The story, then, is not simply the tragedy of an individual; Naboth is only the most obvious victim. The religious uniqueness of Israel, rooted in covenant and enshrined in law and tradition, is equally assaulted. The royal house undermines the very structures of social stability it has the obligation to uphold.

And what of the main character? Here, too, there are hidden depths. Jezebel is clearly the active force in the story. She appears in three scenes and is mentioned in a fourth. In each of the scenes in which she appears, she takes the initiative in speaking or acting, and the scene in which she is mentioned unfolds in strict conformity with her directives. If action is the criterion, she is clearly the protagonist. Yet we have already raised the possibility that Ahab's apparent passivity may mask a subtle form of manipulation. He, too, appears in four scenes. His moods move Jezebel, and his desires determine the outcome of the plot. In its most basic terms, this story is "Ahab wants the vineyard; Ahab gets the vineyard." If the criterion is the shaping and directing of events, Ahab may well be the main character. Yet behind both Jezebel and Ahab stands another character with at least an equal claim to primacy. Though Naboth is almost entirely passive, he is mentioned by name in all six scenes, often with a title, "the Jezreelite." His name occurs first and last in the story and, surprisingly, more often than the names of Ahab and Jezebel combined! It even occurs six times in the three verses after he is dead (vv. 14-16); "Naboth the Jezreelite" haunts the narrative like an unpeaceable ghost. If sheer dominance in the text is the criterion, then this is indeed (as we most often call it) the story of Naboth.

The recognition that we can identify several different characters in the narrative as central, each in his or her own way, is not a sign of disunity in the story. Rather it is a measure of the richness of a compelling narrative that it can offer satisfying readings on several levels. As we shall see, this richness continues in the second part of the chapter, the prophetic condemnation.

Prophetic Condemnation: 21:17-29

The second half of the story tells how Yahweh sends Elijah to announce a word of condemnation to Ahab and how Ahab responds to the prophet's message. The material is in six symmetrical sections:

A. Yahweh's word to Elijah (21:17-19)
  B. Elijah's words to Ahab (21:20-22)
    C. The punishment of Jezebel and Ahab's house (21:23-24)
    C'. The evil of Jezebel and Ahab (21:25-26)
  B'. Ahab's reaction to Elijah's words (21:27)
A'. Yahweh's word to Elijah (21:28-29)

The two central sections comprise different sorts of evaluative pronouncements. Section C' is not a "scene" in the strict sense, since it is a narrator's aside to the reader. As we shall see, the narrative status of section C (vv. 23-24) is more problematic. It may be the continuation of Elijah's speech, as the NRSV takes it, or it may be another narrator's aside.

YAHWEH'S WORD TO ELIJAH: 21:17-19

The narrator's opening words mark what follows as a classic prophetic story. "The word of Yahweh came to . . ." is the standard formula for a prophet's reception of an oracle. The prophet is "Elijah the Tishbite" (for this term, see the discussion of 17:1). The narrator uses the identifying title because he is introducing Elijah for the first time in this story. Yahweh's word consists of a command to Elijah (v. 18) and two messages for Ahab (v. 19).

Yahweh commands Elijah to confront Ahab about the crime against Naboth. His first words link the tale of prophetic condemnation to the story of Naboth by echoing the sounds of Jezebel's words to Ahab in verse 15: Jezebel told Ahab *qûm rēš* ("Arise, take possession"; NRSV, "Go, take possession"); Yahweh tells Elijah *qûm rēd* ("Arise, go down"; NRSV, "Go down"). God refers to Ahab by the king's usual title, "King of Israel," but expands it with the words "who is in Samaria" (NRSV, "who rules in Samaria"). The phrase is unnecessary for two reasons: it does not form part of the usual royal title, and Ahab is in fact not in Samaria but in Naboth's vineyard in Jezreel. Because it is extraneous, it attracts attention and, by the reference to Samaria, recalls the uncommon royal title in verse 1, "King of Samaria," and Ahab's alienation from Israelite tradition that that title insinuated. Yahweh's next words go on to clarify that Ahab is at the moment in Naboth's vineyard "to take possession," again echoing language from the end of the preceding narrative and establishing the prophetic condemnation story as its further development. (This observation is more significant than at first appears, since there is nothing after verse 19 to indicate any connection with the Naboth story.)

In verse 19 Yahweh gives Elijah two oracles intended for Ahab. They are presented in parallel fashion:

> A. "You shall say to him,
> B. 'Thus says Yahweh:
> C. "Have you killed . . ."'
> A'. You shall say to him,
> B'. 'Thus says Yahweh:
> C'. "In the place . . . ."'"

The repeated introductions, A and A', and the repeated traditional prophetic formulas, B and B' (on this "messenger formula" see the remark on 20:13), separate the two oracles and give them the character of independent aphorisms.

The first saying is a terse rhetorical question—only three words in Hebrew, one of which simply adds emphasis. The two main words rhyme with each other, giving the whole phrase a gnomic quality: *hărāsáhtā wĕgam-yārāštā* (note the strong alliterative sequence *r-ṣ-t/r-š-t* and the almost unbroken sequence of *a*-type vowels). The content, too, is gnomic. Both main words have a certain ambivalence surrounding their core meaning. The first, *rṣḥ*, means "to kill," but it can be used of both willful murder and involuntary manslaughter. Since the reference here is to the judicial murder of Naboth, of which Ahab may or may not have been aware (or at least suspicious), the verb is exquisitely appropriate. The second word, *yrš*, means "to take possession," but it can be used of forcible seizure or of legal inheritance. Again, the ambivalence is precisely appropriate for the crown's confiscation of Naboth's vineyard on a perjured charge of *lèse majesté*. The NRSV's translation accurately reflects the basic meaning of the sentence but loses the ironically pertinent ambivalence as well as the aural elegance. A paraphrase could retain something of those qualities: "Did you kill to get your will?"

Yahweh formulates the second saying as a statement of punishment. This implies a positive answer to the preceding rhetorical question: Yes, Ahab is guilty of murder for the sake of gain. The phrasing links Ahab's crime and punishment in two ways: the king will be punished in the same place and in the same manner (dogs licking up the blood) in which Naboth died. The Hebrew ends with an emphatic pronoun that stresses the correspondence: " . . . dogs will lick up your blood—*yours* too." The stress on the commensurability of Ahab's and Naboth's fate points to the legal principle of the law of talion, which stipulates that the punishment must be proportionate to the crime ("an eye for an eye," etc.).

ELIJAH'S WORDS TO AHAB: 21:20-22

The story leaps abruptly to Elijah's encounter with Ahab, omitting any account of Elijah's journey to Jezreel. The effect is to suppress narrative in favor of dialogue, and thus to give the whole prophetic condemnation section a relatively slow tempo. Ahab's hostile opening words sound a similar note to his greeting of Elijah in 18:17, but with a significant difference. In chapters 17–19 the horizon of events is all Israel: at issue is Israel's worship of Baal and the drought that has affected the whole people, and Ahab addresses Elijah as the "troubler of Israel." Here the horizon is Ahab himself, his sin and his punishment; and he addresses Elijah as "my enemy." Elijah's reply simply repeats the main word from Ahab's question ("I have found you"), which is the normal Hebrew way of saying yes.

Elijah continues with a lengthy condemnation that begins as his own words but quickly becomes divine speech. He mentions Yahweh by name in verse 20b (NRSV, "the LORD"), but throughout verses 21-22 "I" is Yahweh (as is commonly true in prophetic oracles). The shift from prophet's words to God's is accompanied by a shift to the vivid present: "Because you have sold yourself to do evil in the sight of Yahweh, here I am, bringing evil on you." The wording here, too, alludes to the law of talion ("evil" for "evil"), though the NRSV obscures the effect by translating the word "disaster" in verse 21.

The entire condemnation in verses 21-22 explicitly refers to two earlier scenes whose words it echoes: the condemnation of Jeroboam's dynasty by Ahijah of Shiloh (14:10-11) and of Baasha's dynasty by Jehu, son of Hanani (16:2b-4). (In fact, verse 24 will continue the echo. See the discussion below for the connection between verses 23-24 and verses 21-22.) The repeated oracle of condemnation points to a tragic pattern in the royal houses of Israel. Jeroboam, founder of the first dynasty of the northern kingdom, was succeeded by a son who reigned only two years; the dynasty ended with the son's assassination. Baasha, founder of the second dynasty, was succeeded by a son who reigned only two years; this dynasty also ended with the son's assassination. The third dynasty will fare only slightly better. Founded by Ahab's father, Omri, it will last three generations. Ahab will be succeeded by a son, Ahaziah, who will reign only two years and who will die as the result of injuries sustained in a fall (2 Kgs 1). Ahaziah will be succeeded by another son of Ahab, Jehoram, with whose assassination the dynasty of Omri and Ahab will end (2 Kgs 9). (For a fuller treatment of this oracle of dynastic condemnation, see the discussion of 14:10-11.)

The Punishment of Jezebel and Ahab's House: 21:23-24

The first question we must address concerning verses 23-24 is whose words these are. The NRSV treats them as the continuation of Elijah's speech to Ahab. Above I suggested that they may be a narrator's aside to the reader. The truth is that it is impossible to be sure. Verses 20b-22 are clearly Elijah's words, and the retrospective tone of verses 25-26 makes it equally clear that they are not. There are no indications in the Hebrew text of where Elijah's speech ends and the narrator's remarks begin (Hebrew does not use quotation marks); the shift of speaker from Elijah to the narrator may occur at the beginning of verse 23 or at the beginning of verse 25.[11] The lack of syntactic markers has an effect on the way we read this passage, but that effect is foreclosed by the NRSV's use of quotation marks to include verses 23-24 unambiguously within Elijah's speech. Without such indicators, we first read verses 23-24 under the assumption that they are Elijah's words. We note that he shifts back to third-person references to Yahweh in verse 23 and to Ahab in verse 24, but since he used such third-person references already in verses 20 and 21, this is not exceptionable. However, when we discover that the narrator is speaking in verses 25-26, we realize that the speaker may have changed earlier, and the third-person references in verses 23-24 could be a sign that they are no longer Elijah's words to Ahab but the narrator's words to us. The net result is not to nullify the possibility of reading verses 23-24 as Elijah's words but to allow us to hear *both* voices, Elijah's and the narrator's, in the verses. We will consider the effect this complicated process

[11]Theoretically the shift could also occur at the beginning of verse 24, but the repetition of "the dogs shall eat" in verses 23 and 24 makes it difficult not to read them as a single unit.

of reading and rereading has on the narrative flow after we have discussed verses 25-26.

The word order in verse 23 puts emphasis on the phrase "also to Jezebel." (The NRSV renders this "also concerning Jezebel," but that is a less likely translation of the Hebrew.) The inference is that just as Yahweh sent Elijah to Ahab with oracles of condemnation and punishment, so also he sent this oracle of punishment to Jezebel. Her crime is not specified, but the parallels between her punishment and Ahab's (both will be punished in Jezreel, and both will be consumed by dogs; see v. 19) imply that the crime is the same: the murder of Naboth. Verse 24 repeats the graphic poetic couplet that ends the condemnations of Israelite dynasties in 14:11 and 16:4. In the present context it continues a gradual expansion of the circle of punishment from Ahab himself (vv. 17-22) to Jezebel (v. 23) to Ahab's entire household (v. 24).

The Evil of Jezebel and Ahab: 21:25-26

Two formal considerations reveal ways in which the narrator draws our attention to these verses. First, the narrator "breaks frame," that is, he steps out of the story, as it were, to address the reader directly. The retrospective tone of the first words ("there was no one like Ahab") marks them as a later evaluative reflection on Ahab's reign and thus situates the speaker (and reader) at some significant remove in time from the narrated events. Second, verses 25-26 are unusually complex grammatically. Each verse comprises a main clause and two subordinate clauses linked to a "like" phrase, as the following literal translation shows:

> However, there was none *like Ahab*
> > *who* sold himself to do evil in Yahweh's sight,
> > *whom* his wife Jezebel induced,
> And he committed great abomination by going after idols *like everything*
> > *which* the Amorites did,
> > *whom* Yahweh dispossessed in favor of the children of Israel.

The grammar is further complicated by ambiguity in the relationship between the two verses. To what is the verb "and he committed great abomination" linked? Hebrew syntax allows us to read it as coordinate to any of the three verbs in verse 25:

1) "There was none like Ahab . . . . And he committed great abomination . . . ."

2) "who sold himself to do evil . . . and committed great abomination
. . . ."

3) "whom his wife Jezebel induced . . . and he committed great abomination . . . ."

(The NRSV follows the first alternative.) The first two readings are similar: the judgment that Ahab was unique in his degree of evil is based on his "great abomination," which is then identified as idolatry. The third, however, is quite different. It means that Ahab's abominable idolatry was the result of Jezebel's influence on him. All three readings are possible. The syntax of verses 25-26, like the story of Naboth in verses 1-16, portrays the royal couple as enmeshed in bonds of mutual guilt too knotty to be clearly disentangled.

The NRSV takes the first word of verse 25 as a simple emphatic ("Indeed"), but the Hebrew adverb actually draws a contrast between what follows and what precedes. Here the contrast is between Ahab's household (v. 24) and Ahab himself. Though all those associated with Ahab will suffer the horrible punishment of having their unburied bodies eaten by scavengers, Ahab's evil exceeded theirs. In fact, as verses 20-22 make clear, Ahab's evil is the reason for the punishment of the others of his house. The narrator repeats the phrase Elijah used in verse 20 (Ahab "sold himself to do evil in the sight of Yahweh"), thereby confirming Elijah's judgment with his own narrative authority. (Compare this to the effect of the appearance of the narrator's term "scoundrels" in Jezebel's letter in verse 10; see p. 325.)

The last words of verse 25 are problematic. They put the major part of the blame for Ahab's evil on Jezebel: the verb "induced" (NRSV, "urged on") includes nuances of deception and misleading influence. Since, as the next verse will show, the evil in view is idolatry, this is not without foundation: Jezebel is a devotee of Baal and aggressively promotes his cult (see 16:31 as well as 18:19). But the literary context of chapter 21 has not yet indicated that idolatry is the issue. We still assume Ahab's evil to be the murder of Naboth. Jezebel is certainly no innocent in the matter, as verses 8-10 demonstrate. However, to say she "induced" Ahab is to misrepresent the case. She does not lead Ahab to do anything; he remains essentially inactive throughout verses 1-16. If anyone induces anyone, Ahab induces Jezebel by his petulant behavior and misleads her by misreporting Naboth's speech.

We have here, then, a striking *non sequitur*. In verses 1-16 the narrator allowed us to entertain two possible understandings of the events: Ahab is passive and oblivious to events, and Jezebel is the evil genius behind the murder of Naboth; or Ahab is the manipulative puppetmaster who plays on Jezebel's wifely devotion and thereby maneuvers her into plotting Naboth's downfall. In verse 25 the narrator implies that Ahab himself has done something actively evil in Naboth's murder but blames Jezebel as the guilty one working behind the scenes—a scenario that simply does not fit the facts of verses 1-16 at all. Yet the stratagem of blaming woman for the sins of man is certainly no stranger to human society, including biblical tradition (see, for example, 1 Timothy 2:14!). And so in the very verse that voices the strongest possible condemnation of Ahab ("there was none like him"), the narrator plants the seeds of an excuse by invoking the rationalization of *cherchez la femme.*

The narrator's next verse unexpectedly specifies Ahab's central evil as idolatry. This was implied in chapters 17–19, where Ahab tolerated the worship of Baal and Asherah, but there has not been the slightest allusion to idolatry in chapter 21. The phrase "committed great abomination" (NRSV, "acted most abominably") is a technical term for heinous religious or ethical wrongdoing; and the word used for idols *(gllym)* is the same as in 15:12 and is a further echo of the scatological language *(gll,* "dung") of the dynastic condemnation formula in 14:10.

The reference to Yahweh's dispossessing the Amorites in favor of the Israelites contains two potent allusions, one verbal and one substantive. The statement that Yahweh "dispossessed" (Hebrew, *yrš;* NRSV, "drove out") the Amorites explicitly echoes God's description of Ahab's crime in verse 19: "Have you killed, and also taken possession?" (Hebrew, *yrš).* More profoundly, Yahweh's action in awarding possession of the land to the Israelites rather than the Amorites was the basis of the principle of ancestral inheritance enshrined in the laws of patrimony that Ahab and Jezebel circumvent in order to take possession of Naboth's vineyard.

What is the effect of these central sections on the narrative flow of verses 17-29? In fact, there are several effects, and they are quite similar to those discussed earlier in regard to verses 8-14. The most obvious result of the material in verses 23-26 is that the action of the story comes to a complete halt. The next section will begin, "When Ahab heard those words . . ." (v. 27); the words referred to are Elijah's condemnation of Ahab in verses 20-22. No narrative time at all passes while we attend to verses 23-26; yet the complexities of these verses require a careful reader to spend considerable time on them, reading and rereading verses 23-24 to try to determine who the speaker is and unraveling the syntactic convolutions of verses 25-26. In other words, the central sections of the prophetic condemnation story distract us from the action and thus weaken the story's dramatic cohesion, much as Jezebel's too explicit letter in verse 10 undermines the narrative tension of the story of Naboth's vineyard.

Other effects also are similar to those in verses 8-14. First, the circle of responsibility is broadened: not only Ahab but his dynasty, his wife, and his entire household fall under Yahweh's condemnation. Second, the interjection of a long series of asides to the reader puts distance between us and the action by foregrounding people (Jezebel, Ahab's household) and issues (retrospective evaluation, idolatry) that do not figure in the surrounding verses. (There is one notable difference from the distancing in verses 1-16, however. There Jezebel's letter undercut narrative tension by spelling out in advance what was to take place. Here narrative tension is held in abeyance—and thus actually sharpened—by allowing us to wonder for several verses how the hostile king will respond to Elijah's unconditional condemnation.) A third effect is to introduce into that distance elements of reflective judgment, especially on Jezebel and Ahab. Finally, as also in verses 8-14, there is a blurring of the lines between character and narrator: the narrator's language shows up in Elijah's speech ("sold himself to do evil in the sight of Yahweh," vv. 20 and 25), and the ambiguity of speaker in verses 23-24 is ultimately unresolved. In short, the effect of the central sections on the whole narrative of verses 17-29 is to transform it from a story of Yahweh's condemnation of Ahab for the murder of Naboth into a story of the downfall of Ahab's dynasty because of his idolatry, with a sort of subtext laying at least some of the blame for Ahab's evil upon Jezebel.

Ahab's Reaction to Elijah's Words: 21:27

The first words of verse 27 are identical to those in verse 16: "As soon as Ahab heard . . ." (NRSV, "When Ahab heard . . ."). Just as Ahab's response to Jezebel is immediate and unquestioning, so too, unexpectedly, is his response to Elijah. Of course, the "words" that Ahab hears cannot be the narrator's aside in verses 25-26, nor are they likely to be the ambiguously voiced words in verses 23-24, which do not have in view the individual punishment of Ahab. They are Elijah's pronouncement of doom on Ahab and his dynasty in verses 20-22. This verse, then, leaps back over verses 23-26 to pick up the story at the point where the lengthy central digressions interrupt it.

The verse ignores the central sections in another sense too. The narrator has just told us that Ahab is guilty of evil unparalleled in the history of Israel (v. 25), yet now he shows us Ahab undertaking humble acts of grief and penance. This apparent discrepancy in the image of Ahab is difficult to resolve (and, in fact, the narrator will never clearly resolve it), but it opens the way for a variety of conjectures. Is the narrator so set against Ahab that he dismisses the king's penitence as trivial? Or does the narrator want us to surmise that Ahab's penance is insincere? Or is Ahab's evil so consummate that even his abject repentance cannot offset it? We shall examine this question again in a moment.

Ahab's penitential practices are several. He tears his garments, a conventional sign of grief in ancient Israel. He puts on "sackcloth" (the translation of Hebrew *śaq* is traditional; we do not know whether the term refers to a type of cloth or a style of clothing); this too was a sign of mourning, much like wearing black in some contemporary Western cultures. Frequently in the Hebrew scriptures (as here), there is mention of wearing sackcloth next to the skin, maybe to indicate that it was a coarse, rough fabric whose discomfort externalized the mourner's grief. Ahab fasts—a conventional sign of penance, comparable to the public fast Jezebel engineered in verses 9-12. He lies in the sackcloth—that is, he wears it day and night, not just during the day as was customary. He goes about meekly. (The meaning of the word is disputed, but words like "gently" and "quietly" cover its other appearances in the Hebrew Bible; the NRSV's "dejectedly" is an overinterpretation.) This last phrase probably refers to the sort of withdrawal from everyday activities that often characterizes a period of mourning or penitence.

Ahab's repentance introduces an unexpected twist to the plot. Up to this point we have had a more or less straightforward tale of royal crime and divine condemnation. The story is tragic, and the wrong to Naboth can never be made right; but the punishments decreed for Ahab and Jezebel at least partially satisfy our sense of justice. Now, however, Ahab's apparent contrition complicates the situation and changes the dynamics of the plot. We value the king's remorse and the divine mercy to which it makes appeal, but we also value the divine justice that would claim eye for eye, tooth for tooth, life for life. It is difficult to imagine any outcome that will completely satisfy the demands of both.

YAHWEH'S WORD TO ELIJAH: 21:28-29

The scene opens with the same conventional formula as in verse 17, including the identification of Elijah by the title "the Tishbite." The title was useful in verse 17, which reintroduced Elijah to us after a long absence; here, however, it serves only to emphasize the connection between verses 17 and 28, and thus to signal the chiastic structure of verses 17-29.

Yahweh begins by commenting on Ahab's self-abasement, which grounds Yahweh's decision to defer the decree of punishment to the next generation. Several comments are in order. First, in terms of the conjectures we entertained above, it is clear that Yahweh considers Ahab's repentance neither trivial nor insincere. Therefore, the third explanation for the narrator's discrepant pictures of Ahab seems most likely: Ahab's evil was so great that it could not be undone by repentance, but the repentance did have the effect of granting the dynasty one more generation of existence. On the other hand, we cannot entirely rule out the possibility that the narrator has reservations about Yahweh's readiness to accept Ahab's remorse and give him a reprieve.

This leads to the second comment. As the narrator reports them, Yahweh's words to Elijah sound self-centered and just a bit smug. "Have you seen how Ahab has humbled himself before me? Because he has humbled himself before me . . . ." Certainly this is a pleased appreciation of human virtue, but the repetition of "humbled himself before me" also rings with a certain tone of self-satisfaction. (Compare Yahweh's similar smugness about Job in Job 1:8 and 2:3.) We are a little dismayed that Yahweh seems more interested in Ahab's subservience than in redressing the injustice to Naboth.

This in turn leads to the third comment. Yahweh's satisfaction makes sense if the offense God has in mind is idolatry rather than Naboth's murder. In verses 25-26 the narrator specified idolatry as Ahab's greatest evil; and Ahab's submission to Yahweh here is a direct reversal of his "going after idols." Yet, by echoing verse 17 in verse 28 the narrator also reminds us that Yahweh's opening words condemned Ahab specifically for Naboth's murder, something that has not been mentioned since verse 19. The narrator seems to be suggesting that Yahweh's primary concern is his own supremacy (compare Yahweh's attitudes in 20:13 and 20:28), and that Ahab's self-abasement so pleases God in this regard that he does not again bring up the unsettled matter of Naboth.

Yahweh's decision to defer the dynastic disaster until the days of Ahab's son is less than congenial to a modern, more individualistic sense of justice. However, the ancient world widely accepted the idea of inheritance of guilt as well as of blessing. In Exodus, for example, Yahweh describes himself as "keeping steadfast love for the thousandth generation," while only remembering sins "to the third and fourth generation" (Exod 34:7). The decision to punish the next generation is, therefore, quite admissible in the theology of the day. It has, moreover, a significant narrative function as well. Ahab's bequest of punishment to his sons is symmetrical to Naboth's inheritance of the vineyard from his fathers. (In verses 1-4 the phrase "ancestral inheritance" is, literally, "inheritance of my fathers.") Both point to the broader, ongoing history of the people of Israel within which this event is an emblematic incident: the oppositions of king and prophet,

of power and weakness, of monarchy and Yahwistic tradition, of idolatry and fidelity, will mark the histories, and eventually the downfalls,
of both Israel and Judah.

The Whole Chapter

Unlike chapters 20 and 22, where the episodes of prophetic condemnation do not have symmetrical structures, both parts of chapter
21 are symmetrically organized. Moreover, the two parts are parallel.
Each contains six chiastically arranged sections; both begin with an
undesirable situation for Ahab and end with a reversal of that situation; both involve dialogues between Ahab and another person; and
both have central scenes whose narrative effects are comparable in
several ways. This parallel symmetry reinforces the fundamental correspondence of the two parts as crime and punishment; it also invites
further comparisons. Such comparison is particularly fruitful in considering the motif of eating, which, in various manifestations (eating,
not eating, being eaten), pervades both parts of the chapter. In verses
1-16 it appears in possession of the vineyard (a source of food and
drink), in Ahab's refusal to eat (v. 4), and in the public fast (v. 12). In
verses 17-29, too, Ahab fasts (v. 27), but otherwise the motif appears
primarily in passive form: Ahab, Jezebel, and Ahab's household are all
condemned to be eaten (vv. 19, 23, 24), and Yahweh's condemnation of
Ahab reveals that Naboth too was eaten (v. 19). The motif clusters particularly around the figures of Ahab and Naboth, and it develops
through the story in tandem with the characters' destinies.

If we compare the development of the motif of eating as it applies
to Naboth and Ahab in verses 1-16, we see a contrasting parallelism:

Naboth		Ahab
+ eat (has vineyard)	v. 1	- eat (lacks vineyard)
Naboth fasts (v. 12)		Ahab fasts (v. 4)
- eat (loses vineyard)	v. 16	+ eat (gains vineyard)

The contrasting extremes are not surprising, since Naboth's loss of the
vineyard and Ahab's acquisition of it form the main tension of the plot.
What is surprising is the function of fasting as the effective turning
point in each character's development. Naboth fasts along with the
rest of the Jezreel assembly, but this fast, unknown to him, is a trap that
costs him his vineyard and his life. Ahab refuses to eat when he cannot have Naboth's vineyard; this fast spurs Jezebel to devise the plot

that eventually gets Ahab the vineyard he covets.

We find Ahab involved in a similar pattern in verses 17-29, though here the motif takes a passive form:

Ahab

+ be eaten (v. 19)
Ahab fasts (v. 27)
- be eaten (v. 29)

Yahweh condemns Ahab in terms that relate the punishment to the crime, Naboth's murder. Just as dogs licked up Naboth's blood, says Yahweh, so will they lick up Ahab's. Ahab performs acts of penance, including a fast, and this moves Yahweh to delay the punishment until the next generation.

This complementary set of motif patterns leads to a further insight. In our discussion of verses 1-16 above, we saw that the first part of the story can be read with Ahab or with Naboth as the main character. If we read verses 1-16 as Naboth's story and compare it with verses 17-29 as Ahab's, then Ahab's fasting in verse 27 is parallel to Naboth's in verse 12: a sincere act of penance (at least as far as Naboth was concerned) that brings about a reversal of fortune. If, on the other hand, we read both parts as primarily stories of Ahab, then Ahab's fasting in verse 27 is parallel to his refusal to eat in verse 4: in both cases the king's behavior results in somebody else doing what he wants and gaining him something he could not obtain on his own. Since we have already suggested that Ahab's refusal to eat in verse 4 may be a subtle manipulation of Jezebel's wifely compassion, this reading invites us to ask whether his fasting in verse 27 may not be a similar manipulation of Yahweh's divine mercy. In other words, the motif of eating and fasting mirrors in its own complex way the same ambivalence about Ahab's character we have already noted.

These observations do not exhaust the richness of the motif, however. When we consider the development of the motif through the chapter as a whole instead of focusing on the two parts separately, it takes on an entirely new and deeper significance. The method we can use to analyze this level of narrative power is somewhat technical but not difficult to understand. It is a diagram, based on the logical "square of opposition" that goes back to Aristotle, if not before. It consists, in technical terms, of arranging two contraries and their respective contradictories in a square matrix. An example will make the idea clearer:

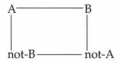

In this diagram, "A" and "B" stand for two elements that are alternatives (that is, logical contraries), though not absolutely contradictory to
each other. The diagram makes it possible to integrate two forms of the
same motif (in the present case, "able to eat" and "liable to be eaten")
into a single analysis and to trace more complex patterns of motif development.

When we plot the course of the motif as it clusters around the figure of Ahab, this pattern results:

Figure 3

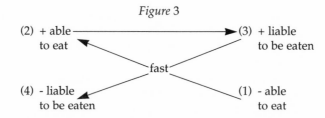

Ahab begins lacking the vineyard (- able to eat). By fasting (v. 4) he
obtains the vineyard (+ able to eat). Because of the crime by which
Ahab acquired the vineyard, Yahweh condemns him to the same sort of
death Naboth suffered (+ liable to be eaten; v. 19). By fasting (v. 27),
Ahab avoids this fate (- liable to be eaten). His journey on the "square
of opposition" is complete and coherent. The diagram explains our feeling that the story of Ahab reaches closure at the end of the narrative;
and if we are somewhat dissatisfied with the ease with which Ahab escapes punishment for his crime, we nevertheless recognize that the
story of Yahweh, abounding in mercy, underwrites the final step.

When we plot the course of the motif as it pertains to Naboth, however, we find something different:

Figure 4

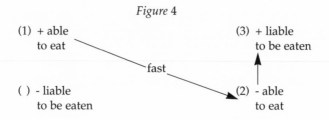

Naboth begins in possession of the vineyard (+ able to eat). He fasts along with the Jezreel assembly (v. 12) and, as a result, loses vineyard and life (- able to eat). We learn in verse 17 that when Naboth died, dogs licked up his blood (+ liable to be eaten). But his story ends there, leaving us with a sense of incompleteness—of wrong not righted and injustice not redressed. While we may be able to accept the final step of Ahab's story as the triumph of divine mercy over divine justice, the missing final step of Naboth's story cries out for completion. Neither the narrator nor we can do anything about Naboth's life or about his vineyard. But we can at least reestablish his good name by exposing the plot to which he fell victim, and thereby demonstrating publicly that he did not deserve his fate (that is, he was really "- liable to be eaten"). We do this by reading and telling his tale. Thus the handing on of Naboth's story is the act of public penitence that corresponds to the public assembly of verse 12 and redeems its hypocrisy. In this way the narrator coopts us and incorporates us into the story itself. Our role as readers and bearers of tradition is neither innocent nor neutral; it is essential to completing the story and restoring justice.

Chapter 21

WAR WITH ARAM: AHAB'S DEFEAT AND DEATH

1 Kings 22:1-40

The story of Ahab returns to international affairs and the continuation of the war with Aram first recounted in chapter 20.[1] After three years of peace (during which we are to assume the Naboth incident took place), hostilities resume between Aram and Israel. Like the narratives in chapters 20–21, this account of the battle of Ramoth-gilead is symmetrically structured, with an episode of prophetic condemnation outside the symmetry. Unlike chapters 20–21, the prophetic condemnation does not follow the Ahab narrative but interrupts it quite early on.

A. Ahab's preparations in Samaria (22:1-4)
-. Prophetic condemnation (22:5-28)
    B. Ahab's strategy—disguise (22:29-31)
       C. The battle (22:32-34)
    B'. Ahab's death—disguised (22:35-36)
A'. Ahab's burial in Samaria (22:37-38)

The formulaic notice of Ahab's death follows the narrative (vv. 39-40). The rest of chapter 22 turns to the reigns of other kings of Israel and Judah. We shall discuss them in the next chapter.

Ahab and the War with Aram, beginning: 22:1-4

In the NRSV the opening verse sounds like an opening verse, but in Hebrew it is cryptic and makes sense only in light of chapter 20: literally,

---

[1]The historical problems mentioned above in regard to chapter 20 (see p. 293) are equally present here. One sign that the stories in this chapter may have been transferred to Ahab from some other king is the fact that except for Ahab's name in 22:20, the narrator names neither the king of Israel nor the king of Aram in 22:1-38.

"And they sat for three years. There was no war between Aram and Israel." The undefined "they" and the three years of peace presume Ahab's earlier victory over Ben-hadad and the treaty they agreed on in 20:34. In this way the narrator reminds us of the larger context within which the current story is placed, namely, the cycle of stories that recount Israel's changing political fortunes vis-à-vis Aram. The three years of peace also allow Ahab time to concentrate on such internal affairs as obtaining property for a vegetable garden next to his palace in Jezreel.[2]

AHAB'S PREPARATIONS IN SAMARIA: 22:2-4

Jehoshaphat "comes down" to visit Ahab in Israel. (It is conventional in Hebrew to treat Jerusalem as the highest point in the land: one "goes up" to Jerusalem and "comes down" from there.) The story moves quickly to the main point. The king of Israel puts a question to his "servants" (that is, his advisers; the same term describes Ben-hadad's advisers in 20:23) about Ramoth-gilead. Ramoth-gilead (in English, "Gilead Heights"), located southeast of the Sea of Galilee, was one of Solomon's chief administrative cities in Transjordan (4:13), but Aramean forces now occupy it. This is apparently one of the cities Ben-hadad promised to return to Israel (20:34), but he has not done so. Ahab's question is rhetorical, and he neither expects nor waits for an answer. The complaining tone of his words ("we are doing nothing") indicates that he wants to do something.

His next question, to Jehoshaphat, is not rhetorical; he asks for Judah's aid in a campaign of conquest. Jehoshaphat's reply is a striking formulation in Hebrew. The NRSV captures the sense correctly, but the stylistic polish is untranslatable. Literally, Jehoshaphat says: "Like me, like you; like my people, like your people; like my horses, like your horses." Since Jehoshaphat is agreeing to cooperate in a military effort, we are to understand "people" as "troops" and "horses" as "chariotry." The personal reference ("like me, like you") means that Jehoshaphat himself will participate in the campaign just as Ahab will. There is an irony in the phrase, as we shall see: Ahab's plans for the battle will involve very different forms of participation for himself and for Jehoshaphat.

[2]The awkwardness of the undefined pronoun "they" may be a vestige of a level of tradition when this story immediately followed that in chapter 20. As we noted in the last chapter, the double introduction to the Naboth story in 21:1 may indicate that the present arrangement of materials is due to a later editor inserting chapter 21 into a preexisting account of Ahab and the Aramean wars.

What is the relationship between Jehoshaphat and Ahab? Are they "brothers"—that is, political peers? Or is Jehoshaphat dependent upon, perhaps even a vassal of, Ahab? These opening verses contain nothing decisive, but several elements point toward dependency. First, Jehoshaphat visits Ahab, not the other way around. State visits certainly can be made between peers and do not imply political inequality. Nevertheless, the relationship of host to guest is an essentially unequal one. As visitor, Jehoshaphat is dependent upon Ahab, and this raises the possibility that the dependency may be reflected in the political realm as well. Second, the narrator tells us that "Jehoshaphat came," and then the king of Israel "said to his servants." The sentence order leads us to expect that the king of Israel will address his recently arrived royal guest, and we can wonder whether the "servants" to whom Ahab speaks include Jehoshaphat. In other words, does Ahab direct his two questions to different addressees, his own court advisers first, and his fellow king second? Or does he direct them to the whole group of his advisers first, then to the chief among them, his vassal Jehoshaphat? Third, Jehoshaphat's words in verse 4b sound a strongly subservient note; compare Ahab's words to his overlord Ben-hadad in 20:4. Finally, though this is further along in the narrative, Jehoshaphat will call Ahab "the king" in verse 8. Is this noblesse oblige between monarchs or a profession of fealty comparable to Ahab's addressing Ben-hadad as "my lord the king" in 20:4 and 9? None of these elements is determinative in itself, but the cumulative impression is of Ahab's hegemony over Jehoshaphat.

Prophetic Condemnation: 22:5-28

The action of the plot, which has moved fairly quickly to this point, slows considerably. The long prophetic condemnation episode is almost entirely speeches: consultation of prophets by kings, speeches by prophets, arguments between prophets. The episode does not have a clearly marked structure, but we can conveniently subdivide it on the basis of the principal characters in each subdivision:

1. Ahab and Jehoshaphat (22:5-9)
2. Interludes (22:10-14)
3. The kings consult Micaiah (22:15-18)
4. Micaiah's monologue (22:19-23)
5. Reactions to Micaiah's monologue (22:24-28)

After examining each of these subdivisions, we will consider the effect of this whole section on the development of the narrative.

AHAB AND JEHOSHAPHAT: 22:5-9

At Jehoshaphat's urging, Ahab agrees to consult his prophets about the proposed campaign. There is one subtle thread to trace through these verses: the use of the name "Yahweh." Jehoshaphat specifically wishes to consult an oracle of Yahweh. Ahab gathers (Hebrew, *qbṣ*) four hundred prophets together, but the narrator does not further identify their divine loyalties. In fact, the alert reader will not miss the echoes of 18:19-20, where Ahab gathered (Hebrew, *qbṣ*; NRSV, "assembled") four hundred fifty prophets of Baal and four hundred prophets of Asherah to Mount Carmel. Elijah killed the four hundred fifty prophets of Baal (18:40); but we were not told the fate of the four hundred prophets of Asherah, and the coincidence of numbers is suggestive.

Ahab's question is straightforward: "Should I attack or not?" The prophets' answer seems clear, but in fact it is not. There are three ambiguities. First, the prophets do not name the "lord" who will deliver the victory.[3] Second, there is no direct object for the verb "deliver." English requires a direct object here, and the NRSV's "it" clearly points to Ramoth-gilead. The Hebrew, however, does not specify what will be delivered. Third, the prophets do not identify "the king" who will gain the victory either. Ahab certainly understands it to be himself, but the prophets do not in fact say so.

Jehoshaphat may be more sensitive to the ambiguities of the oracle than Ahab, for he does not seem satisfied. He asks for another prophet. His phrasing is diplomatic: it neither concedes nor denies the Yahwistic

---

[3]This is a rather technical point, but its importance in the narrative warrants discussion. The name of Israel's God in the Hebrew Bible is *yhwh* (the vowels are unsure; most scholars today vocalize the word "Yahweh"). Ancient tradition avoided pronouncing the sacred name and substituted instead either *'ădōnāy*, "Lord," or *'ĕlōhîm*, "God." Most English translations, including the NRSV, follow this custom and render *yhwh* with either "Lord" or "God." Note the small capitals; such translations use them to distinguish these renderings of *yhwh* from the same words used to translate *'ădōnāy* or *'ĕlōhîm*. In the present case, the NRSV uses "Lord" to indicate that the Hebrew text has *yhwh*. But the situation is more complex than that. While many ancient Hebrew manuscripts read *yhwh* here, the best ones read *'ădōnāy*; and textual scholars must make a judgment which of those readings is more original and which is secondary. Some judge that *yhwh* was original and that later scribes changed it to *'ădōnāy* to remove the sacred name from the mouths of "false" prophets. This choice underlies the NRSV's translation. It does not explain, however, why *yhwh* was retained in verses 11-12, where all manuscripts agree in reading *yhwh*. Others judge that *'ădōnāy* was original and later scribes changed it to *yhwh* under the influence of the very similar words in verse 12. This choice underlies the present commentary.

attachments of the four hundred but insists politely on an oracle explicitly from Yahweh. Ahab responds grudgingly that there is "one
man" (NRSV, "one other"; is Ahab being petty in not calling him a
"prophet"?) through whom one can consult Yahweh. "But," Ahab continues, "*I* hate him" (emphatic pronoun). The pronoun and the following explanation show that Ahab's focus is on himself, not on the truth
or falsehood of this prophet's oracles. Because the man regularly
prophesies things Ahab doesn't want to hear, the king rejects him.
("Hate" is too severe a translation. The Hebrew word can convey this
strong emotion, but it can also mean to spurn, disdain, or reject someone out of dislike.)

There is a touch of suspense in the Hebrew that is lost in the NRSV:
Ahab delays naming this uncooperative prophet until the very end of
his speech. We know that he can be consulted for a word from Yahweh,
we know that Ahab does not like him, and we know that he regularly
prophesies disaster for Ahab—all before we know his name, Micaiah
son of Imlah. In the larger context, especially after Elijah's condemnations of Ahab in 21:20-22, we expect Ahab to name Elijah as his neme-
sis. "Micaiah son of Imlah," of whom we have never heard, comes as
an intriguing surprise. Who is this other prophet, and what is his history of antagonism with Ahab? We never learn anything of Micaiah beyond the present story, but the narrator's allusions to Micaiah's earlier
prophecies against Ahab remind us that our texts point to a world beyond themselves, and that there is more in that world than appears in
our texts. The world that the text implies is much larger than the world
that the text describes.

Jehoshaphat utters a polite demurrer from Ahab's explanation but
does not withdraw his request. And so Ahab sends for Micaiah. He
does so in a command to a courtier that is more clipped and curt than
the NRSV reflects: "Hurry! Micaiah son of Imlah!"

INTERLUDES: 22:10-14

At this point the narrator indulges in a bit of clever delay. The king
of Israel has summoned a prophet for whom he has nothing but antipathy. While we wait eagerly for the inevitable confrontation of
prophet and king, the narrator temporizes with two separate episodes.
First we survey the scene where the four hundred prophets continue
prophesying before the two kings. Then the scene shifts to where the
messenger has found Micaiah. As the messenger brings Micaiah back
to the kings' presence, he advises him of the situation he is about to
walk into.

The first scene begins with descriptive sentences; in Hebrew verse 10 contains no narrative verbs. We see the two kings sitting on thrones in formal regalia. They are outside, in the large public square just inside the city gate. (The Hebrew term can mean a "threshing floor," as the NRSV renders it, but here, as in some other passages, it seems to refer to a large, open, heavily trafficked area.) The outdoor site is much more commodious than the palace audience chamber for entertaining four hundred hyperactive prophets: the word that the NRSV translates "prophesying" in verse 10 connotes prophetic behavior that is uncontrolled and frenetic; it is often translated "rave" (see, for example, 18:29).[4] Amid the frenzy, two prophetic pronouncements stand out. First, one prophet, Zedekiah son of Chenaanah, performs a symbolic action, that is, a prophecy that consists principally of a gesture rather than a word, though an interpretative word may accompany the gesture, as it does here. Zedekiah fashions a pair of horns (for the coalition of the two kings?) and makes goring gestures with them. The detail that the horns are made of iron stresses their sharpness and deadliness, since the other commonly available metal for cutting instruments, bronze, could not be tempered and honed to an equal edge. In explanation of his action, Zedekiah utters in Yahweh's name an oracle guaranteeing Ahab's victory over Aram. The gesture and its interpretative oracle echo ancient Israelite tradition (see Deut 33:17). Second, the rest of the prophets repeat their original oracle from verse 6, but with two significant changes: the addition of "and triumph" removes the ambiguity of the original oracle about who will be the victor, and now the prophets name the "lord" who will give the victory as Yahweh (NRSV, "LORD"; see note 3). It is notable that only now, after Jehoshaphat has expressed in their presence his desire for an oracle from Yahweh, do Ahab's prophets identify Yahweh as their inspiring divinity.[5]

---

[4]Ahab used the same word in reference to Micaiah's prophesying (v. 8). This suggests that "ecstatic prophecy" (the technical term for prophesying in an altered state of consciousness, whether active and frenzied or passive and entranced) was standard in Ahab's court. The alternative, namely, rational delivery of verbal oracles, characterizes Elijah in chapters 17–19 and 21.

[5]Is it coincidence that Zedekiah (whose name is explicitly Yahwistic: "Yahweh is Righteousness") is the son of "Chenaanah" (Hebrew, *kĕnaʿănâ*), whose name sounds suspiciously like "Canaanite" (Hebrew, *kĕnaʿănî*)? The continuing problem during Ahab's reign has been the tendency to blur the distinction between Israelite Yahwism and Canaanite Baalism (including the worship of Asherah), even to merge them into a polytheistic system. Are Ahab's prophets equally at the service of Yahweh and of Baal or Asherah, depending on which deity the king wishes to consult at any given moment?

The second scene does not follow the first chronologically. The Hebrew grammatical construction breaks the narrative flow from one event to the next and suggests in this way that the two interlude scenes are simultaneous. An English translation could capture this nuance by inserting "Meanwhile" at the beginning of verse 13. This scene shows us the messenger who has gone in search of Micaiah son of Imlah speaking politely to him. (The messenger uses the polite particle *nāʾ* twice; on this particle see the remarks on 20:31.) He does not seem to be threatening Micaiah so much as forewarning him. Yet the very fact that a royal messenger assumes that prophets tailor their message to the king's desires speaks volumes about the sort of prophets and prophecy Ahab's court was accustomed to. The word "favorable" (Hebrew, *ṭôb*, "good"), which the messenger uses twice, echoes Ahab's original complaint against Micaiah, that he never speaks anything favorable *(ṭôb)* about Ahab (v. 8). Micaiah's reply is not a rebuke to the messenger but spells out forcefully Micaiah's commitments: he is a prophet of Yahweh (he uses the divine name twice in his brief speech), and he will speak what Yahweh commissions and only that. The NRSV's word order accurately reflects the emphasis the Hebrew places on the word "that" in the phrase *"that* I will speak."

THE KINGS CONSULT MICAIAH: 22:15-18

Micaiah comes before the king, who addresses him by name and asks him the same question he has already asked the four hundred prophets. There is however, one change. To the four hundred prophets he spoke only of himself ("Shall I go to battle . . . ?"); to Micaiah he speaks of the coalition ("Shall we go to battle . . . ?").[6] Ahab hopes, it seems, that Micaiah will be more favorable to a campaign involving Jehoshaphat than to one involving only Ahab. Micaiah's reply repeats almost exactly the oracle given by the four hundred prophets in verse 12, including their use of the name of Yahweh.

Now comes an interesting twist. Ahab, who accepted the favorable oracle from the four hundred prophets, does not believe the same oracle when Micaiah speaks it, and he insists that Micaiah tell him only the truth. How does Ahab infer that Micaiah is not telling the truth? Is it because Micaiah so predictably prophesied disaster for Ahab in the

---

[6]The NRSV's change from "to battle against Ramoth-gilead" (v. 6) to "to Ramoth-gilead for battle" (v. 15) is based on a difference of a single preposition in Hebrew (in fact, a single letter). Literally, verse 6 reads "against Ramoth-gilead for battle" and verse 15 reads "to Ramoth-gilead for battle."

past (v. 8) that a favorable prophecy is automatically suspect? Or should we read between the lines to hear sarcastic intonations in Micaiah's words? The narrator does not tell us but leaves us with the paradoxical, almost titillating picture of a prophet who has just declared his absolute fidelity to Yahweh's words apparently prophesying falsely, and a king who has shown himself more interested in approval than in truth demanding truth instead of endorsement. We shall examine this puzzle more closely below.

The last words of Ahab's speech are grammatically ambiguous: what is done "in the name of Yahweh"? Does Ahab make Micaiah swear in the name of Yahweh, or does he make him swear to tell only the truth when he speaks in the name of Yahweh? Certainly the latter, but perhaps the narrator wishes us to hear both possibilities at once. In either case, the remark makes Ahab's bona fides plain.

In reply, Micaiah recounts a vision he had and an accompanying divine word of interpretation. "All Israel" here probably has the military connotation we saw in 16:16-17 and 20:15: Micaiah's vision is of Ahab's army scattered leaderless like a flock of sheep bereft of any shepherd. (The metaphor of "shepherd" is a commonplace in Ancient Near Eastern literature for a king.) That the sheep are scattered "on the mountains" is foreboding, since Ahab's target, "Gilead Heights," sits on an upland plateau. Yahweh's word of interpretation contains an unsettling ambiguity. Literally it begins, "These have no masters" (NRSV, "master"). The word "master" can be used in the plural to refer to a single individual (a sort of "plural of rank"), and therefore the NRSV's singular rendering is quite possible. But in this context, where Ahab has pointedly referred to the plurality of kings who would be leading the coalition ("Shall *we* go," v. 15), the plural form "masters" has an ominous ring: the king of Israel will certainly die in the battle; Jehoshaphat may too. Yahweh's word continues with a declaration that the army should (or perhaps "will") return home. (The distributive force of "each one to his own home" reminds us of the combined nature of the army, drawn from Judah as well as Israel.)

Ahab's comment to Jehoshaphat is, in essence, "I told you so!" It repeats his complaint of verse 8 verbatim. What this reveals about Ahab is devastating. As Ahab's retort to Micaiah in verse 16 shows, he knows full well that Micaiah's oracle in verse 15 (and, by implication, the four hundred prophets' identical oracle in verse 12) is untrue. His demand that Micaiah speak only the truth opens the possibility that despite his personal antipathy for Micaiah, Ahab might be willing to listen to Yahweh's word. His comment in verse 18 suggests, however, that he pressures Micaiah for a true oracle, not because he intends to follow it—subsequent developments will confirm that he does not—

but simply in order to prove his claim to Jehoshaphat that Micaiah always prophesies disaster!

MICAIAH'S MONOLOGUE: 22:19-23

But Micaiah is not through. His next speech is unsolicited and unexpected, although its first word, "therefore," links it to his previous speech as an explanation. That connection in turn gives Ahab's comment to Jehoshaphat in verse 18 the feel of an aside, as if Micaiah's speech continues from verse 17 to verse 23, and verse 18 is merely a parenthetical interruption. (The lack of a subject in verse 19 strengthens this impression. The NRSV adds "Micaiah" to clarify who is speaking, but the Hebrew has only "Then he said.")

Micaiah has another vision to recount, one that explains why his foresight differs from that of the four hundred prophets and why he foresees disaster for Ahab. He introduces the vision as a *dābār* (NRSV, "word") of Yahweh, though he does not use the standard messenger formula, "Thus says Yahweh." This may well be because Micaiah is in fact not delivering a message entrusted to him by Yahweh for Ahab; rather he is recounting a story about Yahweh (the Hebrew *dābār* can mean "story" as well as "word") that Ahab is not really supposed to know about, namely, how Yahweh has conspired to trick Ahab to his death. Commentators regularly interpret Micaiah's vision as revealing much about the Israelite understanding of prophecy, and indeed it does; compare Amos's claim in Amos 3:7: "surely the Lord Yahweh does nothing without revealing his secret to his servants the prophets." But within the present narrative context it has a more important function. It presents a formidable challenge to Ahab's readiness to follow the optimistic oracle of the four hundred prophets. By explaining how the four hundred prophets have been misled and have in turn misled Ahab, Micaiah exposes the divine trap and virtually dares Ahab to fall into it. If Ahab now goes ahead with his campaign against Ramoth-gilead, he does so fully warned that Yahweh has decreed his death.

Micaiah describes a scene in the heavenly court. (Compare Isaiah's more majestic depiction of the divine court in Isaiah 6 and Ezekiel's baroque symbolic elaboration of the same basic scene in Ezekiel 1.) Yahweh sits on a throne surrounded by his courtiers, who stand "above him" (NRSV, "beside him," but the preposition in Hebrew reflects the fact that Yahweh is seated and the courtiers are standing). The echo of verse 10 is significant: Micaiah is addressing two kings who sit on their respective thrones surrounded by courtiers. The parallelism of the scenes reminds the reader that the monarchs of both Israel and Judah hold their thrones under the higher court of Yahweh and subject to God's will. Just as it evokes the subordination of Ahab and Jehoshaphat to Yahweh, so it also points up the inferiority of the human monarchs' advisers, four hundred raving prophets, to the heavenly ones.

Yahweh seeks advice from the court, as any wise monarch would. God wishes to "entice" Ahab: the word connotes using misleading positive promises to trick the king into doing something disastrous. Even God's opening words are duplicitous: he wishes Ahab to "fall upon Gilead Heights," that is, both to attack it and to be felled there (the NRSV's "fall at Ramoth-gilead" misses the double meaning of the preposition). When various courtiers have proposed various stratagems, one, called "the spirit," claims to have the solution. The definite article indicates that this is the only "spirit" in Yahweh's court. In other words, it is "the spirit of Yahweh," the spirit to which prophets regularly ascribe their divine inspiration. The spirit is confident: "*I* will entice him" (emphatic pronoun: *my* advice will work; all of these others' proposals will not). When Yahweh asks the spirit for details, the spirit replies that it will become a "deceptive spirit" (NRSV, "lying spirit") speaking through Ahab's prophetic advisers.

Yahweh approves the plan and commissions the spirit to carry it out. This stratagem explains the ambiguities of the four hundred prophets' original oracle. It is not—or it is not only—a matter of prophetic vagueness about which divine "lord" will act and which king will prevail. It is also the deceptive spirit inspiring the prophets with enticing words and thus allowing Ahab to infer promises that are not in fact being made. The last words of Micaiah's monologue point this out to Ahab.

Reactions to Micaiah's Monologue: 22:24-28

There are two different reactions to Micaiah's revelation. First, Zedekiah son of Chenaanah takes umbrage at the implication that his oracle is untrue. He abuses Micaiah physically, with a slap across the face, and verbally, with a sarcastic question that implies that Micaiah is the one possessed by a lying spirit of Yahweh, not Zedekiah. Micaiah's response is that Zedekiah, too, will not escape. It begins with the vivid present construction, which is virtually untranslatable in this instance (literally, "Look! You are seeing it on that day when . . ."). The phrase "when you go in to hide in an inner chamber" is very similar to that used of Ben-hadad in 20:30 (literally, "when you go in room by room to hide").

The second reaction is Ahab's. He has Micaiah incarcerated until after the battle. Amon and Joash are otherwise unknown. The first is a municipal official; the second's title, "king's son," may reflect blood relationship, or it may refer to an office of oversight for political prisoners (compare the same title in Jeremiah 36:26 and 38:6, where the prophet Jeremiah is similarly imprisoned for preaching against the king). The king orders that Micaiah receive "bread that is affliction and water that is affliction" (a similar but not identical phrase occurs also in Isaiah 30:20); the NRSV's "reduced rations" captures the meaning but loses the graphic quality of the image. When the king says "until I come in peace," he is calling Micaiah's bluff. It may be that he hopes to pressure Micaiah into reversing the oracle he has given, in order to assure Ahab's safety and consequently Micaiah's own release. Or it may be that the king wishes to detain Micaiah until after the battle; when the king returns safely, he intends to punish Micaiah for false prophecy. This seems to be Micaiah's understanding, for his defiant reply is that should the king return safely, Micaiah is indeed guilty of false prophecy. If that is Ahab's idea, it implies much about his condescending attitude toward Yahweh. As verse 16 shows, Ahab knows that Micaiah's oracle of disaster is probably true, but he expects to be able to elude Yahweh's trap.

The last words attributed to Micaiah, "Hear, you peoples, all of you," do not belong to the story. They are in fact a citation of the first words of the book of the prophet Micah (1:2). Some later scribe, confusing Micaiah son of Imlah and Micah of Moresheth because of the similarity of names,[7] made a marginal cross-reference to the Book of Micah, thinking it contained further prophecies of the prophet. Eventually the marginal gloss crept into the text of the narrative.

The Whole Section

This long section does little to advance the plot of the story. Ahab clearly intends to wage war against Aram at Ramoth-gilead before Jehoshaphat asks for a divine oracle, and after lengthy, complex, and contradictory advice from various prophets, Ahab goes ahead with his military campaign. Yet the section comprises almost two-thirds of the story! And the fact that it is almost entirely dialogue brings the scenes

---

[7]"Micaiah" means "Who is like Yah(weh)?" (*mî-kā-yāhû*). "Micah" is the shortened form of the same name, with the divine element missing: "Who is like?" (*mî-kâ*). Compare "Michael": "Who is like El?" (*mî-kā-'ēl*). El was another of the Canaanite gods, often identified in Israelite tradition with Yahweh.

much closer to the reader than they would be if merely recounted by the narrator. A dialogue scene mirrors the events for the reader in both pace and presentation: dialogue takes approximately as much time to read as it does to happen, and we "hear" it in the same way and at the same time as the participants. Literary critics distinguish between the immediacy of "showing" and the distance of "telling"; these scenes *show* us what is happening, they do not simply tell us about it. Why, if this section does not advance the plot, does the narrator make it so prominent and present?

One reason is that the information Micaiah reveals sets a context within which we will understand the rest of the story of Ahab's defeat and death. As we shall discuss below, this context completely reverses the way we perceive and evaluate Ahab's behavior during the battle and the way we interpret its outcome. But there is more. One of the themes of this entire episode is the difficulty of separating true from false prophecy. The tale cautions us that the issue is not as simple as it may appear. It is not, for instance, a matter of identifying "true prophets" and "false prophets," for in the present tale the four hundred prophets are in fact true prophets. The spirit of Yahweh inspires them, and they speak (at least in their first ambiguous oracle) what the spirit gives them to speak. If what they are given to speak is deceptive, the untruth is God's responsibility, not the prophets'. If anyone in this story deserves to be called a "false prophet," it is Micaiah, who reveals Yahweh's secrets to Ahab without divine permission; but the secrets he reveals are in fact true.

The narrator brings the ambiguities of right and wrong home to the reader in pointed fashion in verses 15-16. Micaiah prophesies in accord with the divinely mandated falsehood, which is also what Ahab wants to hear. Is this true prophecy or false? And Ahab rejects Micaiah's prophecy (though he has accepted the identical oracle from the four hundred prophets) and demands truth. Is this a rejection of the divine word or a reverence for it? When a true prophet speaks a false word and an unfaithful king appears insistently devout, all neat compartmentalizations of good and evil dissolve. Our bewilderment at that point enables us to sympathize with Ahab's dilemma, faced with contradictory oracles in Yahweh's name.

Ultimately, the story tells us, there is no foolproof way to distinguish true and false prophecy. Even Micaiah himself can only appeal to future events as validating or invalidating his prophecy. His warnings to Zedekiah (v. 25) and to Ahab (v. 28a) both mean the same thing: when my prophecy is fulfilled, it will be proven valid.

Ahab and the War with Aram, continued: 22:29-38

The narrative returns to the war with Aram and recounts the rest of the story quickly but with pervasive irony. Ahab devises a strategy of disguise that protects him in battle. Yet he is wounded, as if by chance, dies, and is buried.

AHAB'S STRATEGY—DISGUISE: 22:29-31

Ahab's speech begins with two ambiguous grammatical forms, although the NRSV does not preserve the ambiguity. The verbs "disguise oneself" and "go (into battle)" can be parsed either as imperatives or as infinitives. The most natural reading is to take them as imperative verbs directed to Jehoshaphat, telling him to disguise himself and enter the battle: "The king of Israel said to Jehoshaphat, 'Disguise yourself; go into battle . . . .'" When Ahab continues, however, with an emphatic pronoun, "*you* wear your robes," we realize that the preceding words must speak of Ahab himself, and we reconstrue the forms as infinitives thus: "The king of Israel said to Jehoshaphat, 'To disguise oneself and to go into battle . . . ,'" as if Ahab is mulling over his own plans before turning to direct Jehoshaphat, "'but *you* wear your own robes.'" The narrator confirms this revised understanding by telling us with the same words that Ahab disguised himself and entered the battle.

The effect of this grammatical ploy is noteworthy. By allowing us to understand the words one way, then requiring us to reconstrue them quite differently, the narrator forces us to attend to the question of motivation. How do we understand Ahab's words when we read them as orders directed to Jehoshaphat? The position of the king in battle is important. Arrayed in his royal gear, he is easily identified on the battlefield. He acts as cynosure and rallying point for his forces. At the same time, by reason of rank as well as of being a rallying point, he is the safest person on the field, surrounded and protected by the mass of his army as well as by his personal bodyguard. Our first reading of Ahab's words understands him to be ordering Jehoshaphat to enter the battle on a par with the rest of the troops. Ahab retains for himself the position of visibility and safety and sends Jehoshaphat into unnecessary danger. Our reaction is disapproval of Ahab's apparent cowardice and disdain for his royal ally's well-being. However, as soon as we realize that it is Ahab who intends to enter the battle, our disapproval changes to admiration: Ahab is ceding to his ally the place of visibility and safety in order to brave the dangers of battle himself.

Grammatical forms invite us to compare and contrast the speech of the king of Aram (v. 31) with that of the king of Israel (v. 30). (The NRSV reflects this by the past perfect verb "had commanded" in verse 31, implying that the king of Aram's speech is simultaneous with the king of Israel's.) The comparison proves richly ironic. At the very moment when the king of Israel is deciding to enter the battle incognito, the king of Aram is directing his officers to concentrate on finding and killing the king of Israel. It seems that Ahab's noble and brave gesture is to receive an unanticipated reward; it will conceal him from an unexpected Aramean tactic aimed at him personally. And then the deeper irony hits. In the light of Micaiah's prophecy, Ahab knows that he is in personal jeopardy in this battle: his sheep will be left without a shepherd. Could it be that his apparently brave plan is actually cowardice? Could he be setting Jehoshaphat up in his place, hoping that Jehoshaphat will draw whatever stroke Yahweh intends for Ahab? (And at this point we remember our question in chapter 21, whether the real motivating force behind the plot against Naboth might have been Ahab himself, not Jezebel. The man works by devious ways.) The narrator leaves us hopelessly unsure of Ahab's motivations but very clear about what is likely to happen. Whether through bravery or cowardice, Ahab will probably escape the lethal attentions of the king of Aram.

BATTLE: 22:32-34

The account of the battle begins by following the Aramean officers as they press their attack against the royal personage they believe is Ahab. The narrator's word order emphasizes their misidentification. What the NRSV translates as a narrative verb is actually an aside: "When the captains of the chariots saw Jehoshaphat (but *they* [emphatic pronoun] said, 'It is surely the king of Israel'), they turned to fight against him." When Jehoshaphat cries out, the narrator does not bother to tell us whether he cries a defiant battle cry or a fearful cry for help. Jehoshaphat's character is not the narrator's business in this story of Ahab. The cry is enough to alert the Arameans to their error. Note the parallel in the opening words of verses 32 and 33: "When the captains of the chariots saw . . ."; in this way the narrator emphasizes that the key to this whole battle scene is the identity of the king. The king of Aram's strategy is not "kill the head and the serpent dies"; if it were, killing Jehoshaphat, the visible royal cynosure and rallying point of the army, would have the desired result. The king of Aram's target is specifically and personally Ahab. When it is clear that the royal figure is not he, the captains abandon the attack. Ahab's stratagem of disguise saves him.

The narrator uses the same grammatical construction in verse 34 as in verse 31, and to the same effect: to compare and ironically contrast two scenes. In verses 29-31 it was the speeches of the two kings. Here it is the concentrated but abortive attack on Jehoshaphat and the chance but successful arrow that fells Ahab. The attack is by "somebody" (even the NRSV's "a certain man" is more concrete than the vague Hebrew) who draws his bow "to the full" (or perhaps, as the NRSV interprets it, without knowing the identity of his target; either translation is possible[8]) and hits Ahab in the vulnerable place where two parts of his armor leave a gap. Ahab is wounded and orders his charioteer to pull back out of the battle. (Actually in the Hebrew text Ahab says "out of the camp [mḥnh]," which is puzzling, since Ahab is not in the camp. Almost all modern versions follow the ancient Greek translation and read "out of the battle [mlḥmh]." If we wish to make sense of the Hebrew text, perhaps we must think of Ahab as disoriented by the shock of his wound.) A seemingly random arrow at a seemingly undistinguished Israelite chariot-rider, and Ahab's carefully woven stratagem of disguise unravels. When one's enemy is divine, camouflage avails nothing.

AHAB'S DEATH—DISGUISED: 22:35-36

The irony deepens. If Ahab is able to pull back from the front and seek medical attention, perhaps he will survive. But all things conspire to accomplish the divine decree of death. The fighting becomes so intense that his charioteer cannot withdraw. Even Ahab's decision to enter the battle works against him. The king stands propped up in the chariot, not in order to inspire his troops (presumably he is still incognito) but because the press is so great that he has no room to collapse. While he stands there, he slowly dies. Thus the stratagem of disguise reaches its ultimate irony: the king who pretended not to be a king is now a corpse pretending not to be dead.

The narrator says that Ahab dies at evening, which makes it clear that the arrow does not penetrate any vital organ and kill him immediately. The next clause, about the blood flowing into the king's chariot,

---

[8]The strikingly different possibilities for the translation of this phrase are due to the cryptic quality of the Hebrew. The word means literally "to his wholeness." If "wholeness" is understood physically, as "full strength," it means that the archer pulls his bow to its maximum tension; this would explain how the arrow manages to pierce the king's armor and inflict a fatal wound. If, however, it is taken mentally, as "integrity, innocence," it means that the archer is not aiming at Ahab because he recognizes him but simply because he is an enemy soldier; the fact that the target is Ahab is the mysterious working out of Yahweh's oracle.

implies that he bleeds to death. The NRSV strengthens this impression by the past perfect, "had flowed," and by the phrase "from the wound," as if the narrator had reversed the order of events by putting the effect, Ahab's death, first, and the cause after it. But the Hebrew reads otherwise. The syntax clearly describes the flow of blood as following the king's death, and the Hebrew speaks of blood "of" the wound, not "from" it. The inference remains that the king bleeds to death; the emphasis, however, is not on the flowing of blood "from the wound" but on the pooling of the wound's blood in the bottom of the chariot. This points forward to the next scene (v. 38), where the chariot is washed out and the blood features in a prophecy fulfillment.

Once evening falls, the camp (that is, the camp of Israel, since Aram is in possession of Ramoth-gilead and would not have a "camp" at the battlefield) rings with the shout to abandon the campaign. "Every man to his city and every man to his country" reflects that the Israelite forces are drawn not just from the cities of the northern kingdom, Israel, but from the southern kingdom, Judah, as well. Who sounds the retreat? The narrator personifies the shout itself, as if no identifiable individual is actually responsible for it: "A shout went through the army." Both the anonymity of the cry and its content evoke Micaiah's first vision. Leaderless Israel, scattered like sheep without a shepherd, hears the word Yahweh spoke: "These have no master; let each man go home in peace" (v. 17).

Ahab's Burial in Samaria: 22:37-38

The first words of verse 37 reprise the statement of Ahab's death from verse 35. The repetition is necessary to maximize the sardonic quality of the next words. The NRSV's translation, "So the king died, and was brought to Samaria," modifies the Hebrew text slightly and in so doing misses the mockery. The Hebrew text says simply, "So the king died and came to Samaria," as if nothing so trivial as death could interfere with his determination to return. The allusion is to the king's parting words in verse 27, when he put Micaiah in prison "until I come in peace." He has "come," but hardly in the "peace" he anticipated. He is buried in Samaria, the capital city founded and built by his father (16:24).

The next verse adds a gruesome postscript. The king's chariot, filled with Ahab's dried blood, must be washed. The pool of Samaria provides ample water for the task. (We are probably not to think of a local cistern or reservoir whose water would be used for drinking and cooking, but of a public catch basin used for bathing, for laundry, and the like.) Dogs lap up the bloodied runoff, and prostitutes bathe in it. The narrator explains these grotesque images as fulfillments of a divine word. The first element (dogs licking up Ahab's blood) corresponds to Yahweh's word to Elijah in 21:19, although there is an explicit deviation: according to 21:19, this was to occur "in the place where dogs licked up the blood of Naboth," in other words, in the city of Jezreel (21:1); but according to 22:38, it takes place in Samaria. The narrator's unconcern about this divergence in detail is revealing. Prophecy is not a mechanical process but a living word. Fulfillment need not mesh with prediction like complementary gears: if the central thrust of the prophecy is realized, variations in circumstantial detail are irrelevant. The second part of the image, prostitutes bathing in the bloody water, does not correspond to any prophecy in our texts. The narrator reminds us that the text assumes a larger world than it describes (see the remarks above on verse 8) and that we, as readers, must actively collaborate with the narrator in constructing that larger world on the basis of the limited materials the narrator offers us. Somewhere, the narrator tells us, there was a prophetic word spoken against Ahab about prostitutes bathing in his blood, even though we have not heard the story.

The Whole Story

What is the effect of the combination of war story and prophetic condemnation episode? In chapters 20 and 21 the effect was clear, because the prophetic condemnation episode came after the Ahab story was completed; in this chapter, however, it comes early in the narrative and colors everything that follows. One way to discern its effect is to examine a hypothetical version of the story that would not include verses 5-28. (We used this technique in the last chapter when we contrasted 21:1-16 with a hypothetical version of the story lacking verse 10.) Without verses 5-28 the story is symmetrically organized and narratively whole. (Note how smoothly verse 4 connects to verse 29.) Ahab and his vassal Jehoshaphat agree to undertake a campaign against Ramoth-gilead. Ahab determines to disguise himself and join the fighting, leaving Jehoshaphat to hold the position of visibility and safety. Without the divine threat in verses 5-28, we have no reason to question Ahab's motives: he is acting nobly and courageously. Nor do we have any reason to see in the arrow that kills him anything more than fatal chance. His charioteer's inability to extricate the dying king from the press of battle is a tragic consequence of the king's brave but foolhardy decision to place himself in danger. In short, the characterization of Ahab is essentially positive, with perhaps a rueful sigh over the difficulty of distinguishing royal boldness from rashness. Even the final remarks (v. 38), which recall prophetic predictions about Ahab's blood after his death, do not suggest that the death itself was divinely engineered.

The prophetic condemnation episode in verses 5-28 precludes the possibility of such a reading. Knowing that Yahweh intends Ahab to fall at Ramoth-gilead, and knowing that Ahab knows it as well, we cannot avoid wondering about Ahab's motivation in disguising himself or about the providential design behind the arrow that fells him. We inevitably read the entire battle story as the working out of the divine plan revealed in Micaiah's visions. When, in verse 38, we see that other prophetic predictions too are fulfilled in the aftermath of Ahab's death, it confirms our belief that the whole course of events is divinely directed. In short, the presence of verses 5-28 in the narrative effects a complete reversal of the characterization of Ahab and of our understanding of its events. He is not a brave and noble monarch who dies tragically in the hazards of battle but a man under divine condemnation who strives unsuccessfully to thwart Yahweh and escape his fate.

Ahab's Death Notice: 22:39-40

The story of Ahab's reign concludes with the formulaic notice of his death, burial, and successor. (On these formulas, see p. 206 above.) Two cryptic notices remark on "the ivory house that he built" and "the cities that he built." In this way the narrator suggests two things: first, that Ahab's greater reputation is for his building projects; second, that the stories of Ahab's reign that the narrator has told are intended to balance that fame with an equally important, if less complimentary, picture. Excavations in Israel enable us to put flesh on the bare bones of this reputation for building, with which the original readers would no doubt have been familiar. Ahab's "ivory house" was his palace in Samaria, which was built of stone, of course, but lavishly decorated with inlaid panels and furnishings of ivory. Archaeologists have unearthed several exquisite examples of this ivory work in the ruins of the Omrid palace in Samaria. Ahab's "cities" include Samaria itself; Omri, Ahab's father, died only six years after founding the city (16:23), leaving Ahab to accomplish the major part of the construction work. Other cities in Israel, notably Megiddo and Hazor, also show extensive and ambitious remains from Ahab's time.

Ahab "slept with his ancestors," that is, he is buried in the family tomb. The plural "ancestors" is conventional, since this is in fact a relatively new tomb. Ahab's father and predecessor Omri founded Samaria as a new city, capital of his new dynasty. Presumably he is the first and only "ancestor" of Ahab as yet buried there. (An even more inaccurate use of the same conventional formula marked Omri's own burial in 16:28.) Ahab's son Ahaziah succeeds his father.

Chapter 22

THE WHOLE AHAB STORY

1 Kings 16:29–22:40

MORE KINGS OF JUDAH AND ISRAEL

1 Kings 22:41-53

Like the stories of Elijah in chapters 17–19, the narratives that deal with the reign of Ahab are nested like a series of Chinese boxes. First, the three stories in chapters 20–22, each with its associated episode of prophetic condemnation, make up a single narrative unit. There are several indications of this unity: the common setting of chapters 20 and 22 in the wars with Aram; the link forged between the two chapters by the mention of three years of peace in 22:1, alluding to the treaty of 20:34; the dominance of the figure of Ahab in all three chapters; and the common structure of symmetrical Ahab story plus separate prophetic condemnation episode in all three chapters. Second, the whole reign of Ahab constitutes a still larger unit that begins with the formulaic introduction to Ahab's reign (16:29) and ends with its formulaic conclusion (22:39-40), incorporating within its boundaries the large story complexes about Elijah (chs. 17–19) and about Ahab and the prophets (20:1–22:38). Third, there are still larger units that extend into 2 Kings, such as the story of the Omrid dynasty, which begins in 1 Kings 16:21 and ends only with Jehu's coup d'état in 2 Kings 9–11. In this chapter we shall consider the first two narrative units, and then look briefly at the more formulaic treatments of the reigns of Jehoshaphat and Ahaziah with which 1 Kings closes. In the next chapter we shall consider narrative units whose boundaries extend beyond 1 Kings.

Ahab and the Prophets: 1 Kings 20–22

Chapters 20–22 portray the last three years of Ahab's reign as a time of shifting fortunes in international politics. Israel rises from vassalage to Aram to a political ascendancy over Judah that, as we shall see in 22:41-50, is quickly lost. The focus of the chapters, however, is not the political realm. The military conflict between Israel and Aram is entirely absent from chapter 21, and the details of negotiations, tactics, and casualty statistics that fill chapter 20 are lacking in chapter 22. The threads that bind all three chapters together are the person of King Ahab and the hostility between him and the prophets of Yahweh.

The movement from chapter 20 to chapter 22 is progressive in several ways. The prophetic condemnation episode, for instance, comprises a significantly greater proportion of the narrative in each chapter: in chapter 20 it is approximately one-fifth of the whole; in chapter 21 it is almost half; and in chapter 22 it is nearly two-thirds of the entire story. The impression this conveys is that the rift between prophets and king deepens rapidly toward the end of Ahab's reign. At the same time, the prophetic prediction itself becomes more pointed. In chapter 20 Ahab learns that he and his people will suffer for his release of Ben-hadad; but the prophet does not specify the punishment further ("your life shall be for his life" is not a death sentence in 20:42 any more than it is in 20:39), nor does he indicate when it shall ensue. In chapter 21 the divine oracle about dogs licking up Ahab's blood (21:19) points to the king's death, as do the repeated allusions to the law of talion, which would demand Ahab's life for Naboth's. Elijah's invocation of the dynastic condemnation formula extends Ahab's punishment to his whole dynasty. But still no term is set for Ahab's personal punishment, although Yahweh eventually appoints the next generation as the time for the dynastic downfall. In chapter 22 Micaiah speaks clearly, though allusively, of Ahab's death ("like sheep that have no shepherd," 22:17; "fall upon Gilead Heights," 22:20), and announces that it is imminent: "If you return in peace, Yahweh has not spoken by me" (22:28).

The characterization of Ahab is a further example of progression in the three chapters. In 20:1-34 the portrayal of the king is generally positive. Through prophets, Yahweh favors him with reassuring oracles, tactical advice, and miraculous military victories. Ahab shows himself courageous and noble in vassalage and merciful and generous in victory. Only with the prophetic condemnation episode in 20:35-43 do we perceive in retrospect that Ahab failed Yahweh's expectations, and even then we infer that he did so unawares and with the best of intentions.

In chapter 21 the portrayal is generally ambiguous, though neither reading is complimentary. We can see Ahab as petty, petulant, and passive, ignorant of the evil deeds of an unscrupulous wife who usurps his royal authority. Or we can see him as cleverly manipulative of Jezebel, actively permitting her to exercise royal authority in his interests, as long as he remains technically innocent of the crimes she commits in his name. The prophetic condemnation episode in 21:17-29 is even more ambivalent. The narrator condemns Ahab for unsurpassed evil, yet shows him performing acts of repentance that Yahweh credits and rewards.

Finally, in chapter 22 the portrayal is unambiguously negative. By placing the prophetic condemnation episode early in what would otherwise be a positive portrayal of Ahab, the narrator precludes the possibility that we will view Ahab positively as we did in 20:1-34. In chapter 22 as it stands, Yahweh decrees Ahab's death at Ramoth-gilead; no reason is given, and so we take this to be the working out of the punishment announced by Elijah in chapter 21. Although Ahab is aware of Yahweh's decree, he goes ahead with his military plans, menaces the prophet whose oracle he knows is true, and disguises himself in an attempt to defy Yahweh's will.

The three chapters do not agree, however, on the reason for the deteriorating relationship between Ahab and Yahweh. In chapter 20 it is Ahab's readiness to treat Ben-hadad generously. In chapter 21 there are two crimes: the murder of Naboth, which is the basis of the plot, and Ahab's idolatry, which is mentioned in the narrator's parenthetical aside to the reader (21:26). Chapter 22 cites no sins, though it does make an oblique reference to Naboth's murder (22:38, alluding to 21:19). The focus in these chapters is more on the punishment than on the crime. To see more clearly what the narrator considers Ahab's central evil, we must examine the whole account of his reign.

The Reign of Ahab: 1 Kings 16:29–22:40

The whole account of Ahab's reign comprises the two large narrative complexes about Elijah and Ahab framed by the standard regnal formulas (see p. 206):

  A. Formulaic introduction to Ahab's reign (16:29-34)
    B. THE ELIJAH STORY (17:1–19:21)
    B'. AHAB AND THE PROPHETS (20:1–22:38)
  A'. Formulaic conclusion to Ahab's reign (22:39-40).

Elements of form and content link the two large narrative complexes and invite us to read them together. First, there is the converse formal structure of the two complexes. The Elijah story comprises two chapters of private events surrounding one chapter set in the public, political realm. The prophet is the main character; Ahab appears mainly in the central chapter, and then in a secondary role. The Ahab story comprises two chapters of public, political events surrounding one chapter in the private realm. The king is the main character; Elijah appears only in the central chapter, and then in a secondary role. Second, there are several otherwise superfluous details that link the two complexes. "Seven thousand," for instance, is the number of Yahweh's faithful worshipers (19:18) and of Ahab's military forces (20:15). "Four hundred" is the number of Asherah's prophets (18:19) and Ahab's (22:6), and in both cases Ahab "gathers" the prophets together (the Hebrew verb is the same in both places, though the NRSV translates it "assembled" in 18:20). The hostile exchange between Ahab and Elijah in 21:20 is reminiscent of their similar exchange in 18:17-18.

The parallel structures of the Elijah and Ahab stories put the relationship between prophet and king in a singular light. That prophets can oppose and even condemn kings is nothing new. Samuel condemns Saul in 1 Samuel; Nathan condemns David in 2 Samuel 12; Ahijah of Shiloh condemns Solomon in 1 Kings 11 and Jeroboam in 1 Kings 14. There is ample precedent for hostility between prophet and monarch. But the texts do not generally portray the antagonists as literary equals. Here Elijah has his own story complex alongside Ahab's, of similar length and converse structure. In other words, the opposition between prophet and king is expressed also on the textual level: 16:29–22:40 is not simply the story of a king who is opposed by a prophet; it comprises rather the opposition of two contrasting stories—that of the prophet who is almost as great as Moses (see pp. 287–289) and that of the king who is worse than Jeroboam (16:31-33).

As a matter of fact, the thematic center of unity in the account of Ahab's reign is neither Ahab himself (he is only a very minor character in chapters 17–19), nor Elijah (who is entirely absent from chapters 20 and 22), nor the opposition between them (they meet only a few times in the course of the six chapters). The single focus is the struggle between Yahweh and Baal for the loyalties of Israel and its royal house. The prominence of this theme in chapters 17–19 calls attention to its occurrence elsewhere in the account of Ahab's reign as well. Its first appearance is in 16:31-32, where it is the basis for the theological evaluation of Ahab that is part of the conventional regnal formula. The drought story in chapters 17–18 epitomizes the rivalry between Baal, god of fertility and rainfall, and Yahweh, who claims supremacy over all Israel. The people's confession of faith in 18:39 resolves their divided loyalties, at least for the moment, but Ahab's response to Yahweh's demonstration of sovereignty remains unclear (see the remarks on 18:41-42 on p. 286). The king does not seem to undergo a conversion like the people's, however, since in the next chapter Jezebel still feels free to menace Yahweh's prophet (19:2).

Allusions to royal infidelity to Yahweh are present in the three chapters of the Ahab story as well, though they are less prominent. In chapter 20 Ahab is twice told that Yahweh will afford him miraculous help in his battles with Ben-hadad so that "you shall know that I am Yahweh" (20:13 and 28). In other words, Yahweh expects acknowledgment of his sovereignty from both Ahab and the people ("you" is singular in 20:13 and plural in 20:28). In chapter 21 there is a clear reference to Ahab's idolatry (21:26), but the parallel structure of the two parts of the chapter and the parallel references to Jezebel's influence in both parts add a deeper dimension to the issue: they imply that the narrator considers Naboth's murder and the seizure of his ancestral inheritance emblematic of the more fundamental evil of which Ahab is guilty, namely, idolatry. In this regard, we should not overlook the prophetic use of "vineyard" as a symbol of Israel: Naboth's death enabled Ahab to seize the landowner's vineyard, but Ahab's idolatry is metaphorically an expropriation of Yahweh's vineyard. Finally, in chapter 22 the ambiguity of the divine loyalties of Ahab's four hundred prophets hints that, right to the end of his reign, Ahab fails to make a decisive choice between Yahweh and other deities.

More Kings of Judah and Israel: 1 Kings 22:41-53

In the last verses of 1 Kings the tone of the narrative shifts once more, as it did in 14:21, to a brief, almost dry chronicle of the succession of kings in Judah and Israel. See page 206 above for a detailed discussion of the conventional material used to introduce and conclude each regnal account. As before, the kings are treated in order of their accession to the throne, whether they rule over Israel or Judah. Thus we begin with Jehoshaphat, who came to the throne of Judah during the reign of Ahab of Israel; then we turn to Ahaziah of Israel, who succeeded his father Ahab while Jehoshaphat still ruled in Judah.

There is a minor difference in versification between the standard Hebrew text and the translation tradition represented in the NRSV. There is no difference in content, but the Hebrew text divides the sentences in verse 43 (NRSV) between two verse numbers. As a result, verses 43-53 in the NRSV correspond to verses 43-54 in the Hebrew text. In the discussion that follows, we will use the NRSV numbers.

JEHOSHAPHAT OF JUDAH: 22:41-50

The formulaic introduction to the reign of Jehoshaphat of Judah is entirely standard. The narrator gives Jehoshaphat a positive evaluation, comparing his twenty-five-year reign to the even longer forty-one-year reign of his father Asa (15:9-24), with the standard qualification that Jehoshaphat did not remove the high places. The event mentioned from his years is that he "made peace" (or perhaps "was at peace") with Israel, a situation already reflected in the coalition between Ahab and Jehoshaphat described in 22:1-4. In two ways this remark forges a tight link with the chain of Judah's rulers stretching back to Solomon. First, the theme of war between Israel and Judah was a leitmotif in the treatments of the reigns of Rehoboam, Abijam, and Asa of Judah, as well as of Nadab of Israel (see p. 220 above). Second, "made peace" (Hebrew, *yšlm*) plays on the name of Solomon *(šlmh)*. As we shall see, the rest of the account of Jehoshaphat contains several other allusions to Solomon as well.

The formulaic conclusion begins in entirely conventional fashion, with vague comments about Jehoshaphat's power and wars and the usual reference to the standard resource for further information, the Book of the Annals of the Kings of Judah. But the narrator interrupts the conclusion with several remarks inserted before the mention of Jehoshaphat's death, burial, and successor in verse 50. The first remark refers back to 15:12, which reports Asa's campaign to eliminate the *qādēš* (NRSV, "male temple prostitutes," but see the discussion on 14:24 for the uncertainty of this translation) from Israel. Asa's success was incomplete and Jehoshaphat finishes the job. The second remark is an obscure comment about Edom's political situation. It is not as isolated as at first appears: its purpose is to explain how Jehoshaphat is able to initiate a shipping endeavor at the port of Ezion-geber (v. 48), since when Edom is strong it always controls this port. The third remark is about Jehoshaphat's abortive attempt to revive the gold trade with Ophir on the Red Sea. The fourth remark is easily misunderstood in translation. The first word, "then" (Hebrew, *'āz*) does not mean "subsequently," as if Ahaziah waits until Jehoshaphat's ships are wrecked before offering to join the expedition. It means more broadly "That was the time when." In other words, when Jehoshaphat is undertaking this renewal of the Red Sea trading enterprise, Ahaziah proposes that they make it a joint venture (compare the combined fleets of Solomon and Hiram of Tyre mentioned in 9:27-28, 10:11-12, and 10:22), but Jehoshaphat refuses. By inserting these remarks into the conclusion, immediately following the conventional statement about "the rest of the acts of Jehoshaphat," the narrator suggests that these are a selected few of "the rest of the acts," and implies therefore that they do not match in importance the event singled out in verse 44.

What is the point of the remarks? The data listed in verses 46-49 refine the data of verses 43-44. First, verse 43 likens Jehoshaphat to his father Asa, both positively and negatively. Verse 46 tells us that Jehoshaphat not only maintains Asa's reform but prosecutes it more successfully than Asa did. Second, verse 44 reveals that Jehoshaphat heals the breach in the once-united kingdom of Solomon. Verses 47-48 show that he also tries to recapture the glories of the Solomonic empire—control of Edomite territory and revival of the lucrative Red Sea trade—but that he fails in this goal. Finally, verse 49 shows that the peace Jehoshaphat makes with Israel is not the whole story. With the death of Ahab and accession of Ahaziah, Jehoshaphat manages to throw off Judah's subservience to Israel. Where he acquiesced without reserve to Ahab's proposed campaign against Ramoth-gilead (22:4), he can refuse Ahab's son's proposal to join Judah's maritime fleet.

The notice of Jehoshaphat's death, burial, and successor are entirely standard.

AHAZIAH OF ISRAEL: 1 KINGS 22:51-53

The First Book of Kings ends, surprisingly, with the formulaic introduction to the reign of Ahaziah of Israel. It follows the standard form (though there is no mention of the capital city from which Ahaziah rules), includes a negative theological evaluation that compares Ahaziah to Jeroboam, and identifies his crime plainly as the same Baal worship of which his father Ahab was guilty. The only unusual element is the mention of Ahaziah's mother along with his father as the model of evil that Ahaziah follows.

Chapter 23

THE WHOLE OF 1 KINGS AND LARGER UNITS

The pattern we have seen regularly throughout 1 Kings, where short, self-contained stories become component parts of longer narratives, is repeated on an ever larger scale. The "First Book of Kings" comprises the stories of Solomon, Jeroboam, Elijah, and Ahab, along with brief accounts of other kings' reigns in 14:21–16:28 and 22:41-53. A first question we must ask is whether the whole book of 1 Kings can be considered a single story in itself. Then we will look briefly at the larger stories of which 1 Kings is a part.

The Whole of 1 Kings

Despite its name, the "First Book of Kings" is not a self-contained literary unit, that is, it does not constitute a single narrative with a beginning, middle, and end. Particularly at the end of the book, there is no sense of conclusion. Commentators on 1 Kings regularly cite a pragmatic consideration for the division between 1 and 2 Kings, namely, the practical length of a manageable scroll. In the ancient world, scrolls were made of papyrus sheets or leather panels sewn together. Whichever material was used, the resulting scroll became unwieldy beyond a certain length. When one scroll reached that length, the ancient author would begin to write on another. This factor no doubt played a role in the composition and division of the biblical books; for instance, it is probably why 1 Samuel, 2 Samuel, 1 Kings, and 2 Kings are all approximately the same length.

But there is a literary detail at the end of 1 Kings that points to a different issue at work as well. If the scribe wished to give the scroll of 1 Kings a feeling of relative completeness, a more appropriate ending place would have been 22:50, the formulaic conclusion to the reign of Jehoshaphat. Including 22:51-53 on the scroll may have been a penny-wise economizing on a trivial bit of papyrus or leather, but it has a powerful narrative effect as well. Since these verses are the formulaic introduction to the reign of Ahaziah, they forge a strong bond with 2 Kings 1, which continues and concludes that reign, and thereby foil any chance that a reader might find closure at 22:53. The text of 1 Kings itself, then, requires that we include 2 Kings in our considerations of narrative unity.

Before we do so, however, we must examine one element of continuity and development that ties together all the separate narrative complexes in 1 Kings. This is the presence of a single character who, though he almost always remains in the background, nevertheless appears throughout the book—Yahweh. The narrator tells us much about Yahweh both in the narrator's own words and through statements of other characters (some reliable and some not), and on several occasions he shows us Yahweh himself speaking and acting. God's first appearance in 1 Kings is in 3:5, and his last appearance is in 21:28; but he is spoken of by Bathsheba as early as 1:17 and mentioned by the narrator as late as the last verse of the book. In the course of the book we can form a vivid impression of God's character, though, as with any highly developed literary characterization, the complexities of the figure leave many questions unanswered. In discussing the character of Yahweh in 1 Kings, we should not forget that our analysis is necessarily partial. First Kings is not a complete literary unit in itself, and so the portrayal of Yahweh in it is only part of a continuing characterization that extends beyond the confines of the book.

In 1 Kings Yahweh appears in two different sets of relationships. In the first half of the book, he interacts directly with King Solomon. He appears to Solomon (3:5-15; 9:2-9), his word comes to Solomon (6:11-13; 11:9-13), and, according to the narrator, he gives wisdom to Solomon (4:29). In the second half of the book, Yahweh interacts directly with prophets but never with kings or other human beings.[1] This change signals a growing distance between God and king, and a shift to mediated rather than immediate divine intervention in human affairs. Since the major emphasis in the second half of 1 Kings is on the northern realm, we cannot tell whether this divine withdrawal is operative in Judah as well. The stories of 2 Kings, however, will make it clear that it affects both kingdoms and that it intensifies until it culminates in God's apparent abandonment of both kingdoms. Israel, the northern kingdom,

---

[1]In 17:9 Yahweh claims to have given a command to the widow of Zarephath, but her later behavior shows that she knows nothing of such a command. Whatever form of communication Yahweh used, it was not the sort of direct encounter that he has with prophets.

will be obliterated by the Assyrians (2 Kgs 17); Judah, the southern kingdom, will be carried into exile by the Babylonians (2 Kgs 24–25).

Though Yahweh changes his way of relating to human beings in the course of 1 Kings, the narrator characterizes him consistently by focusing on a single unwavering trait, the divine demand for obedience. In each of Solomon's four personal encounters with Yahweh, the deity emphasizes that the king must "walk in my ways, keeping my statutes and my commandments" (3:14; see also 6:12; 9:4; 11:11). The first two encounters do not describe this obedience further, but the third and fourth encounters are explicit about what constitutes violation of God's ways: idolatry (9:6; 11:10). The king is obedient if his worship of Yahweh is pure; he is disobedient if it is contaminated with the worship of other gods. In the second half of the book, cultic fidelity to Yahweh is the single criterion by which all kings of Israel and Judah are judged. In Israel, Yahweh supports Jeroboam's political and military separation from Judah, but when Jeroboam establishes calf sanctuaries at Dan and Bethel, Yahweh repudiates him. All subsequent kings of Israel are likewise condemned for "walking in the way of Jeroboam," that is, for continuing to support the calf sanctuaries. When the narrator condemns Ahab for evil surpassing that of Jeroboam, he has a worse form of idolatry in view, the worship of Baal (16:31). In Judah, the narrator couches royal judgments in terms of whether a king tolerates or removes the worship of other gods, and in particular whether or not he removes the sanctuaries on the high places (see 14:22-24; 15:12-14; 22:43, 46).

In dealing with prophets, Yahweh similarly demands uncompromising obedience. The issue here is not "ways, statutes, and commandments," nor, generally speaking, idolatry. It is absolute compliance with whatever commands Yahweh issues to the prophet in question. The most common picture is of a prophet simply delivering the word Yahweh commissions (Ahijah of Shiloh in 11:29-39 and 14:5; Shemaiah in 12:22-23; Jehu in 16:1-4). But the more complicated pictures also center ultimately on the question of prophetic obedience. The man of God from Judah dies for his disobedience, despite the fact that he is misled by the lies of the old prophet of Bethel; the old prophet is pressed into the service of the very word he tries to circumvent (13:11-32). The frequent command-and-compliance patterns in the Elijah story present his obedience as exemplary, so much so that in many respects he resembles Moses, the paradigmatic Israelite prophet. Yet Elijah's story climaxes in his resolute refusal of Yahweh's commission even in the face of a mysterious self-revelation of God, signaled by the broken command-and-compliance pattern of 19:11 and 13. The hapless prophet in 20:35-36, even more than the man of God in 13:11-32, dies for a disobedience he does not even know he is committing. Finally Micaiah, son of Imlah, articulates what might be called the prophetic oath of honor: to speak all and only what Yahweh commissions the prophet to speak (22:14) .

Whether the issue is royal fidelity to Yahweh's demand for cultic singularity or prophetic submission to Yahweh's word, and whether the king or prophet is praised or condemned, the underlying issue is obedience. Yahweh is a God who will not brook human insubordination. Certainly the Yahweh of 1 Kings has other traits—generosity (3:12-13), faithfulness to his own promises (9:3-5) and to those who are loyal to him (11:34; 15:4-5), compassion for the weak and helpless (14:13; 17:14-16; 17:22; 22:17), jealousy of his own prerogatives (20:42), mercy (21:29), deceptiveness (22:20-23), and so on. But the dominant trait, the one that pervades the book, is Yahweh's concern for his own supremacy and for the loyal obedience of his people.

First and Second Kings

The interdependence of 1 and 2 Kings appears most clearly in the brief account of the reign of Ahaziah, which begins in 1 Kings 22:51 and ends in 2 Kings 1:18. We can discern similar links on more inclusive levels as well, where a symmetrically organized narrative unit begins in 1 Kings and extends into 2 Kings. Since detailed examination of the materials in 2 Kings is beyond the scope of this study, we shall indicate only in a cursory way the shape of two of these larger narrative units.

THE STORY OF THE OMRID DYNASTY: 1 KINGS 16:21–2 KINGS 11:21

Unlike the kingdom of Judah, where the Davidic line held the throne from David until the Exile, the northern kingdom underwent a series of dynastic changes. The narrator has indicated parallels among the first three dynasties, those of Jeroboam, Baasha, and Omri (see the discussion of 1 Kings 21:20-22). The narrator's extensive coverage of the Omrid dynasty suggests that he considers it of first importance in the history of the northern kingdom. He organizes the stories of this dynasty concentrically:

> A. Civil war; the beginning of the Omrid dynasty (1 Kgs 16:21–34)
> > B. Elijah and the Omrid dynasty: Ahab and Ahaziah (1 Kgs 17–2 Kgs 1)

    C. Elisha succeeds Elijah (2 Kgs 2)
    B'. Elisha and the Omrid dynasty: Jehoram (2 Kgs 3–8)
    A'. Civil war; the end of the Omrid dynasty (2 Kgs 9–11)

The story begins and ends in civil war. In 1 Kings 16 Israelite loyalties are divided between Tibni and Omri for five years until Omri emerges victorious, establishes the new capital at Samaria, and founds a new dynasty. In 2 Kings 9–10, Jehu, at the instigation of the prophet Elisha, assassinates the reigning Omrid Jehoram and Jehoram's mother Jezebel. This unleashes a purge that drowns the entire Omrid line in blood. Meanwhile, in Judah, King Ahaziah has died in the same attack that killed Israel's Jehoram. His mother, Athaliah, seizes power in Judah and holds it for six years. She is the last Omrid, since she is the daughter of Ahab of Israel. 2 Kings 11 tells of her seizure of power and her eventual downfall. Connected with this overarching unity is the presence of clear prophecy and fulfillment notices. There are several references in the account of Jehu's coup d'état to prophecies of the downfall of Ahab's dynasty. The citations are not always exact, but they are close enough that the echoes are unmistakable: compare 2 Kings 9:8-10 with 1 Kings 21:21-23; 2 Kings 9:25-26 with 1 Kings 21:19; 2 Kings 9:36 with 1 Kings 21:23; and 2 Kings 10:10-11 with 1 Kings 21:21, 24.

Perhaps the most surprising development on this level of narrative organization is that prophets, not kings, are the determinants of structure. Not all the stories in 1 Kings 17–2 Kings 1 are about Elijah, but they all involve prophets, of whom Elijah is by far the most prominent. Similarly, the stories in 2 Kings 3–8 feature Elisha and the bands of prophets associated with him. The central section (2 Kgs 2) has a strange peculiarity: the narrator places it *outside* the political succession of reigns. Elsewhere the formulaic conclusion to one king's reign is almost always followed immediately by the formulaic introduction to another's—either the former king's successor or the next king of the other kingdom to be treated according to the narrator's scheme. Here, however, the formulaic conclusion to Ahaziah's reign (2 Kgs 1:17-18) is separated from the formulaic introduction to his successor Jehoram's (2 Kgs 3:1-3) by the narrative of the assumption of Elijah and the succession of Elisha to his master's office, and the first stories of Elisha's prophetic deeds. The implication is that the events recounted in 2 Kings 2 fall in some way outside of the normal course of political realities: the prophetic office represents the fixed point around which such ephemera as kings and their succession pivot.

The prophetic stories, too, contain echoes that unify the whole narrative. Elisha's succession to Elijah and the use of Elijah's mantle in that process recall Yahweh's command in 1 Kings 19:16 and Elijah's action in 1 Kings 19:19. When Elisha sends one of his prophetic associates to anoint Jehu (2 Kgs 9:1-13) and incites Hazael to assassinate and succeed Ben-hadad of Damascus (2 Kgs 8:7-15), both actions fulfill commissions Yahweh gave Elijah at Horeb (1 Kgs 19:15-16).

THE WHOLE OF 1 AND 2 KINGS

The whole of 1 and 2 Kings is similarly concentric and tells the tragic story of Yahweh's people from the glories of Solomon's reign through the disintegration of the kingdom to the eventual disappearance of both Israel and Judah into the maelstrom of Ancient Near Eastern political turmoil.[2]

> A. Solomon and the united monarchy (1 Kgs 1–11)
> B. The separation of the northern kingdom (1 Kgs 12)
> C. Kings of Israel and Judah (1 Kgs 13–16)
> D. The Omrid dynasty (1 Kgs 17–2 Kgs 11)
> C'. Kings of Israel and Judah (2 Kgs 12–16)
> B'. The fall of the northern kingdom (2 Kgs 17)
> A'. The kingdom of Judah alone (2 Kgs 18–25)

This pattern reveals a carefully balanced interest in the affairs of the two kingdoms. The kingdom of Judah is the subject of nineteen chapters (sections A and A'), and the kingdom of Israel is the subject of nineteen chapters (sections B, D, and B'). The movement of the whole, however, suggests that a single kingdom ruled from Jerusalem is the fundamental reality and that the existence of a second kingdom in the north is a temporary political expedient. Yahweh's intent in allowing the existence of the northern kingdom is to chastise the Davidic dynasty for the idolatry of Solomon (1 Kgs 11:9-13, 31-36). But when Israel also proves unfaithful, particularly in the Baalism of the Omrids and their successors, Yahweh ends the experiment. Unfortunately by that time Judah has fallen into idolatry as well, particularly during the reigns of Manasseh and his son Amon (2 Kgs 21), and even the unique fidelity of Josiah is not enough to save Judah from destruction (2 Kgs 23:25-27). And so Judah also falls to its enemies (2 Kgs 24–25). Yet here too there is a sense of open-endedness. The story does not end with

---

[2]I have based this outline on one given by George Savran in "1 and 2 Kings," *The Literary Guide to the Bible,* ed. Robert Alter and Frank Kermode (Cambridge, Mass.: Harvard University Press, 1987), p. 148. I have modified Savran's outline in some minor details.

2 Kings 25:21 ("So Judah went into exile out of its land") nor even with the flight of the remaining Judahite leaders to Egypt after they assassinate the king of Babylon's appointee as governor (2 Kgs 25:26). The last four verses of the book hint at hope. In Babylon, thirty-seven years after he went into exile, King Jehoiachin of Judah is released from prison and given a state pension. The Davidic dynasty is in eclipse, but it is not ended; the sun of Yahweh's promise can still shine again.

Larger Narrative Units

The books that follow 1 and 2 Kings do not continue their narrative. In the Hebrew manuscript tradition, the next book is Isaiah, a book of prophecy written mostly in poetry. In many English translations, 2 Kings is followed by the Books of Chronicles.[3] These, like 1 and 2 Kings, are prose narratives, but they do not pick up the story of Israel where 2 Kings leaves off. Rather they return to the beginning of the human story to retell everything since Adam. With 2 Kings, then, we come to the end of a major block of narrative material in the Hebrew Bible.

The books preceding 1 Kings, on the other hand, are continuous with it. One important story that overlaps the beginning of 1 Kings is called "The Succession Narrative" (generally considered as including 2 Samuel 7–20 + 1 Kings 1–2). It recounts the tragedies in the family of David following his adultery with Bathsheba and the murder of her husband, and it implies that those problems are due to David's sin. (On these events see p. 4 above.) Since that turmoil eventually cost David his two eldest sons, one of the continuing sources of dramatic tension in the narrative is determining David's heir: who will succeed David on the throne? The tension climaxes and is resolved in 1 Kings 1–2 when Solomon wins out over Adonijah. Although the first chapters of 1 Kings can be read as self-contained narratives (as we have done in this study), they nonetheless presume the entire complicated history

---

[3]The differences in the order of books are ancient. The Hebrew tradition considers Joshua, Judges, 1–2 Samuel, and 1–2 Kings "prophetic" books and puts them together with, but preceding, the other prophetic books: Isaiah, Jeremiah, Ezekiel, and the minor prophets. The Septuagint (the ancient Greek translation produced in Alexandria, Egypt, during the third and second centuries B.C.E.) considers Joshua, Judges, 1–2 Samuel, and 1–2 Kings "historical" books and puts them together with, but preceding, the other major collection of historical books: 1–2 Chronicles, Ezra, and Nehemiah. Most English translations follow the Greek tradition in this regard.

of adultery and murder, rape and fratricide, rebellion and restoration that is the Succession Narrative.

On a still larger scale, however, the entire first part of the Hebrew Bible can be appreciated as a single continuous narrative. The first eleven books[4] tell a multifarious story that begins with the chaos out of which God creates all things and ends with the chaos of exile into which the history of Israel's sin eventually leads. The grand scale of the story reveals its universal relevance. It is not simply the story of the Israelite monarchy (from 2 Samuel to 2 Kings), nor of the people of Yahweh (from Exodus), nor of the descendants of Abraham (from Genesis 12), but of all the children of Adam and Eve (from Genesis 4), indeed of all creatures (from Genesis 2) and all creation itself (from Genesis 1). Most of all, it is the story of the God whose creative word brought forth the past and whose prophetic word, whether of blessing or punishment, anger or forgiveness, continues to generate the future. It is the story of the God who is faithfully and eternally present to all his works.

---

[4]This includes Genesis, Exodus, Leviticus, Numbers, Deuteronomy, Joshua, Judges, 1 and 2 Samuel, and 1 and 2 Kings. It does not include the Book of Ruth, which is placed elsewhere in the Hebrew ordering of the biblical books. In English translations, which follow the Greek tradition by placing Ruth between Judges and 1 Samuel, Ruth is a sort of vignette of private life during the time of the Judges (see Ruth 1:1) that complements the generally public, political focus of Judges. In the larger sweep of the narrative of Israel's history, the transition from the near extinction of the tribe of Benjamin (Judg 19–21) to the story of Ruth, David's ancestor (Ruth 4:13-22), foreshadows the passing of kingship from the Benjaminite Saul to David.

FOR FURTHER READING

As those familiar with the literature on 1 Kings will recognize, I have drawn on many sources in preparing this study. The following suggestions for further reading do not attempt to exhaust the long list of scholars to whom I am indebted for information and insight. They are intended for the reader who wishes to pursue one or another aspect of the literary appreciation of 1 Kings further than the scope of this commentary allows. For that reason I have limited myself primarily, though not exclusively, to works that take a literary approach to the text, particularly to the final form of the text. I have also restricted myself to works in English.

General Commentaries on 1 Kings

Among the general commentaries on 1 Kings, most of those that have been around long enough to become standards in the scholarly world take a historical approach both to the text and to the events the text describes. Their questions are different from those posed in this commentary. They ask about the sources the author used in composing his work, and about the historical reliability of those sources and of the composite work produced from them. Chief among these commentaries in English are three:

Gray, John. *I & II Kings*. Old Testament Library. 2d ed. Philadelphia: Westminster, 1970.

Jones, Gwilym H. *1 and 2 Kings*. New Century Bible Commentary. 2 vols. Grand Rapids: William B. Eerdmans, 1984.

Montgomery, James A. *A Critical and Exegetical Commentary on the Books of Kings*. Edited by Henry Snyder Gehman. International Critical Commentary. Edinburgh: T. & T. Clark, 1951.

Several more recent commentaries attend to literary considerations to a greater degree than the standard historical critical commentaries. Among these I have found the following most helpful in preparing the present work:

Conroy, Charles. *1–2 Samuel, 1–2 Kings.* Old Testament Message 6. Wilmington: Michael Glazier, 1983.

DeVries, Simon J. *1 Kings.* Word Biblical Commentary 12. Waco: Word Books, 1985.

Long, Burke O. *1 Kings with an Introduction to Historical Literature.* The Forms of the Old Testament Literature 9. Grand Rapids: William B. Eerdmans, 1984.

Nelson, Richard. *First and Second Kings.* Interpretation. Atlanta: John Knox, 1987.

Savran, George. "1 and 2 Kings." *The Literary Guide to the Bible.* Edited by Robert Alter and Frank Kermode. Cambridge, Mass.: Harvard University Press, 1987; pp. 146–164.

Walsh, Jerome T., and Christopher R. Begg. "1–2 Kings." *The New Jerome Biblical Commentary.* Englewood Cliffs: Prentice Hall, 1990; §10.

Studies of Particular Passages

There is a vast literature on the smaller narrative complexes and individual stories within 1 Kings. The following selection of studies includes those that I have found both particularly insightful and not overly technical in their expectations of the reader.

THE SOLOMON STORY: 1 KINGS 1–11

Frisch, Amos. "Structure and Its Significance: The Narrative of Solomon's Reign (1 Kings 1–12.24)." *Journal for the Study of the Old Testament* 51 (1991) 3–14.

Lasine, Stuart. "The Riddle of Solomon's Judgment and the Riddle of Human Nature in the Hebrew Bible." *Journal for the Study of the Old Testament* 45 (1989) 61–86.

Long, Burke O. "A Darkness Between Brothers: Solomon and Adonijah." *Journal for the Study of the Old Testament* 19 (1981) 79–94.

Parker, Kim Ian. "Repetition as a Structuring Device in 1 Kings 1–11." *Journal for the Study of the Old Testament* 42 (1988) 19–27.

Porten, Bezalel. "The Structure and Theme of the Solomon Narrative (1 Kings 3–11)." *Hebrew Union College Annual* 38 (1967) 93–128.

THE JEROBOAM STORY: 1 KINGS 11–14

Barth, Karl. *Church Dogmatics.* Edinburgh: T. & T. Clark, 1936–1977; II/2, pp. 393–409.

Cohn, Robert. "Literary Technique in the Jeroboam Narrative." *Zeitschrift für die Alttestamentliche Wissenschaft* 97 (1985) 23–35.

Lasine, Stuart. "Reading Jeroboam's Intentions: Intertextuality, Rhetoric, and History in 1 Kings 12." In *Reading Between Texts: Intertextuality and the Hebrew Bible.* Edited by Danna Nolan Fewell. Louisville: Westminster/John Knox, 1992; pp. 133–152.

Simon, Uriel. "I Kings 13: A Prophetic Sign—Denial and Persistence." *Hebrew Union College Annual* 47 (1976) 81–117.

Walsh, Jerome T. "The Contexts of 1 Kings xiii." *Vetus Testamentum* 39 (1989) 355–370.

THE ELIJAH STORY: 1 KINGS 17–19

Cohn, Robert. "The Literary Logic of 1 Kings 17–19." *Journal of Biblical Literature* 101 (1982) 333–350.

Hauser, Alan J., and Russell Gregory. *From Carmel to Horeb: Elijah in Crisis.* Journal for the Study of the Old Testament Supplement 85; Bible and Literature 19. Sheffield: Almond, 1990.

Robinson, Bernard P. "Elijah at Horeb, 1 Kings 19:1-18: A Coherent Narrative." *Revue Biblique* 98 (1991) 513–536.

THE AHAB STORY: 1 KINGS 20–22

Long, Burke O. "Historical Narrative and the Fictionalizing Imagination." *Vetus Testamentum* 35 (1985) 405–416.

Walsh, Jerome T. "Methods and Meanings: Multiple Readings of 1 Kings 21." *Journal of Biblical Literature* 111 (1992) 193–211.

Works Relating Literary Theory to Biblical Studies

Alter, Robert. *The Art of Biblical Narrative.* New York: Basic Books, 1981.

Bar-Efrat, Shimon. *Narrative Art in the Bible.* Journal for the Study of the Old Testament Supplement 70. Sheffield: Almond, 1989.

Berlin, Adele. *Poetics and the Interpretation of Biblical Narrative.* Bible and Literature 9. Sheffield: Almond, 1983.

Brichto, Herbert Chanan. *Toward a Grammar of Biblical Poetics: Tales of the Prophets.* New York: Oxford University Press, 1992.

Parunak, H. Van Dyke. "Oral Typesetting: Some Uses of Biblical Structure." *Biblica* 62 (1981) 153–168.

____. "Transitional Techniques in the Bible." *Journal of Biblical Literature* 102 (1983) 525–548.

Sternberg, Meir. *The Poetics of Biblical Narrative: Ideological Literature and the Drama of Reading.* Indiana Studies in Biblical Literature. Bloomington: Indiana University Press, 1987.

GENERAL INDEX

INDEX OF SCRIPTURAL REFERENCES

Note: Biblical books are listed below in the order in which they occur in the Hebrew canon. The order differs in most English translations.